WORLD PIECE

STORY BY
JOSH TIERNEY

ART BY
AGROSHKA

 ORIGINALS

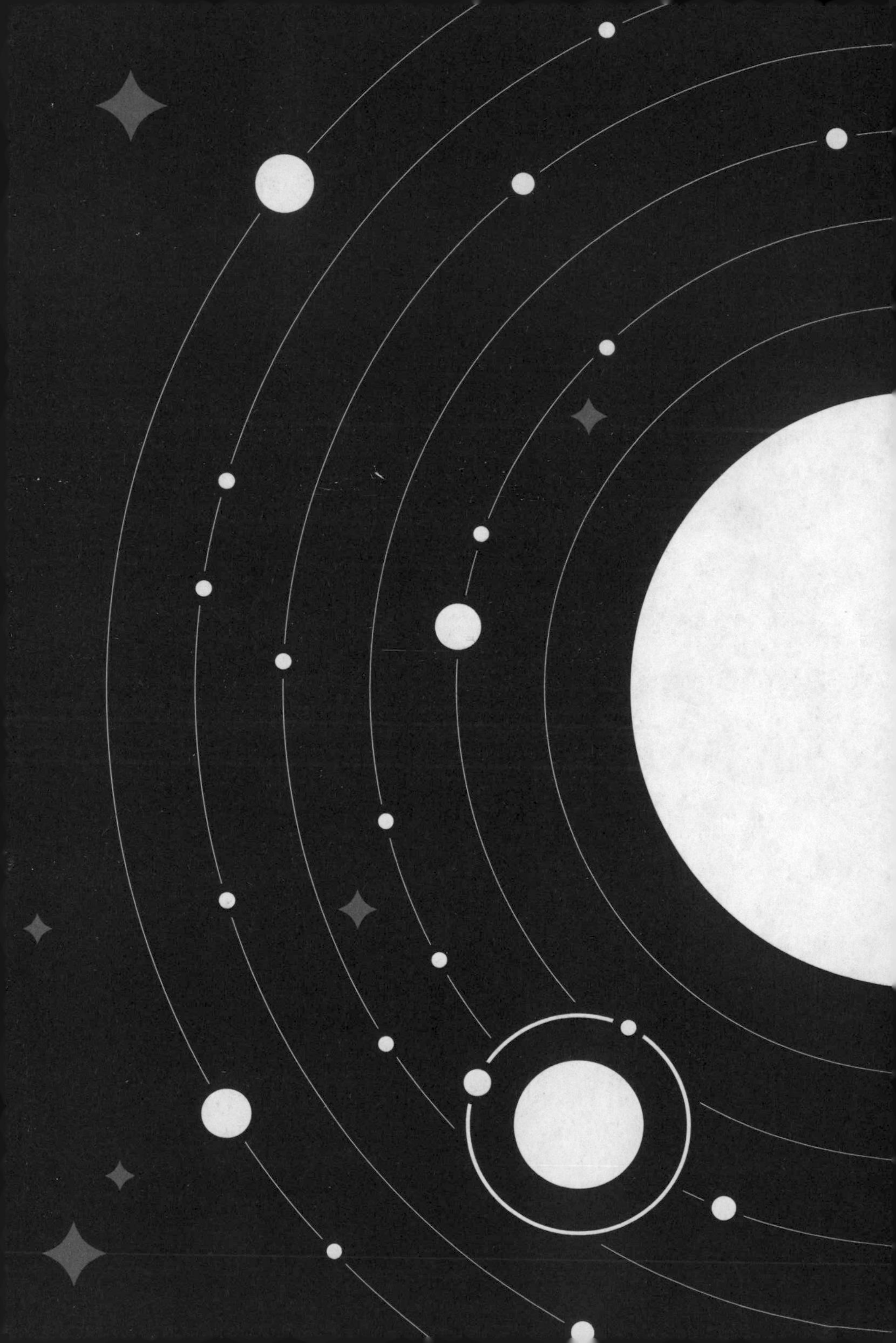

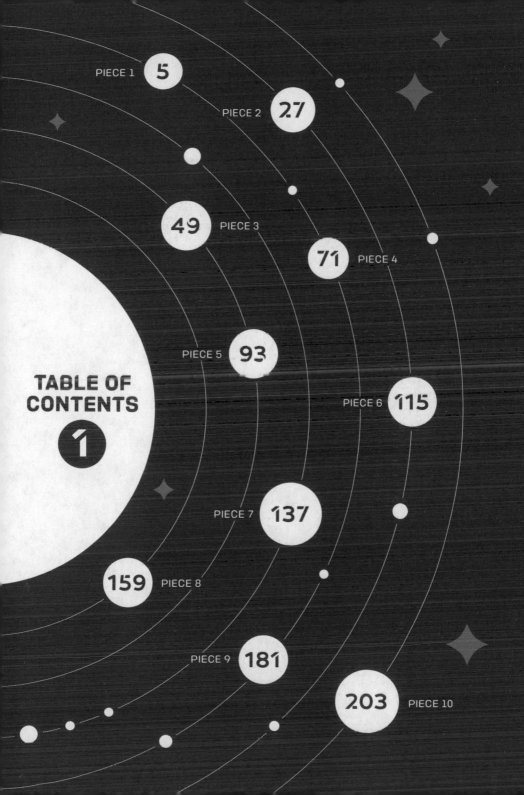

TABLE OF CONTENTS
1

WORLD PIECE

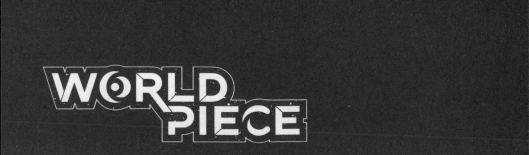

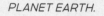

PLANET EARTH.

BUT YOU KNOW THAT ALREADY. YOU LIVE HERE, AFTER ALL.

YOU'VE PROBABLY SEEN IMAGES OF EARTH LIKE THIS...

...BUT VERY FEW HAVE ACTUALLY VIEWED THE PLANET IN ITS ENTIRETY FROM SPACE, SURROUNDED BY STARS.

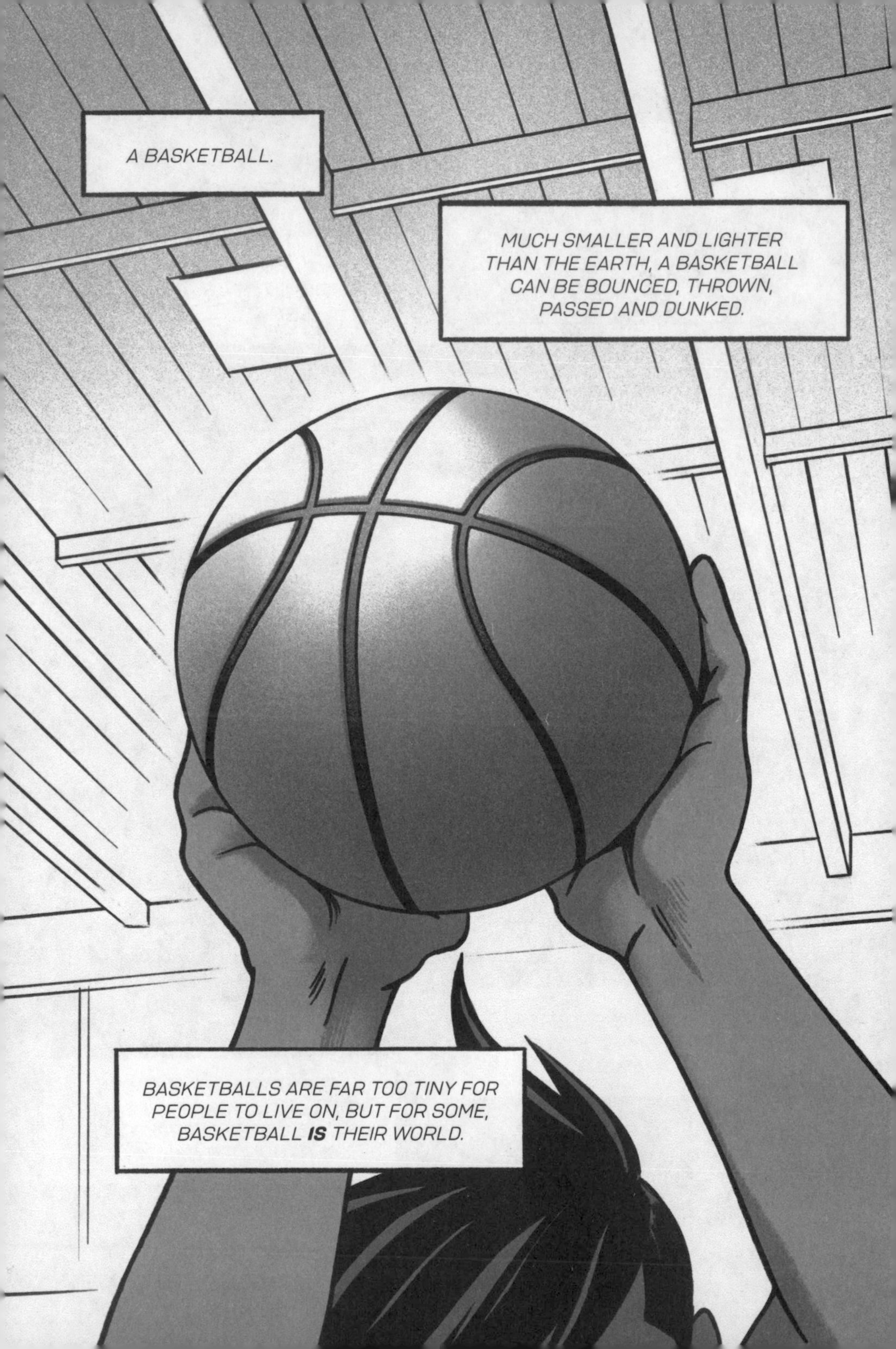
A BASKETBALL.
MUCH SMALLER AND LIGHTER THAN THE EARTH, A BASKETBALL CAN BE BOUNCED, THROWN, PASSED AND DUNKED.
BASKETBALLS ARE FAR TOO TINY FOR PEOPLE TO LIVE ON, BUT FOR SOME, BASKETBALL **IS** THEIR WORLD.

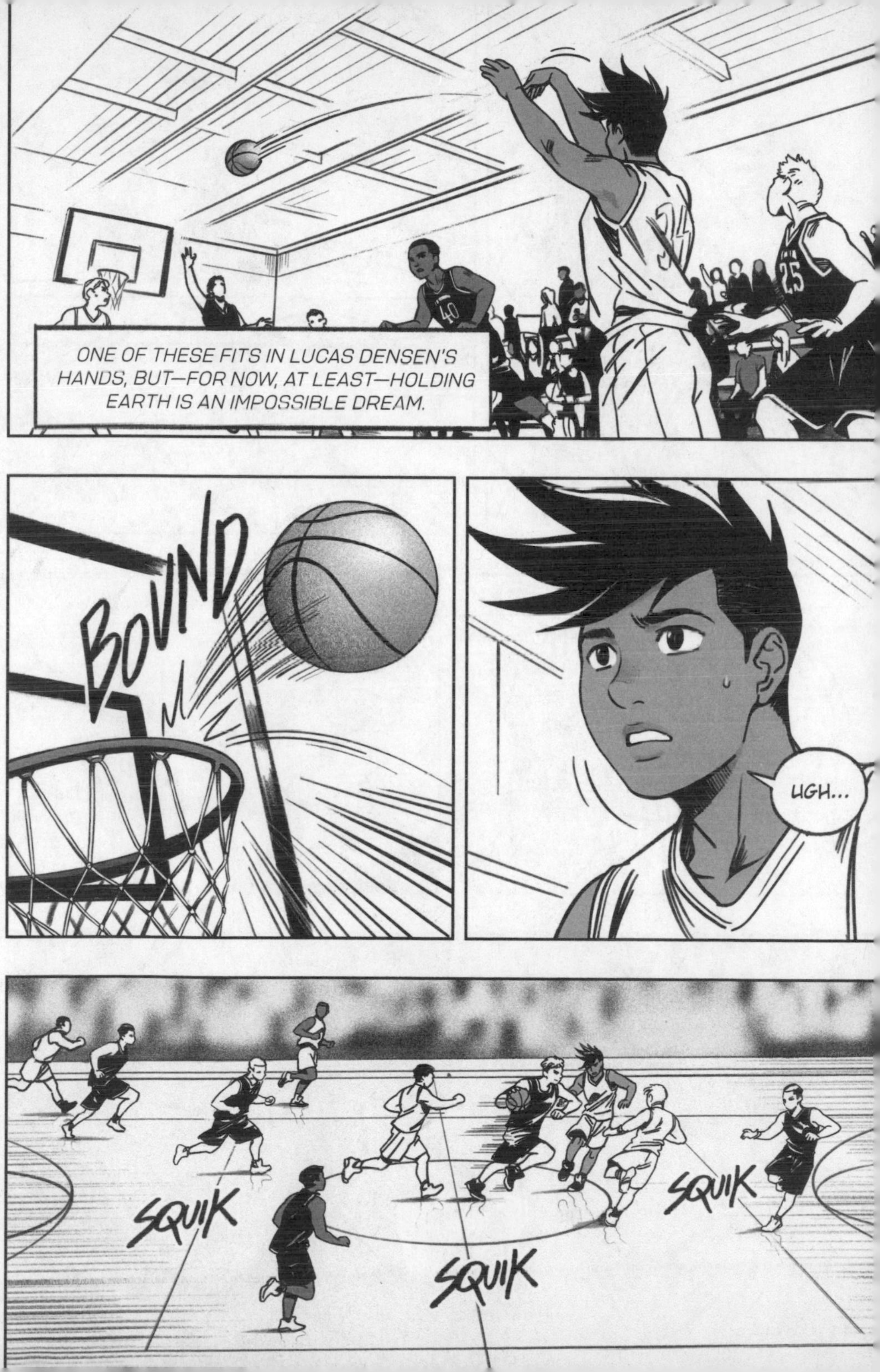
ONE OF THESE FITS IN LUCAS DENSEN'S HANDS, BUT—FOR NOW, AT LEAST—HOLDING EARTH IS AN IMPOSSIBLE DREAM.
BOUND
UGH...
SQUIK
SQUIK
SQUIK

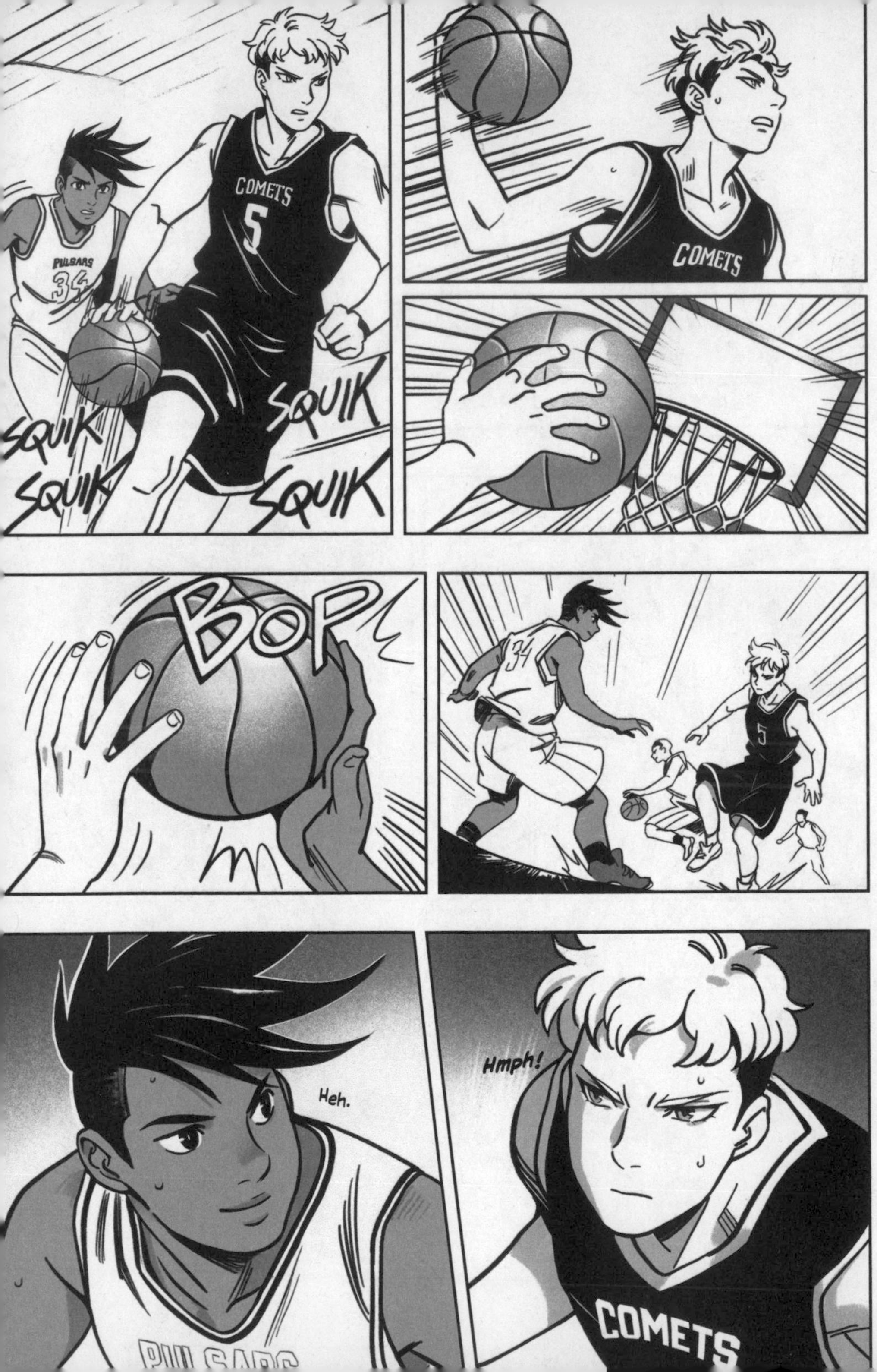

PULSARS
34
COMETS
5
SQUIK
SQUIK
SQUIK
SQUIK
COMETS
BOP
34
5
Heh.
Hmph!
COMETS

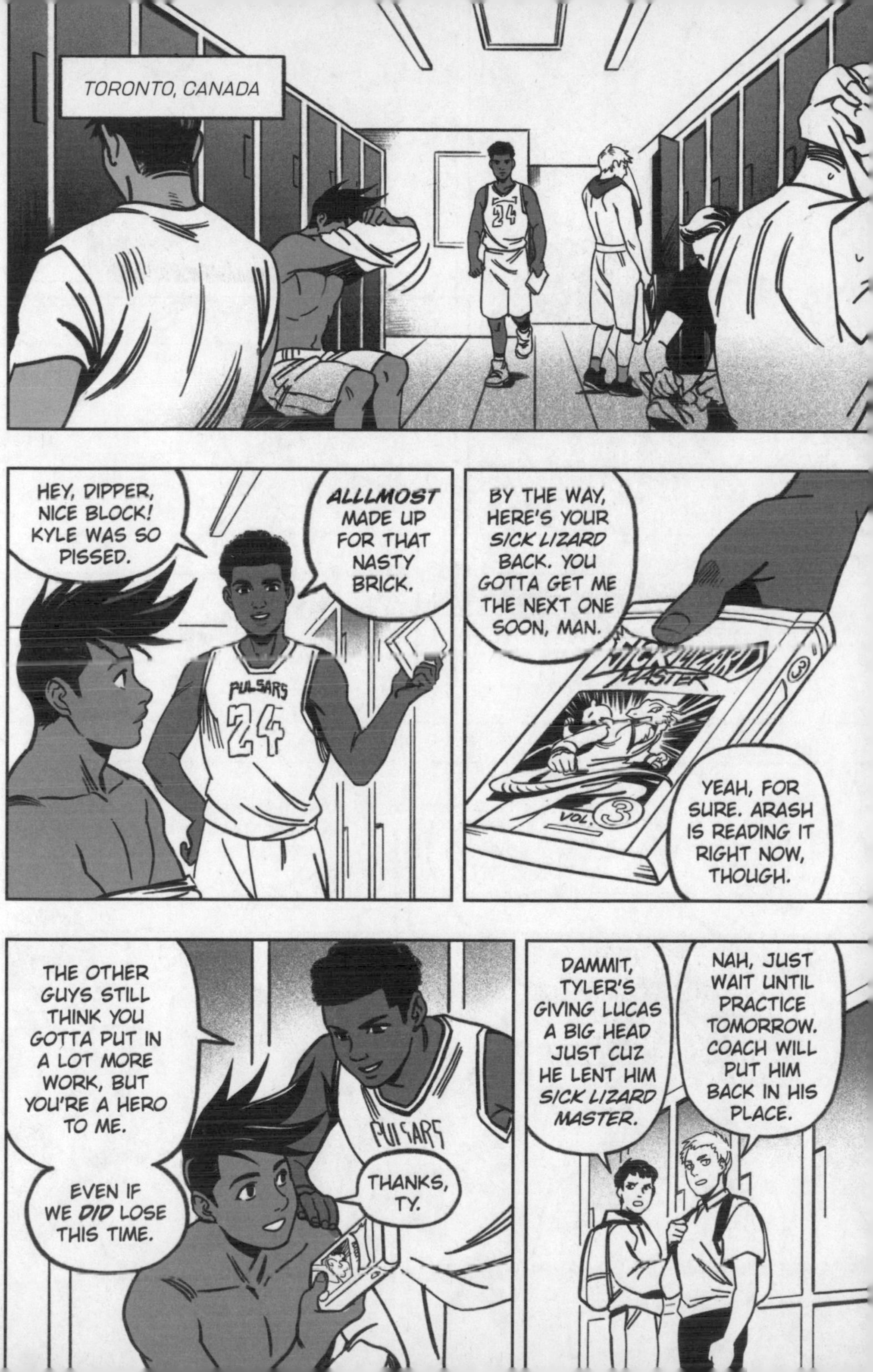
TORONTO, CANADA
HEY, DIPPER, NICE BLOCK! KYLE WAS SO PISSED.
ALLLMOST MADE UP FOR THAT NASTY BRICK.
PULSARS 24
BY THE WAY, HERE'S YOUR SICK LIZARD BACK. YOU GOTTA GET ME THE NEXT ONE SOON, MAN.
SICK LIZARD MASTER
VOL. 3
YEAH, FOR SURE. ARASH IS READING IT RIGHT NOW, THOUGH.
THE OTHER GUYS STILL THINK YOU GOTTA PUT IN A LOT MORE WORK, BUT YOU'RE A HERO TO ME.
EVEN IF WE DID LOSE THIS TIME.
PULSARS
THANKS, TY.
DAMMIT, TYLER'S GIVING LUCAS A BIG HEAD JUST CUZ HE LENT HIM SICK LIZARD MASTER.
NAH, JUST WAIT UNTIL PRACTICE TOMORROW. COACH WILL PUT HIM BACK IN HIS PLACE.

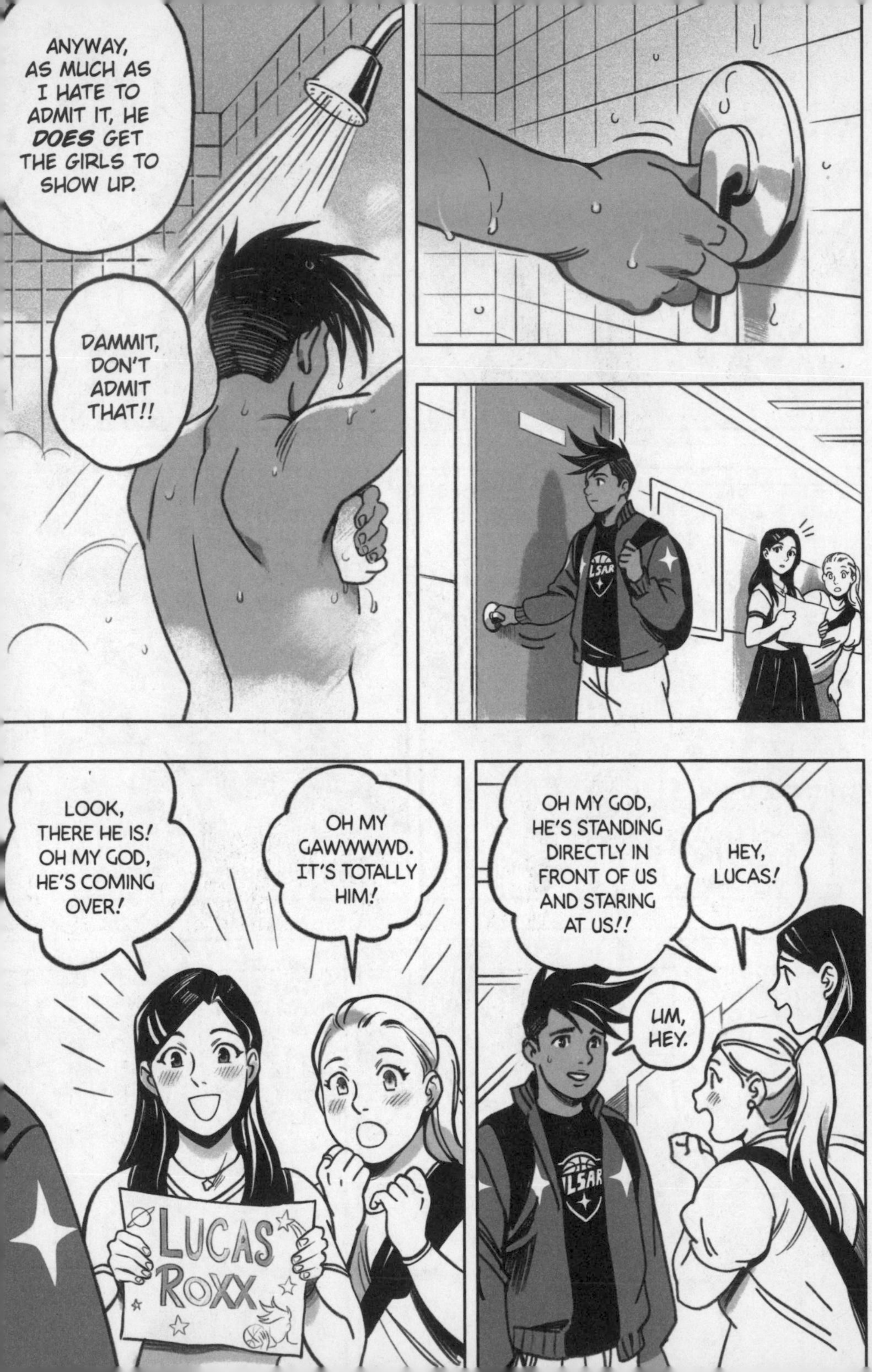
ANYWAY, AS MUCH AS I HATE TO ADMIT IT, HE *DOES* GET THE GIRLS TO SHOW UP.
DAMMIT, DON'T ADMIT THAT!!
LOOK, THERE HE IS! OH MY GOD, HE'S COMING OVER!
LUCAS ROXX
OH MY GAWWWWD. IT'S TOTALLY HIM!
OH MY GOD, HE'S STANDING DIRECTLY IN FRONT OF US AND STARING AT US!!
HEY, LUCAS!
UM, HEY.

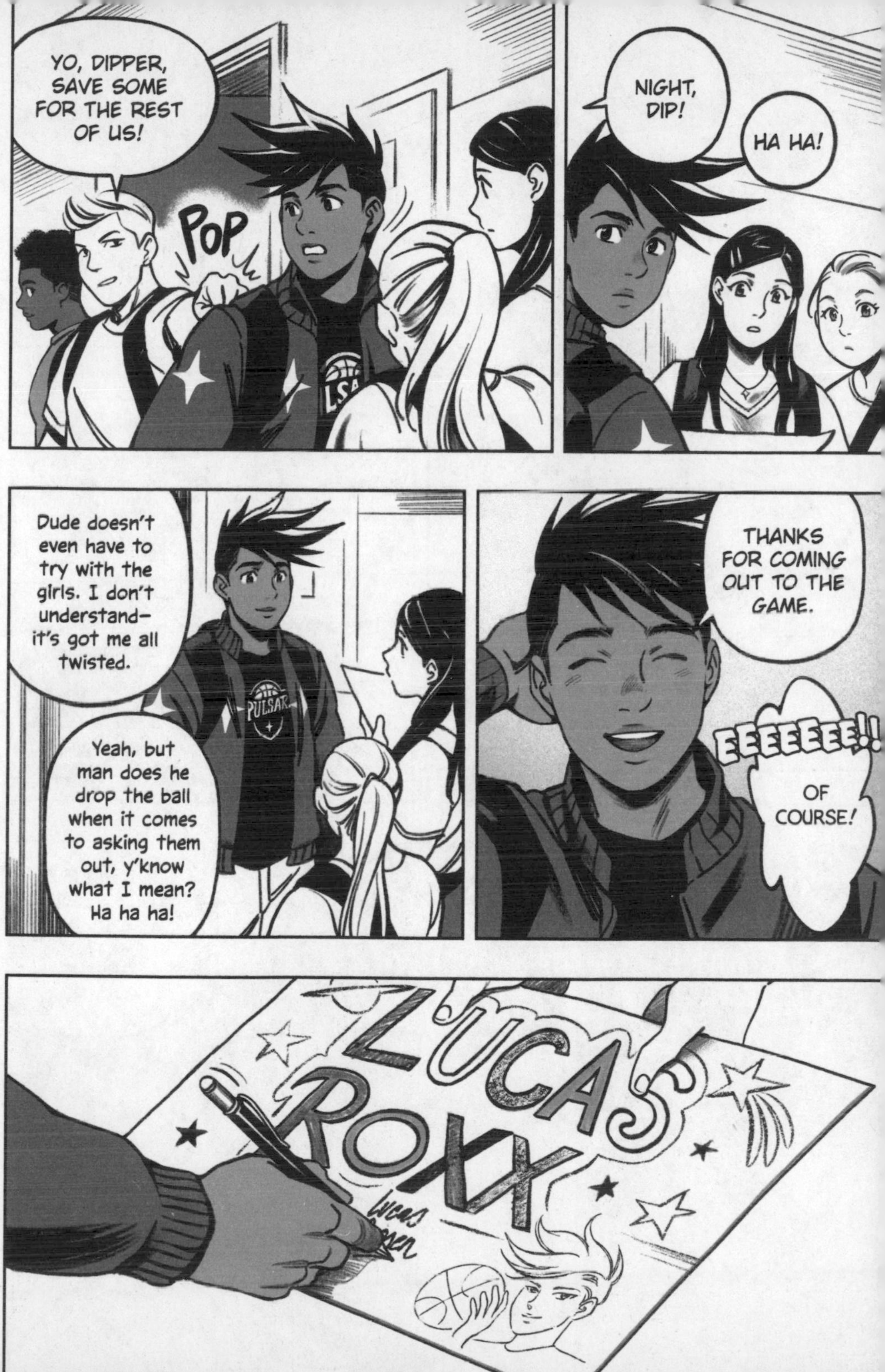
YO, DIPPER, SAVE SOME FOR THE REST OF US!
POP
NIGHT, DIP!
HA HA!
Dude doesn't even have to try with the girls. I don't understand— it's got me all twisted.
PULSAR
Yeah, but man does he drop the ball when it comes to asking them out, y'know what I mean? Ha ha ha!
THANKS FOR COMING OUT TO THE GAME.
EEEEEEE!!
OF COURSE!
LUCAS ROXX

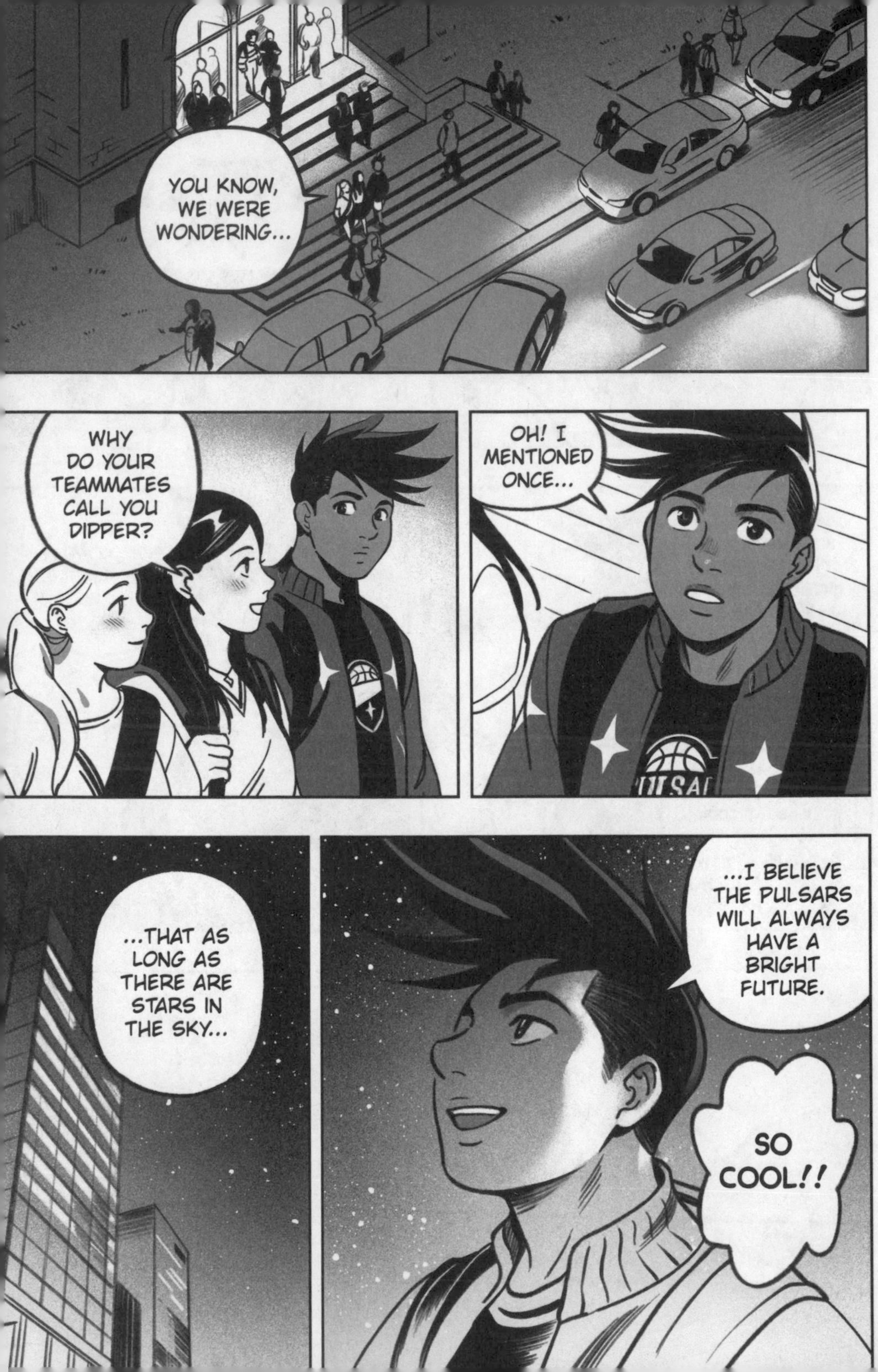
YOU KNOW, WE WERE WONDERING...
WHY DO YOUR TEAMMATES CALL YOU DIPPER?
OH! I MENTIONED ONCE...
...THAT AS LONG AS THERE ARE STARS IN THE SKY...
...I BELIEVE THE PULSARS WILL ALWAYS HAVE A BRIGHT FUTURE.
SO COOL!!

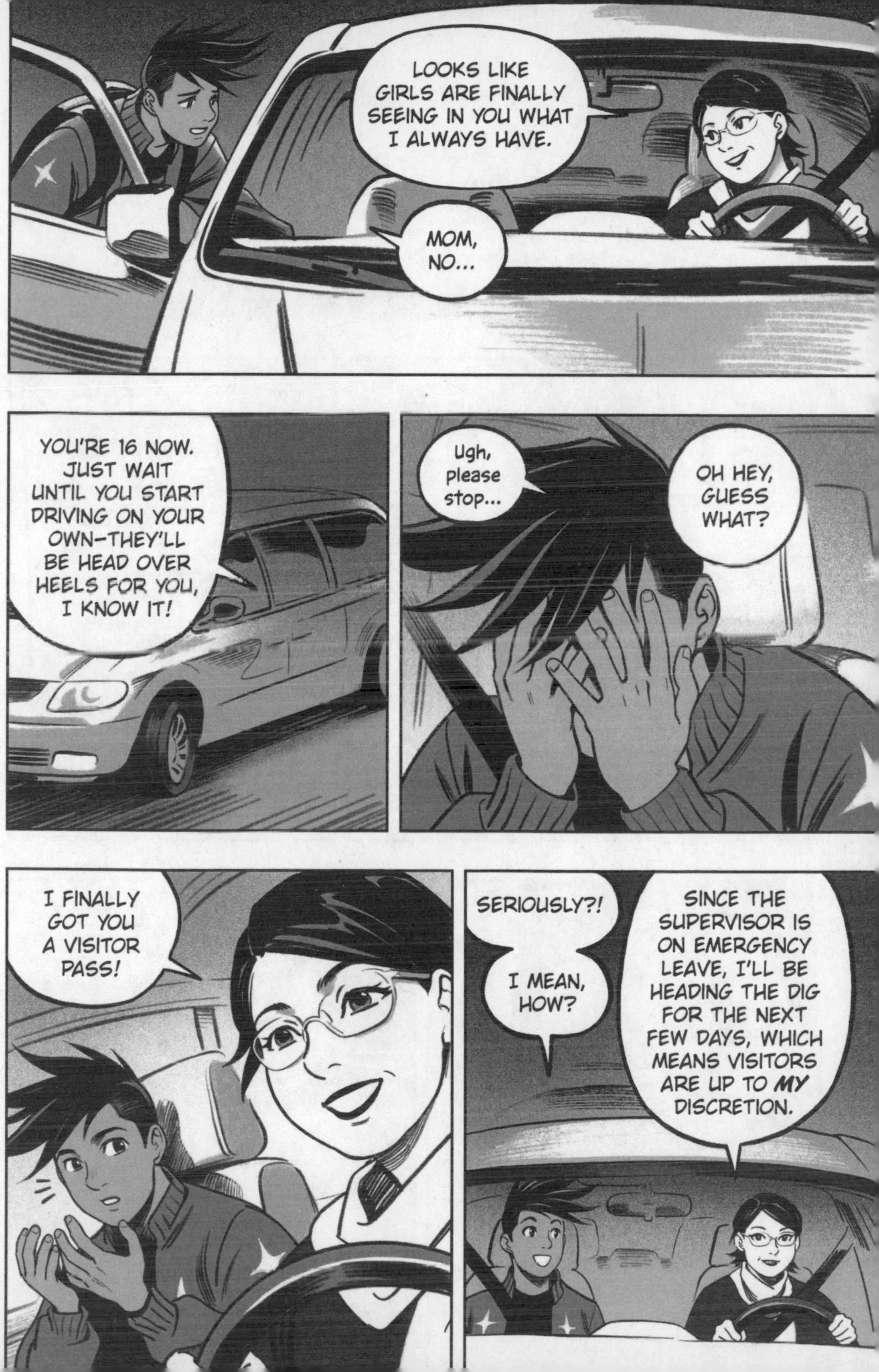
LOOKS LIKE GIRLS ARE FINALLY SEEING IN YOU WHAT I ALWAYS HAVE.
MOM, NO...
YOU'RE 16 NOW. JUST WAIT UNTIL YOU START DRIVING ON YOUR OWN—THEY'LL BE HEAD OVER HEELS FOR YOU, I KNOW IT!
Ugh, please stop...
OH HEY, GUESS WHAT?
I FINALLY GOT YOU A VISITOR PASS!
SERIOUSLY?!
I MEAN, HOW?
SINCE THE SUPERVISOR IS ON EMERGENCY LEAVE, I'LL BE HEADING THE DIG FOR THE NEXT FEW DAYS, WHICH MEANS VISITORS ARE UP TO *MY* DISCRETION.

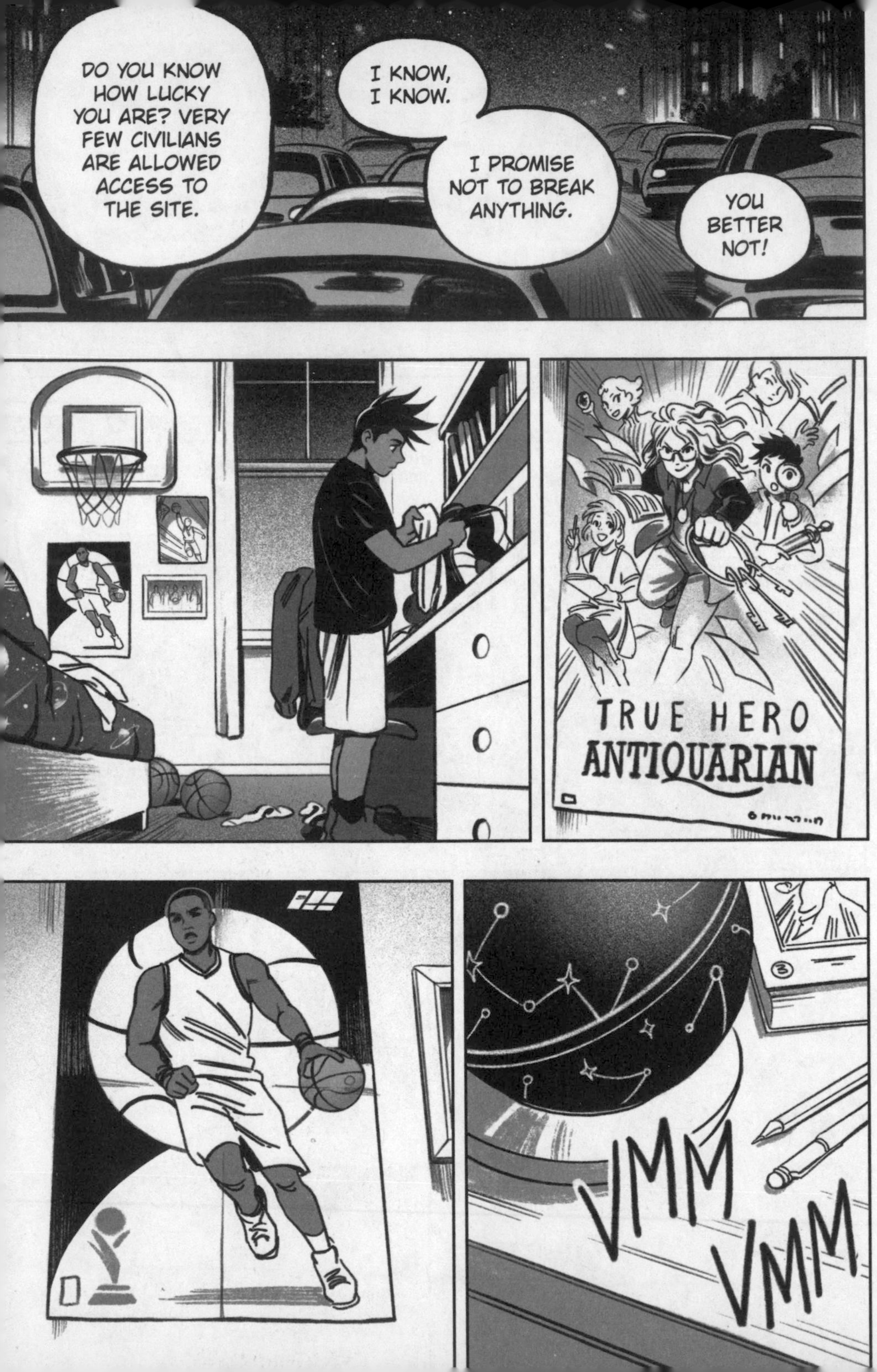
DO YOU KNOW HOW LUCKY YOU ARE? VERY FEW CIVILIANS ARE ALLOWED ACCESS TO THE SITE.
I KNOW, I KNOW.
I PROMISE NOT TO BREAK ANYTHING.
YOU BETTER NOT!
TRUE HERO ANTIQUARIAN
VMM
VMM

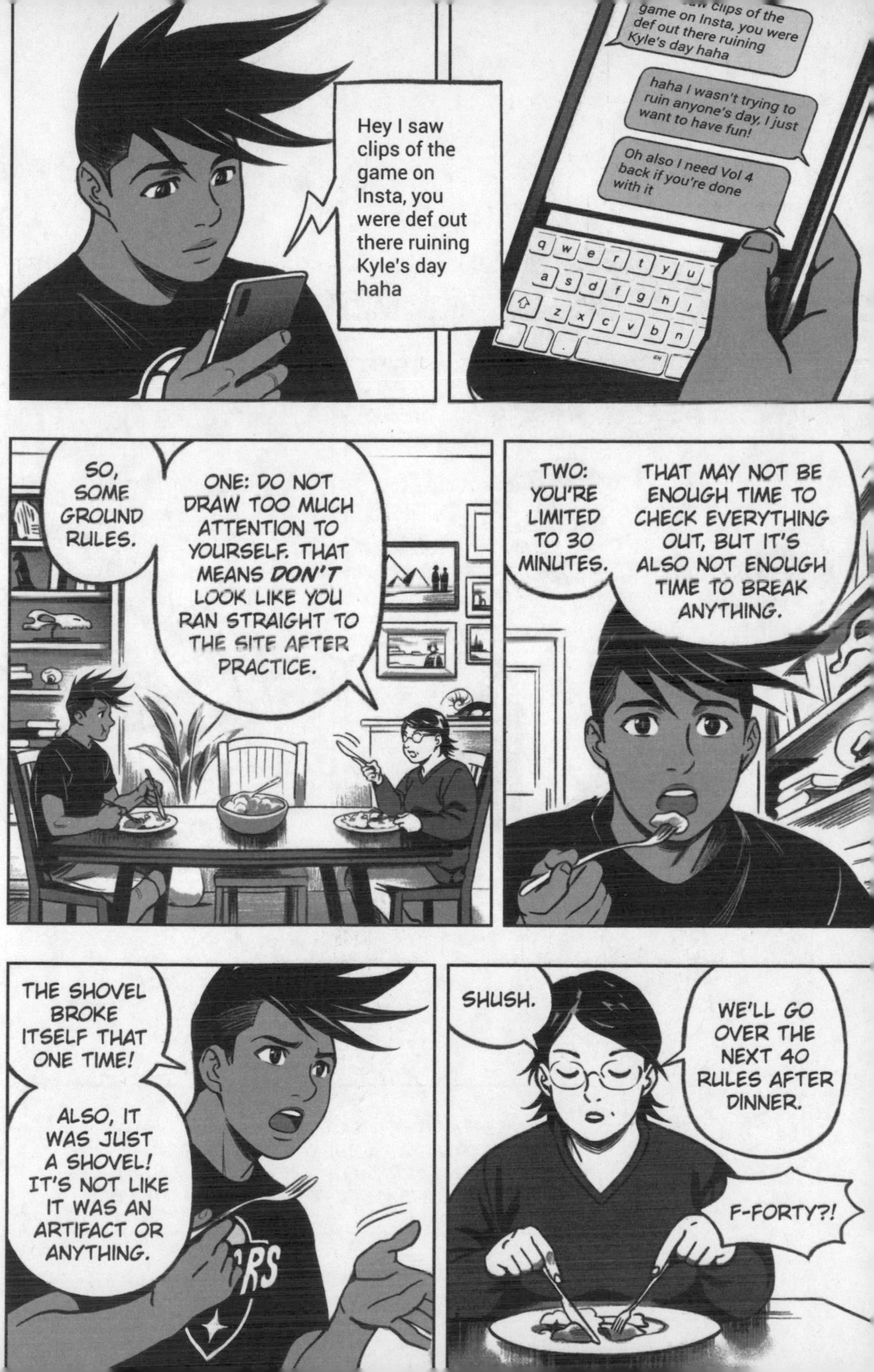
Hey I saw clips of the game on Insta, you were def out there ruining Kyle's day haha
clips of the game on Insta, you were def out there ruining Kyle's day haha
haha I wasn't trying to ruin anyone's day, I just want to have fun!
Oh also I need Vol 4 back if you're done with it
SO, SOME GROUND RULES.
ONE: DO NOT DRAW TOO MUCH ATTENTION TO YOURSELF. THAT MEANS DON'T LOOK LIKE YOU RAN STRAIGHT TO THE SITE AFTER PRACTICE.
TWO: YOU'RE LIMITED TO 30 MINUTES.
THAT MAY NOT BE ENOUGH TIME TO CHECK EVERYTHING OUT, BUT IT'S ALSO NOT ENOUGH TIME TO BREAK ANYTHING.
THE SHOVEL BROKE ITSELF THAT ONE TIME!
ALSO, IT WAS JUST A SHOVEL! IT'S NOT LIKE IT WAS AN ARTIFACT OR ANYTHING.
SHUSH.
WE'LL GO OVER THE NEXT 40 RULES AFTER DINNER.
F-FORTY?!

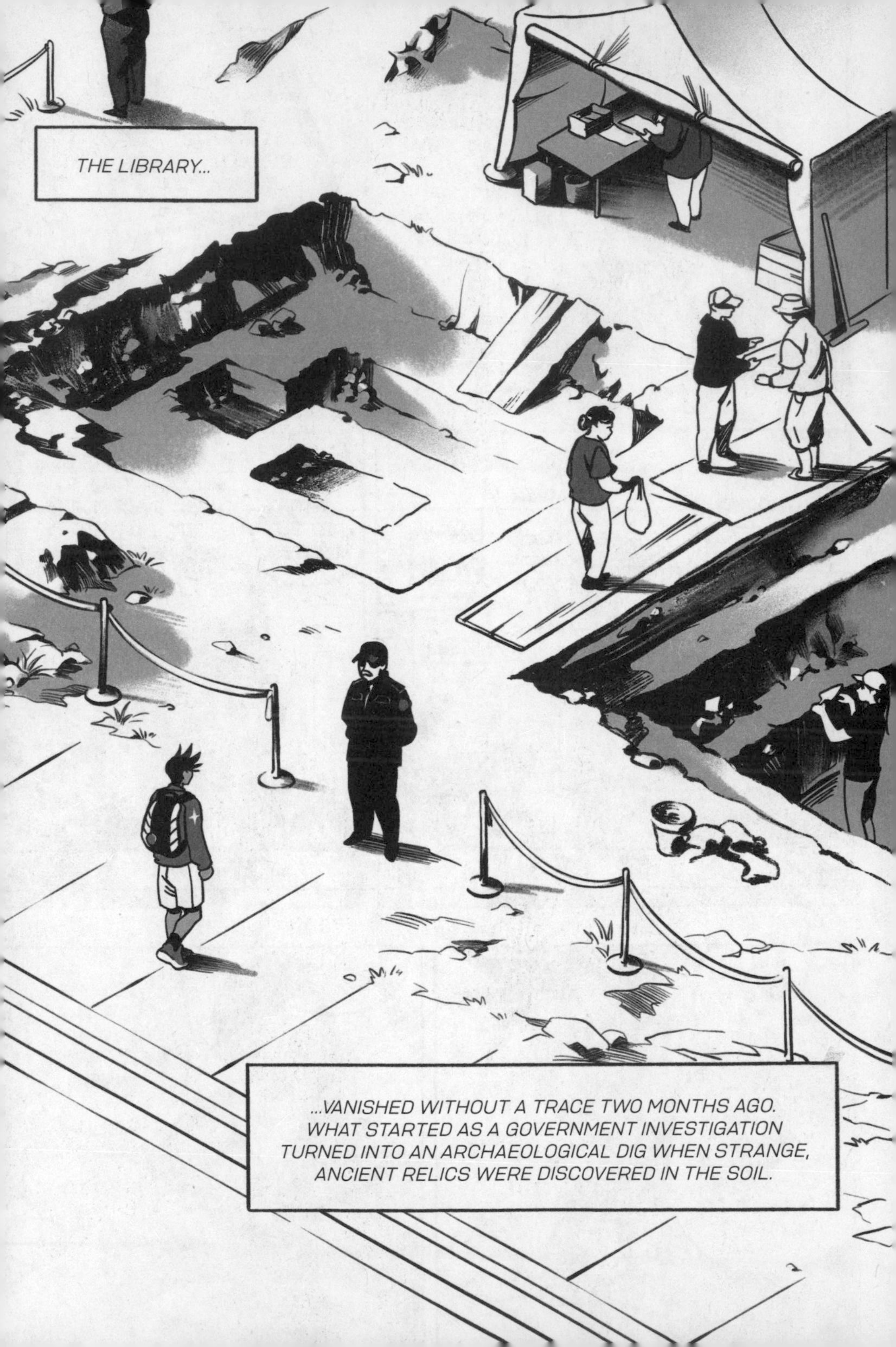
THE LIBRARY...
...VANISHED WITHOUT A TRACE TWO MONTHS AGO. WHAT STARTED AS A GOVERNMENT INVESTIGATION TURNED INTO AN ARCHAEOLOGICAL DIG WHEN STRANGE, ANCIENT RELICS WERE DISCOVERED IN THE SOIL.

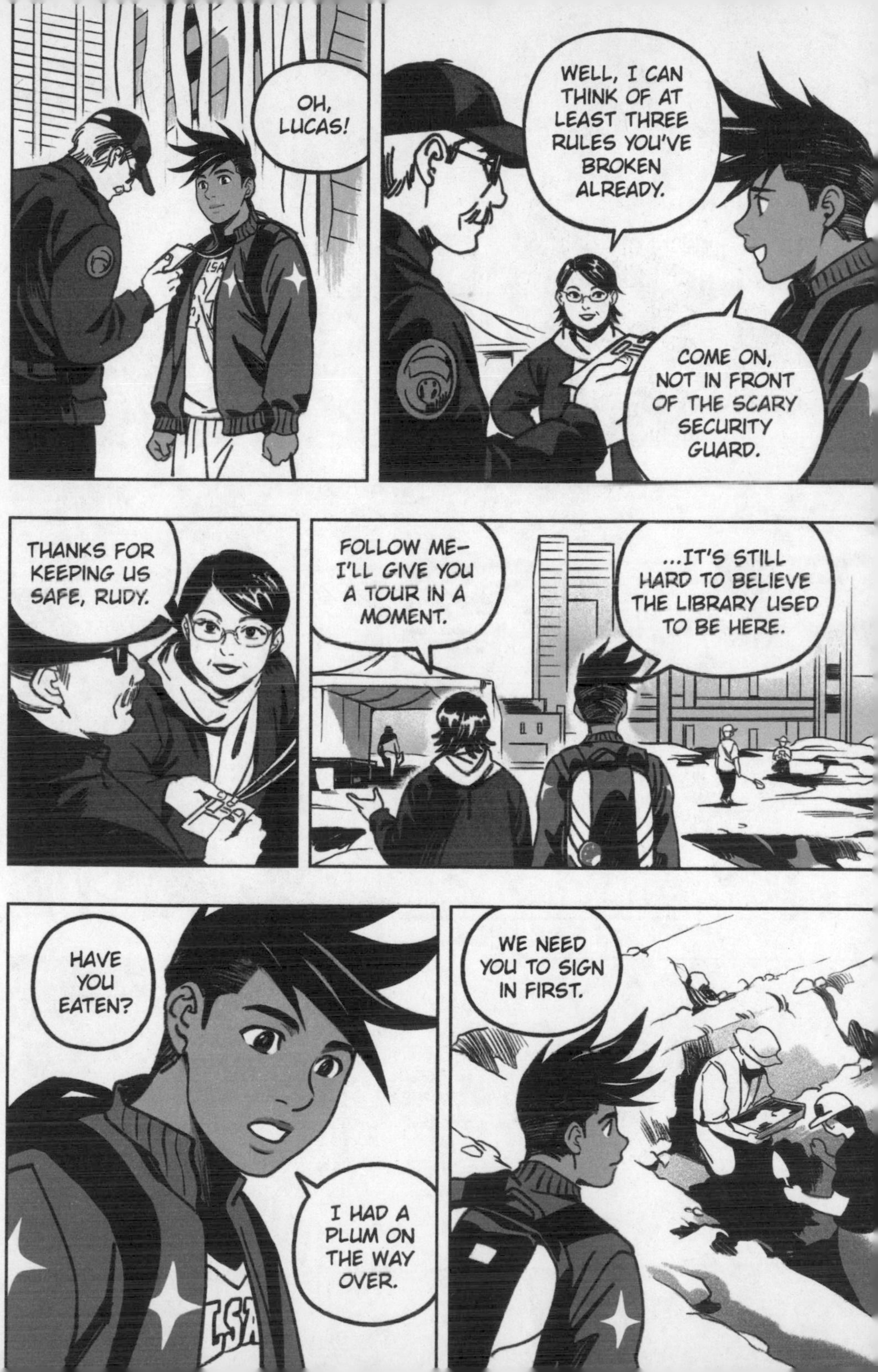
OH, LUCAS!
WELL, I CAN THINK OF AT LEAST THREE RULES YOU'VE BROKEN ALREADY.
COME ON, NOT IN FRONT OF THE SCARY SECURITY GUARD.
THANKS FOR KEEPING US SAFE, RUDY.
FOLLOW ME— I'LL GIVE YOU A TOUR IN A MOMENT.
...IT'S STILL HARD TO BELIEVE THE LIBRARY USED TO BE HERE.
HAVE YOU EATEN?
I HAD A PLUM ON THE WAY OVER.
WE NEED YOU TO SIGN IN FIRST.

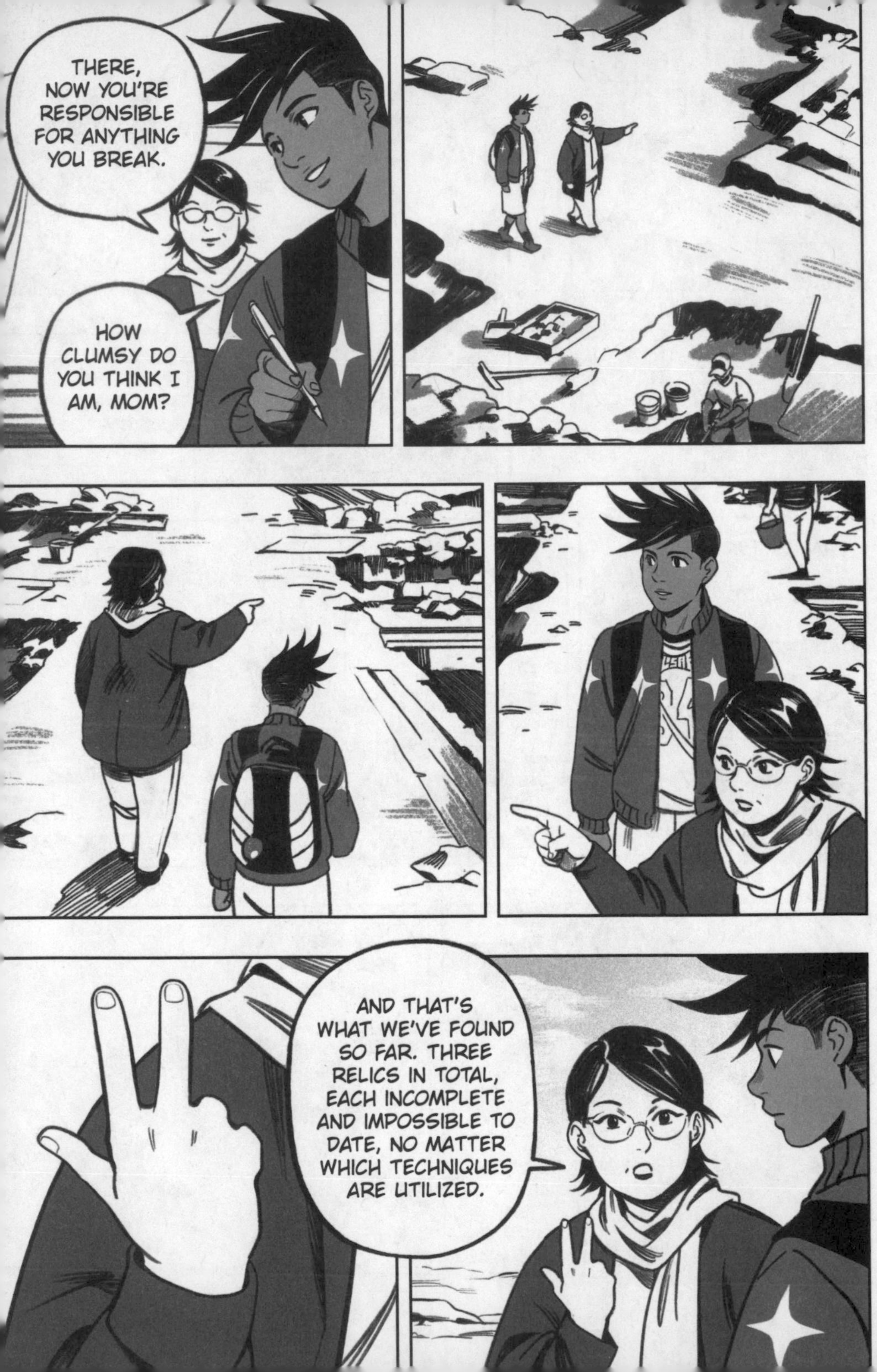
THERE, NOW YOU'RE RESPONSIBLE FOR ANYTHING YOU BREAK.
HOW CLUMSY DO YOU THINK I AM, MOM?
AND THAT'S WHAT WE'VE FOUND SO FAR. THREE RELICS IN TOTAL, EACH INCOMPLETE AND IMPOSSIBLE TO DATE, NO MATTER WHICH TECHNIQUES ARE UTILIZED.

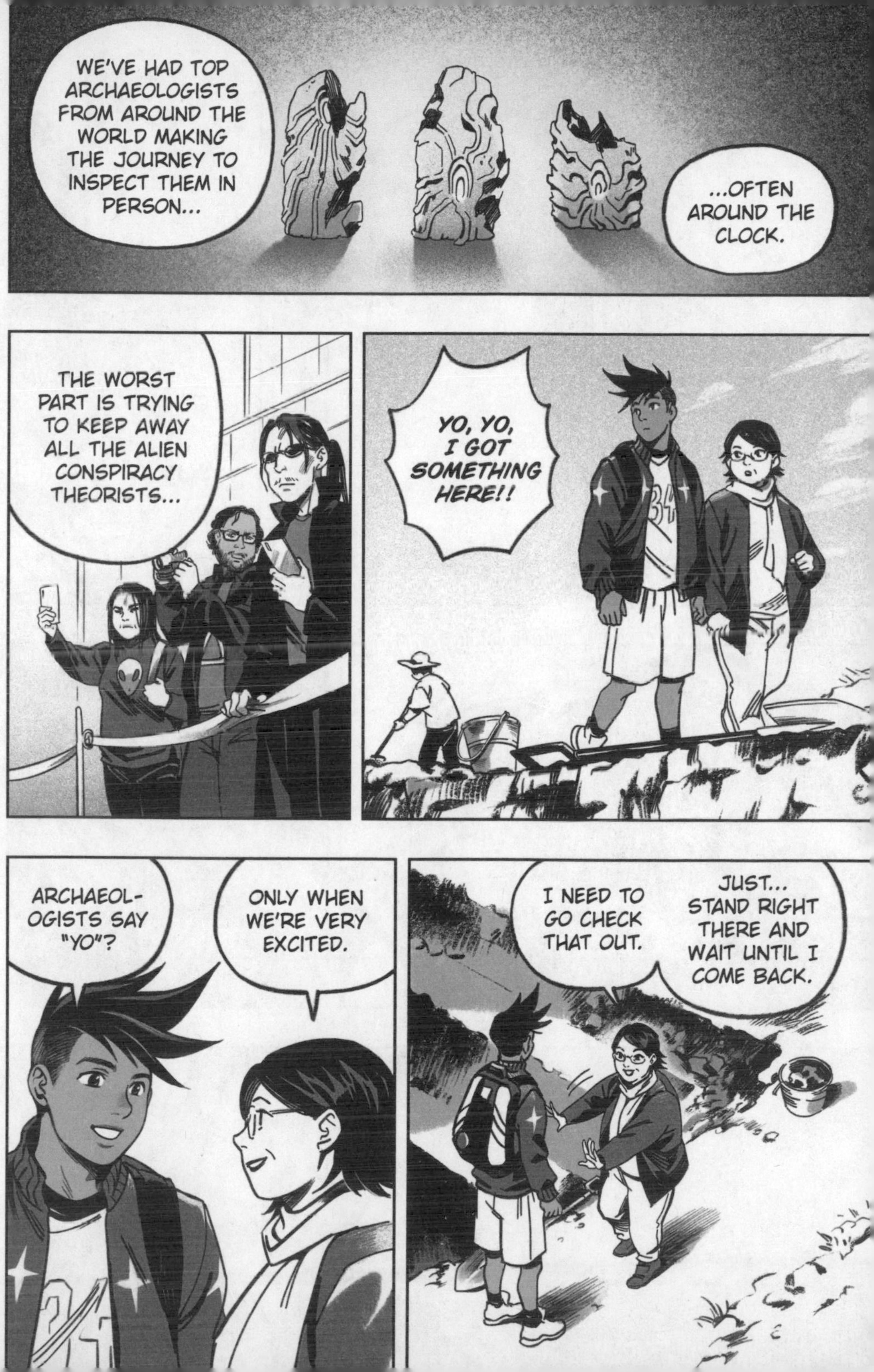
WE'VE HAD TOP ARCHAEOLOGISTS FROM AROUND THE WORLD MAKING THE JOURNEY TO INSPECT THEM IN PERSON...
...OFTEN AROUND THE CLOCK.
THE WORST PART IS TRYING TO KEEP AWAY ALL THE ALIEN CONSPIRACY THEORISTS...
YO, YO, I GOT SOMETHING HERE!!
ARCHAEOL-OGISTS SAY "YO"?
ONLY WHEN WE'RE VERY EXCITED.
I NEED TO GO CHECK THAT OUT.
JUST... STAND RIGHT THERE AND WAIT UNTIL I COME BACK.

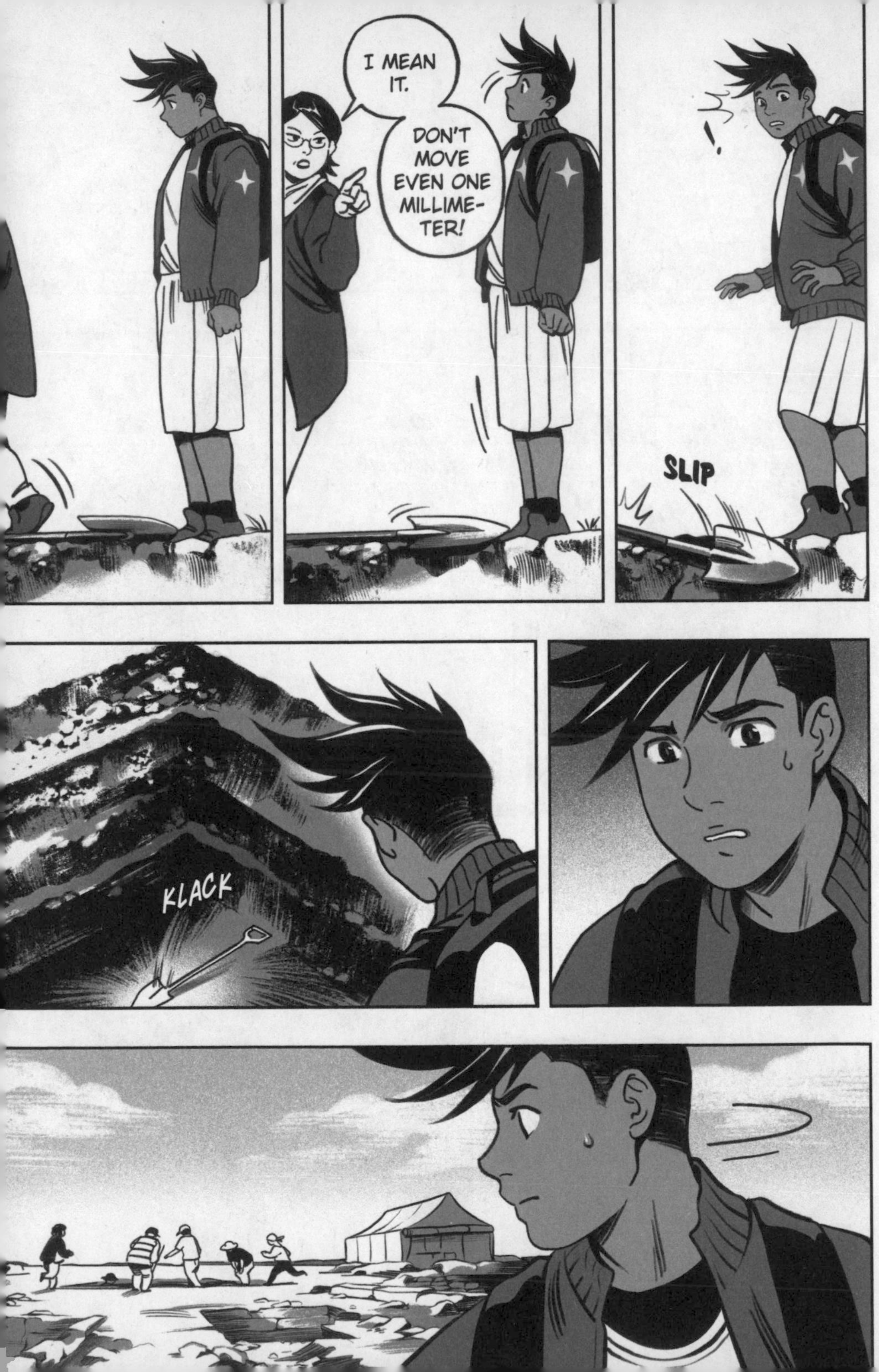
I MEAN IT.
DON'T MOVE EVEN ONE MILLIME-TER!
!
SLIP
KLACK

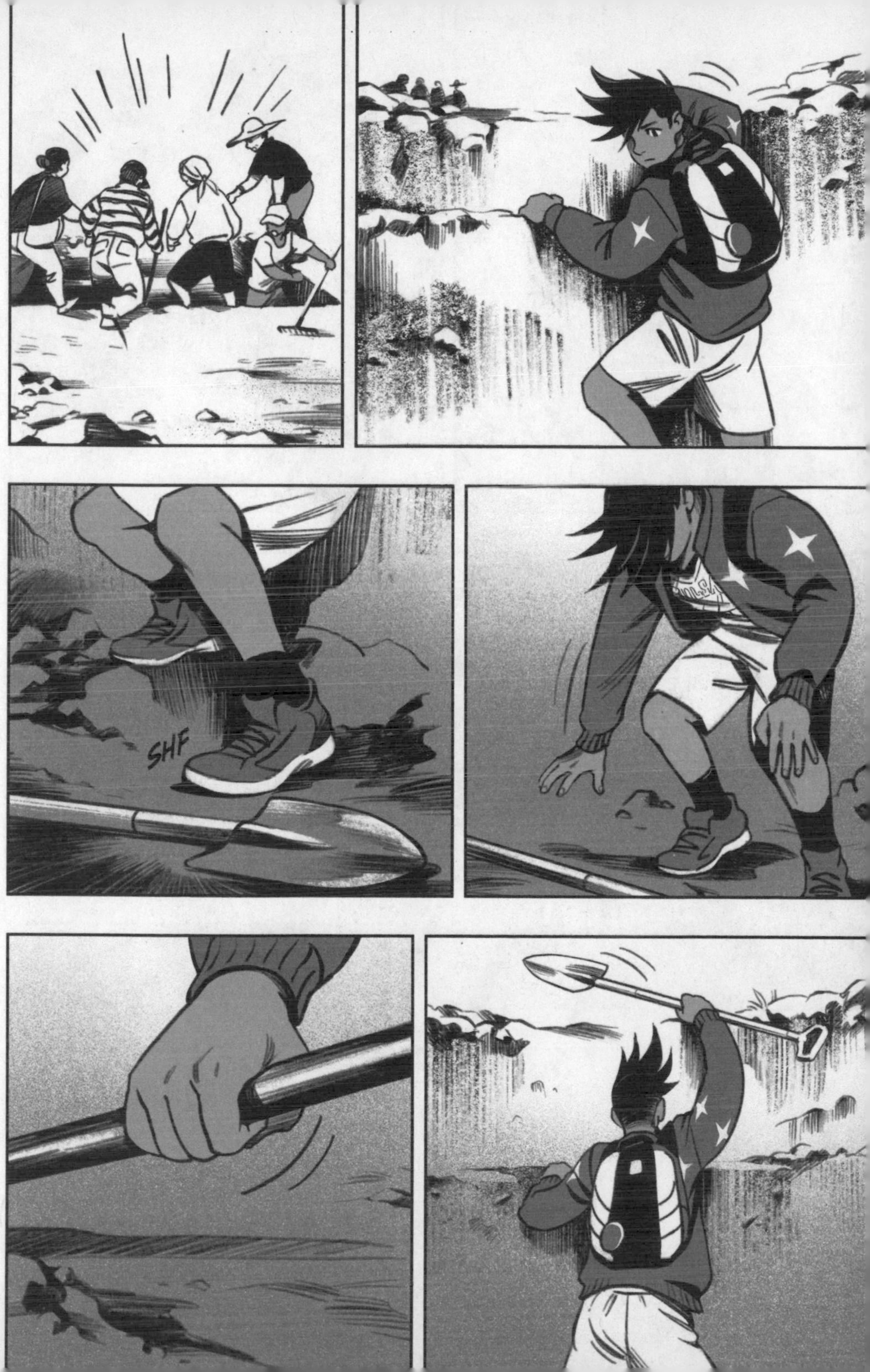
SHF

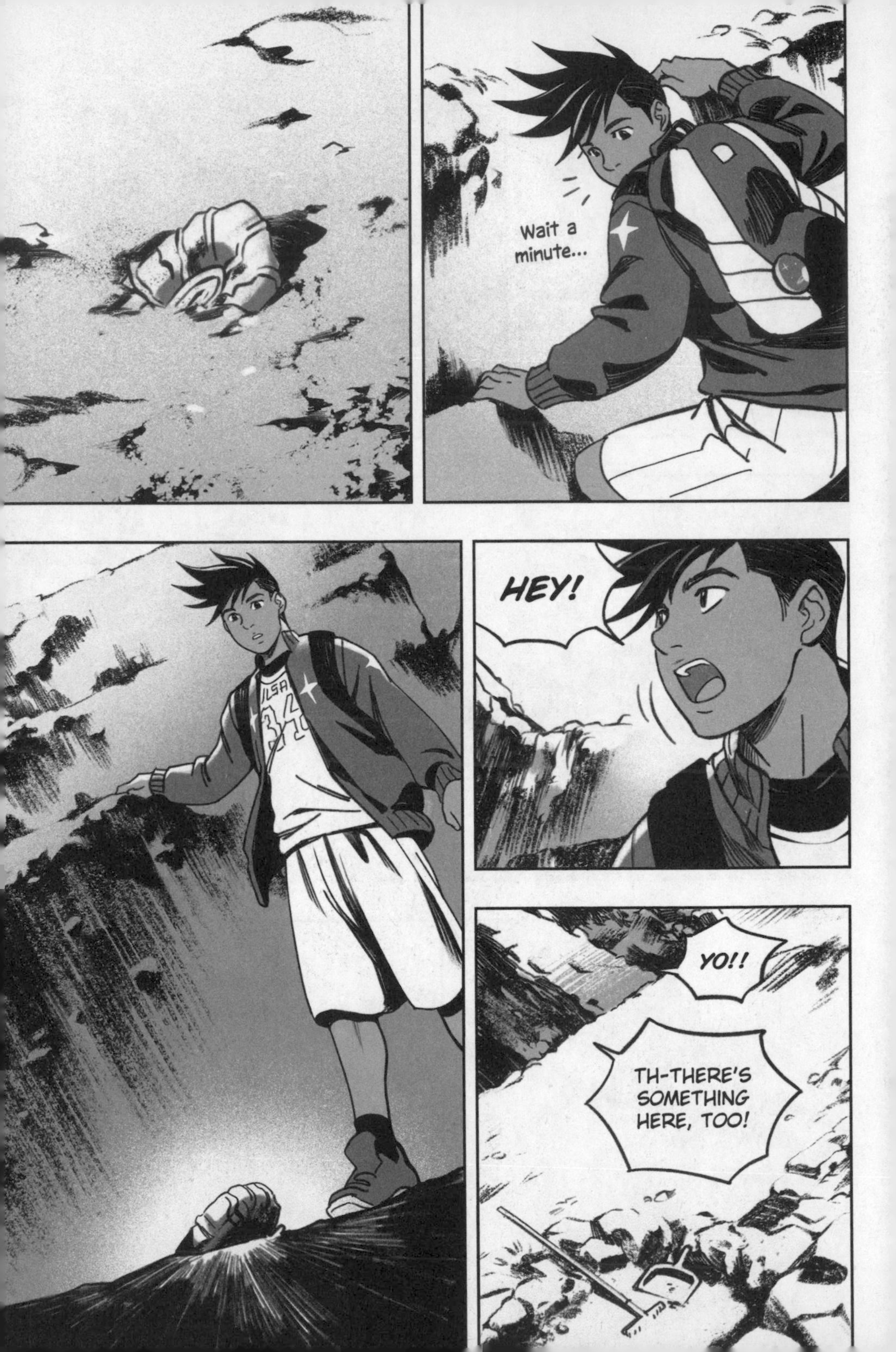
Wait a minute...
HEY!
YO!!
TH-THERE'S SOMETHING HERE, TOO!

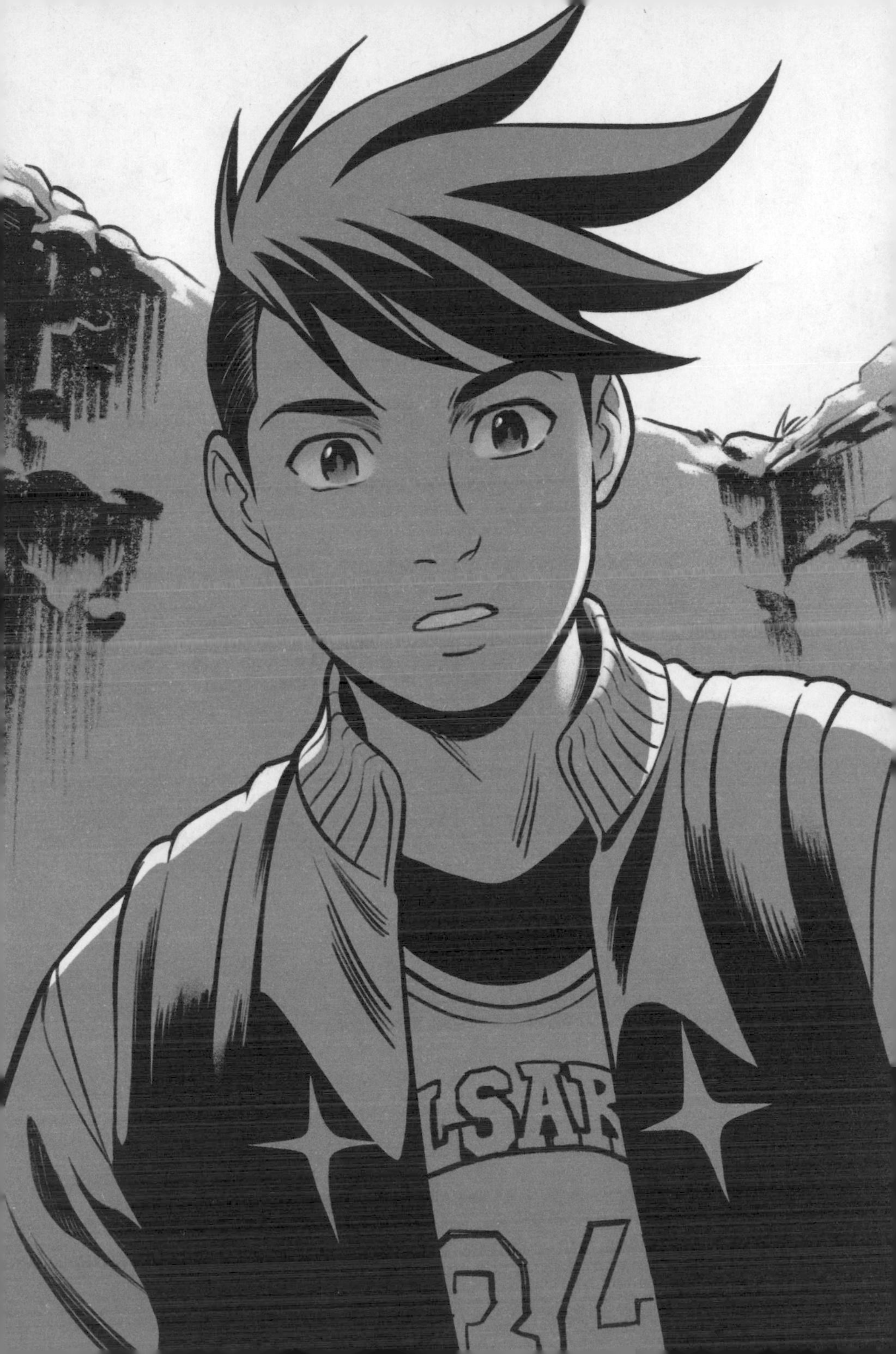

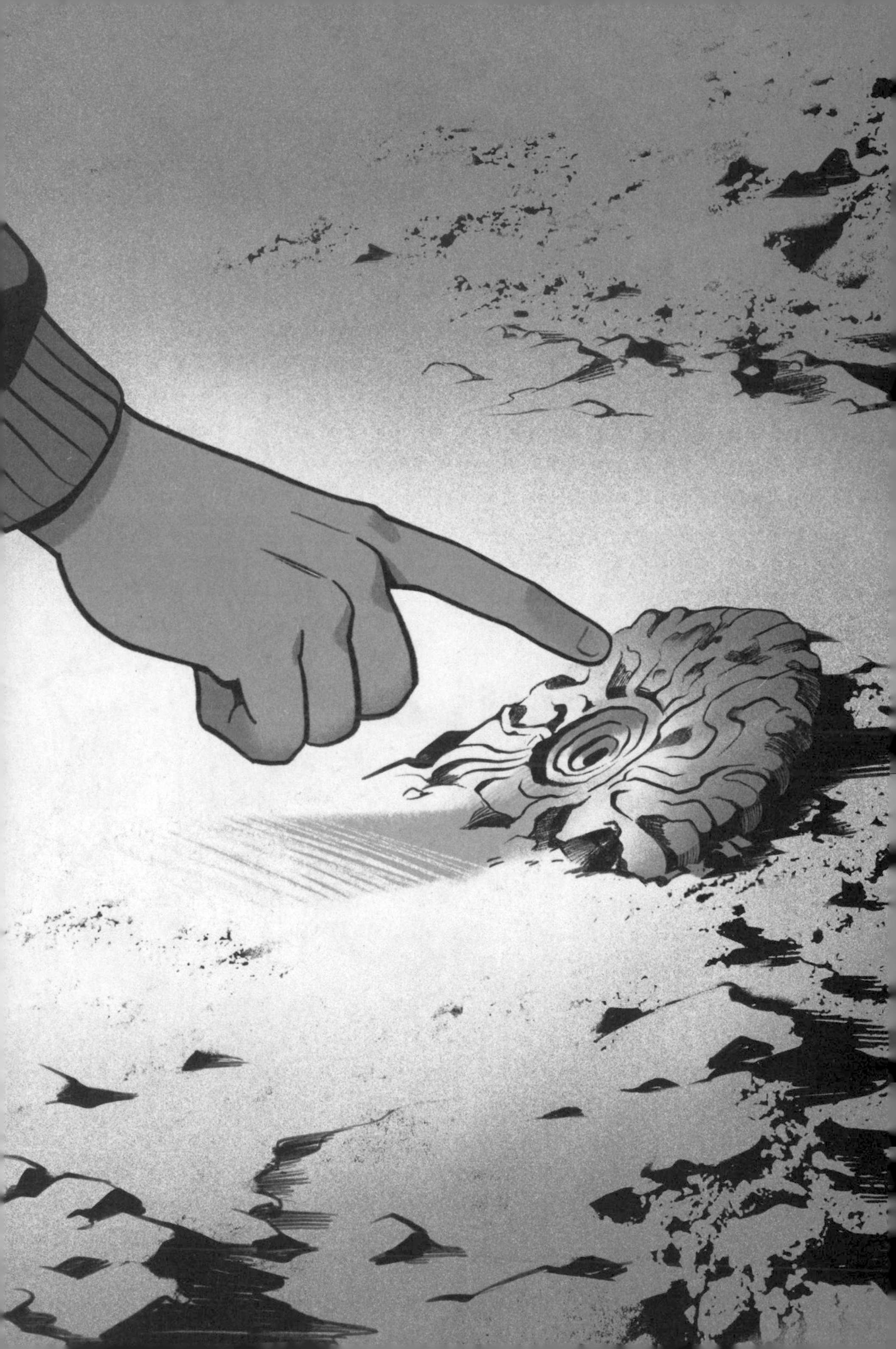

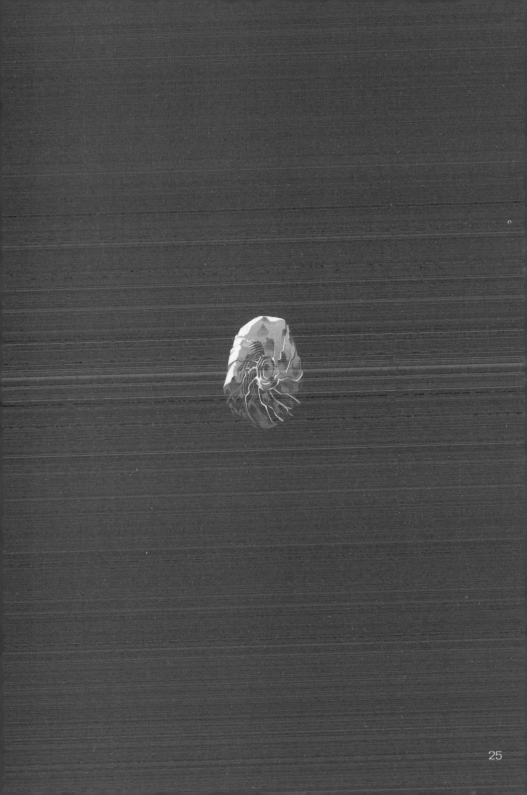

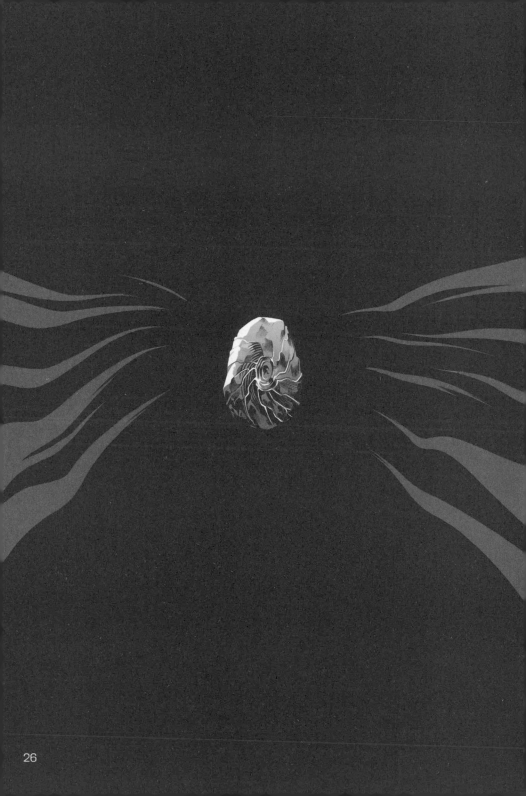

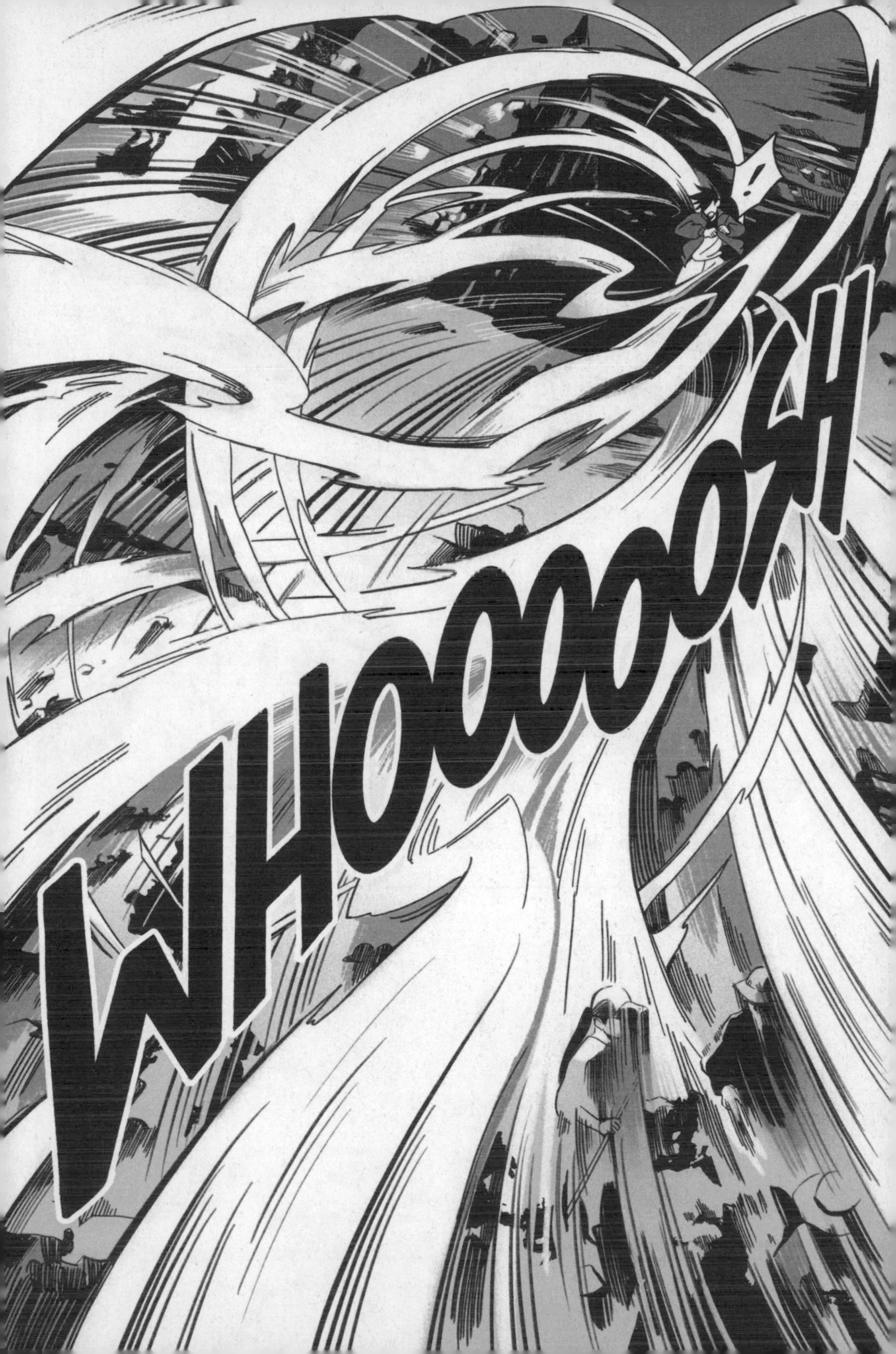
!
WHOOOOOSH

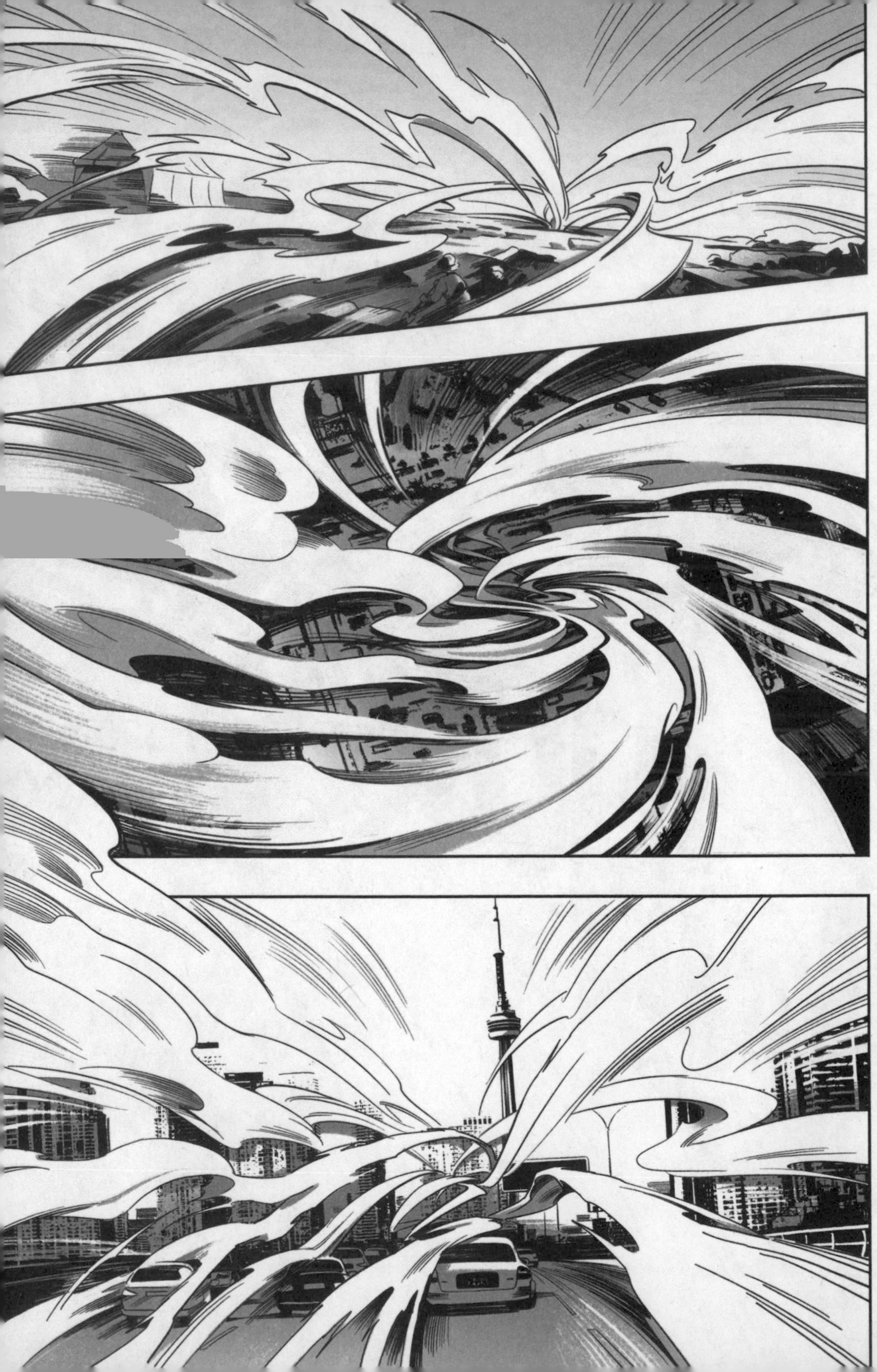

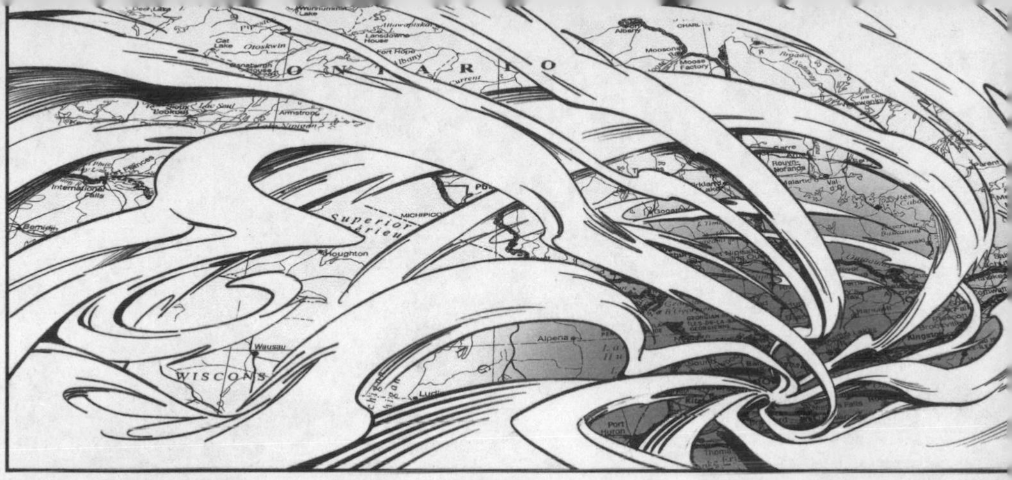
O N T A R I O
Cat Lake
Otoskwin
Lansdowne House
Fort Hope
Moose Factory
Superior
Houghton
Wausau
WISCONS
Alpena
Port Huron

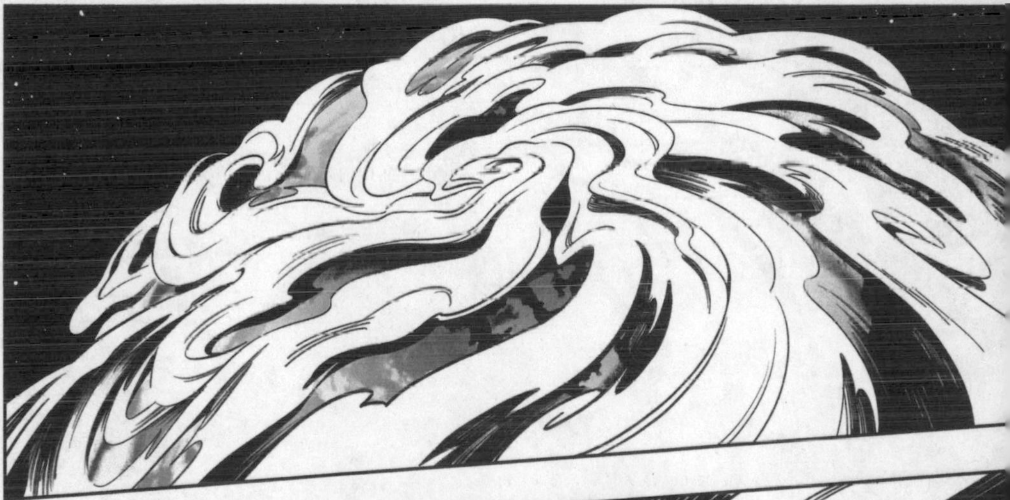

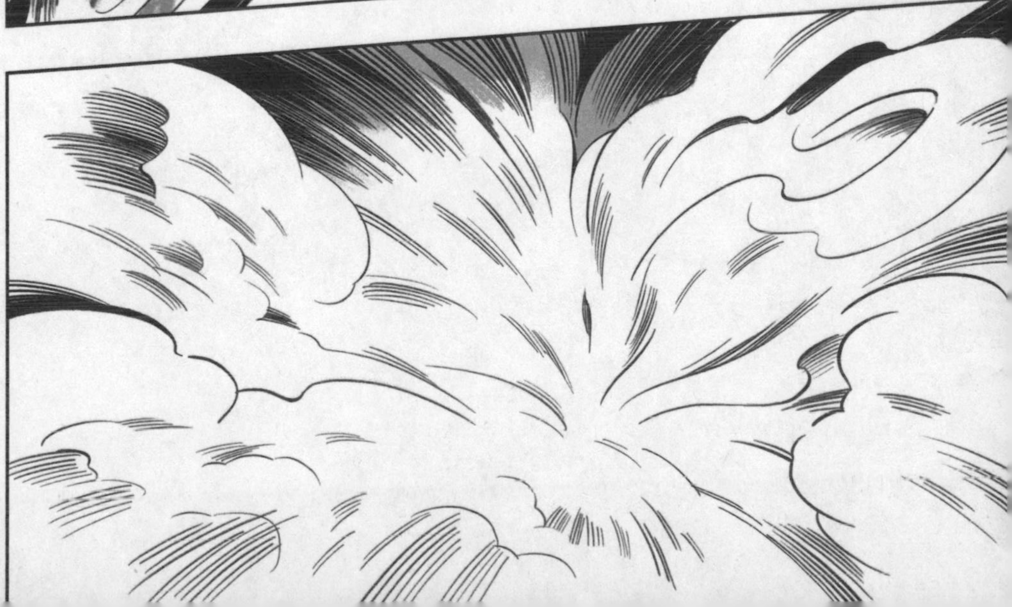

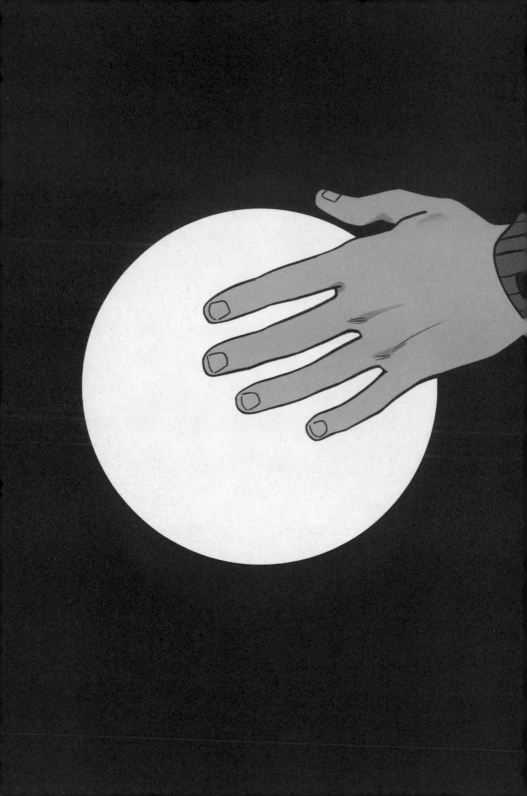

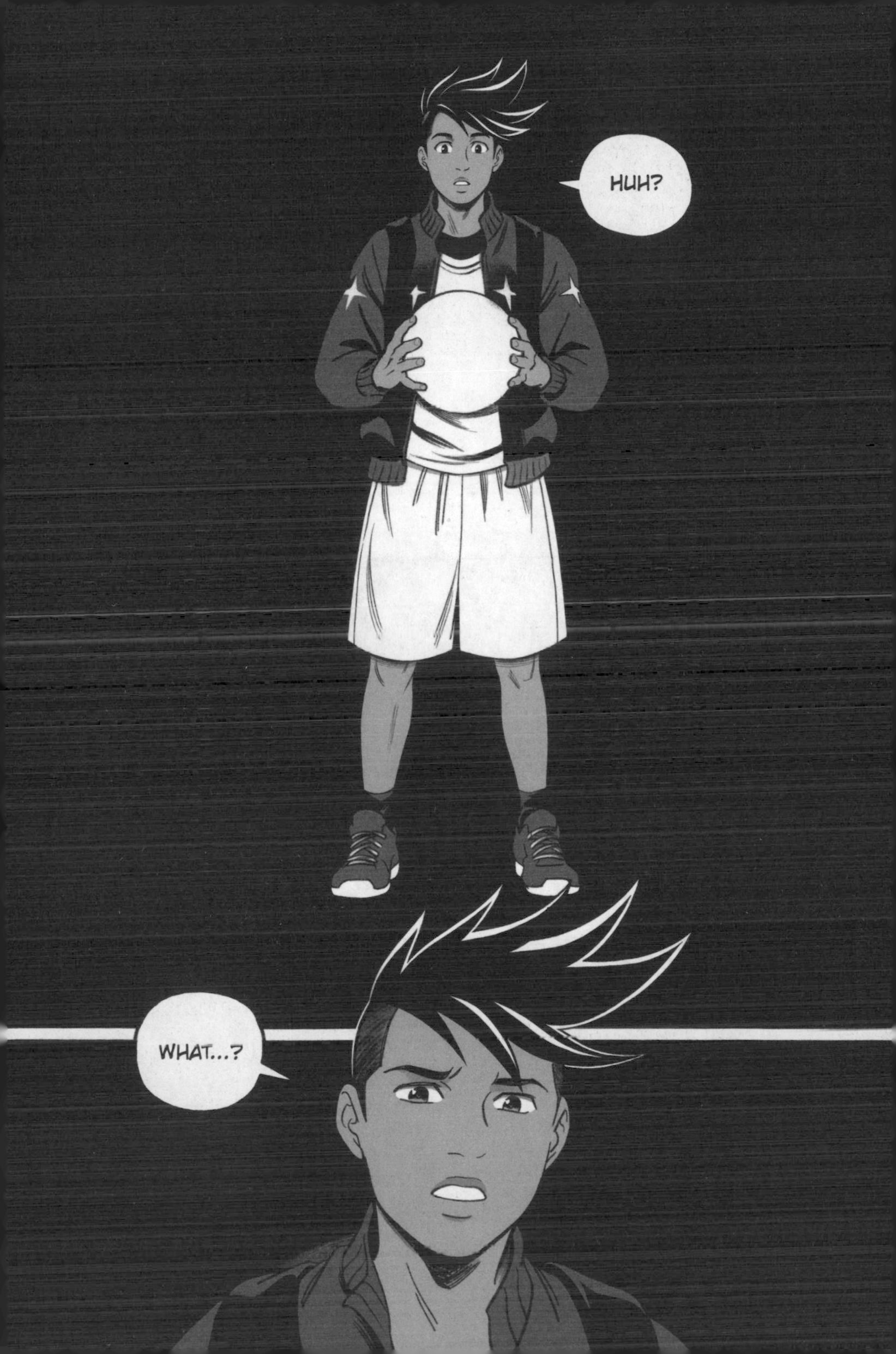
HUH?
WHAT...?

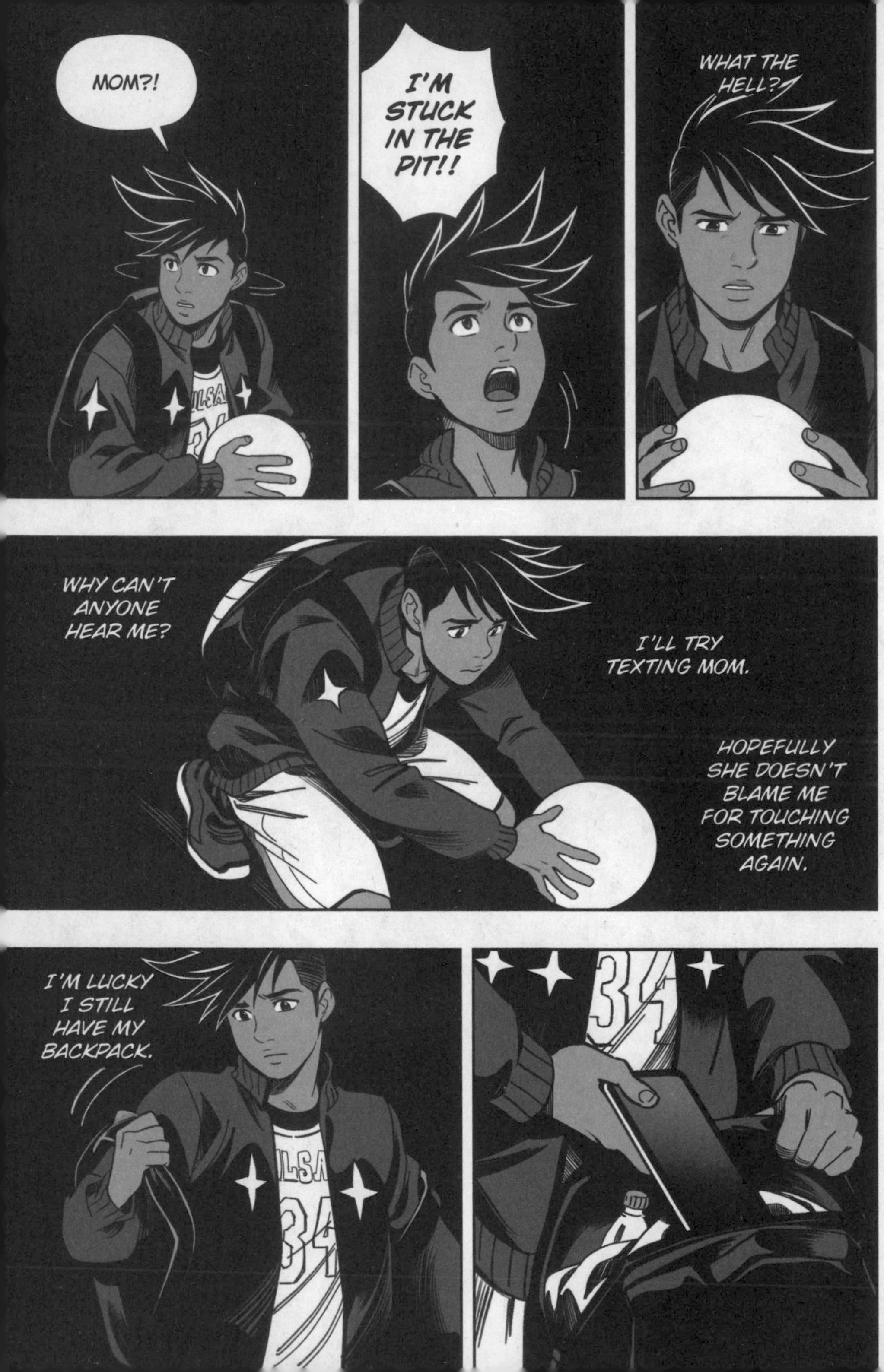

MOM?!
I'M STUCK IN THE PIT!!
WHAT THE HELL?!
WHY CAN'T ANYONE HEAR ME?
I'LL TRY TEXTING MOM.
HOPEFULLY SHE DOESN'T BLAME ME FOR TOUCHING SOMETHING AGAIN.
I'M LUCKY I STILL HAVE MY BACKPACK.

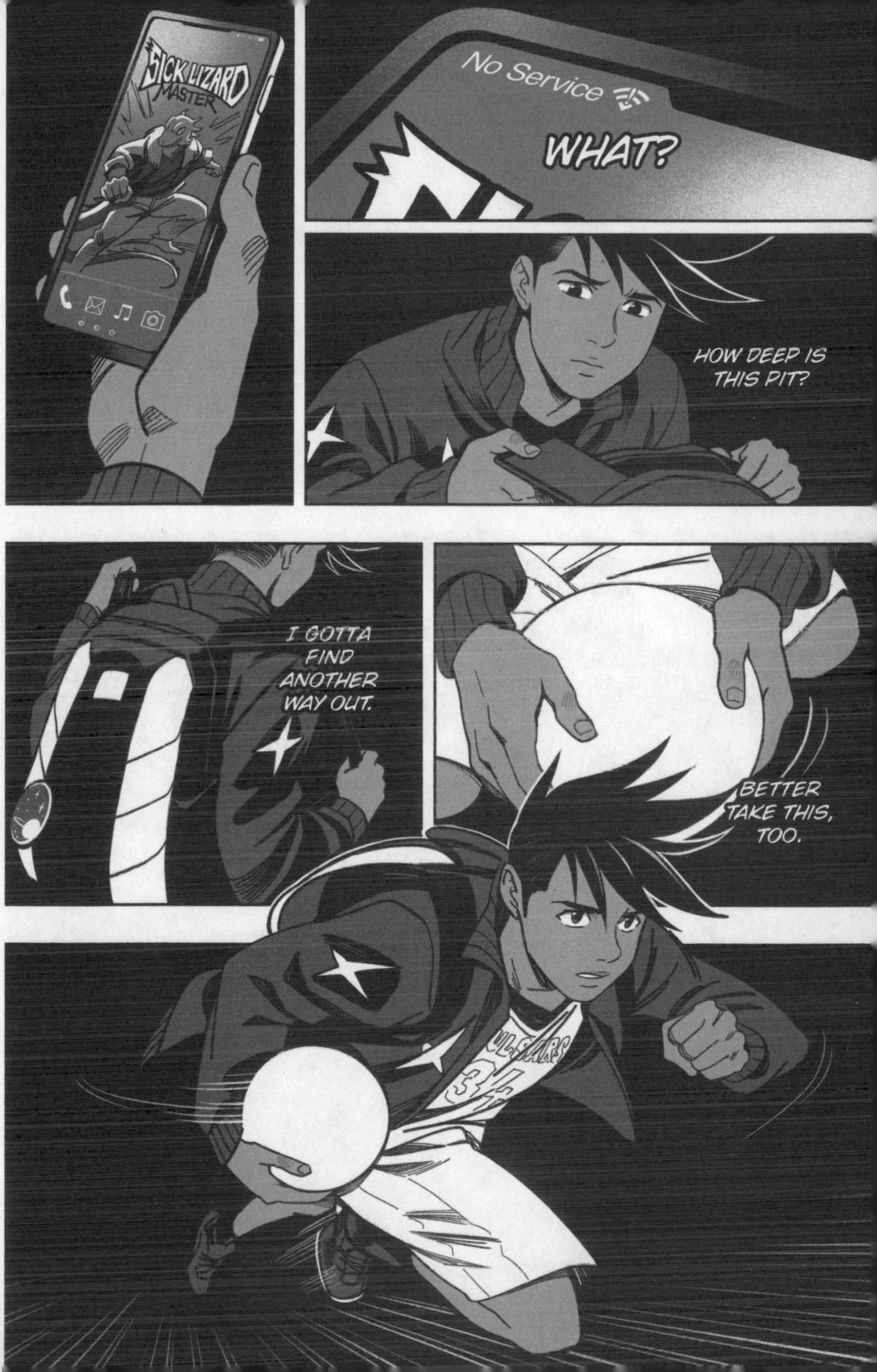
SICK LIZARD MASTER
No Service
WHAT?
HOW DEEP IS THIS PIT?
I GOTTA FIND ANOTHER WAY OUT.
BETTER TAKE THIS, TOO.

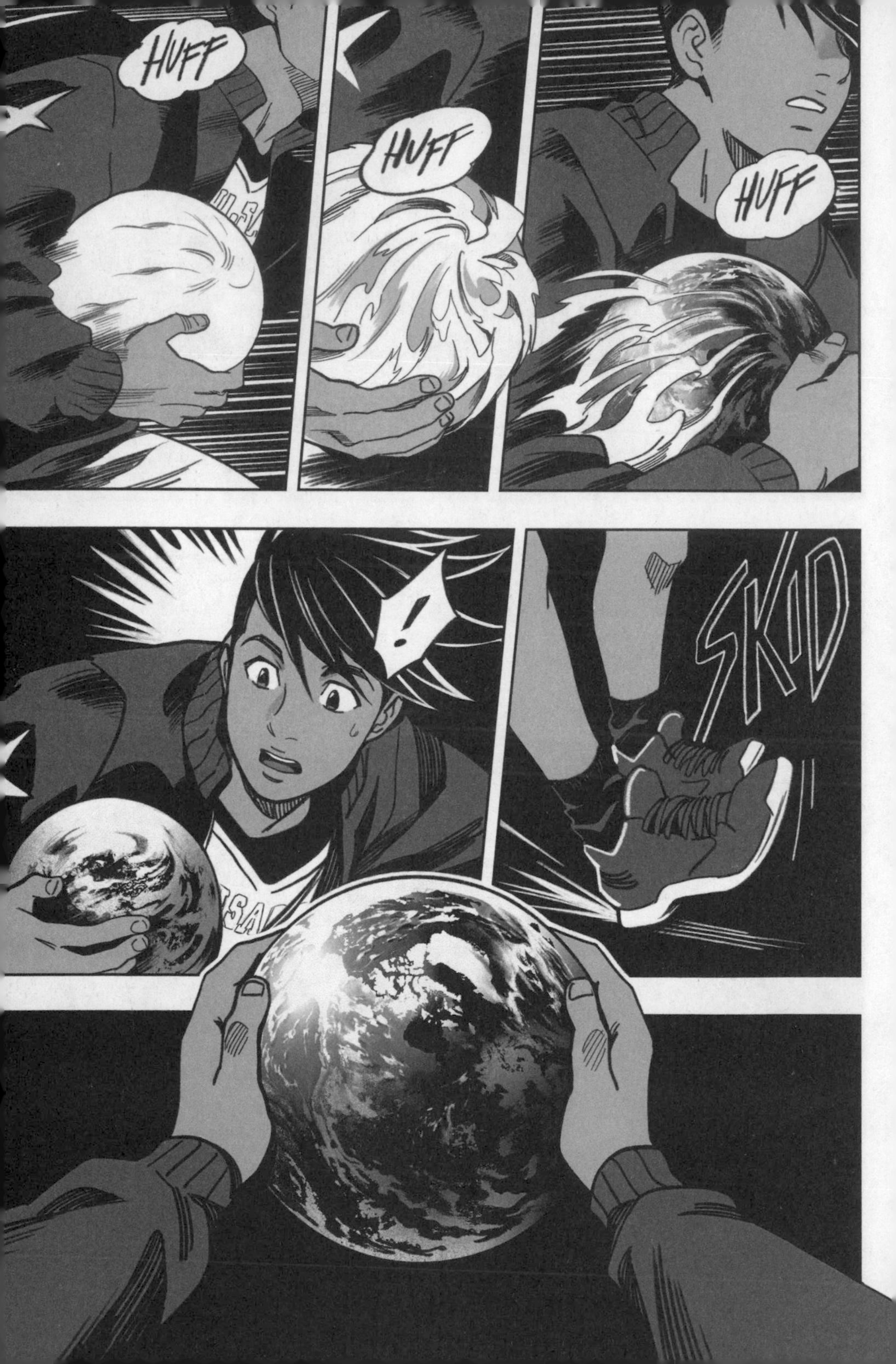
HUFF
HUFF
HUFF
!
SKID

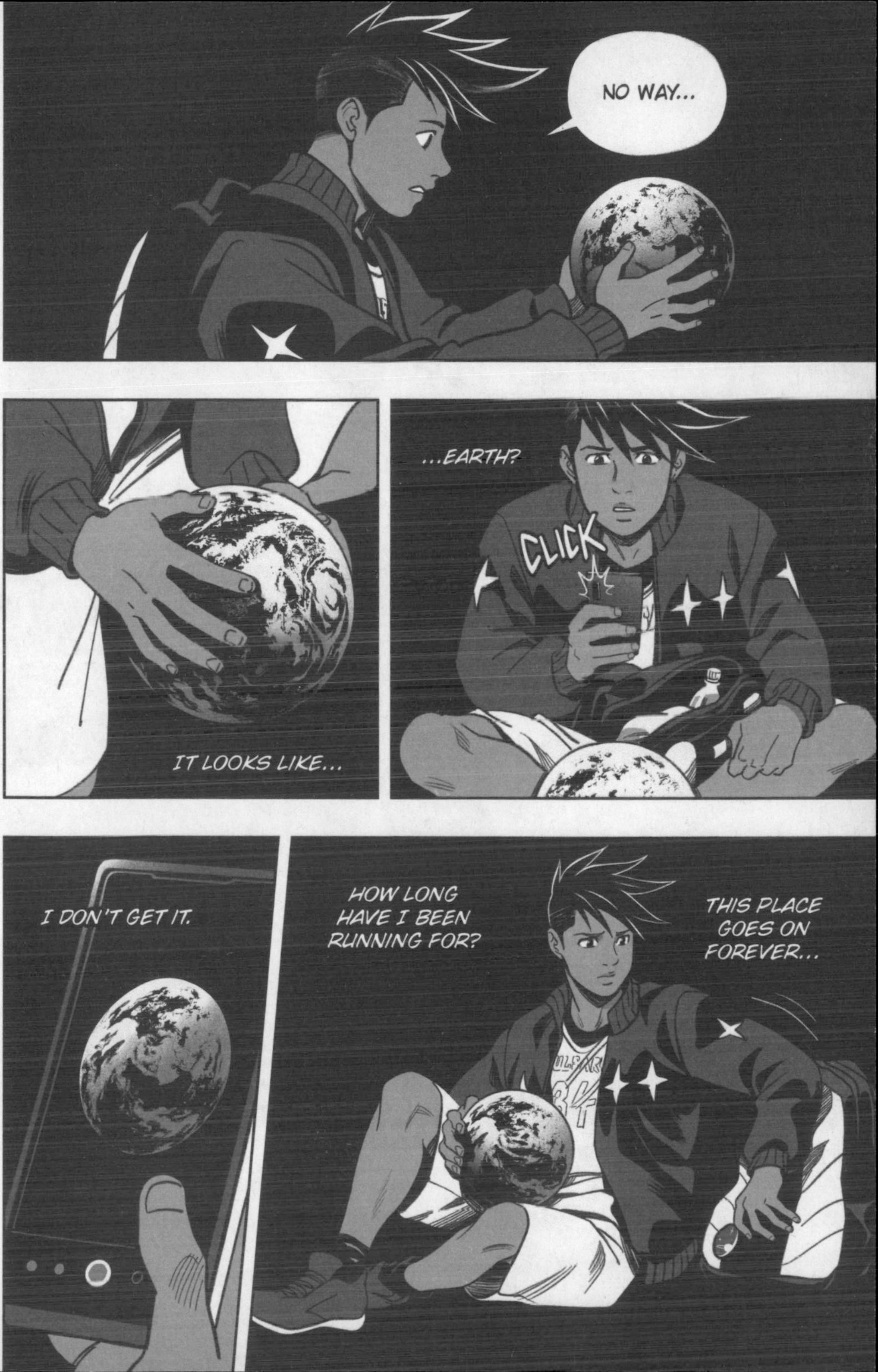
NO WAY...
IT LOOKS LIKE...
...EARTH?
CLICK
I DON'T GET IT.
HOW LONG HAVE I BEEN RUNNING FOR?
THIS PLACE GOES ON FOREVER...

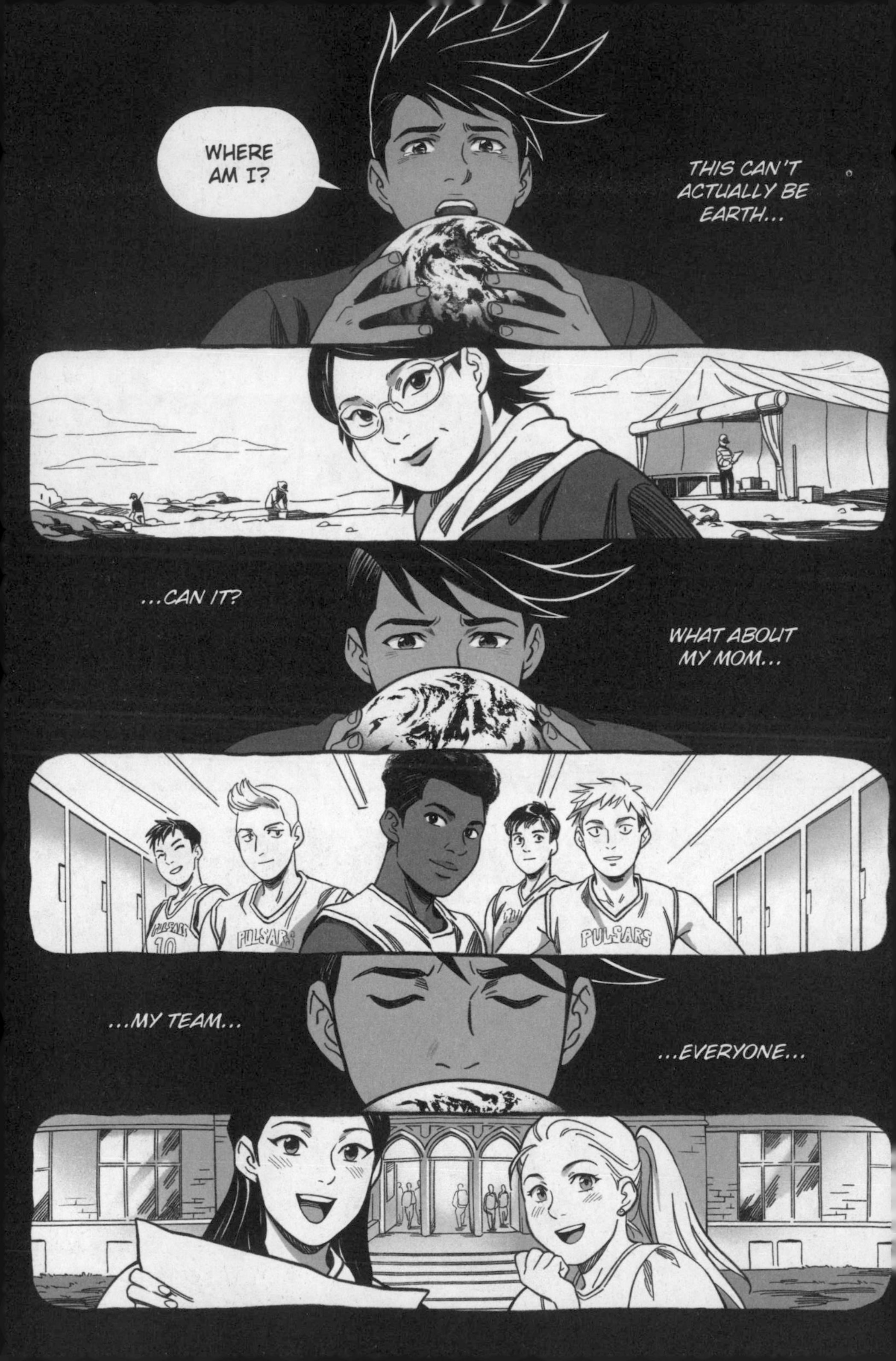
WHERE AM I?
THIS CAN'T ACTUALLY BE EARTH...
...CAN IT?
WHAT ABOUT MY MOM...
PULSARS
10
PULSARS
PULSARS
...MY TEAM...
...EVERYONE...

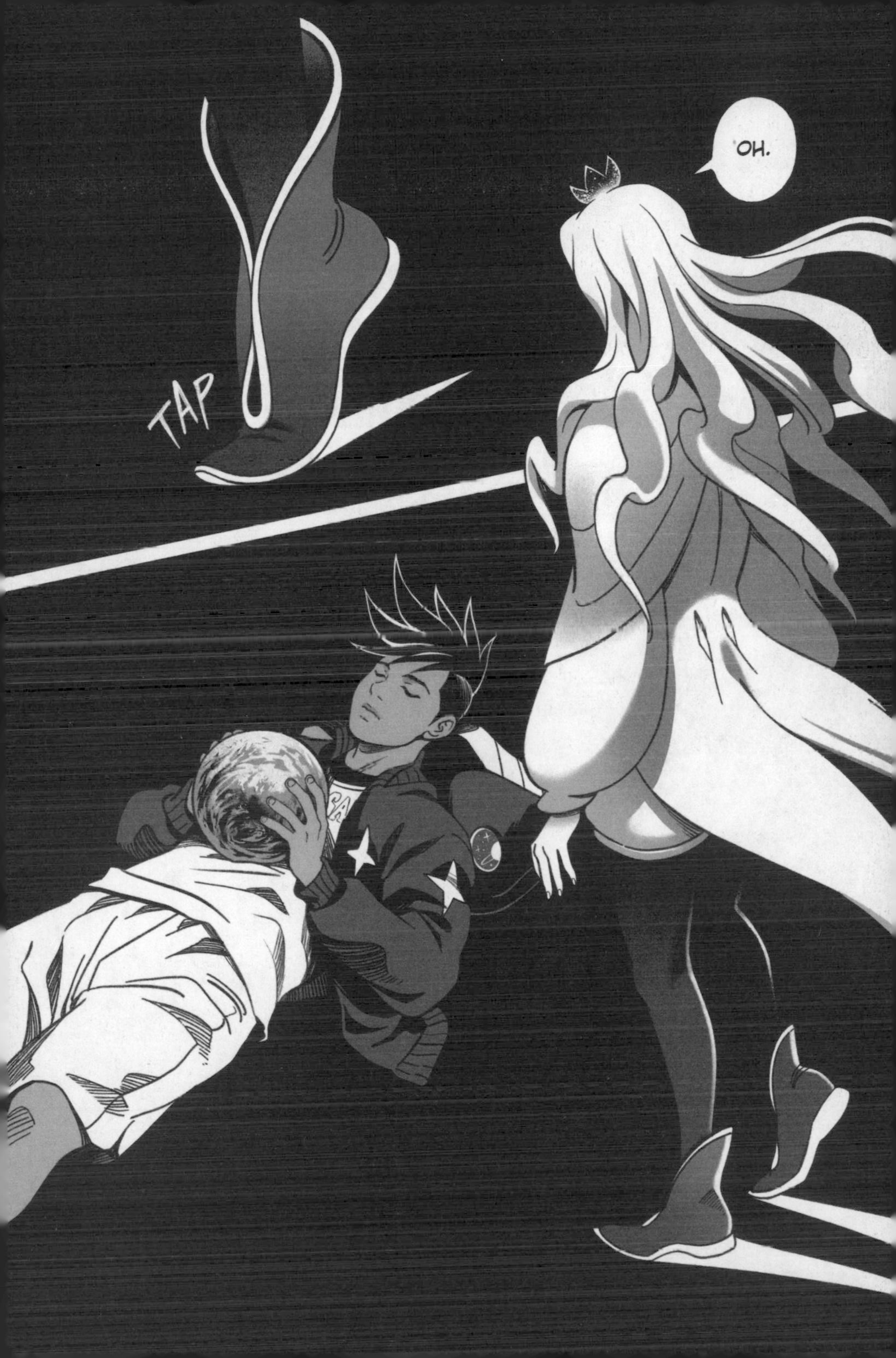
TAP
OH.

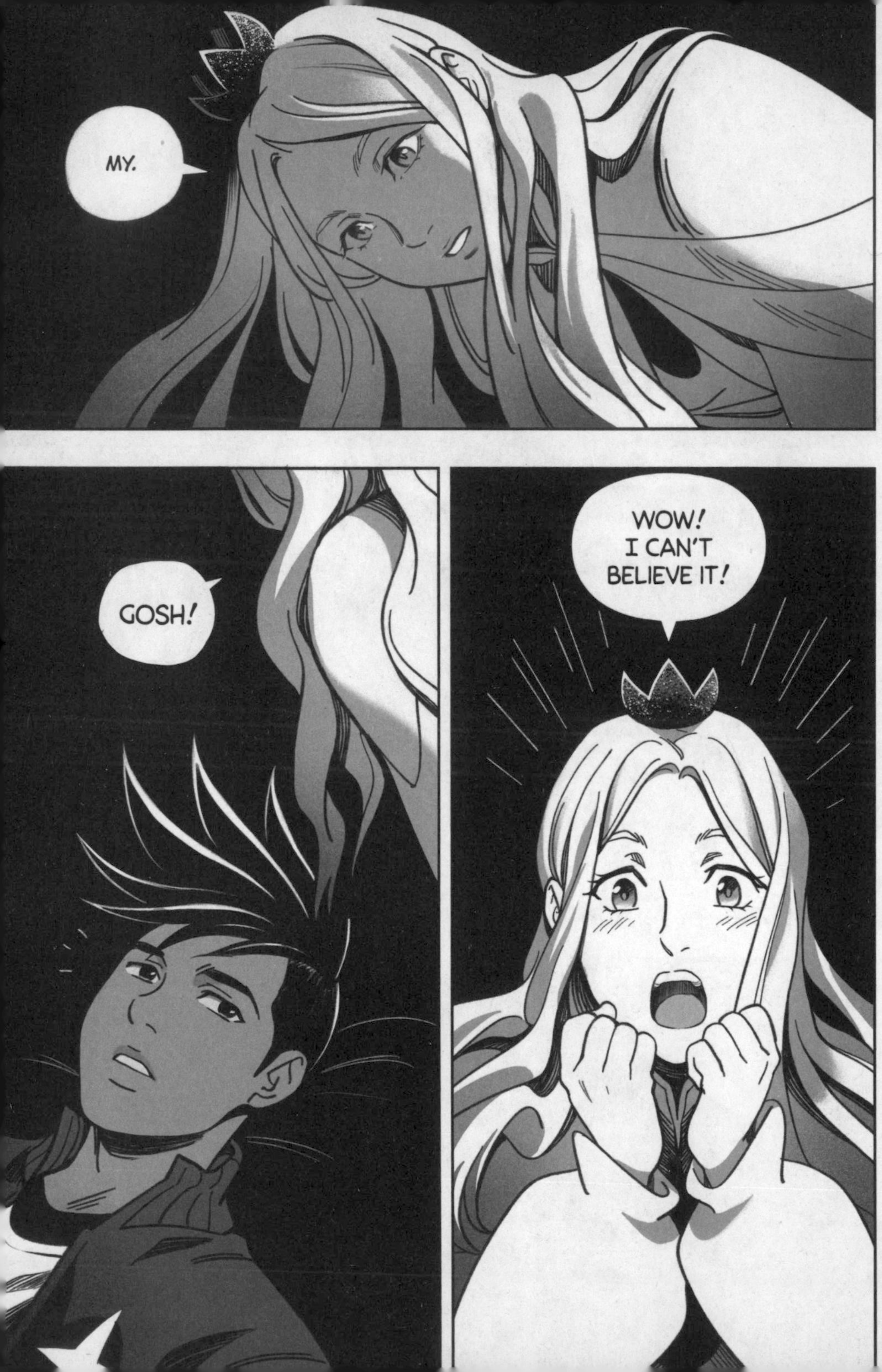
MY.
GOSH!
WOW! I CAN'T BELIEVE IT!

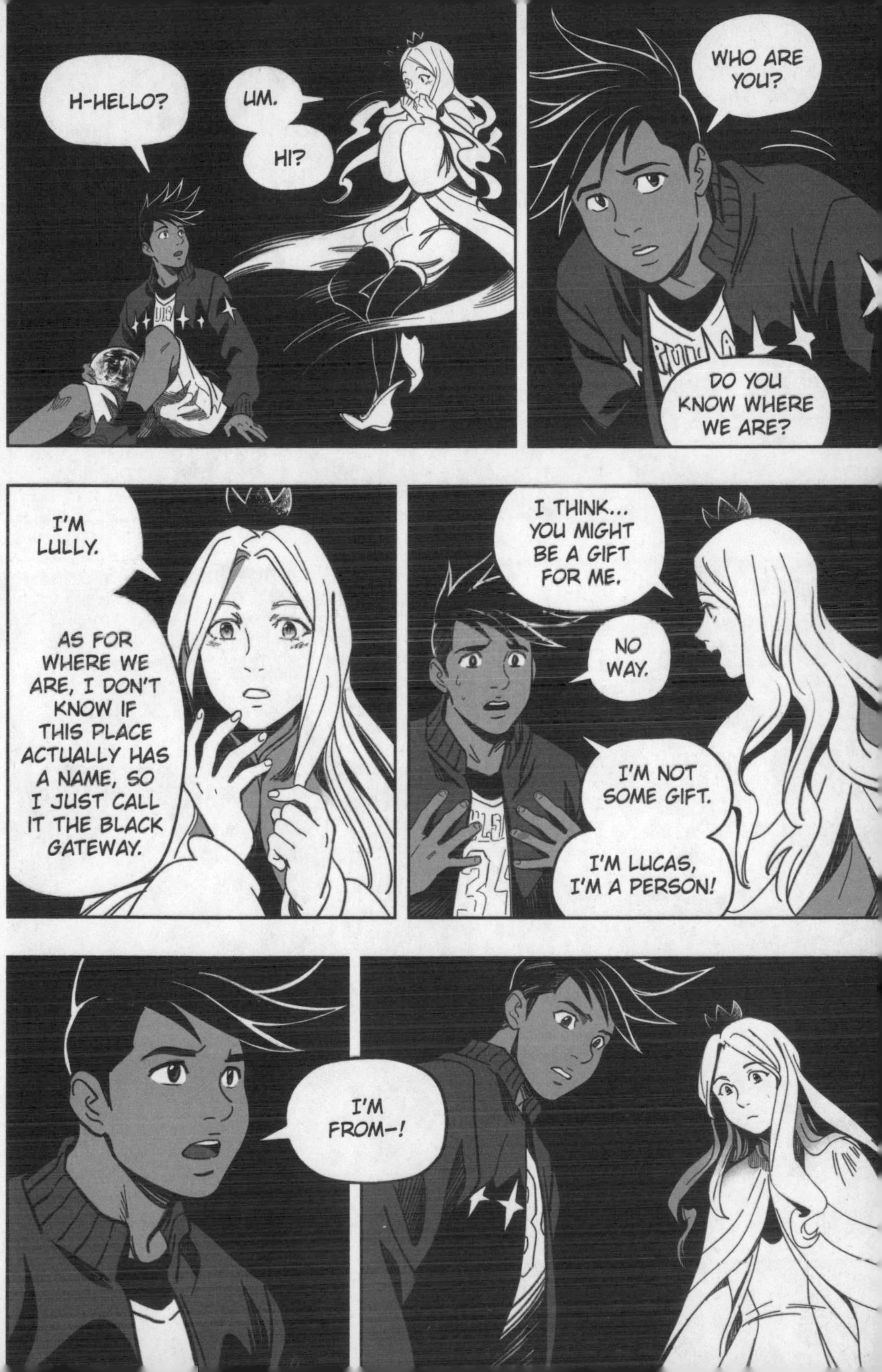
H-HELLO?
UM.
HI?
WHO ARE YOU?
DO YOU KNOW WHERE WE ARE?
I'M LULLY.
AS FOR WHERE WE ARE, I DON'T KNOW IF THIS PLACE ACTUALLY HAS A NAME, SO I JUST CALL IT THE BLACK GATEWAY.
I THINK... YOU MIGHT BE A GIFT FOR ME.
NO WAY.
I'M NOT SOME GIFT.
I'M LUCAS, I'M A PERSON!
I'M FROM-!

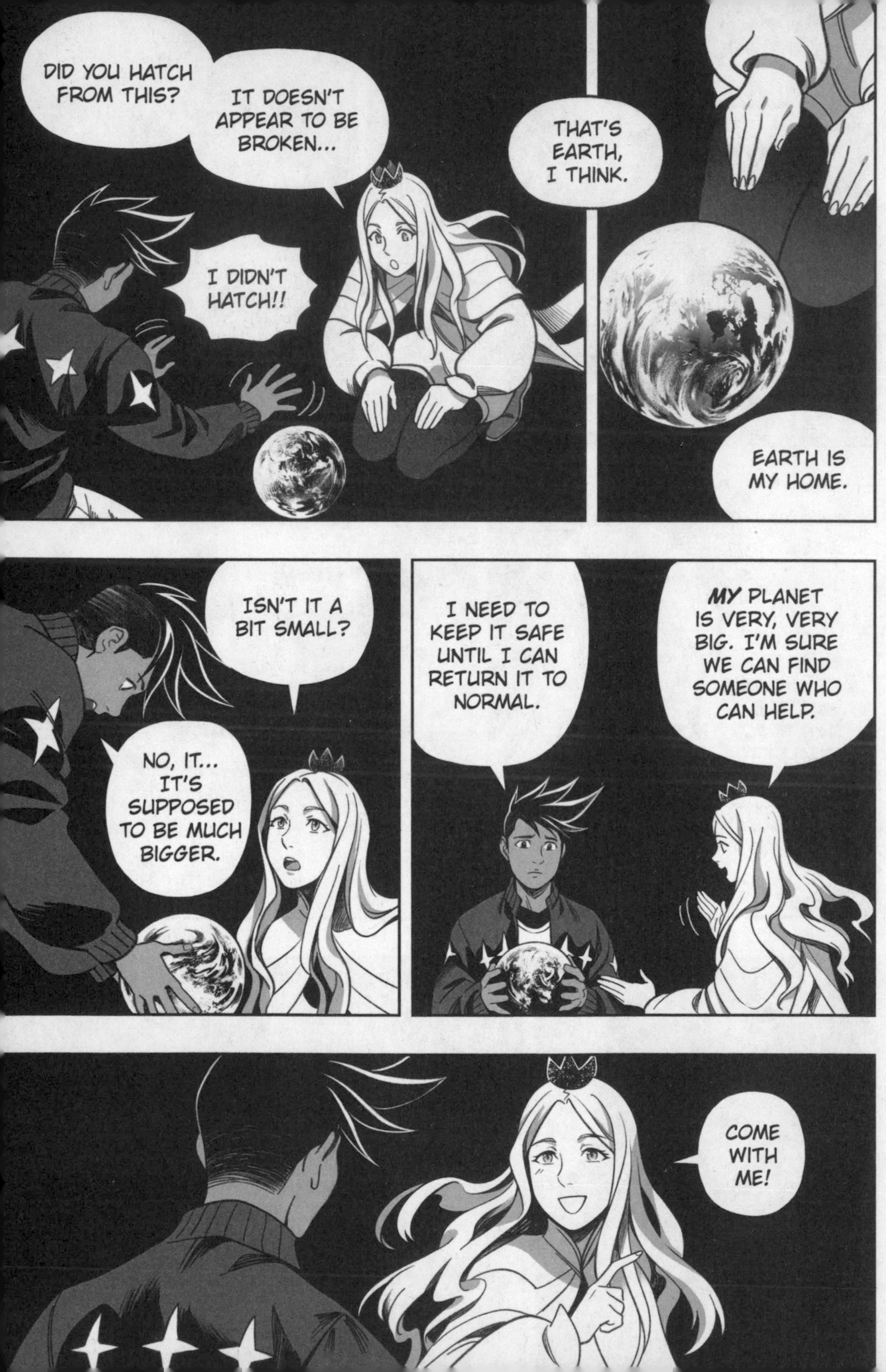
DID YOU HATCH FROM THIS?
IT DOESN'T APPEAR TO BE BROKEN...
I DIDN'T HATCH!!
THAT'S EARTH, I THINK.
EARTH IS MY HOME.
ISN'T IT A BIT SMALL?
NO, IT... IT'S SUPPOSED TO BE MUCH BIGGER.
I NEED TO KEEP IT SAFE UNTIL I CAN RETURN IT TO NORMAL.
MY PLANET IS VERY, VERY BIG. I'M SURE WE CAN FIND SOMEONE WHO CAN HELP.
COME WITH ME!

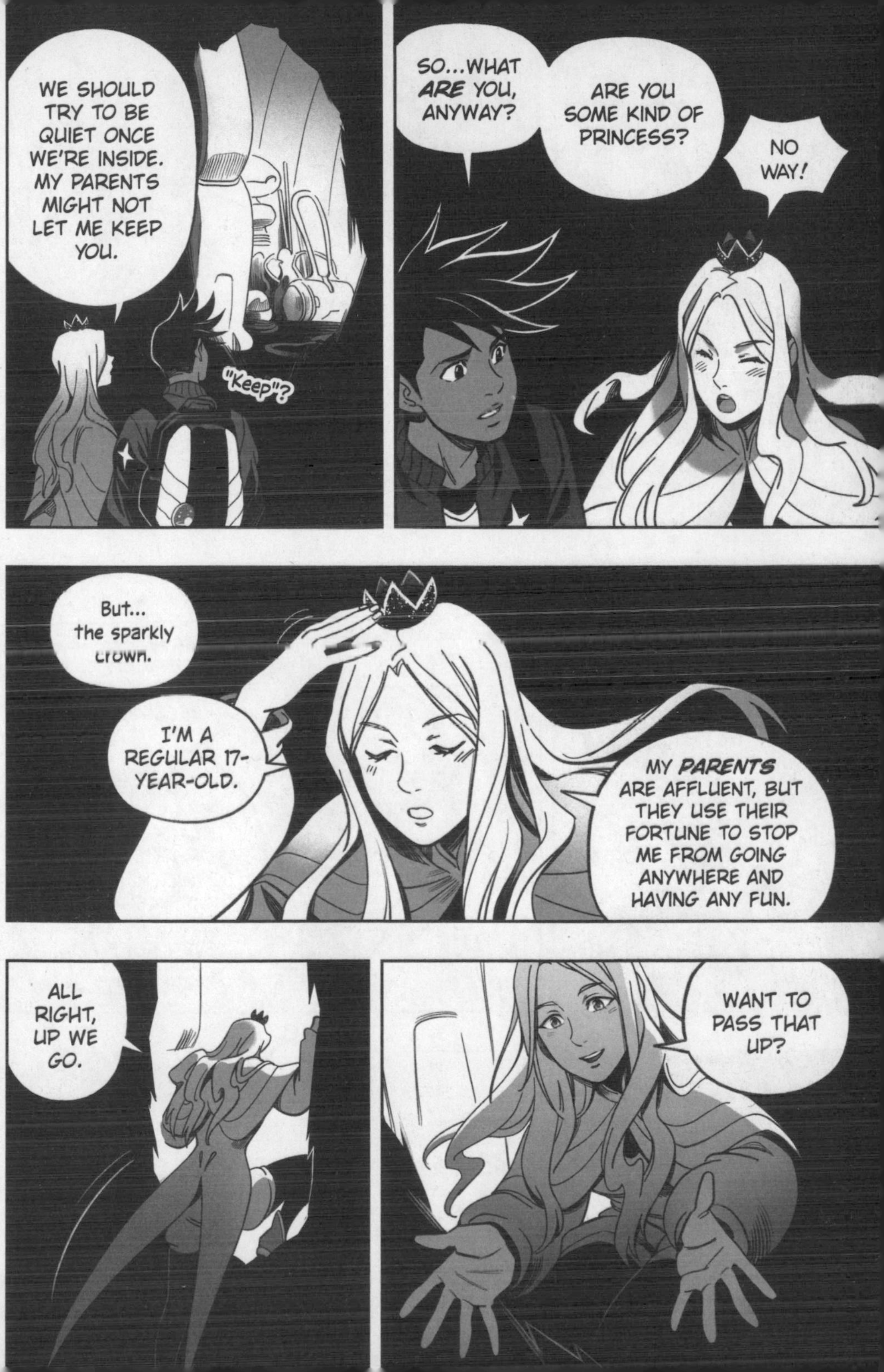
WE SHOULD TRY TO BE QUIET ONCE WE'RE INSIDE. MY PARENTS MIGHT NOT LET ME KEEP YOU.
"Keep"?
SO...WHAT ARE YOU, ANYWAY?
ARE YOU SOME KIND OF PRINCESS?
NO WAY!
But... the sparkly crown.
I'M A REGULAR 17-YEAR-OLD.
MY PARENTS ARE AFFLUENT, BUT THEY USE THEIR FORTUNE TO STOP ME FROM GOING ANYWHERE AND HAVING ANY FUN.
ALL RIGHT, UP WE GO.
WANT TO PASS THAT UP?

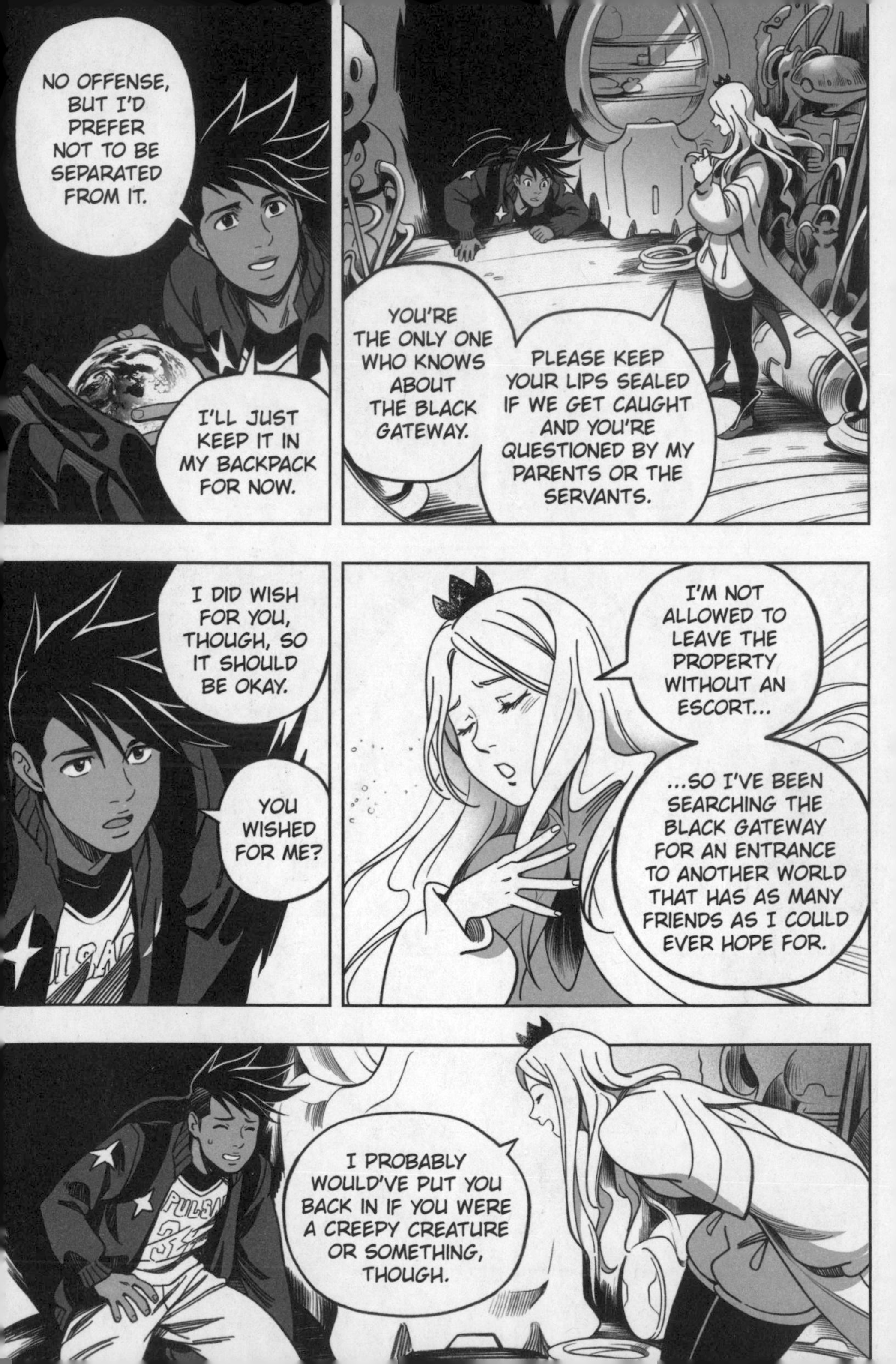
NO OFFENSE, BUT I'D PREFER NOT TO BE SEPARATED FROM IT.
I'LL JUST KEEP IT IN MY BACKPACK FOR NOW.
YOU'RE THE ONLY ONE WHO KNOWS ABOUT THE BLACK GATEWAY.
PLEASE KEEP YOUR LIPS SEALED IF WE GET CAUGHT AND YOU'RE QUESTIONED BY MY PARENTS OR THE SERVANTS.
I DID WISH FOR YOU, THOUGH, SO IT SHOULD BE OKAY.
YOU WISHED FOR ME?
I'M NOT ALLOWED TO LEAVE THE PROPERTY WITHOUT AN ESCORT...
...SO I'VE BEEN SEARCHING THE BLACK GATEWAY FOR AN ENTRANCE TO ANOTHER WORLD THAT HAS AS MANY FRIENDS AS I COULD EVER HOPE FOR.
I PROBABLY WOULD'VE PUT YOU BACK IN IF YOU WERE A CREEPY CREATURE OR SOMETHING, THOUGH.

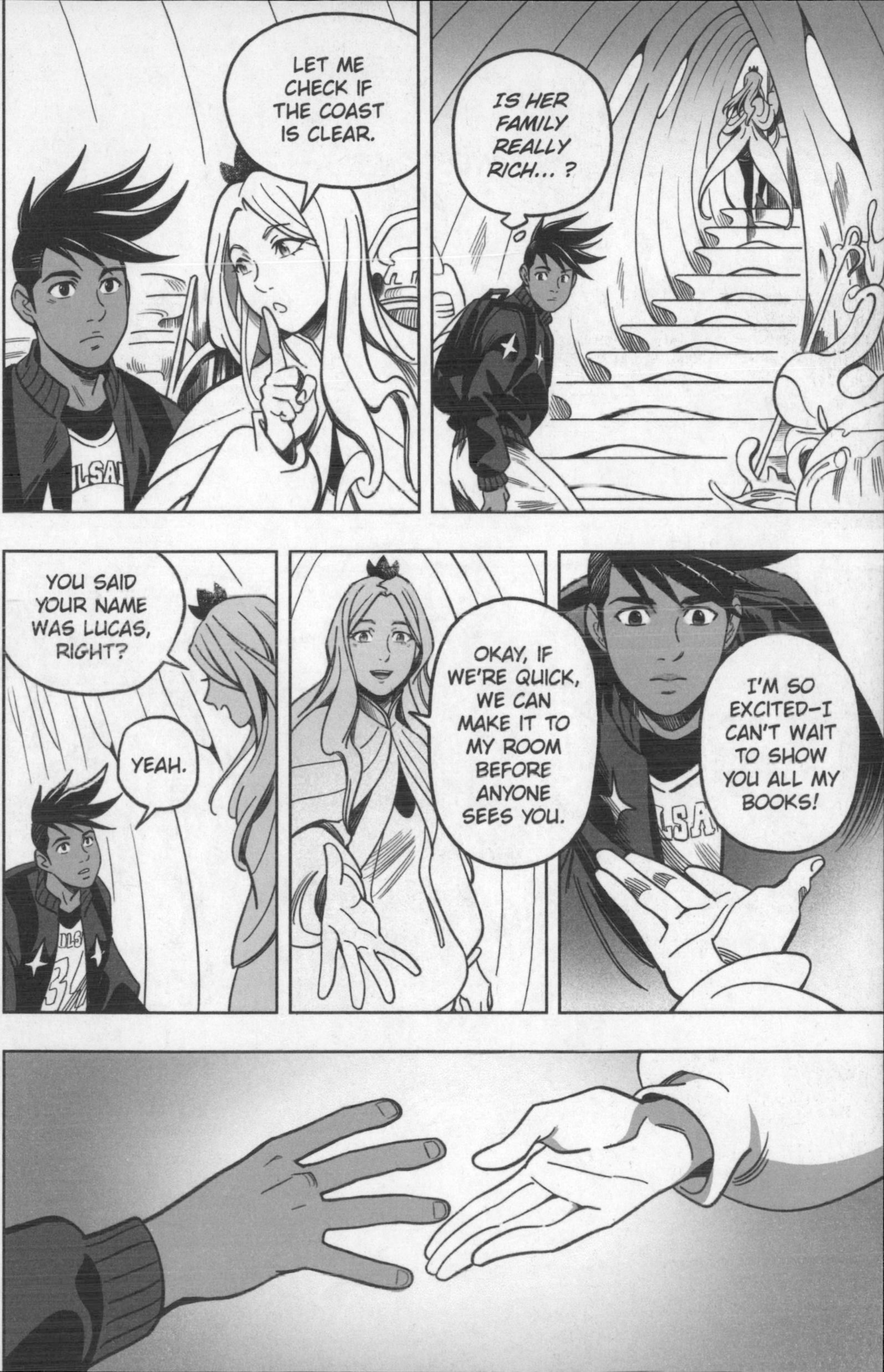
LET ME CHECK IF THE COAST IS CLEAR.
IS HER FAMILY REALLY RICH... ?
YOU SAID YOUR NAME WAS LUCAS, RIGHT?
YEAH.
OKAY, IF WE'RE QUICK, WE CAN MAKE IT TO MY ROOM BEFORE ANYONE SEES YOU.
I'M SO EXCITED—I CAN'T WAIT TO SHOW YOU ALL MY BOOKS!

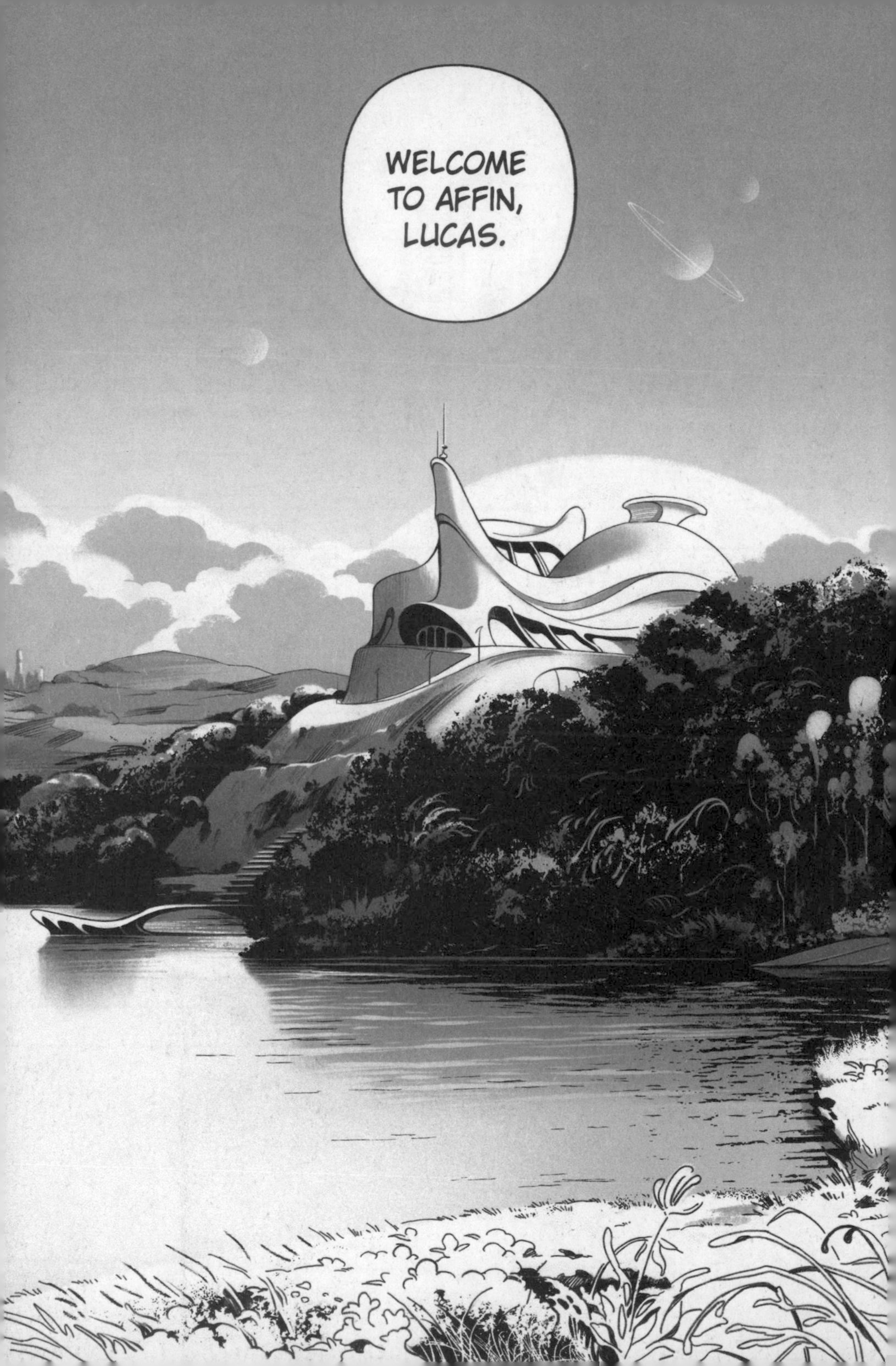
WELCOME TO AFFIN, LUCAS.

WORLD PIECE

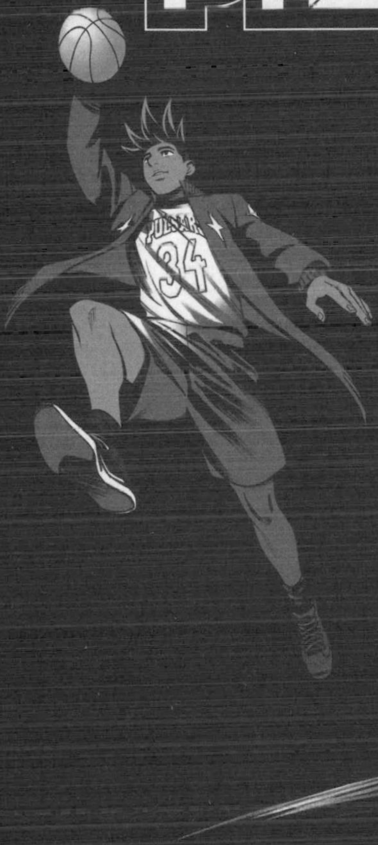

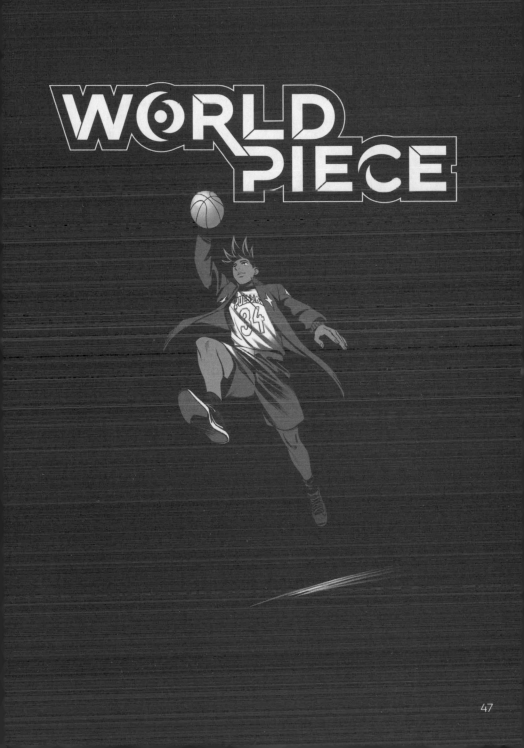

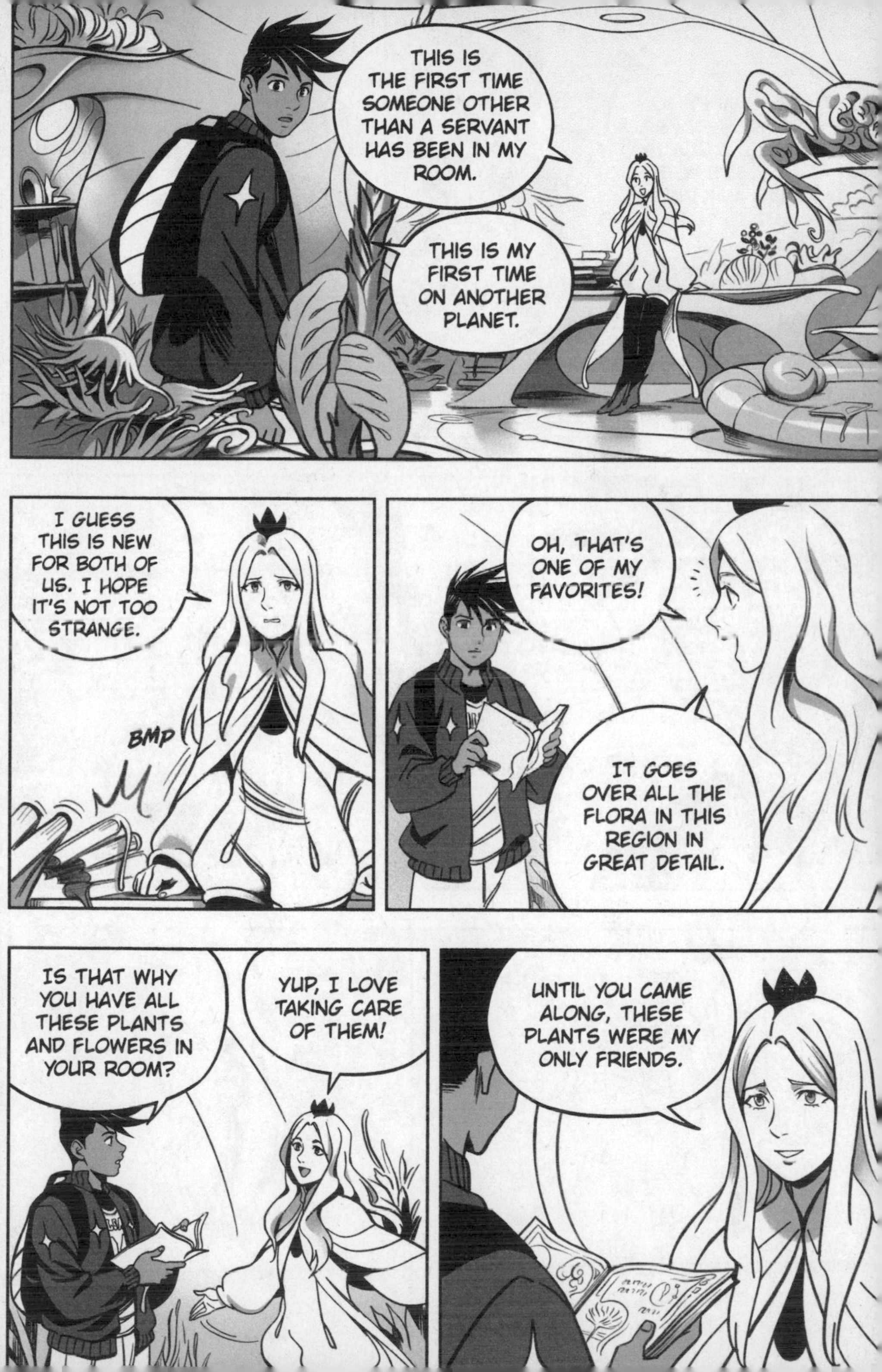
THIS IS THE FIRST TIME SOMEONE OTHER THAN A SERVANT HAS BEEN IN MY ROOM.
THIS IS MY FIRST TIME ON ANOTHER PLANET.
I GUESS THIS IS NEW FOR BOTH OF US. I HOPE IT'S NOT TOO STRANGE.
BMP
OH, THAT'S ONE OF MY FAVORITES!
IT GOES OVER ALL THE FLORA IN THIS REGION IN GREAT DETAIL.
IS THAT WHY YOU HAVE ALL THESE PLANTS AND FLOWERS IN YOUR ROOM?
YUP, I LOVE TAKING CARE OF THEM!
UNTIL YOU CAME ALONG, THESE PLANTS WERE MY ONLY FRIENDS.

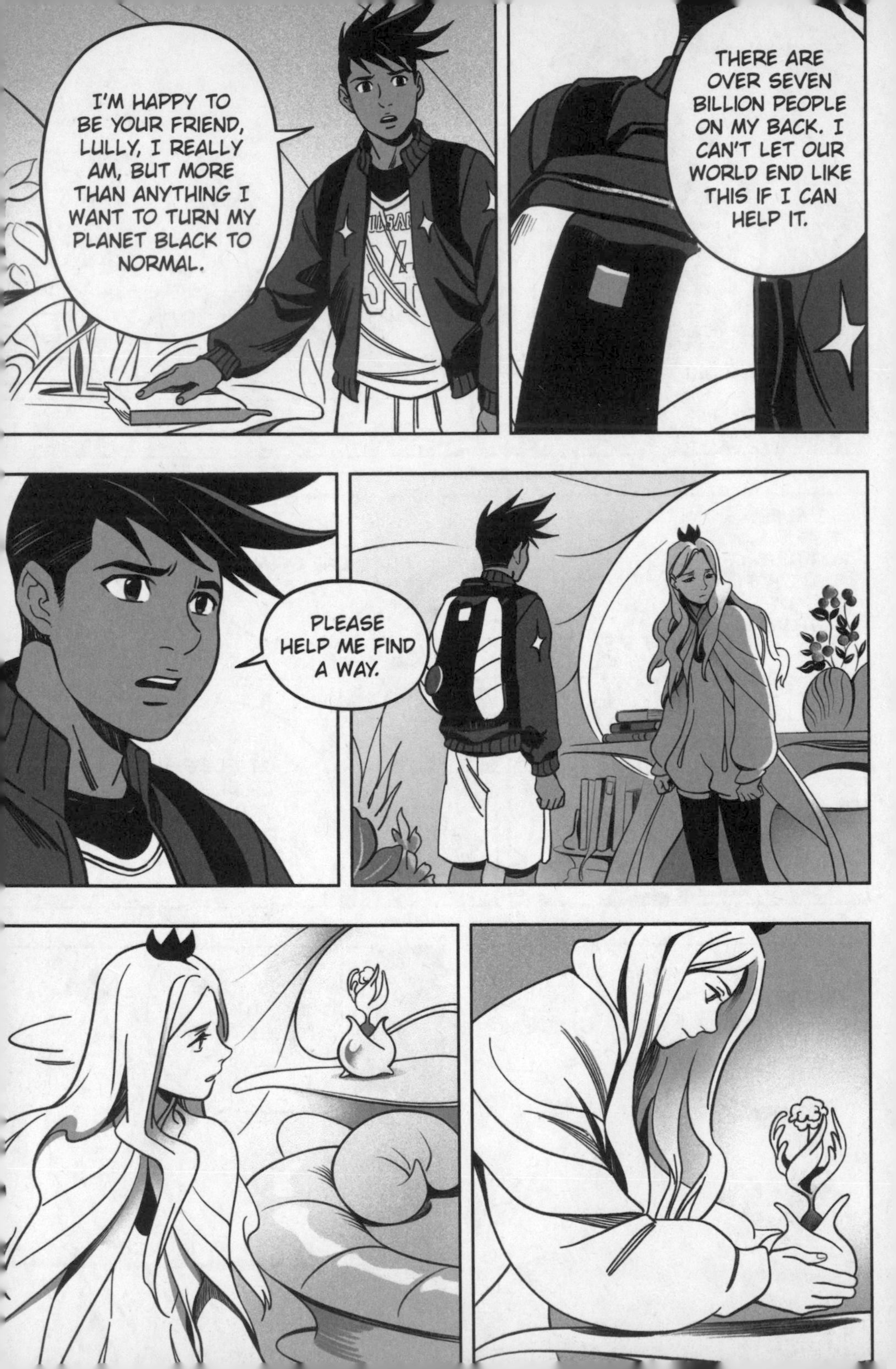
I'M HAPPY TO BE YOUR FRIEND, LULLY, I REALLY AM, BUT MORE THAN ANYTHING I WANT TO TURN MY PLANET BLACK TO NORMAL.
THERE ARE OVER SEVEN BILLION PEOPLE ON MY BACK. I CAN'T LET OUR WORLD END LIKE THIS IF I CAN HELP IT.
PLEASE HELP ME FIND A WAY.

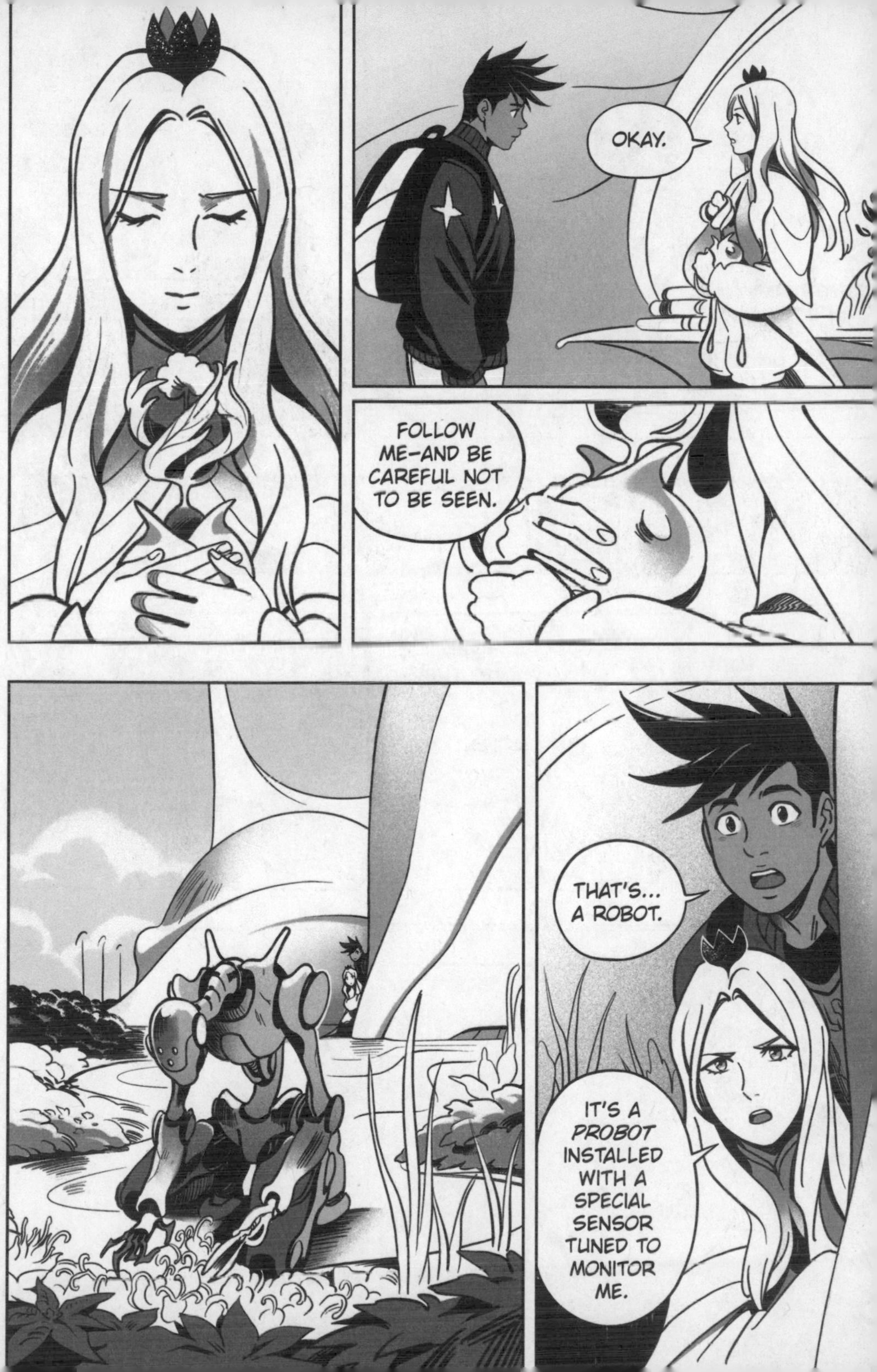
OKAY.
FOLLOW ME—AND BE CAREFUL NOT TO BE SEEN.
THAT'S... A ROBOT.
IT'S A *PROBOT* INSTALLED WITH A SPECIAL SENSOR TUNED TO MONITOR ME.

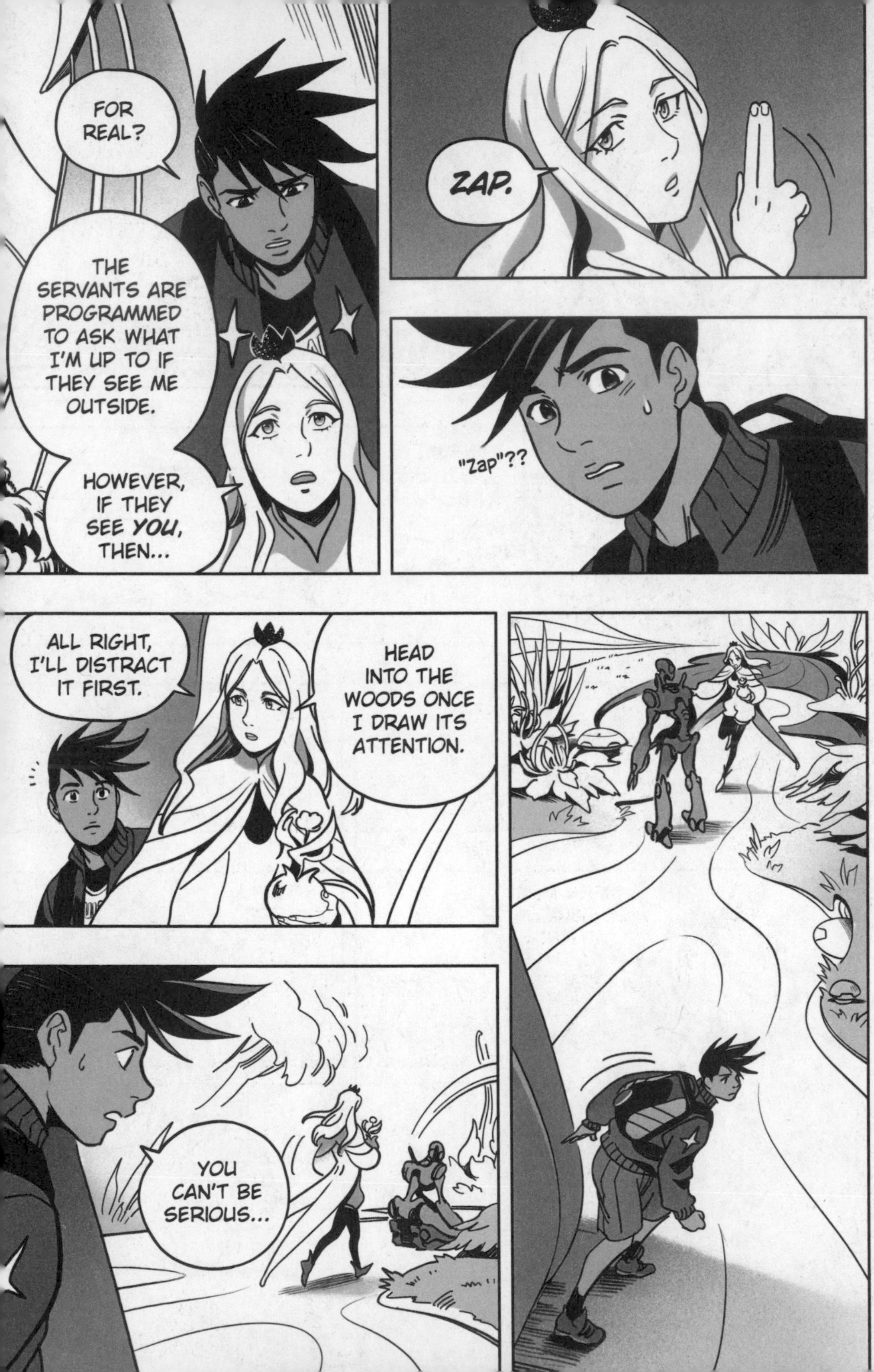
FOR REAL?
THE SERVANTS ARE PROGRAMMED TO ASK WHAT I'M UP TO IF THEY SEE ME OUTSIDE.
HOWEVER, IF THEY SEE *YOU*, THEN...
ZAP.
"Zap"??
ALL RIGHT, I'LL DISTRACT IT FIRST.
HEAD INTO THE WOODS ONCE I DRAW ITS ATTENTION.
YOU CAN'T BE SERIOUS...

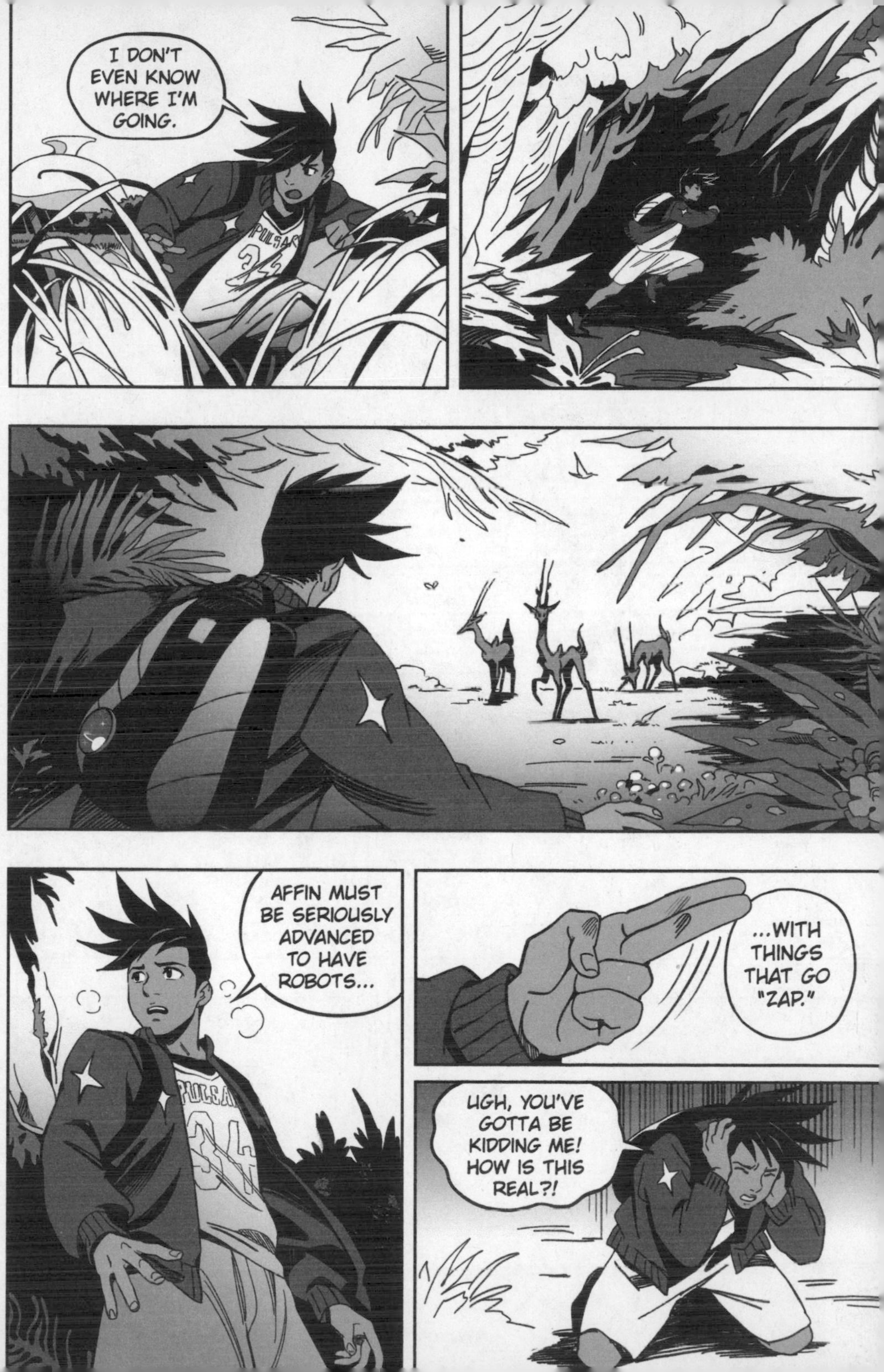
I DON'T EVEN KNOW WHERE I'M GOING.
AFFIN MUST BE SERIOUSLY ADVANCED TO HAVE ROBOTS...
...WITH THINGS THAT GO "ZAP."
UGH, YOU'VE GOTTA BE KIDDING ME! HOW IS THIS REAL?!

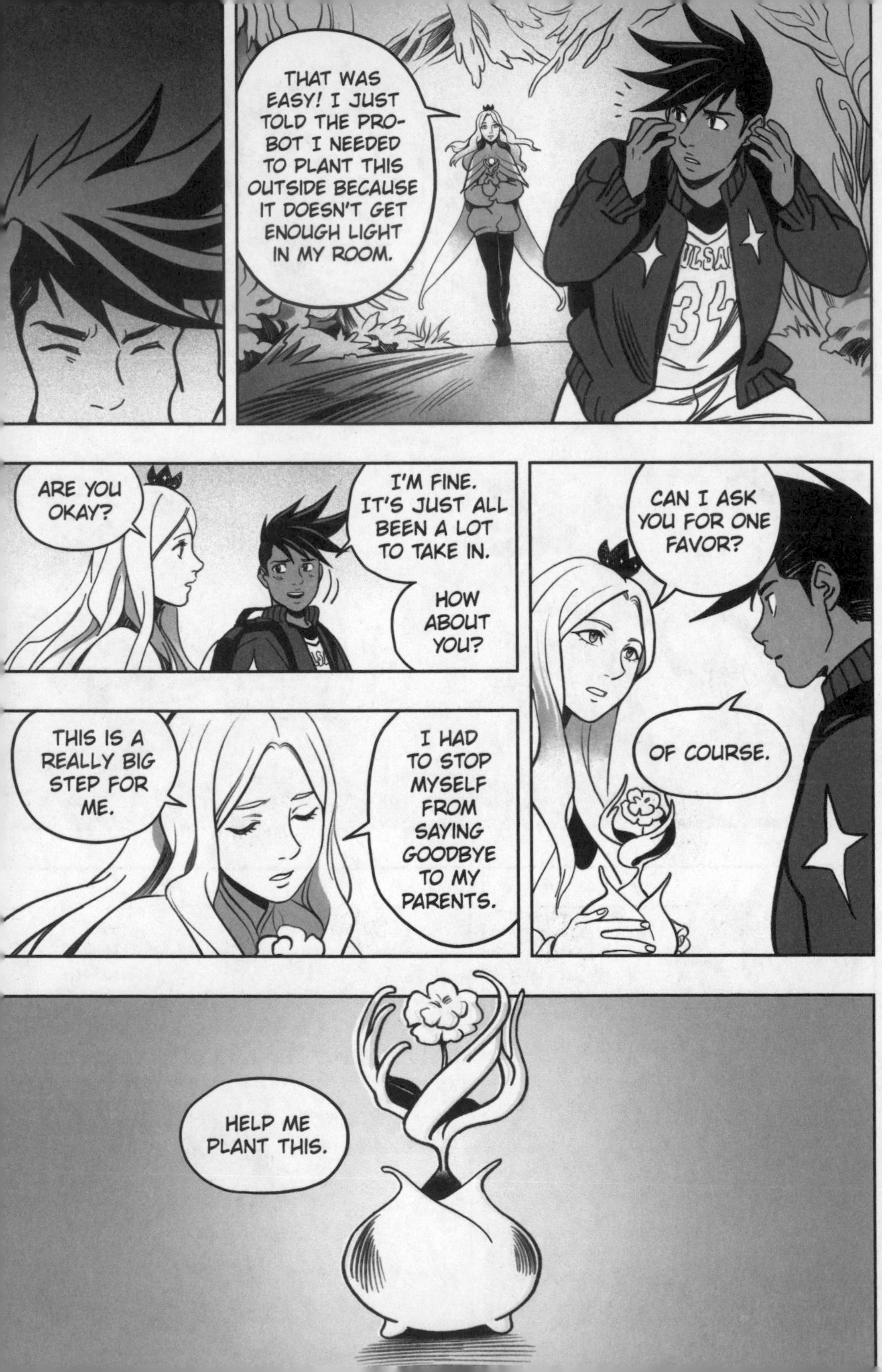
THAT WAS EASY! I JUST TOLD THE PRO-BOT I NEEDED TO PLANT THIS OUTSIDE BECAUSE IT DOESN'T GET ENOUGH LIGHT IN MY ROOM.
ARE YOU OKAY?
I'M FINE. IT'S JUST ALL BEEN A LOT TO TAKE IN.
HOW ABOUT YOU?
THIS IS A REALLY BIG STEP FOR ME.
I HAD TO STOP MYSELF FROM SAYING GOODBYE TO MY PARENTS.
CAN I ASK YOU FOR ONE FAVOR?
OF COURSE.
HELP ME PLANT THIS.

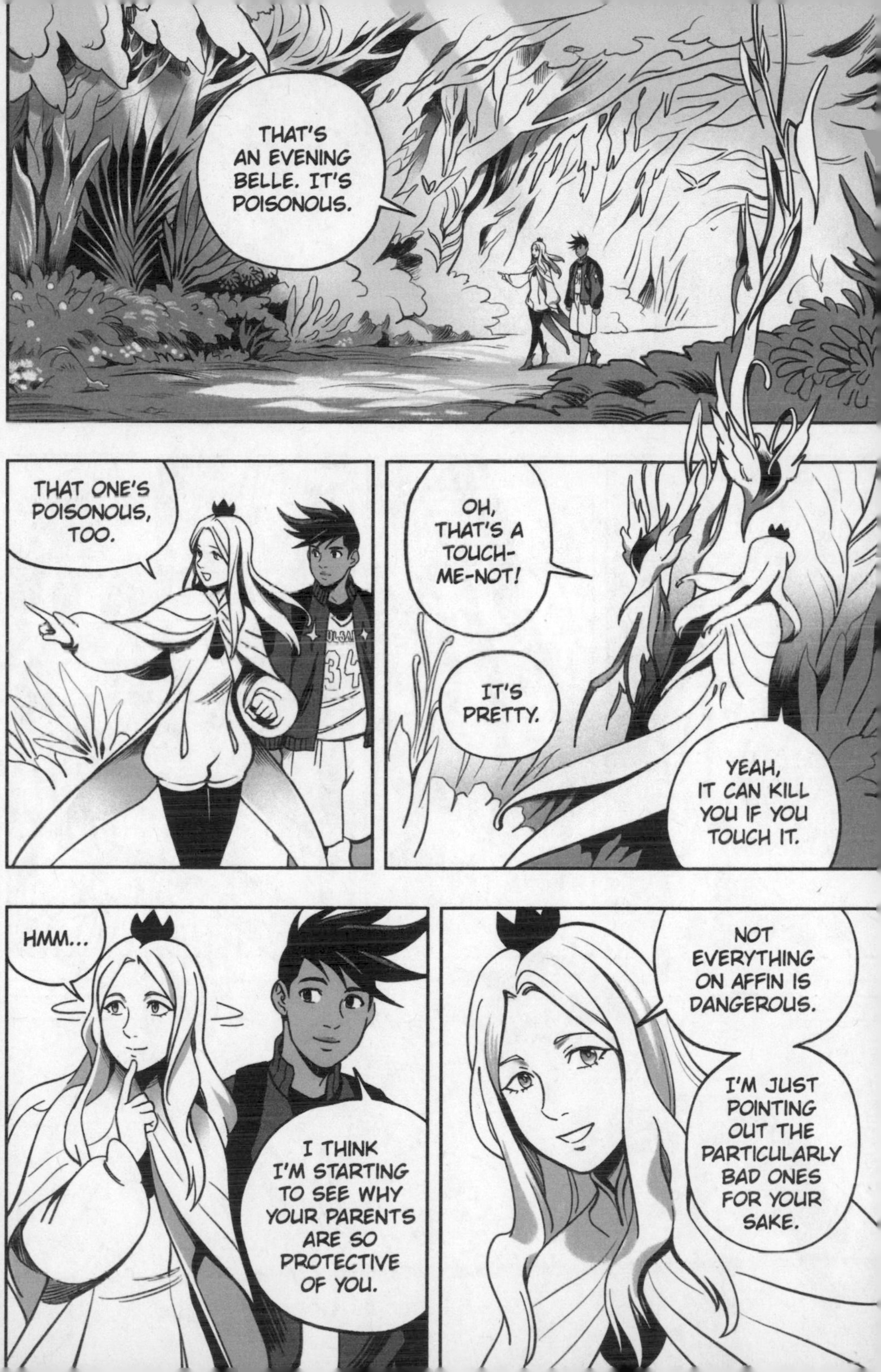
THAT'S AN EVENING BELLE. IT'S POISONOUS.
THAT ONE'S POISONOUS, TOO.
OH, THAT'S A TOUCH-ME-NOT!
IT'S PRETTY.
YEAH, IT CAN KILL YOU IF YOU TOUCH IT.
HMM...
I THINK I'M STARTING TO SEE WHY YOUR PARENTS ARE SO PROTECTIVE OF YOU.
NOT EVERYTHING ON AFFIN IS DANGEROUS.
I'M JUST POINTING OUT THE PARTICULARLY BAD ONES FOR YOUR SAKE.

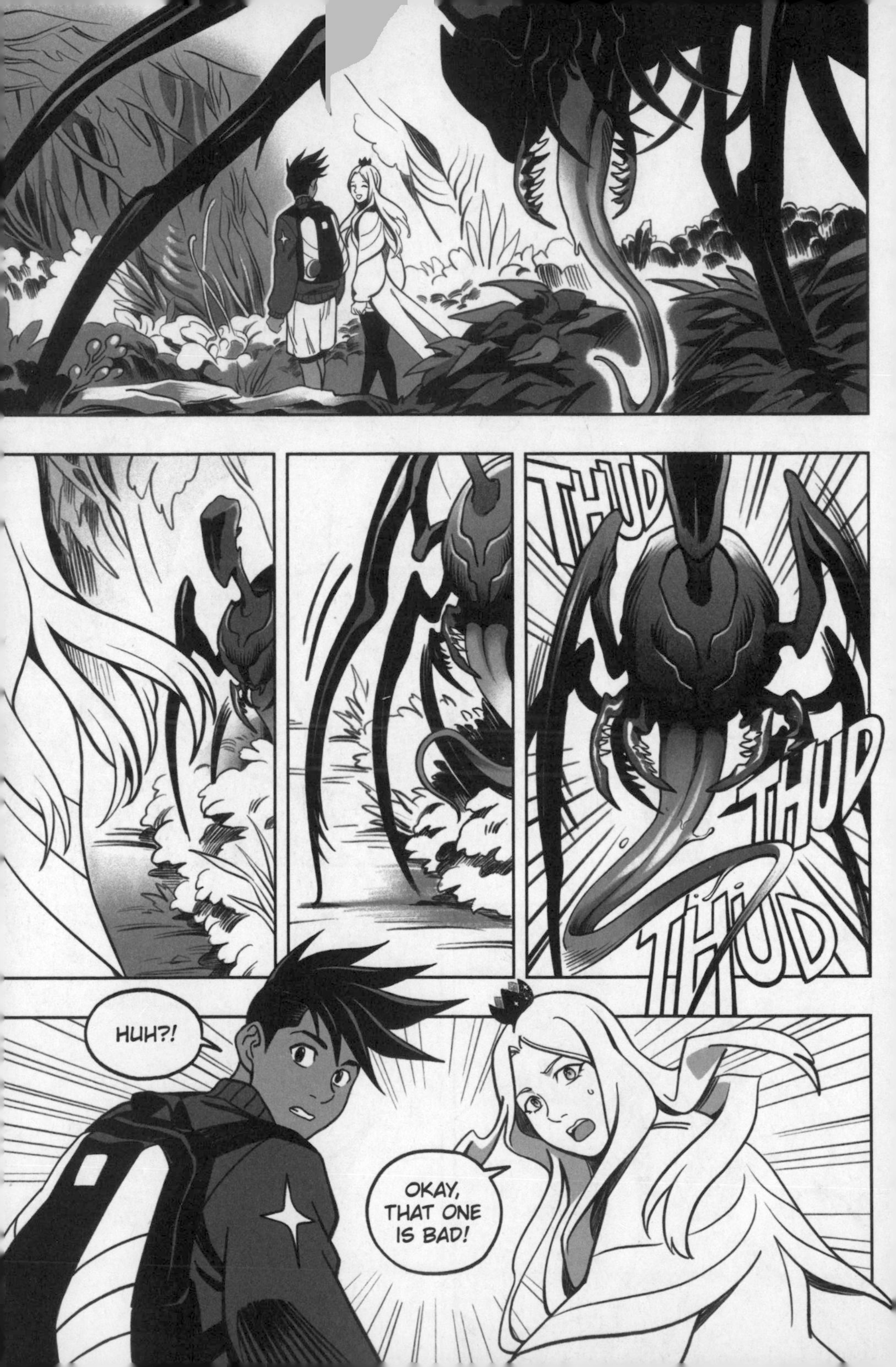
THUD
THUD
THUD
HUH?!
OKAY, THAT ONE IS BAD!

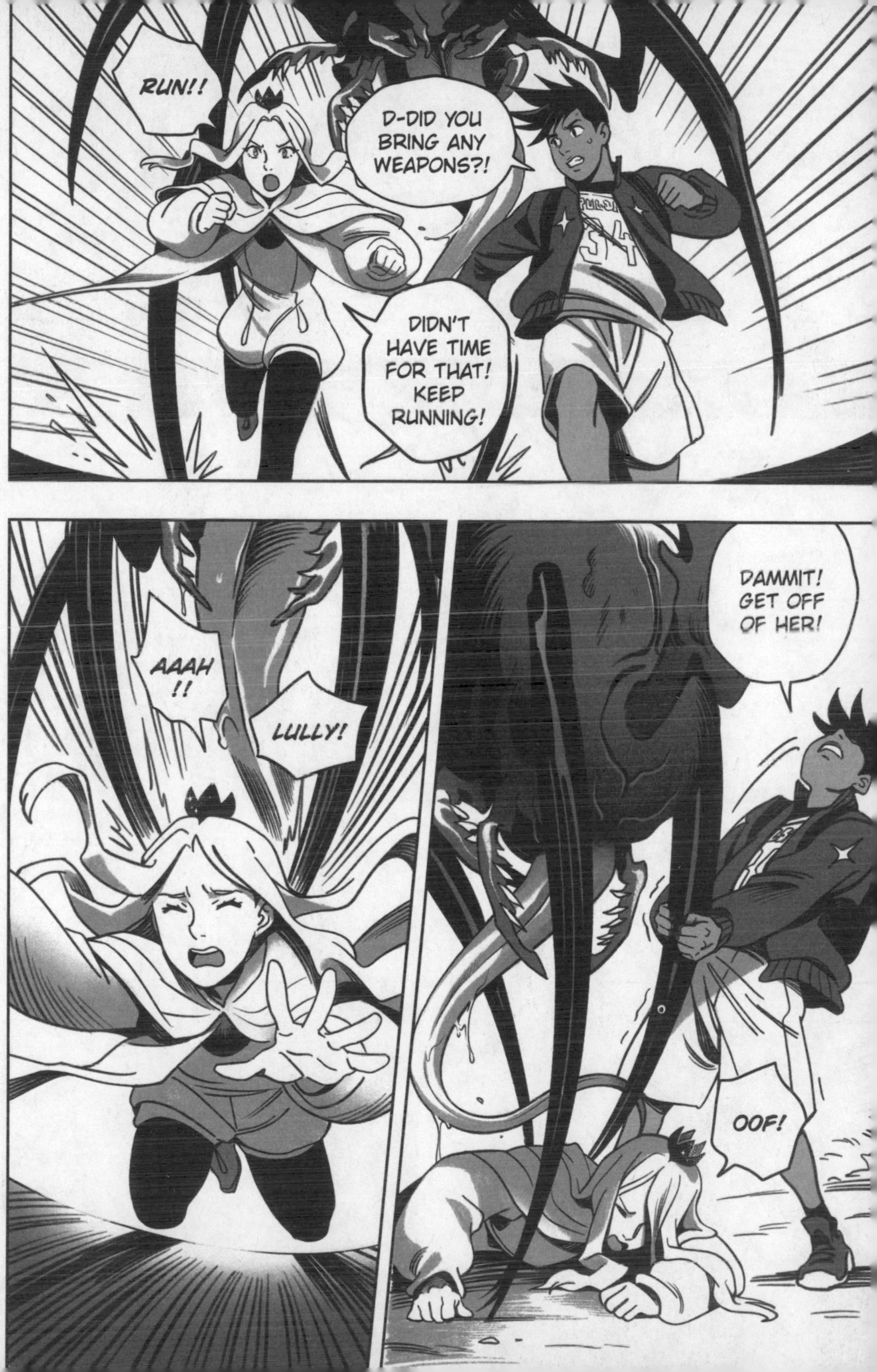
RUN!!
D-DID YOU BRING ANY WEAPONS?!
DIDN'T HAVE TIME FOR THAT! KEEP RUNNING!
AAAH!!
LULLY!
DAMMIT! GET OFF OF HER!
OOF!

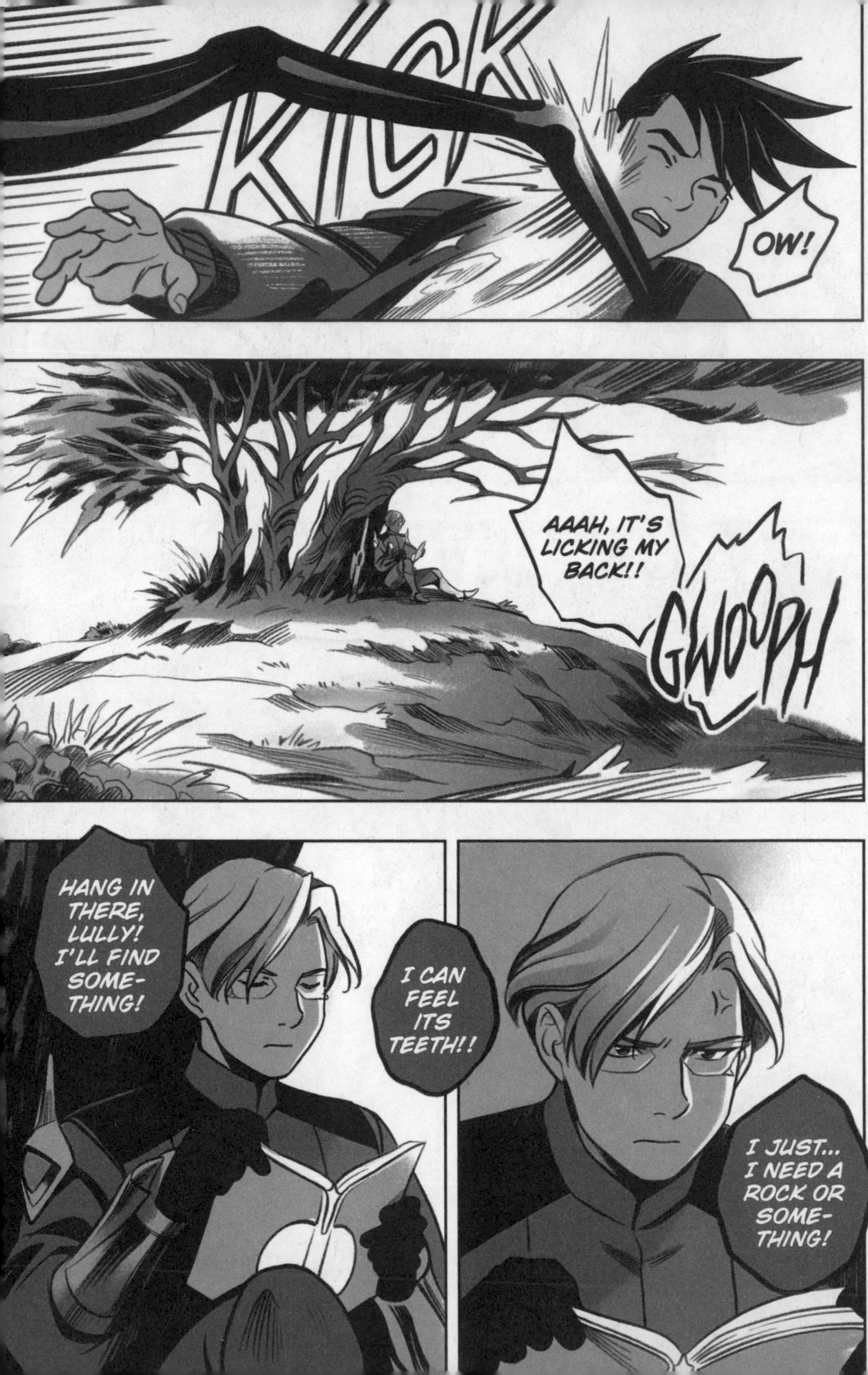
KICK
OW!
AAAH, IT'S LICKING MY BACK!!
GWOOPH
HANG IN THERE, LULLY! I'LL FIND SOME-THING!
I CAN FEEL ITS TEETH!!
I JUST... I NEED A ROCK OR SOME-THING!

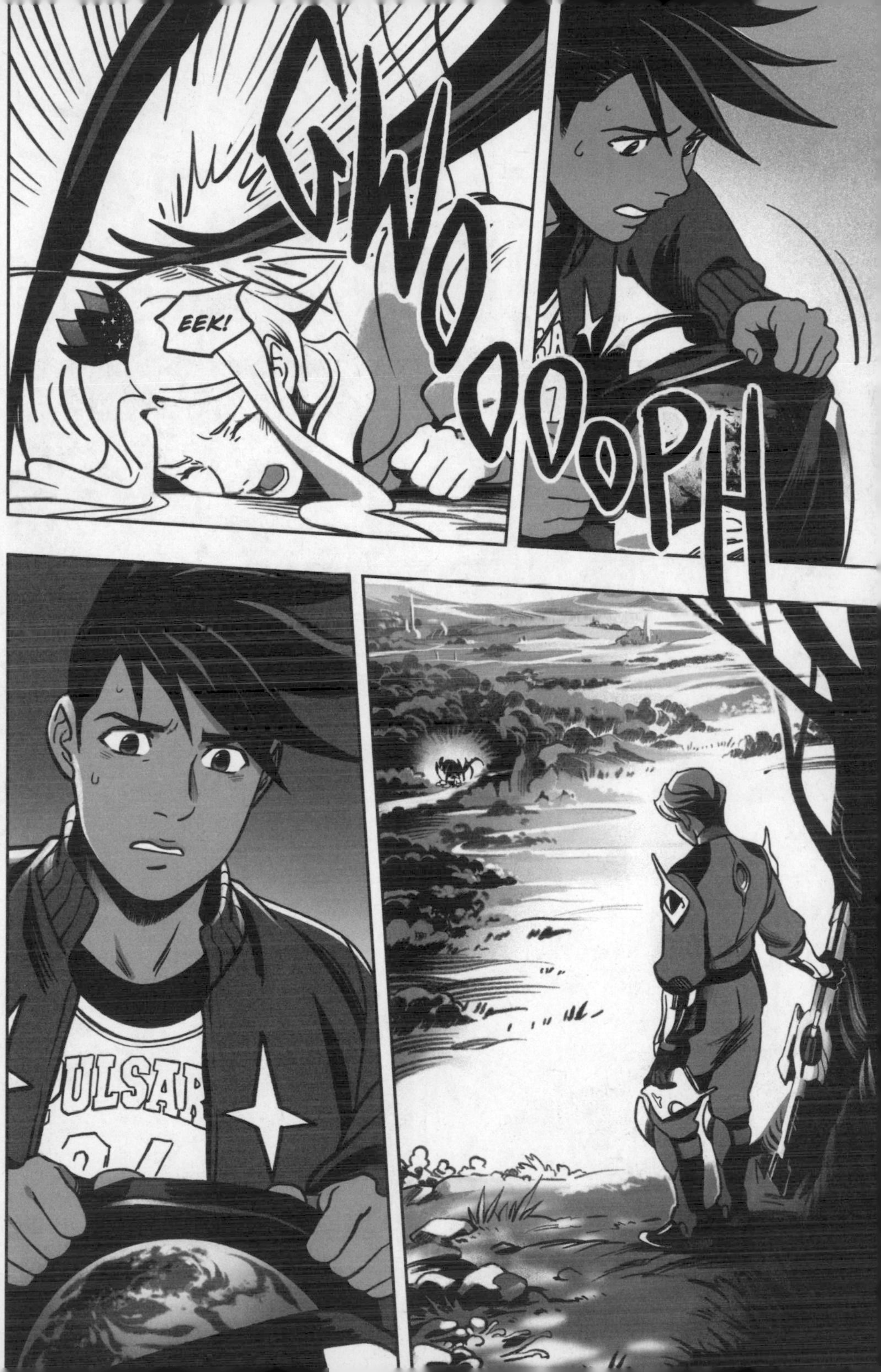
EEK!
GWOOOOPH

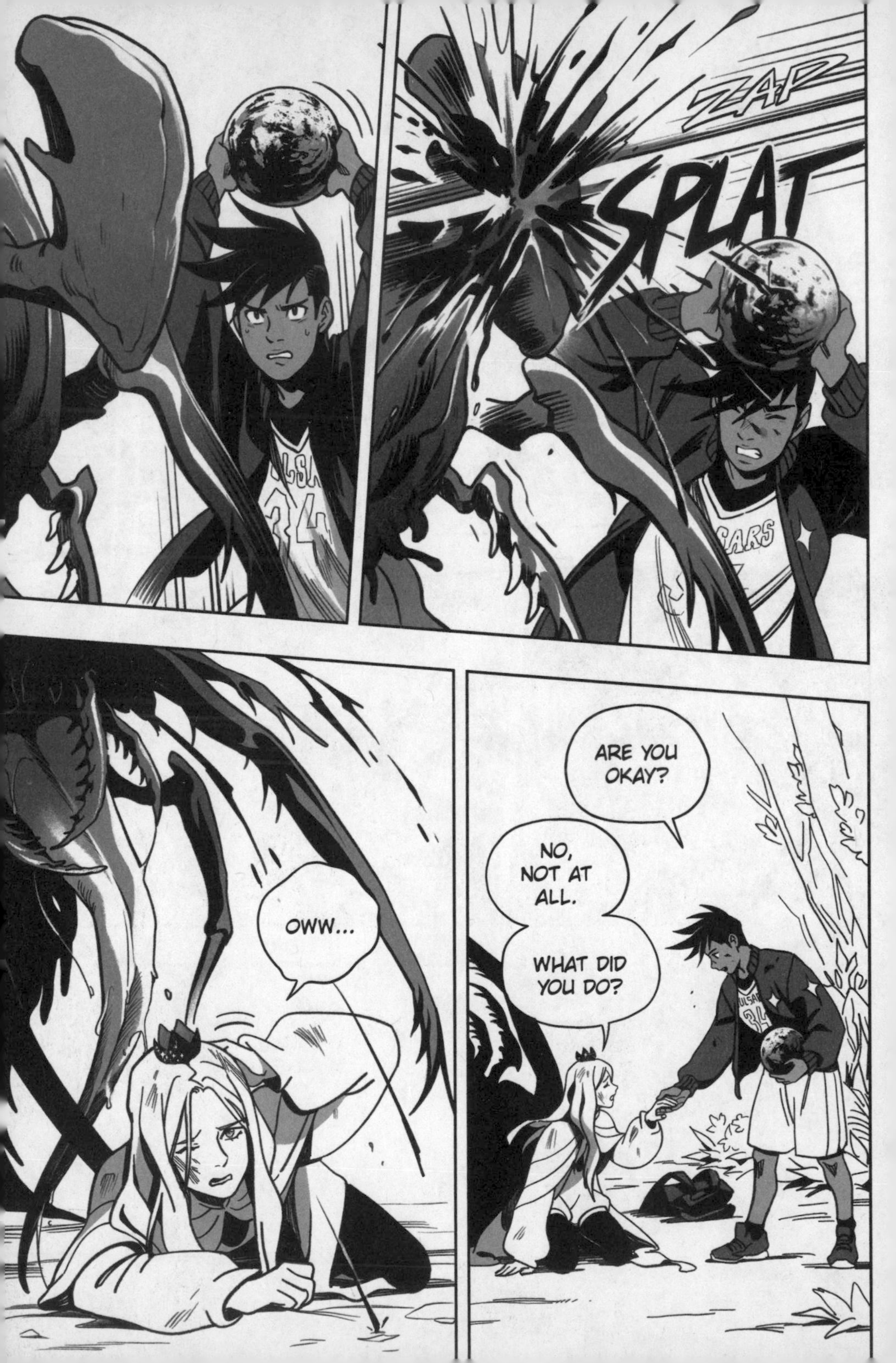
ZAP
SPLAT
OWW...
ARE YOU OKAY?
NO, NOT AT ALL.
WHAT DID YOU DO?

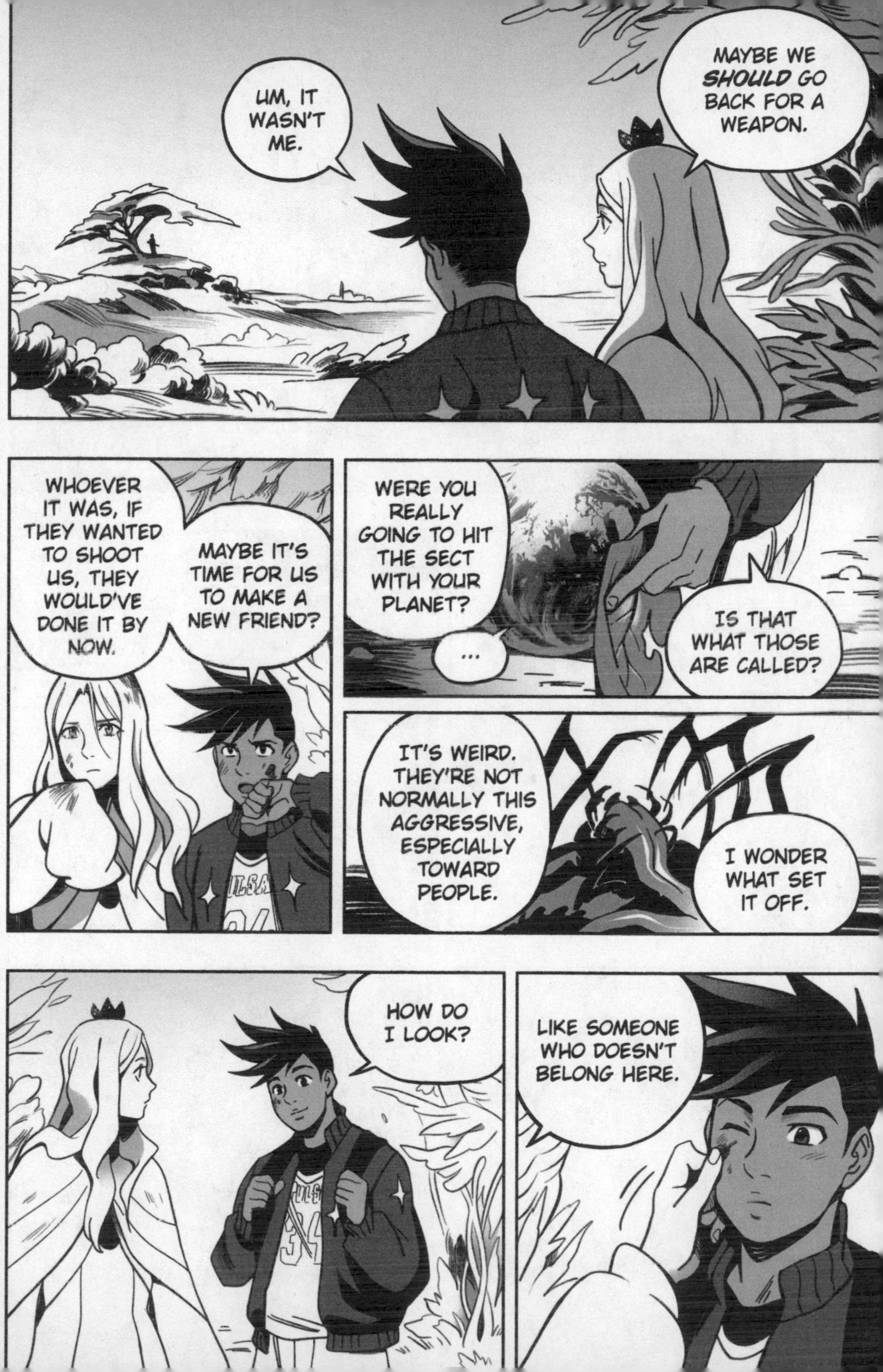
UM, IT WASN'T ME.
MAYBE WE SHOULD GO BACK FOR A WEAPON.
WHOEVER IT WAS, IF THEY WANTED TO SHOOT US, THEY WOULD'VE DONE IT BY NOW.
MAYBE IT'S TIME FOR US TO MAKE A NEW FRIEND?
WERE YOU REALLY GOING TO HIT THE SECT WITH YOUR PLANET?
...
IS THAT WHAT THOSE ARE CALLED?
IT'S WEIRD. THEY'RE NOT NORMALLY THIS AGGRESSIVE, ESPECIALLY TOWARD PEOPLE.
I WONDER WHAT SET IT OFF.
HOW DO I LOOK?
LIKE SOMEONE WHO DOESN'T BELONG HERE.

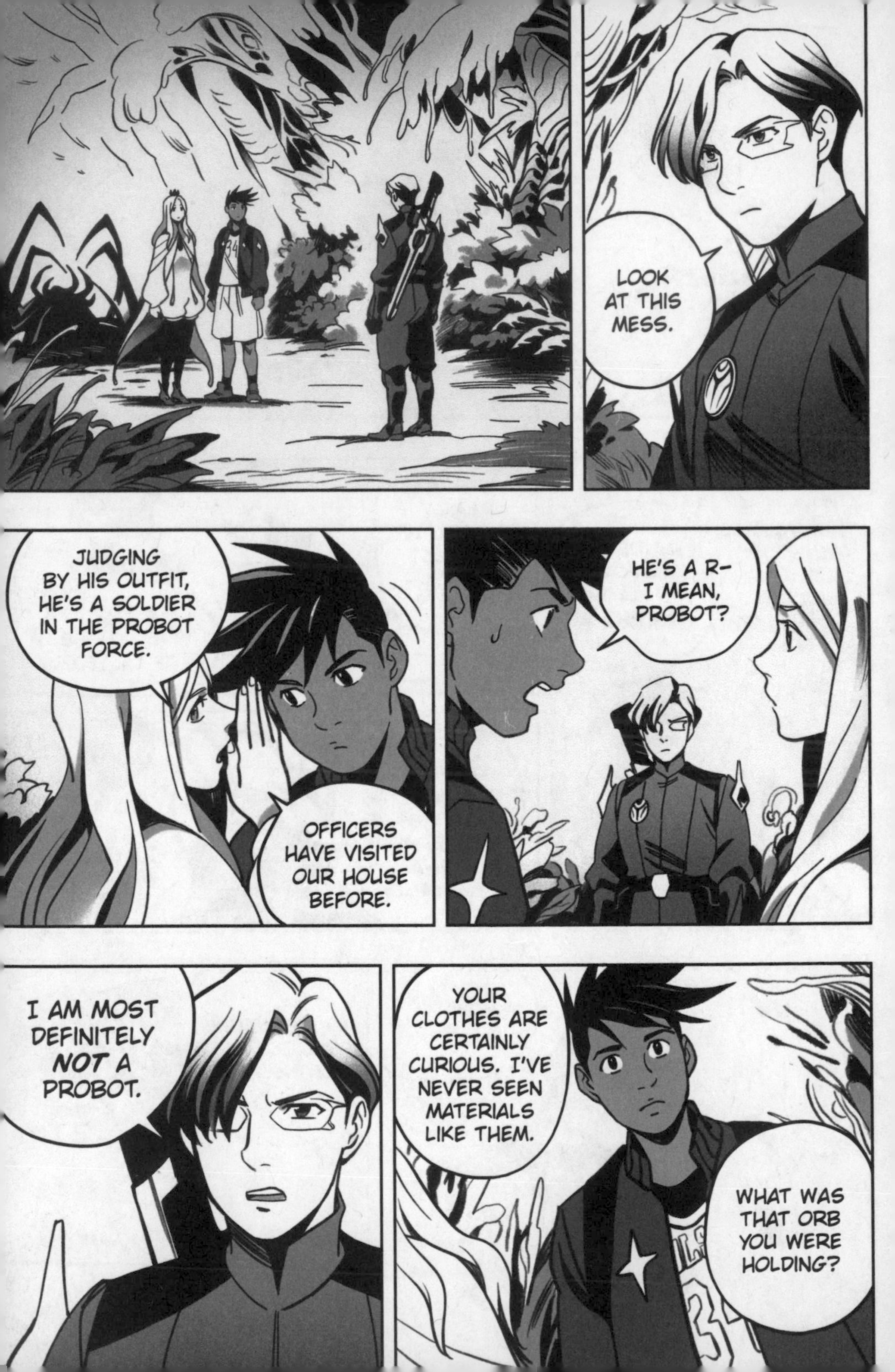
LOOK AT THIS MESS.
JUDGING BY HIS OUTFIT, HE'S A SOLDIER IN THE PROBOT FORCE.
OFFICERS HAVE VISITED OUR HOUSE BEFORE.
HE'S A R– I MEAN, PROBOT?
I AM MOST DEFINITELY *NOT* A PROBOT.
YOUR CLOTHES ARE CERTAINLY CURIOUS. I'VE NEVER SEEN MATERIALS LIKE THEM.
WHAT WAS THAT ORB YOU WERE HOLDING?

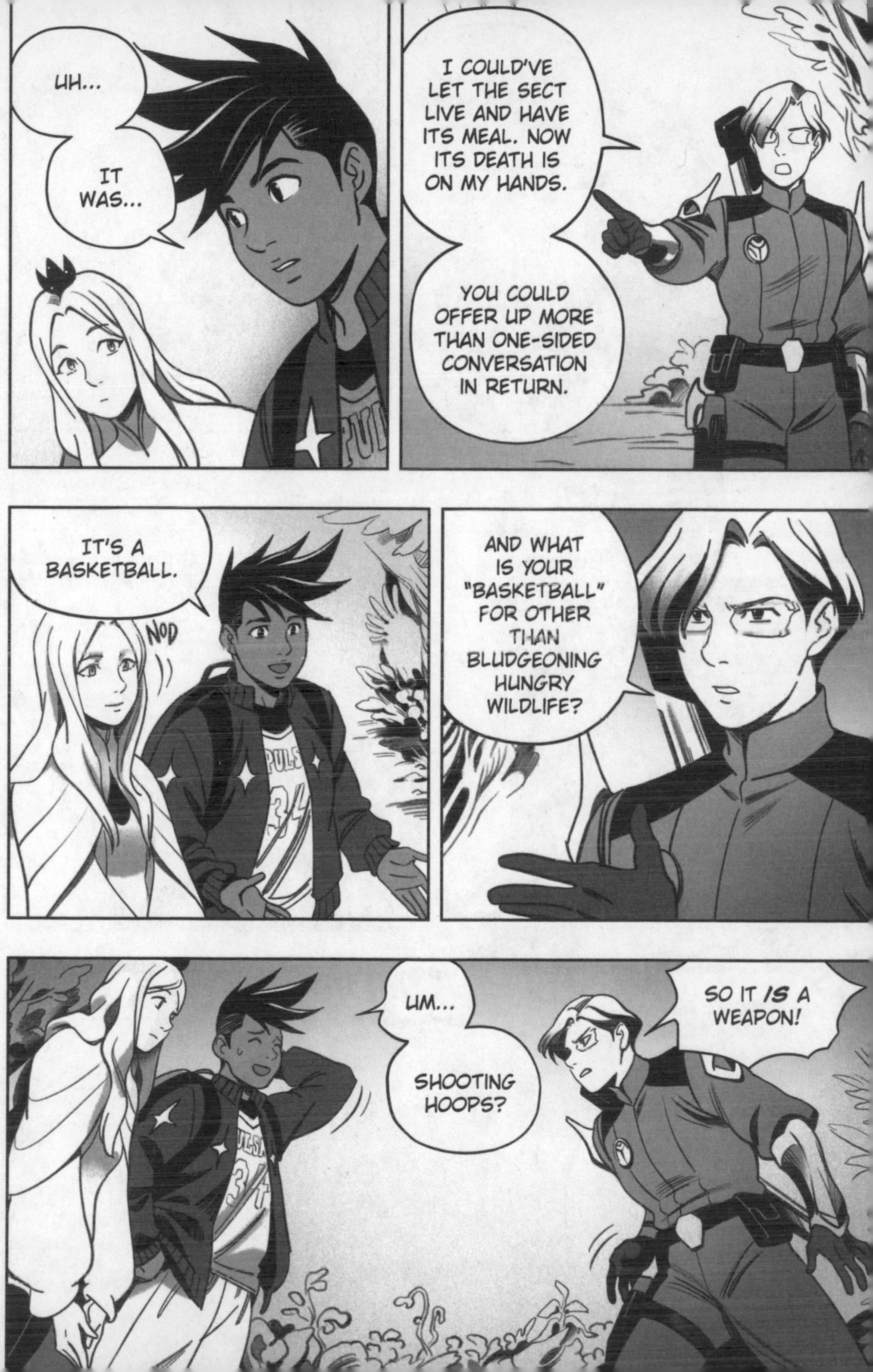
UH...
IT WAS...
I COULD'VE LET THE SECT LIVE AND HAVE ITS MEAL. NOW ITS DEATH IS ON MY HANDS.
YOU COULD OFFER UP MORE THAN ONE-SIDED CONVERSATION IN RETURN.
IT'S A BASKETBALL.
NOD
AND WHAT IS YOUR "BASKETBALL" FOR OTHER THAN BLUDGEONING HUNGRY WILDLIFE?
UM...
SHOOTING HOOPS?
SO IT *IS* A WEAPON!

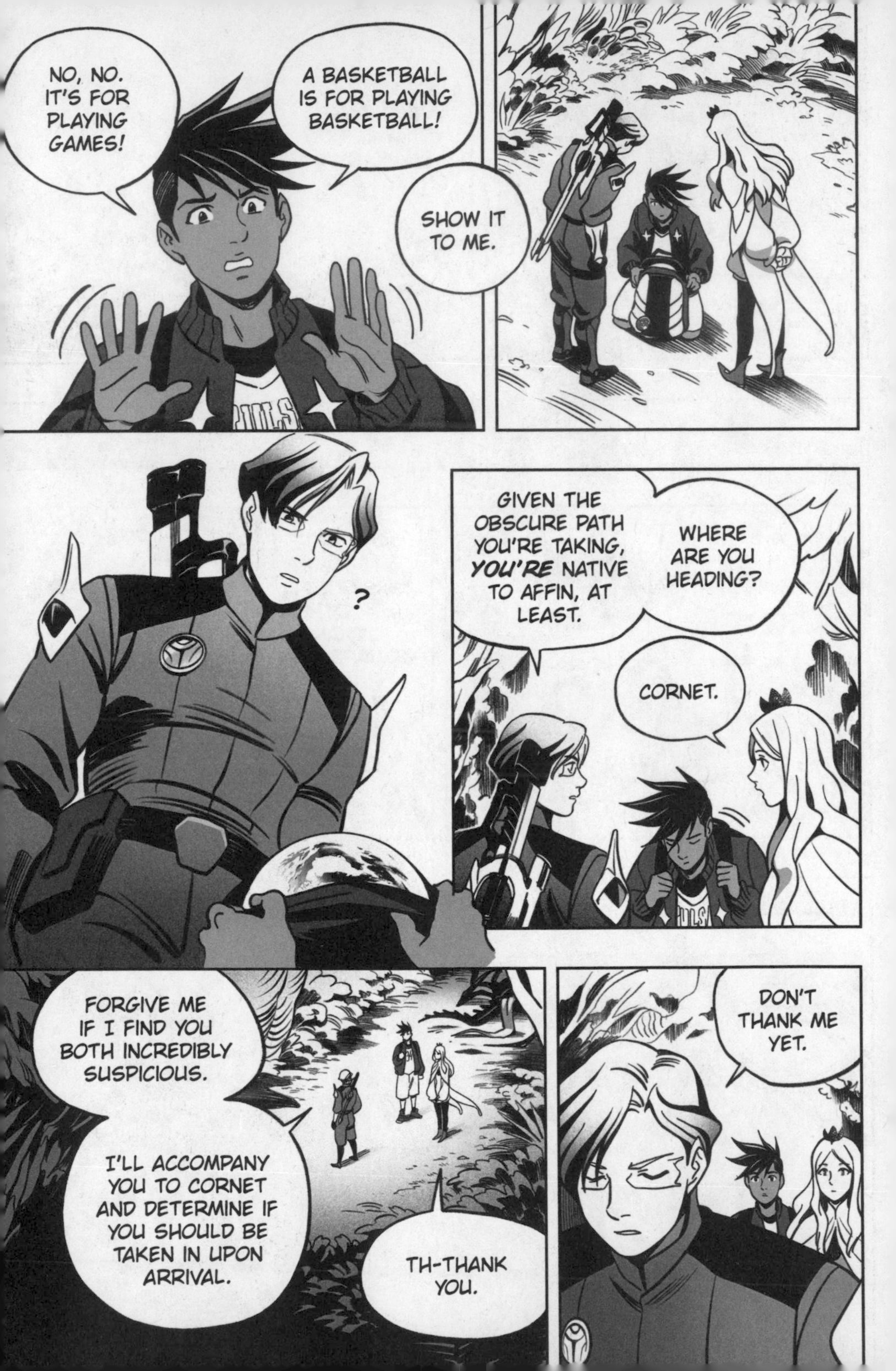
NO, NO. IT'S FOR PLAYING GAMES!
A BASKETBALL IS FOR PLAYING BASKETBALL!
SHOW IT TO ME.
?
WHERE ARE YOU HEADING?
CORNET.
GIVEN THE OBSCURE PATH YOU'RE TAKING, *YOU'RE* NATIVE TO AFFIN, AT LEAST.
FORGIVE ME IF I FIND YOU BOTH INCREDIBLY SUSPICIOUS.
I'LL ACCOMPANY YOU TO CORNET AND DETERMINE IF YOU SHOULD BE TAKEN IN UPON ARRIVAL.
TH-THANK YOU.
DON'T THANK ME YET.

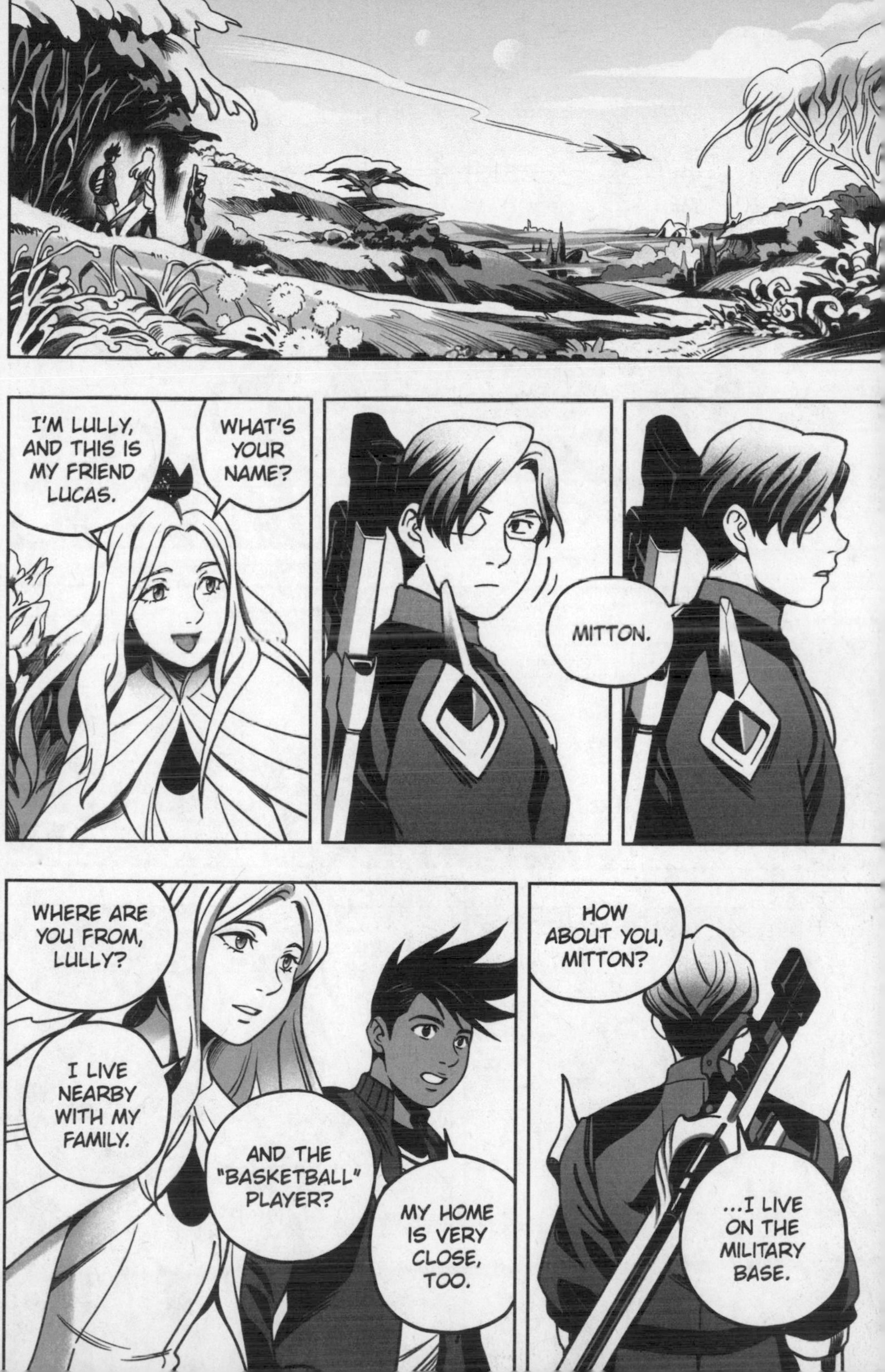
I'M LULLY, AND THIS IS MY FRIEND LUCAS.
WHAT'S YOUR NAME?
MITTON.
WHERE ARE YOU FROM, LULLY?
I LIVE NEARBY WITH MY FAMILY.
AND THE "BASKETBALL" PLAYER?
MY HOME IS VERY CLOSE, TOO.
HOW ABOUT YOU, MITTON?
...I LIVE ON THE MILITARY BASE.

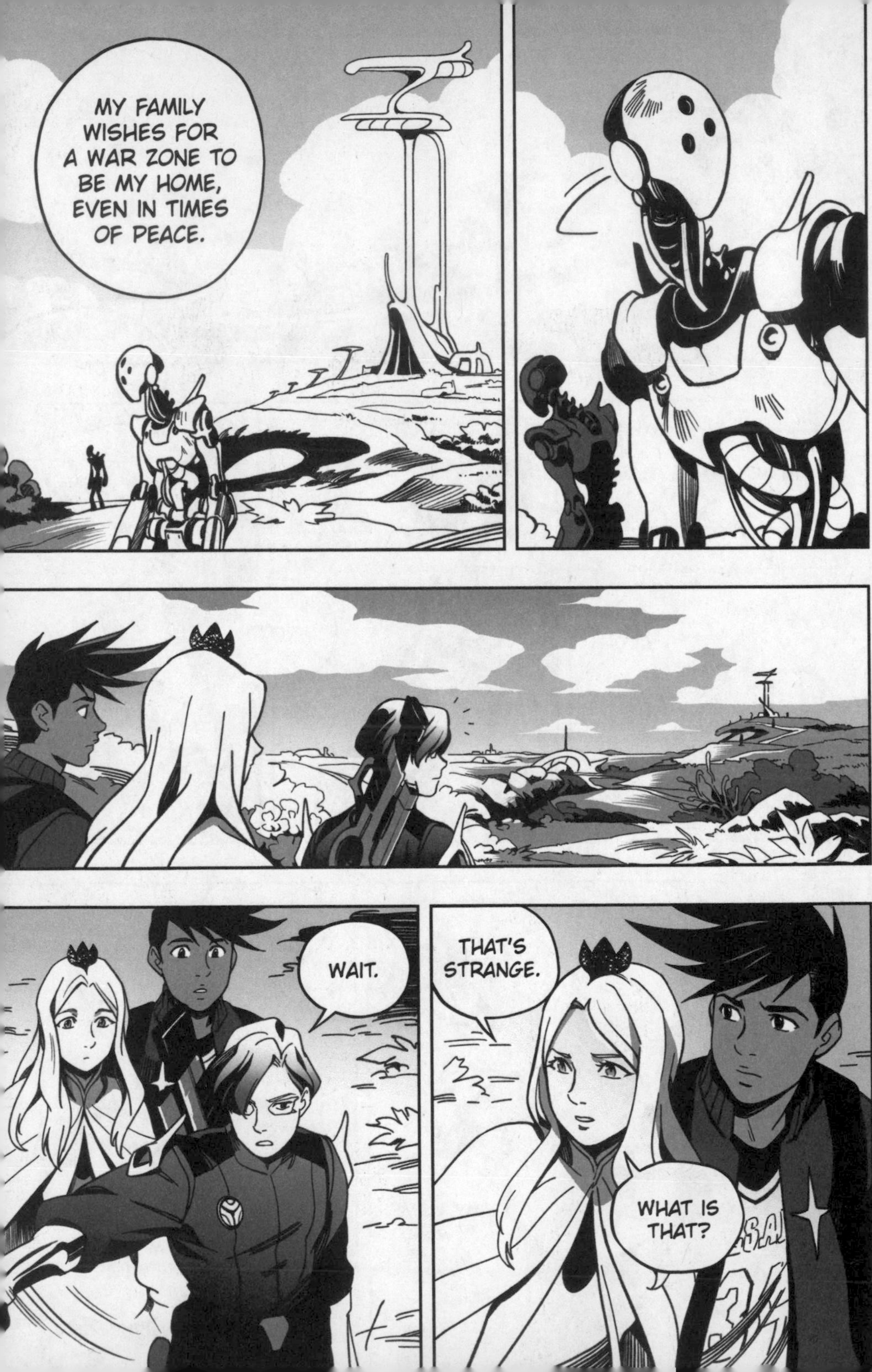
MY FAMILY WISHES FOR A WAR ZONE TO BE MY HOME, EVEN IN TIMES OF PEACE.
WAIT.
THAT'S STRANGE.
WHAT IS THAT?

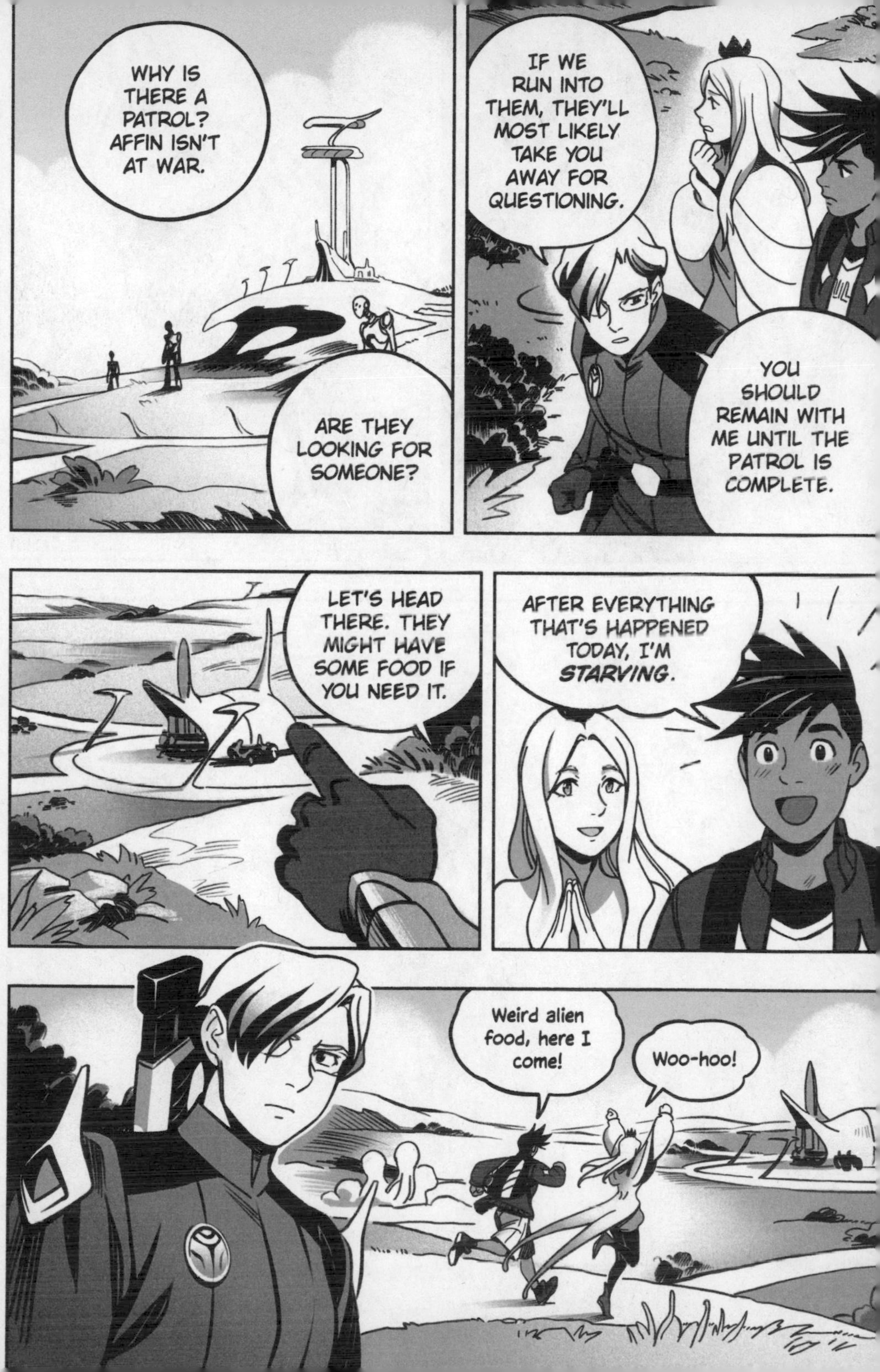
WHY IS THERE A PATROL? AFFIN ISN'T AT WAR.
ARE THEY LOOKING FOR SOMEONE?
IF WE RUN INTO THEM, THEY'LL MOST LIKELY TAKE YOU AWAY FOR QUESTIONING.
YOU SHOULD REMAIN WITH ME UNTIL THE PATROL IS COMPLETE.
LET'S HEAD THERE. THEY MIGHT HAVE SOME FOOD IF YOU NEED IT.
AFTER EVERYTHING THAT'S HAPPENED TODAY, I'M STARVING.
Weird alien food, here I come!
Woo-hoo!

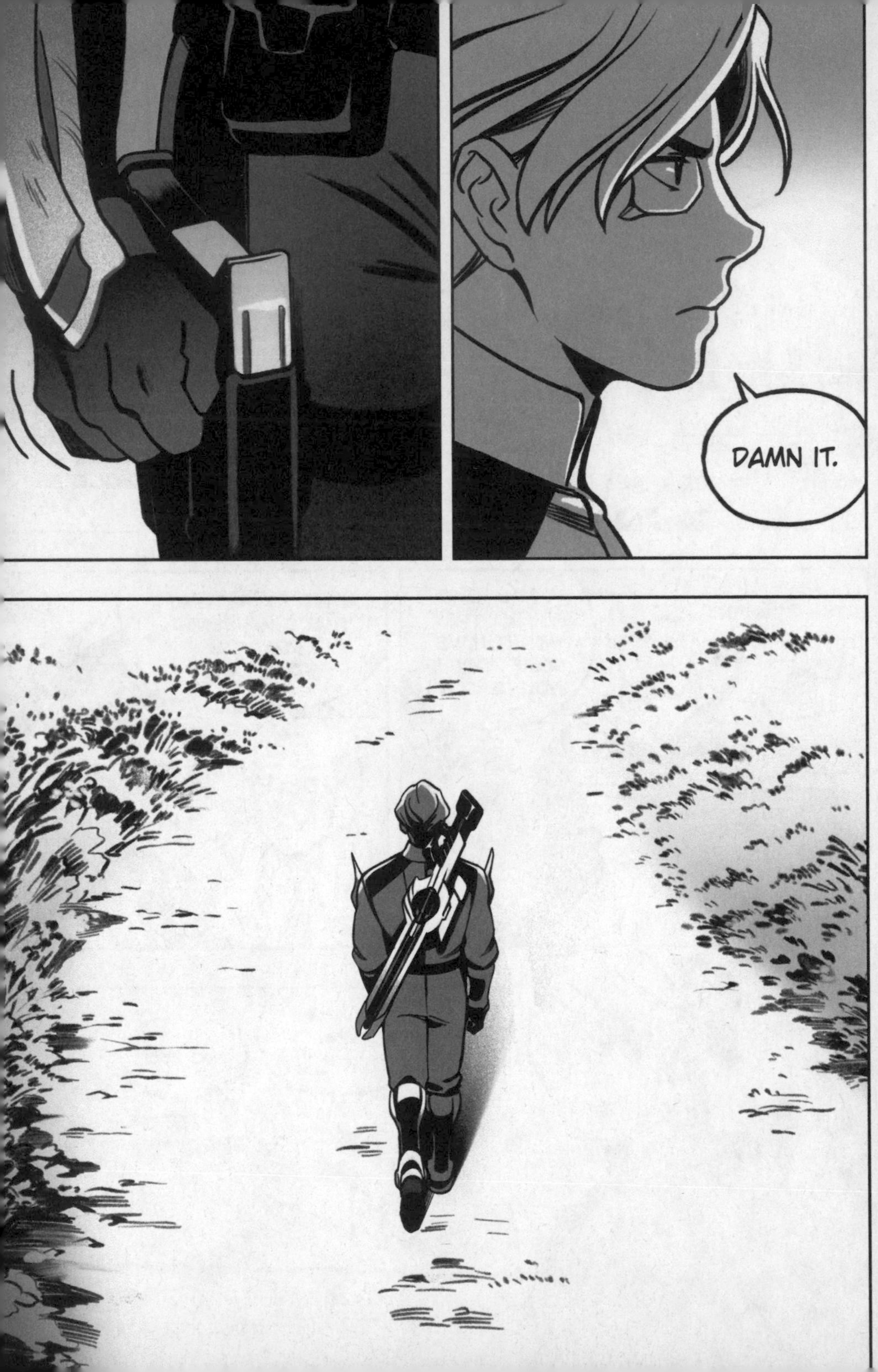
DAMN IT.

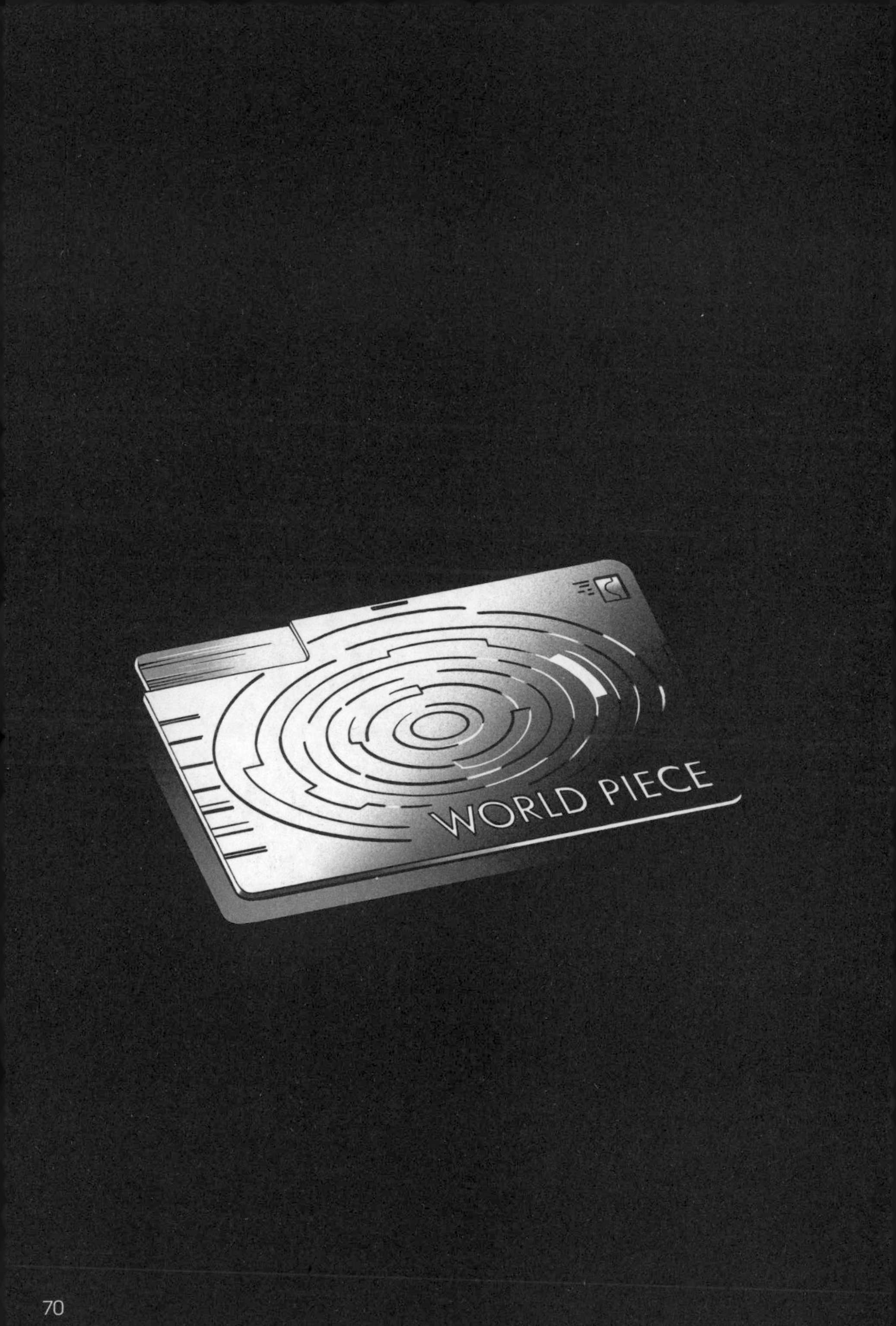
WORLD PIECE

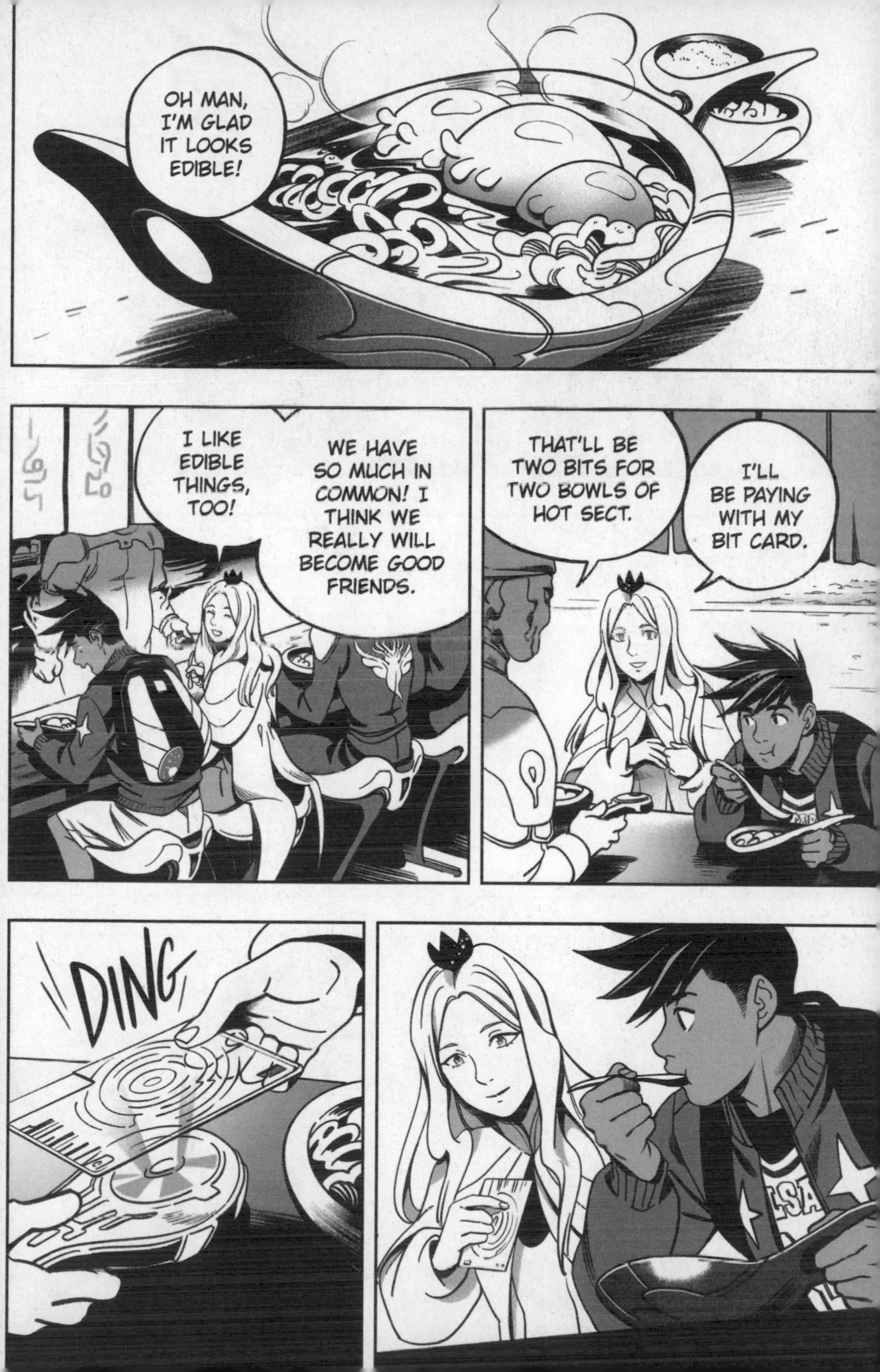
OH MAN, I'M GLAD IT LOOKS EDIBLE!
I LIKE EDIBLE THINGS, TOO!
WE HAVE SO MUCH IN COMMON! I THINK WE REALLY WILL BECOME GOOD FRIENDS.
THAT'LL BE TWO BITS FOR TWO BOWLS OF HOT SECT.
I'LL BE PAYING WITH MY BIT CARD.
DING

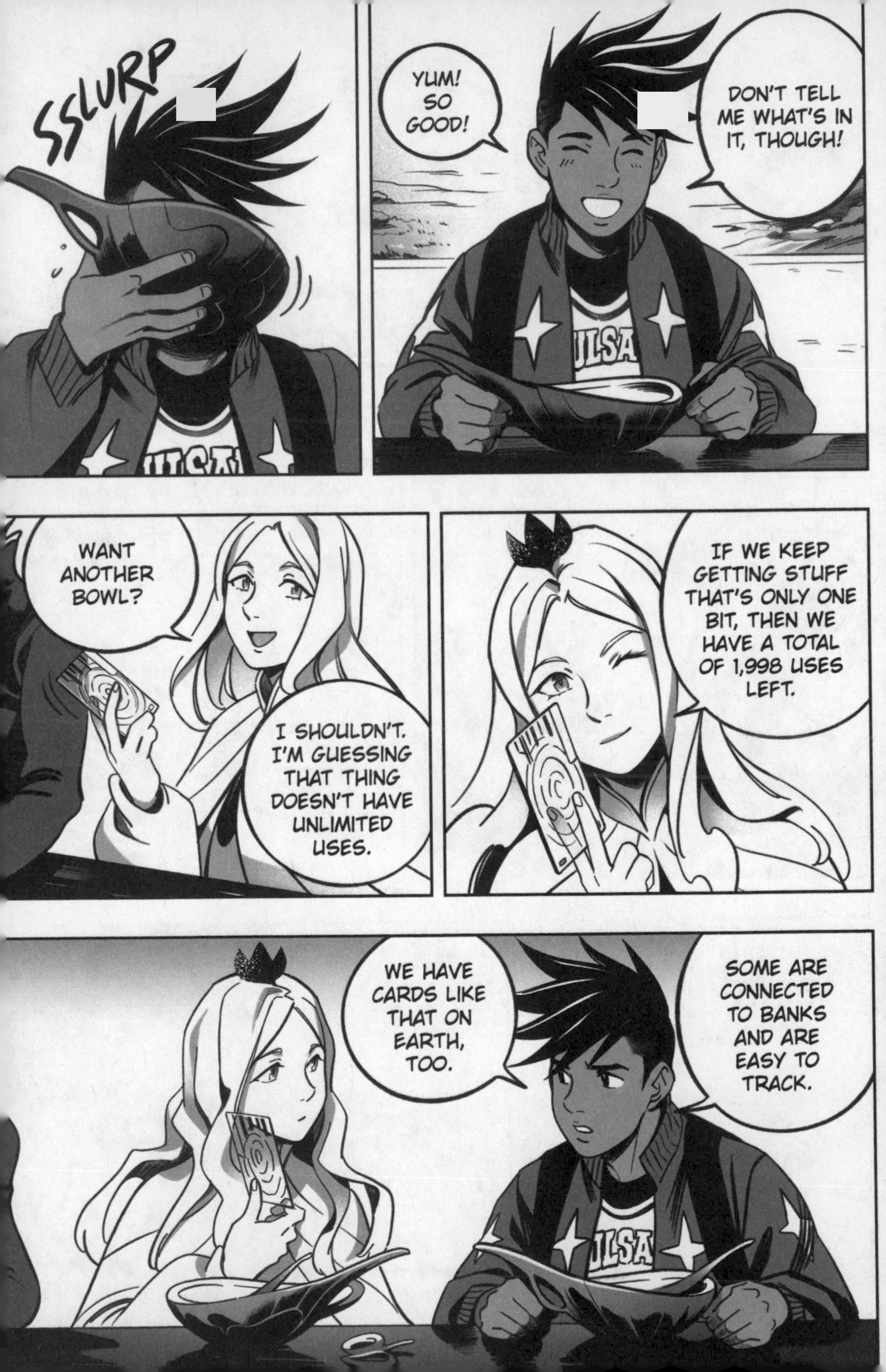
SSLURP
YUM! SO GOOD!
DON'T TELL ME WHAT'S IN IT, THOUGH!
WANT ANOTHER BOWL?
I SHOULDN'T. I'M GUESSING THAT THING DOESN'T HAVE UNLIMITED USES.
IF WE KEEP GETTING STUFF THAT'S ONLY ONE BIT, THEN WE HAVE A TOTAL OF 1,998 USES LEFT.
WE HAVE CARDS LIKE THAT ON EARTH, TOO.
SOME ARE CONNECTED TO BANKS AND ARE EASY TO TRACK.

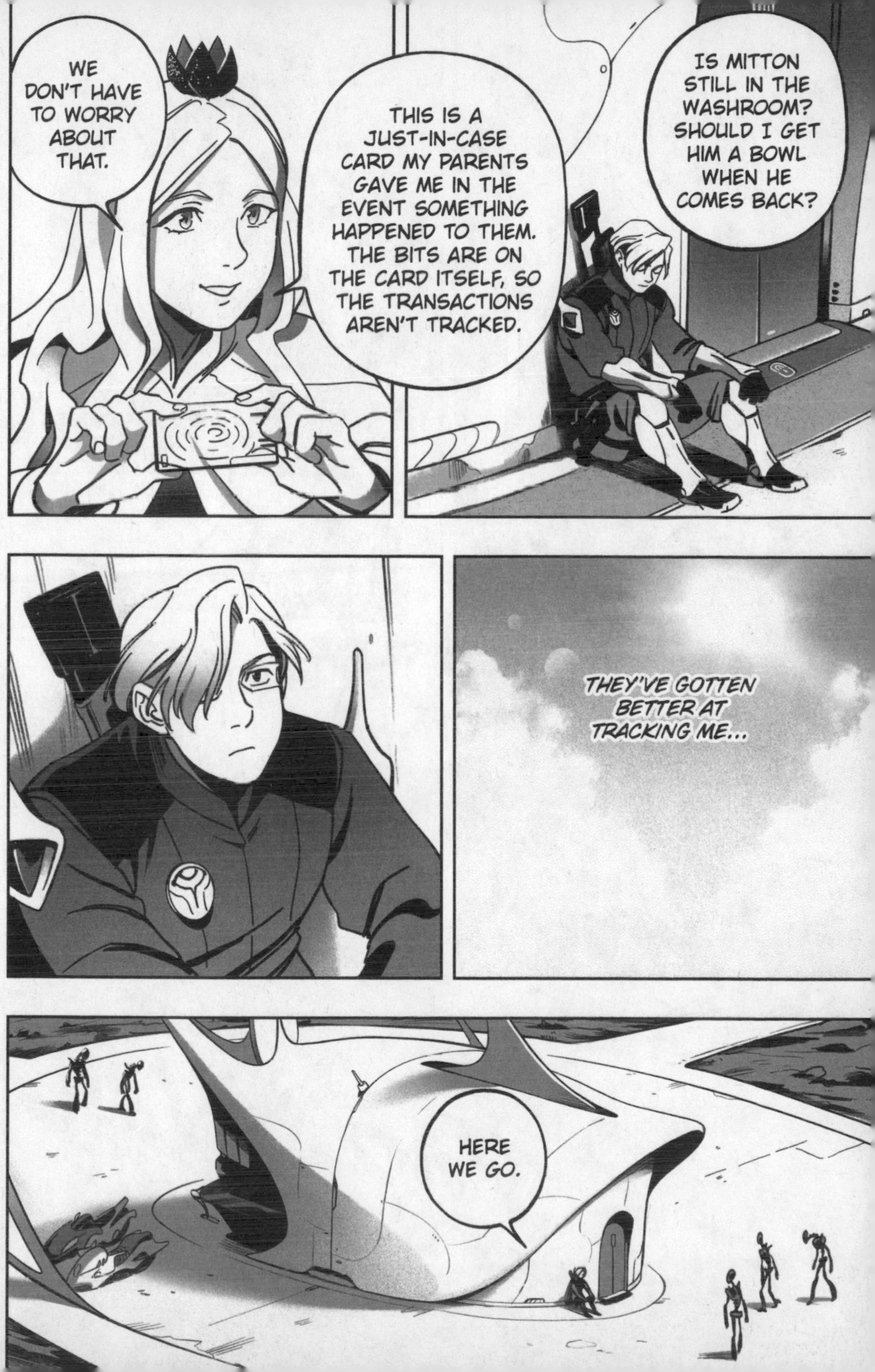
WE DON'T HAVE TO WORRY ABOUT THAT.
THIS IS A JUST-IN-CASE CARD MY PARENTS GAVE ME IN THE EVENT SOMETHING HAPPENED TO THEM. THE BITS ARE ON THE CARD ITSELF, SO THE TRANSACTIONS AREN'T TRACKED.
IS MITTON STILL IN THE WASHROOM? SHOULD I GET HIM A BOWL WHEN HE COMES BACK?
THEY'VE GOTTEN BETTER AT TRACKING ME...
HERE WE GO.

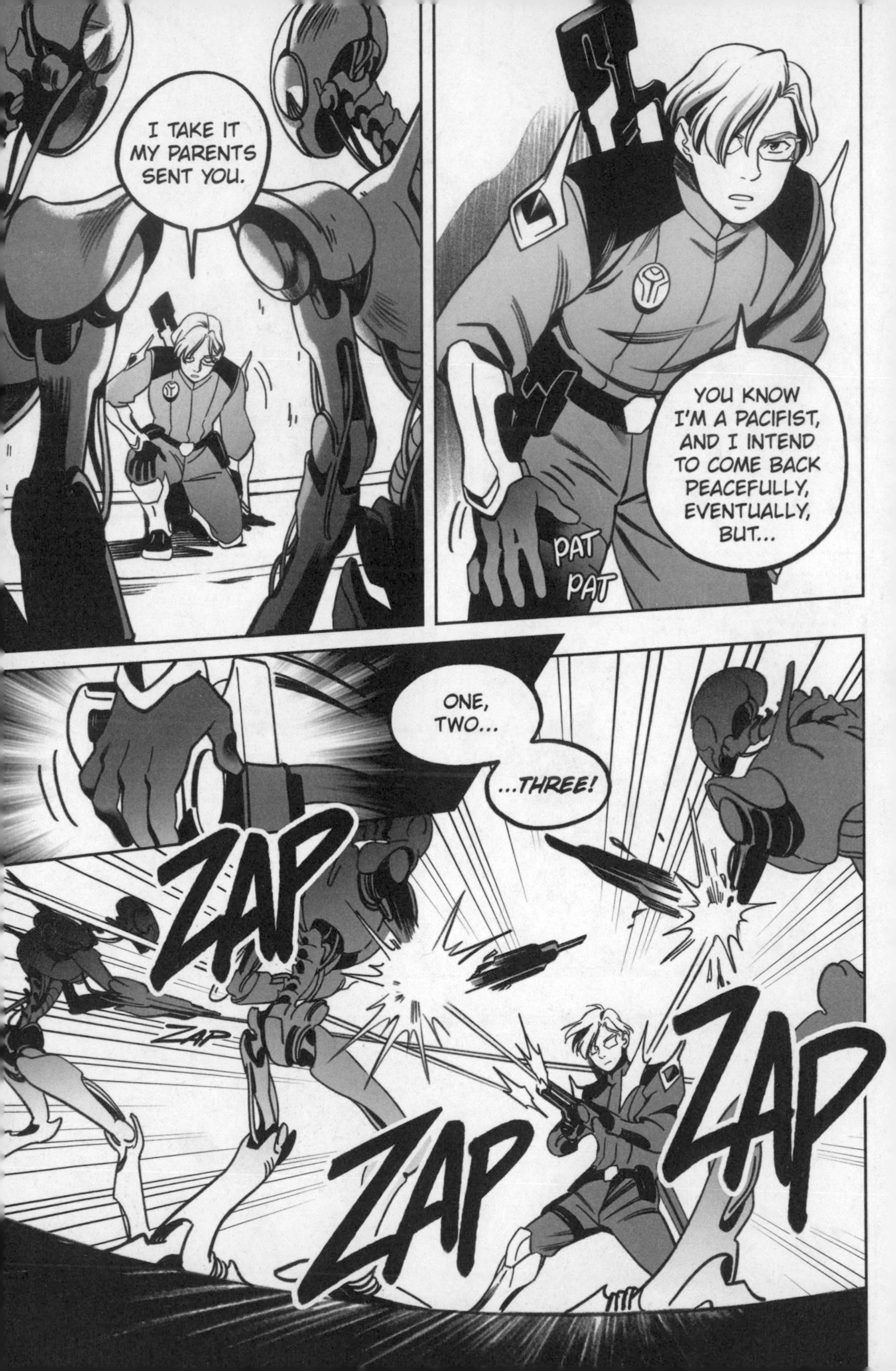
I TAKE IT MY PARENTS SENT YOU.
YOU KNOW I'M A PACIFIST, AND I INTEND TO COME BACK PEACEFULLY, EVENTUALLY, BUT...
PAT PAT
ONE, TWO...
...THREE!
ZAP
ZAP
ZAP
ZAP

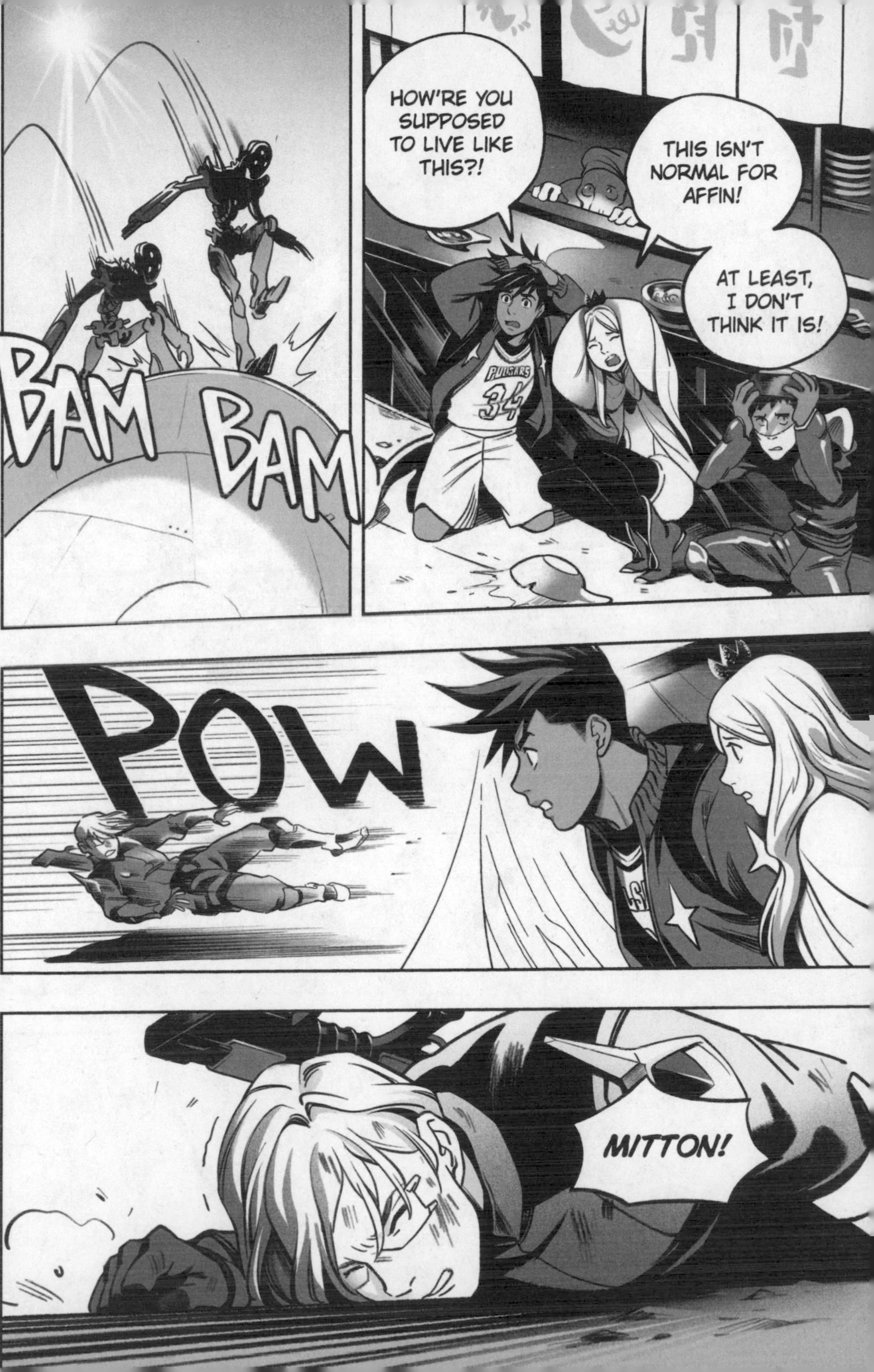
BAM BAM
HOW'RE YOU SUPPOSED TO LIVE LIKE THIS?!
THIS ISN'T NORMAL FOR AFFIN!
AT LEAST, I DON'T THINK IT IS!
POW
MITTON!

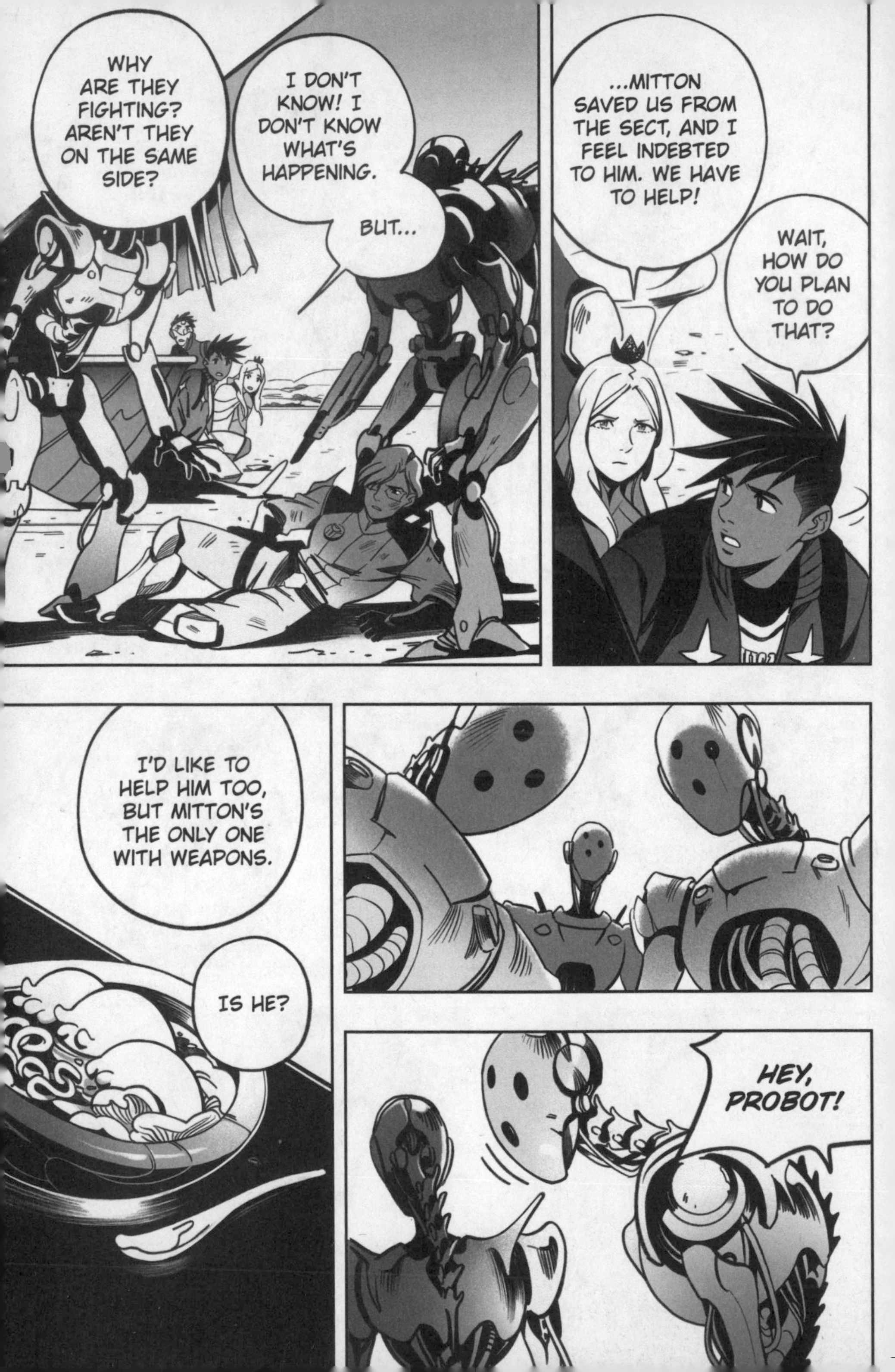
WHY ARE THEY FIGHTING? AREN'T THEY ON THE SAME SIDE?
I DON'T KNOW! I DON'T KNOW WHAT'S HAPPENING.
BUT...
...MITTON SAVED US FROM THE SECT, AND I FEEL INDEBTED TO HIM. WE HAVE TO HELP!
WAIT, HOW DO YOU PLAN TO DO THAT?
I'D LIKE TO HELP HIM TOO, BUT MITTON'S THE ONLY ONE WITH WEAPONS.
IS HE?
HEY, PROBOT!

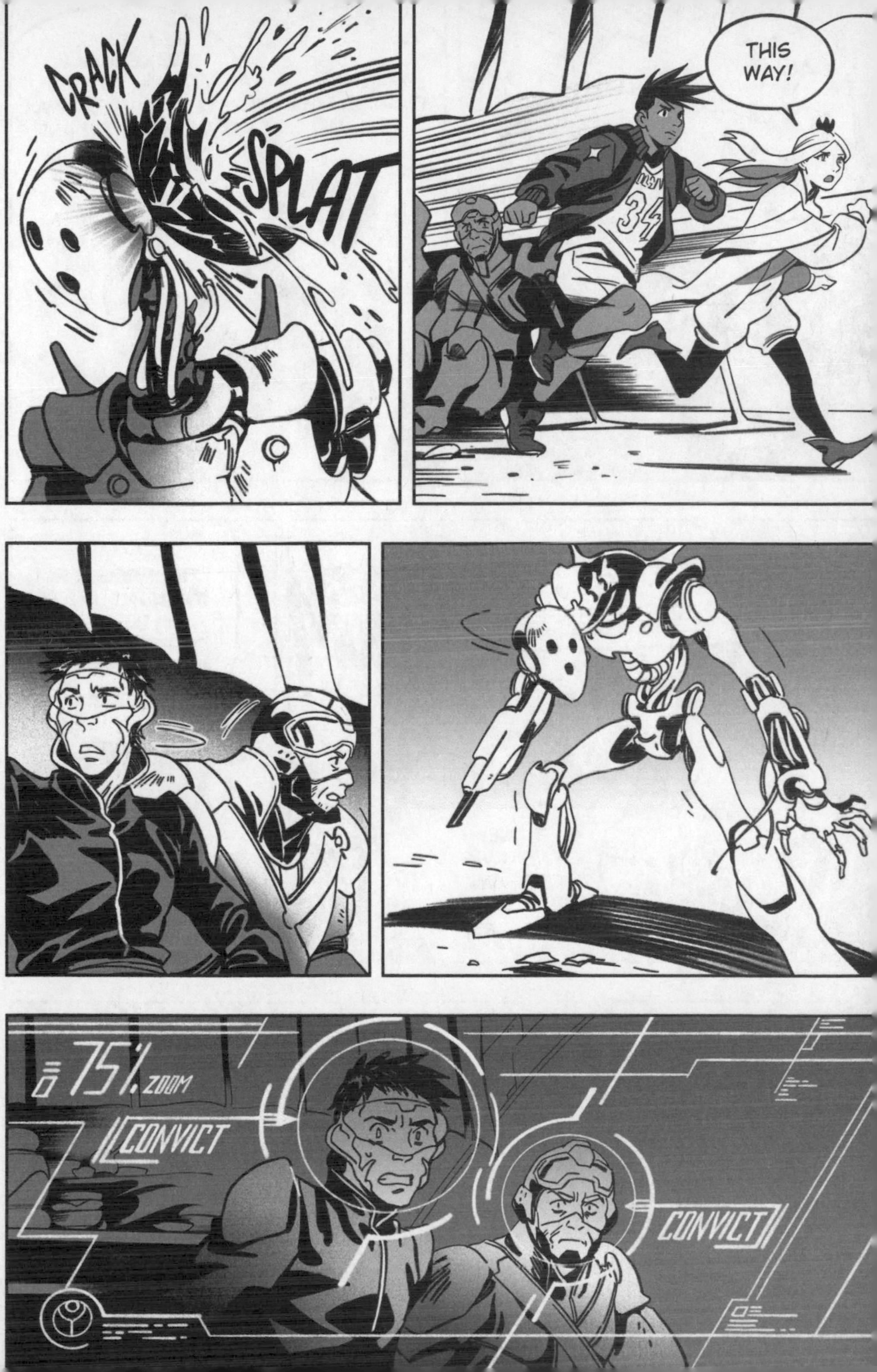
CRACK
SPLAT
THIS WAY!
75% ZOOM
CONVICT
CONVICT

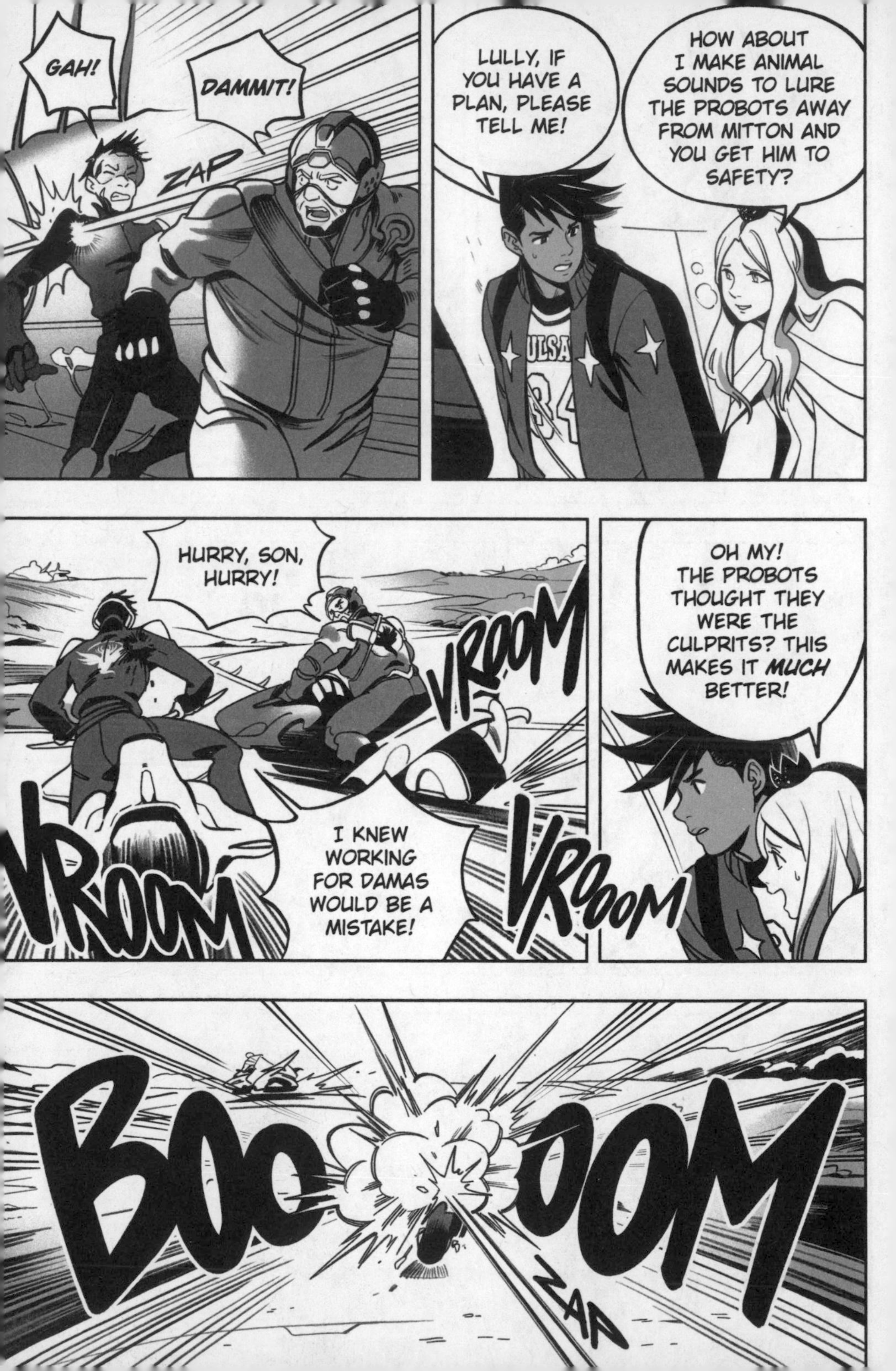
GAH!
DAMMIT!
ZAP
LULLY, IF YOU HAVE A PLAN, PLEASE TELL ME!
HOW ABOUT I MAKE ANIMAL SOUNDS TO LURE THE PROBOTS AWAY FROM MITTON AND YOU GET HIM TO SAFETY?
HURRY, SON, HURRY!
VROOM
VROOM
I KNEW WORKING FOR DAMAS WOULD BE A MISTAKE!
VROOOOM
OH MY! THE PROBOTS THOUGHT THEY WERE THE CULPRITS? THIS MAKES IT *MUCH* BETTER!
BOOOOM
ZAP

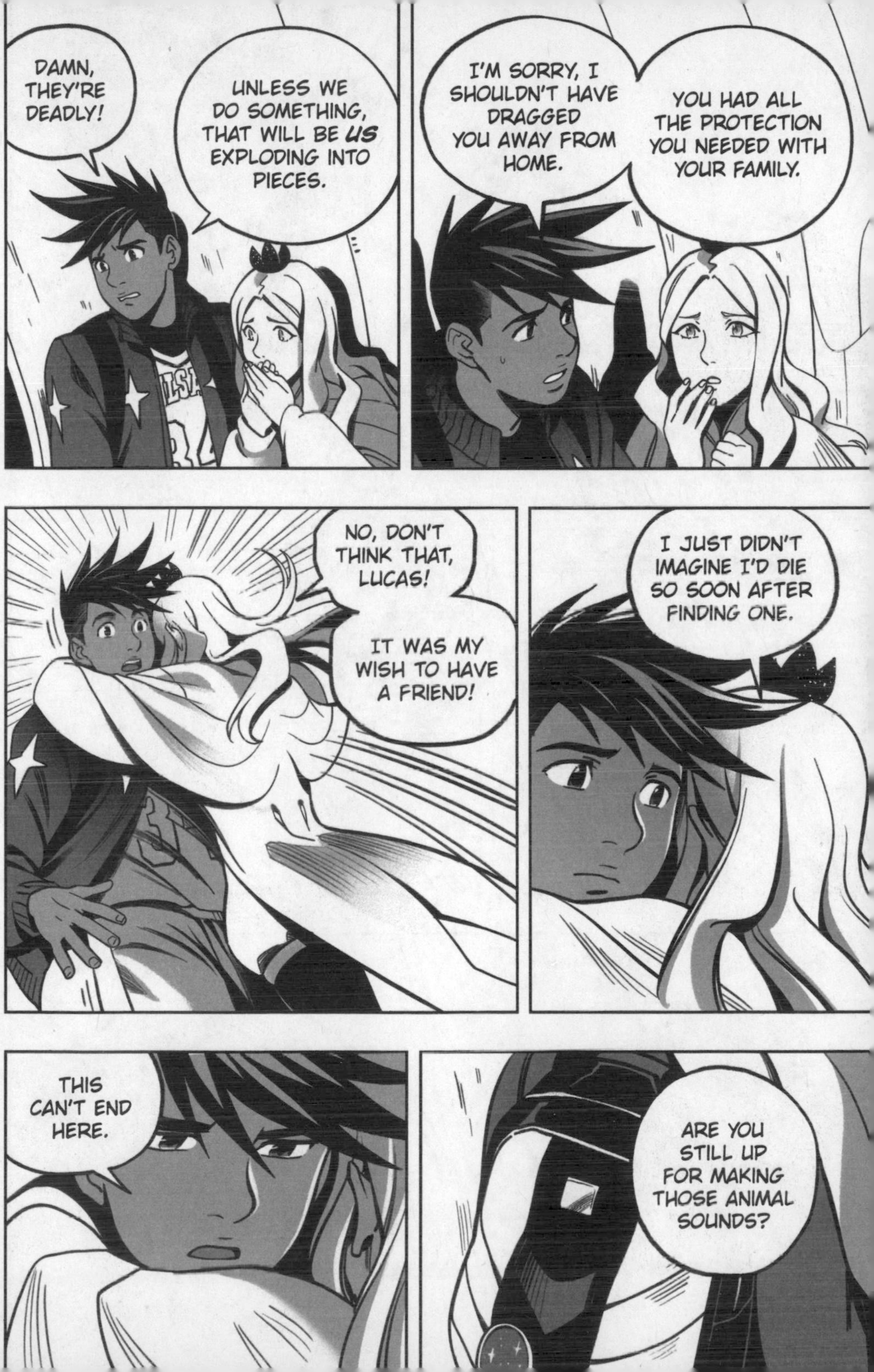
DAMN, THEY'RE DEADLY!
UNLESS WE DO SOMETHING, THAT WILL BE US EXPLODING INTO PIECES.
I'M SORRY, I SHOULDN'T HAVE DRAGGED YOU AWAY FROM HOME.
YOU HAD ALL THE PROTECTION YOU NEEDED WITH YOUR FAMILY.
NO, DON'T THINK THAT, LUCAS!
IT WAS MY WISH TO HAVE A FRIEND!
I JUST DIDN'T IMAGINE I'D DIE SO SOON AFTER FINDING ONE.
THIS CAN'T END HERE.
ARE YOU STILL UP FOR MAKING THOSE ANIMAL SOUNDS?

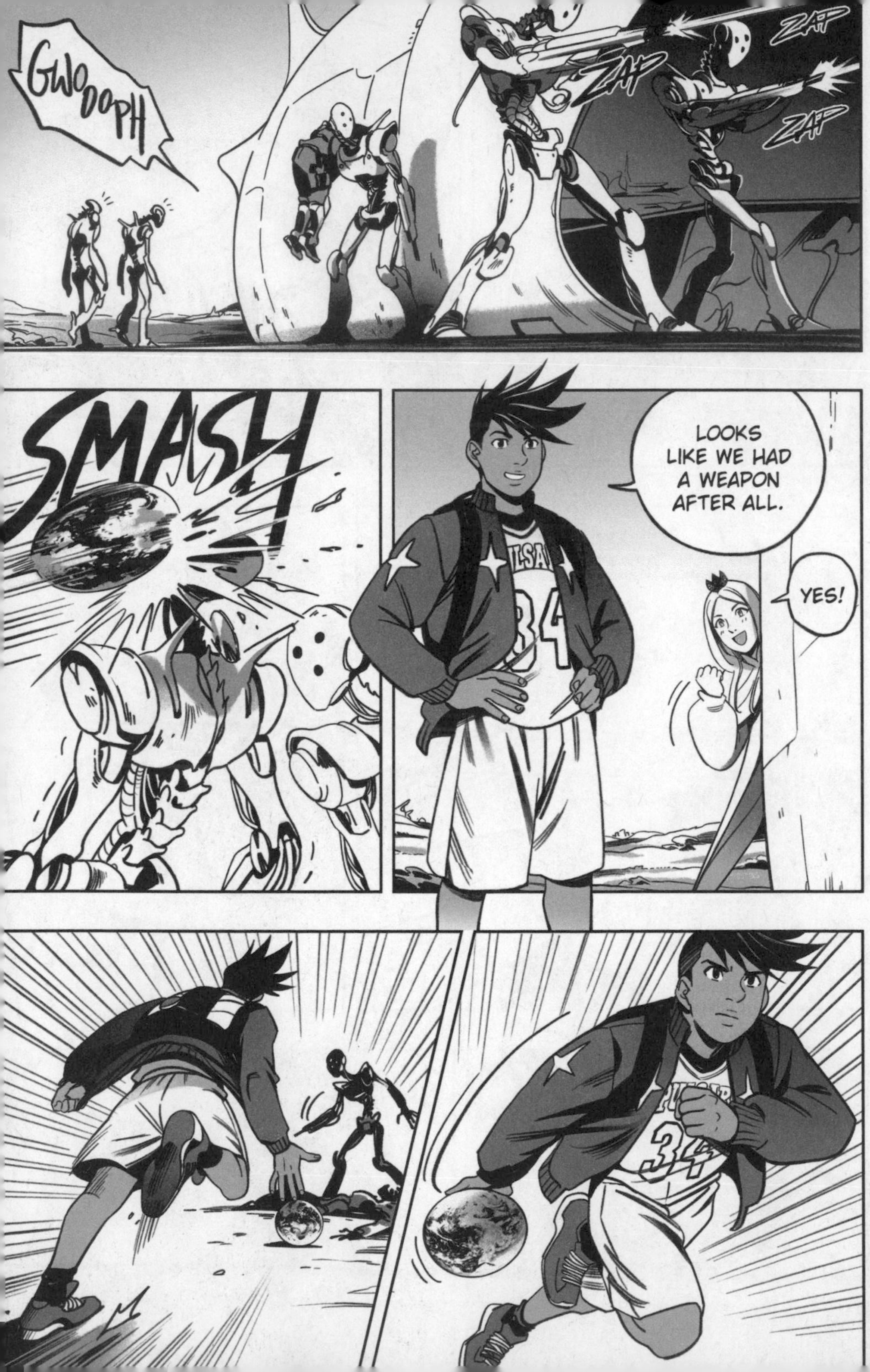
GWOOOPH
ZAP
ZAP
ZAP
SMASH
LOOKS LIKE WE HAD A WEAPON AFTER ALL.
YES!

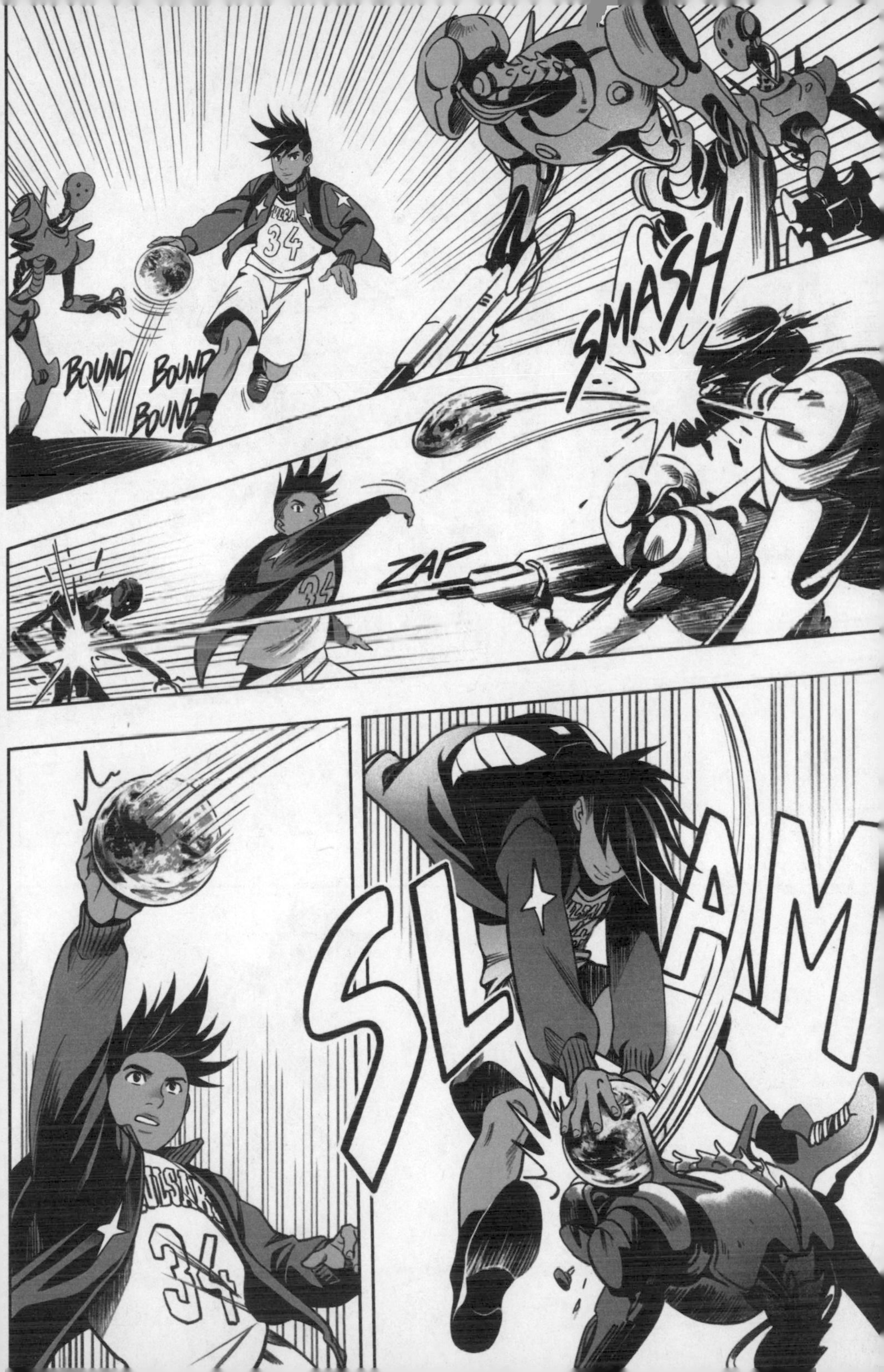
BOUND
BOUND
BOUND
SMASH
ZAP
SLAM

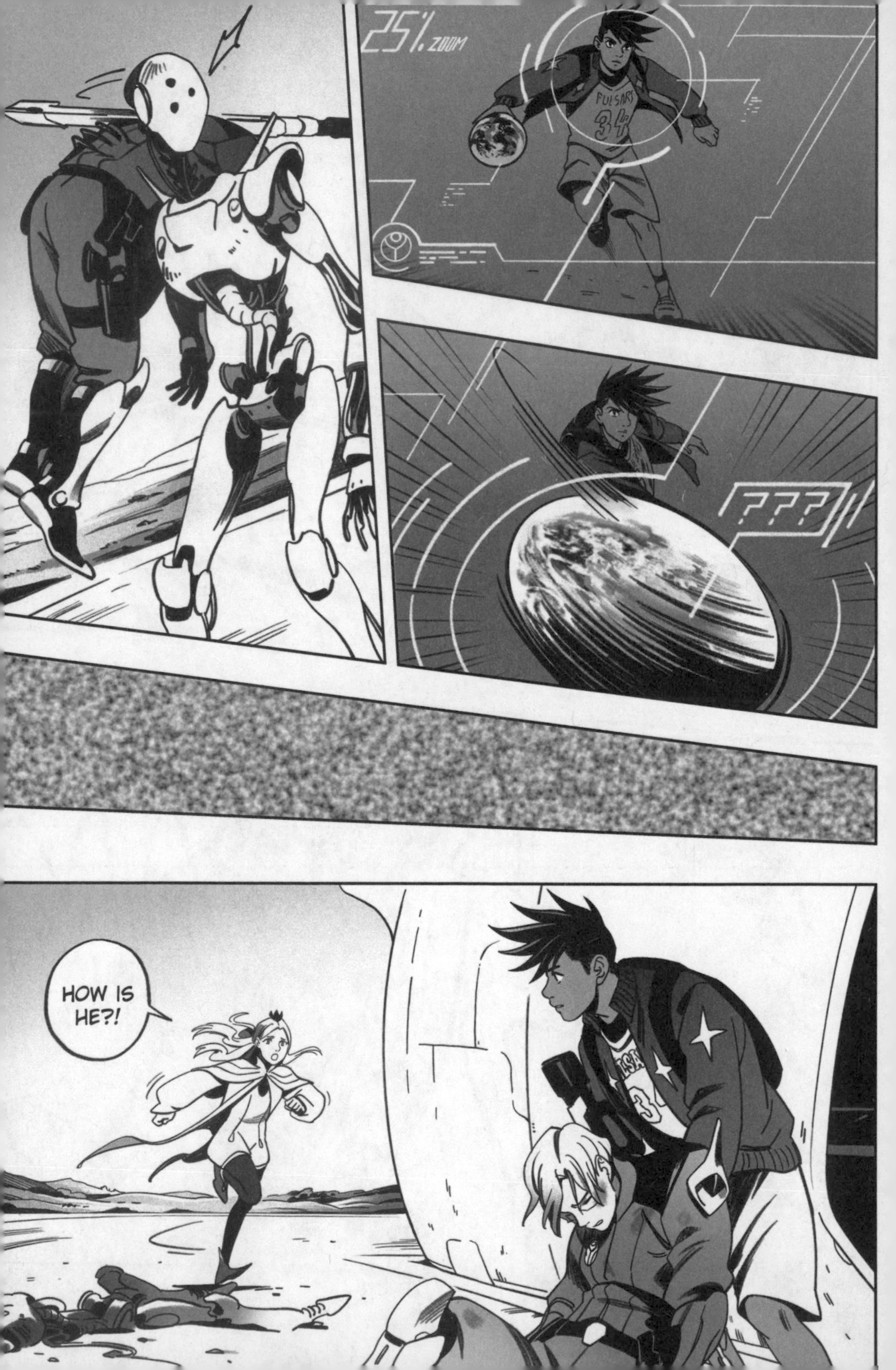
25% ZOOM
PULSARS
34
???
HOW IS HE?!

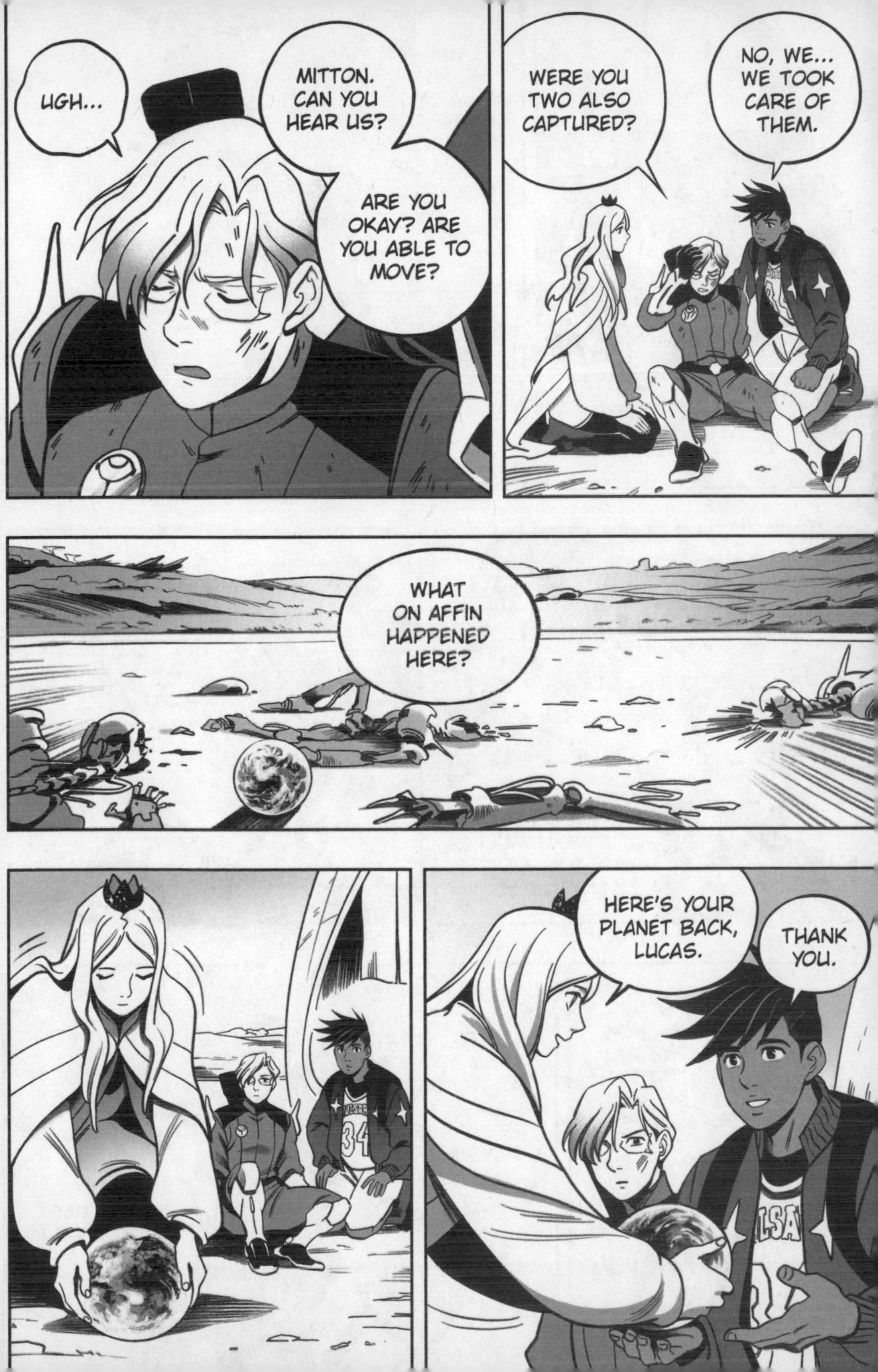

UGH...
MITTON. CAN YOU HEAR US?
ARE YOU OKAY? ARE YOU ABLE TO MOVE?
WERE YOU TWO ALSO CAPTURED?
NO, WE... WE TOOK CARE OF THEM.
WHAT ON AFFIN HAPPENED HERE?
HERE'S YOUR PLANET BACK, LUCAS.
THANK YOU.

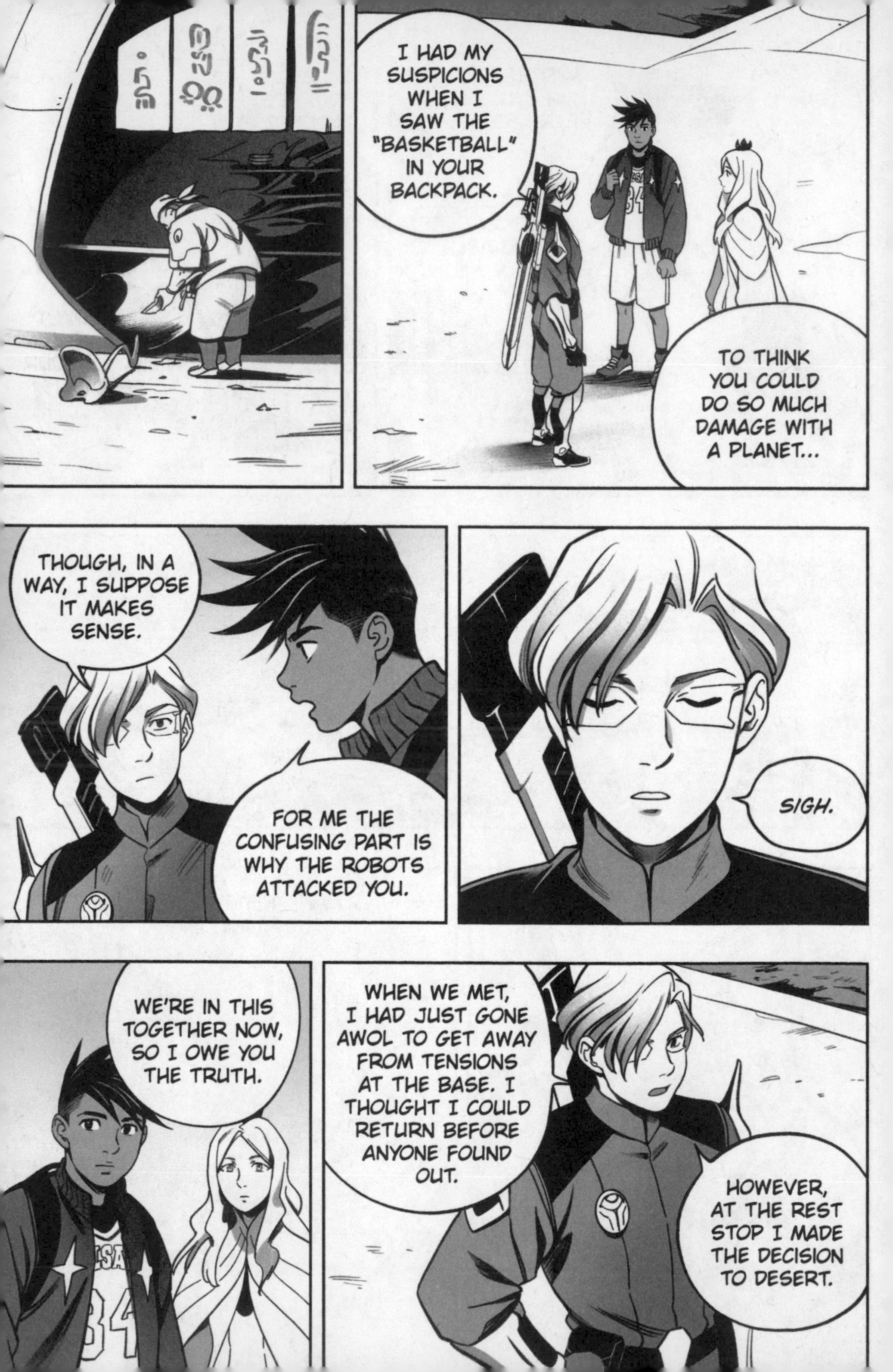
I HAD MY SUSPICIONS WHEN I SAW THE "BASKETBALL" IN YOUR BACKPACK.
TO THINK YOU COULD DO SO MUCH DAMAGE WITH A PLANET...
THOUGH, IN A WAY, I SUPPOSE IT MAKES SENSE.
FOR ME THE CONFUSING PART IS WHY THE ROBOTS ATTACKED YOU.
SIGH.
WE'RE IN THIS TOGETHER NOW, SO I OWE YOU THE TRUTH.
WHEN WE MET, I HAD JUST GONE AWOL TO GET AWAY FROM TENSIONS AT THE BASE. I THOUGHT I COULD RETURN BEFORE ANYONE FOUND OUT.
HOWEVER, AT THE REST STOP I MADE THE DECISION TO DESERT.

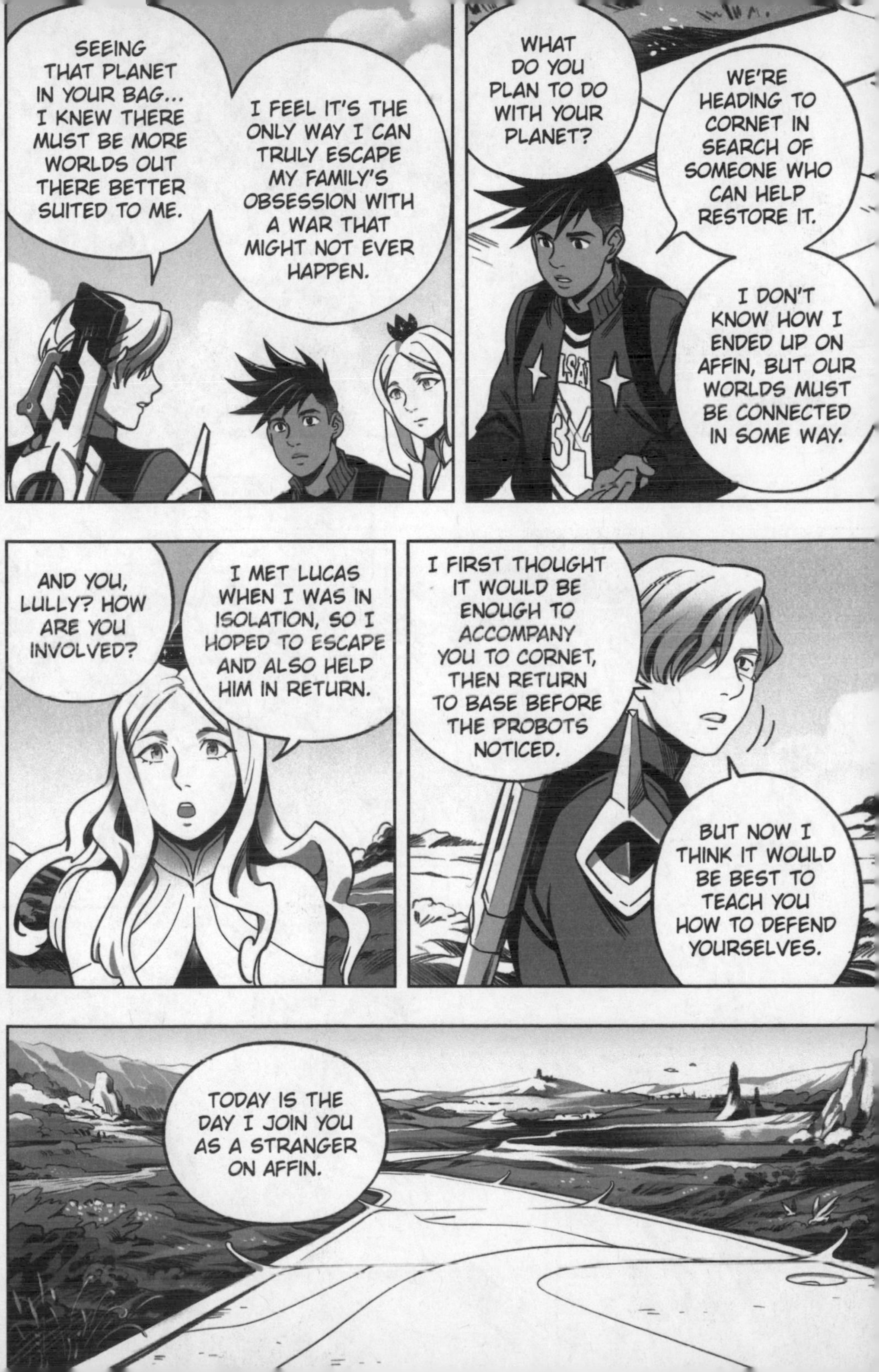
SEEING THAT PLANET IN YOUR BAG... I KNEW THERE MUST BE MORE WORLDS OUT THERE BETTER SUITED TO ME.
I FEEL IT'S THE ONLY WAY I CAN TRULY ESCAPE MY FAMILY'S OBSESSION WITH A WAR THAT MIGHT NOT EVER HAPPEN.
WHAT DO YOU PLAN TO DO WITH YOUR PLANET?
WE'RE HEADING TO CORNET IN SEARCH OF SOMEONE WHO CAN HELP RESTORE IT.
I DON'T KNOW HOW I ENDED UP ON AFFIN, BUT OUR WORLDS MUST BE CONNECTED IN SOME WAY.
AND YOU, LULLY? HOW ARE YOU INVOLVED?
I MET LUCAS WHEN I WAS IN ISOLATION, SO I HOPED TO ESCAPE AND ALSO HELP HIM IN RETURN.
I FIRST THOUGHT IT WOULD BE ENOUGH TO ACCOMPANY YOU TO CORNET, THEN RETURN TO BASE BEFORE THE PROBOTS NOTICED.
BUT NOW I THINK IT WOULD BE BEST TO TEACH YOU HOW TO DEFEND YOURSELVES.
TODAY IS THE DAY I JOIN YOU AS A STRANGER ON AFFIN.

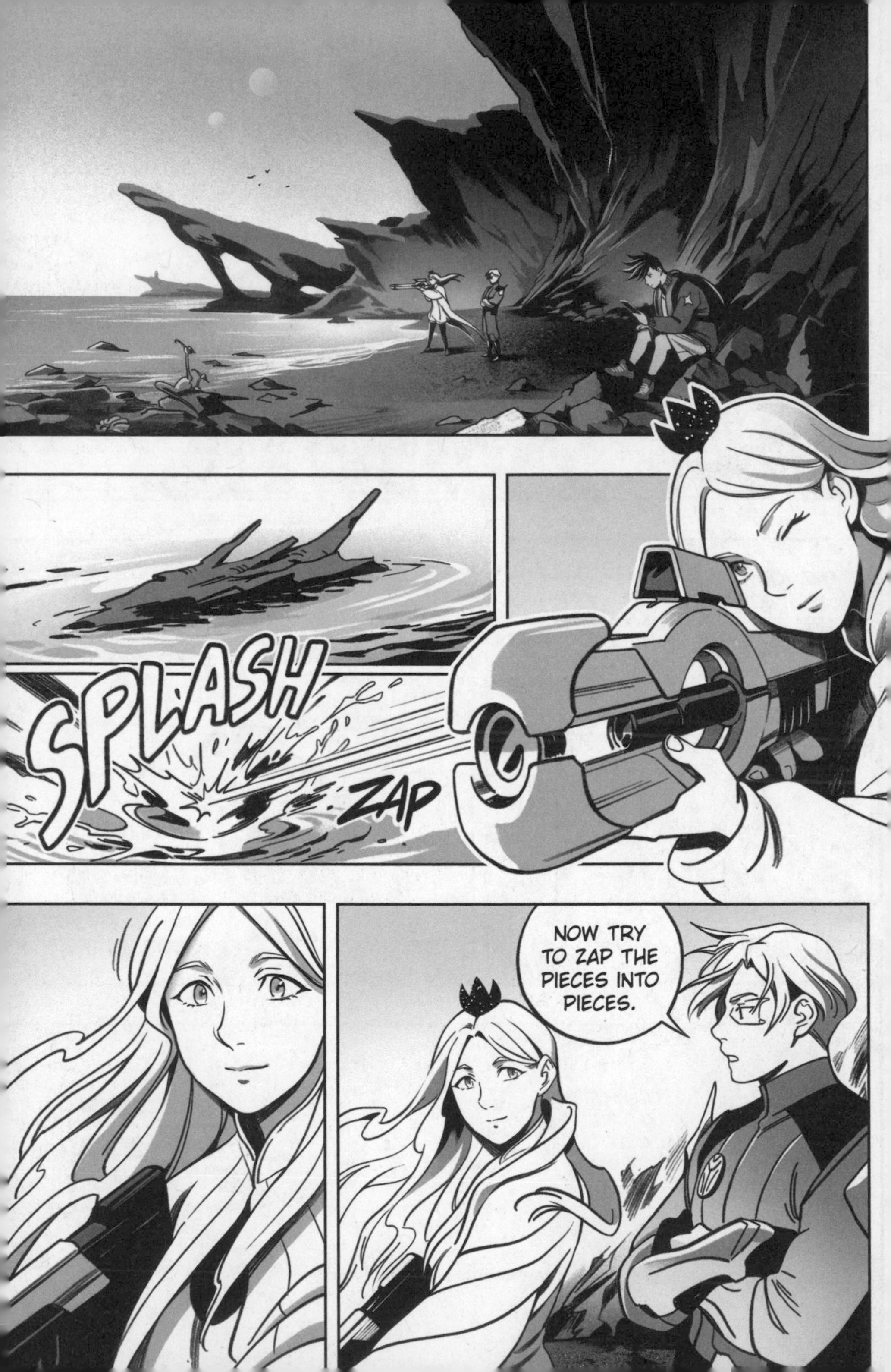
SPLASH
ZAP
NOW TRY TO ZAP THE PIECES INTO PIECES.

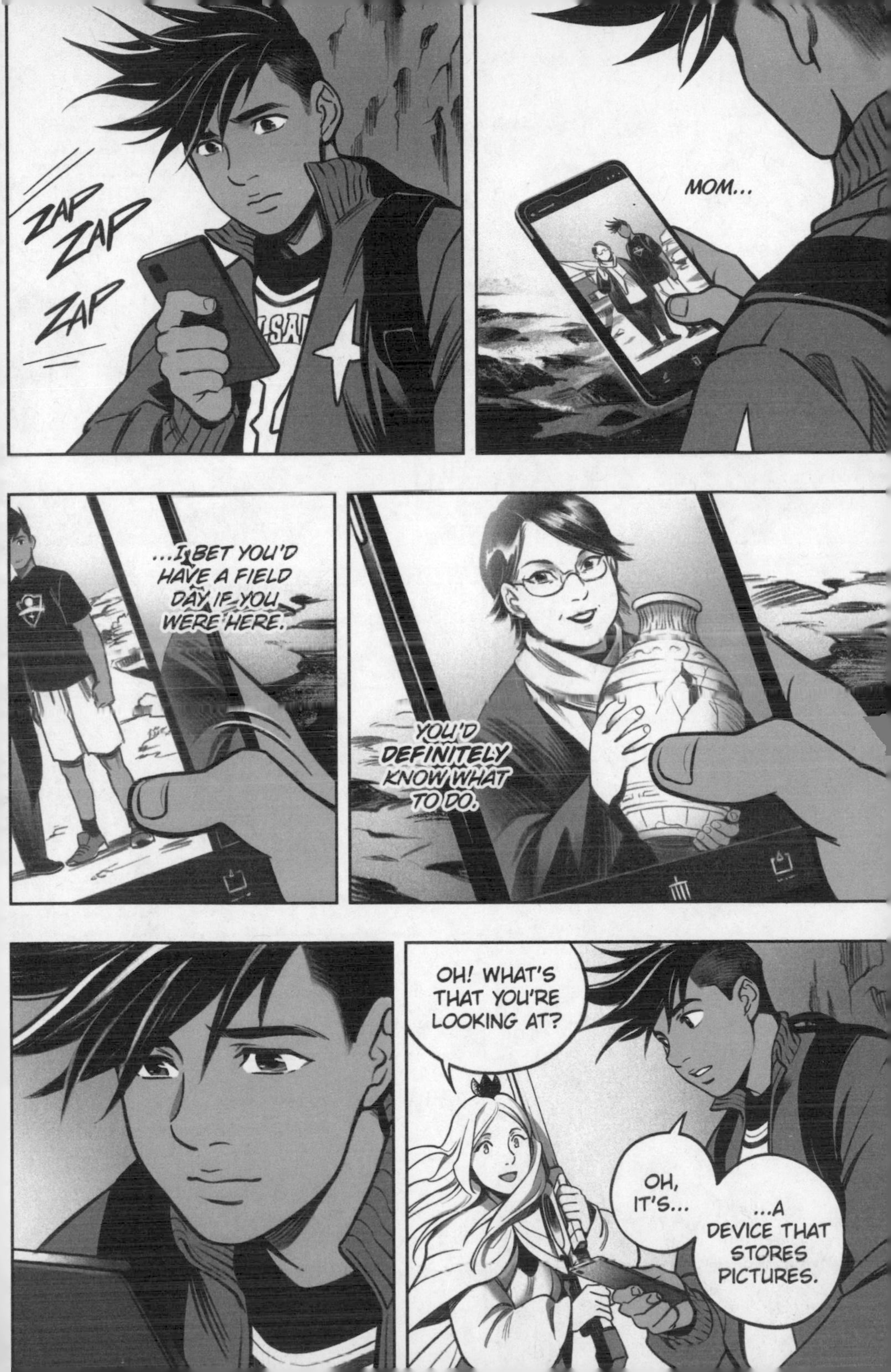
ZAP ZAP ZAP
MOM...
...I BET YOU'D HAVE A FIELD DAY IF YOU WERE HERE.
YOU'D DEFINITELY KNOW WHAT TO DO.
OH! WHAT'S THAT YOU'RE LOOKING AT?
OH, IT'S...
...A DEVICE THAT STORES PICTURES.

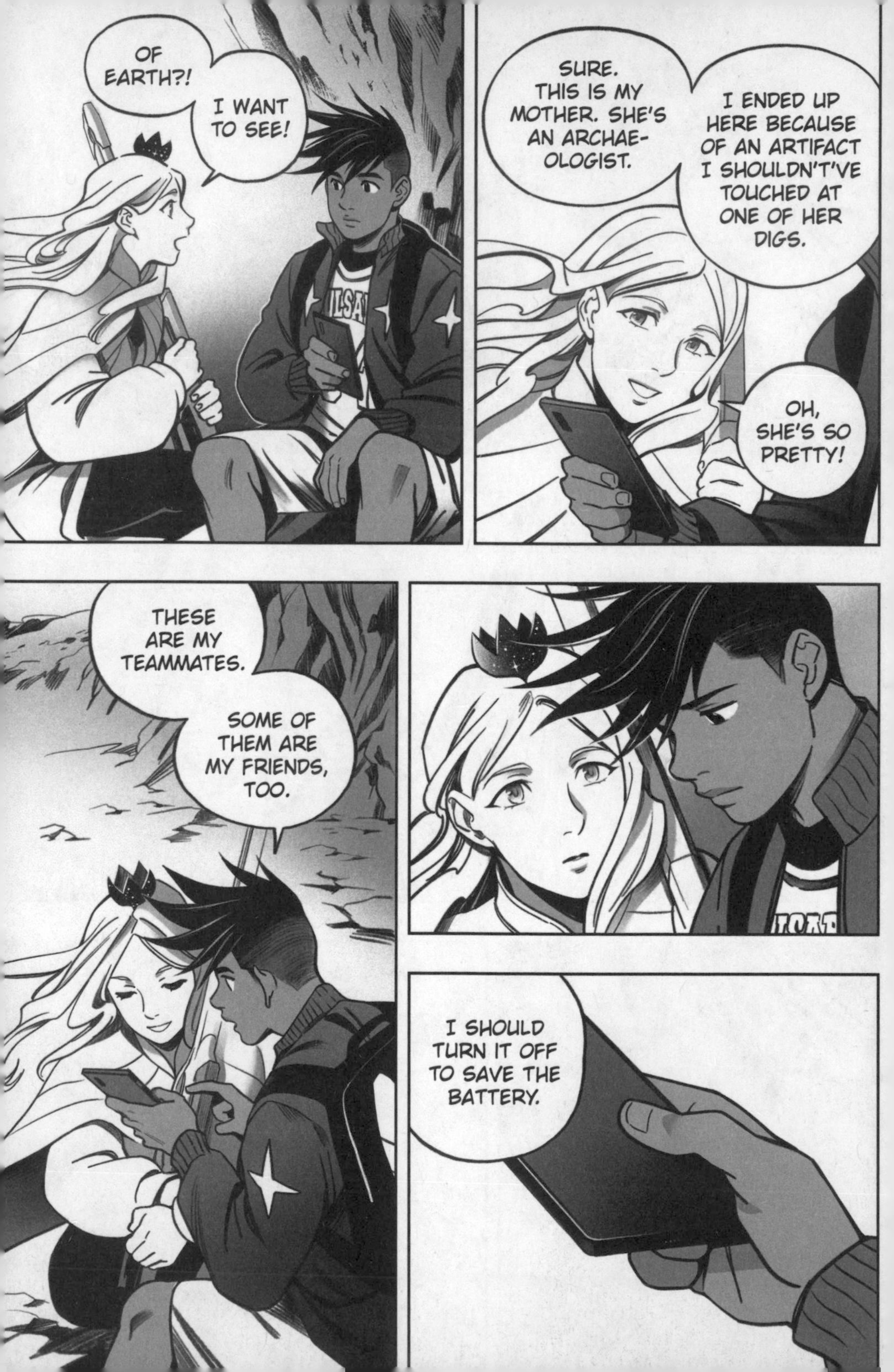
OF EARTH?!
I WANT TO SEE!
SURE. THIS IS MY MOTHER. SHE'S AN ARCHAE-OLOGIST.
I ENDED UP HERE BECAUSE OF AN ARTIFACT I SHOULDN'T'VE TOUCHED AT ONE OF HER DIGS.
OH, SHE'S SO PRETTY!
THESE ARE MY TEAMMATES.
SOME OF THEM ARE MY FRIENDS, TOO.
I SHOULD TURN IT OFF TO SAVE THE BATTERY.

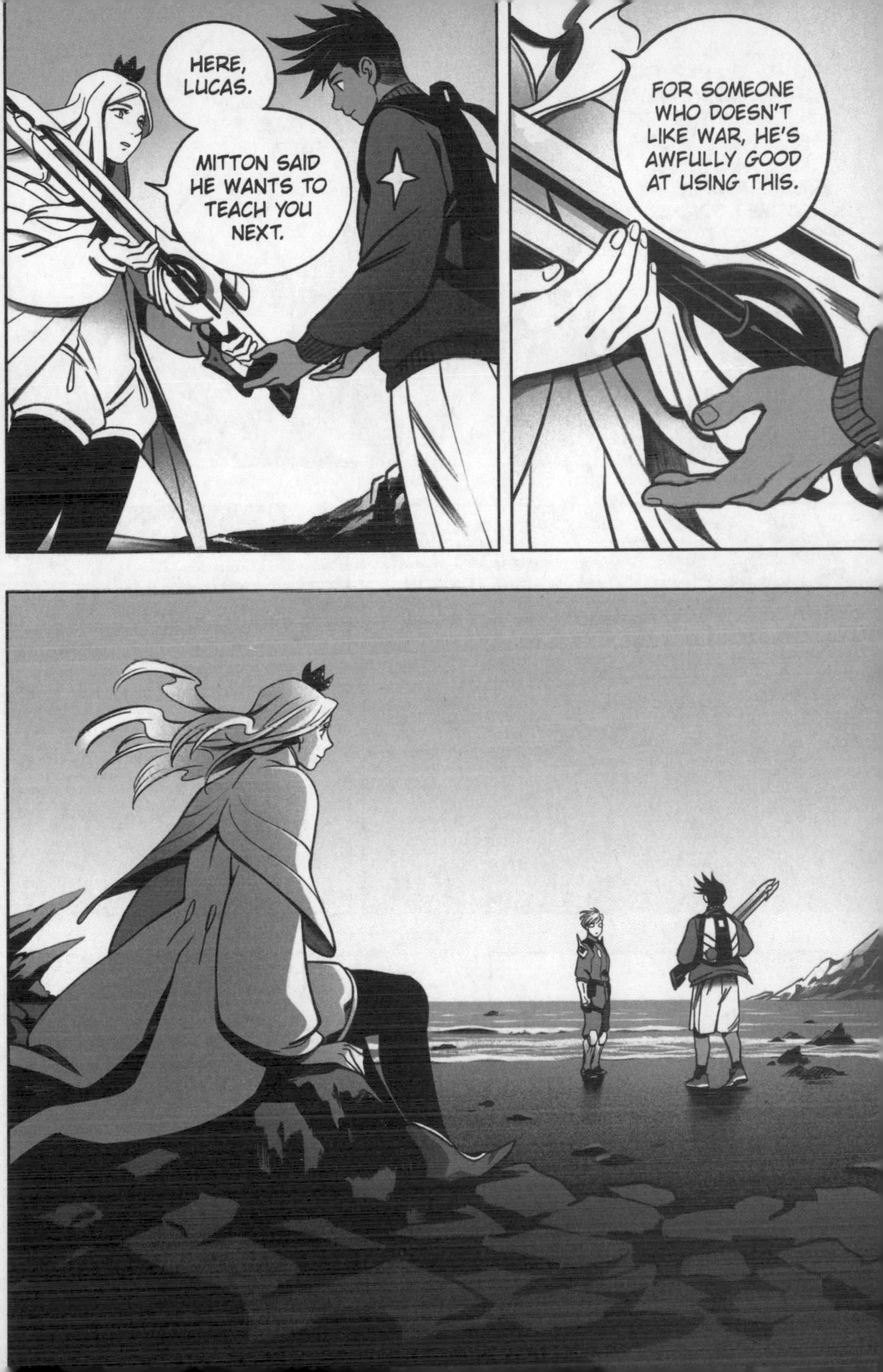
HERE, LUCAS.
MITTON SAID HE WANTS TO TEACH YOU NEXT.
FOR SOMEONE WHO DOESN'T LIKE WAR, HE'S AWFULLY GOOD AT USING THIS.

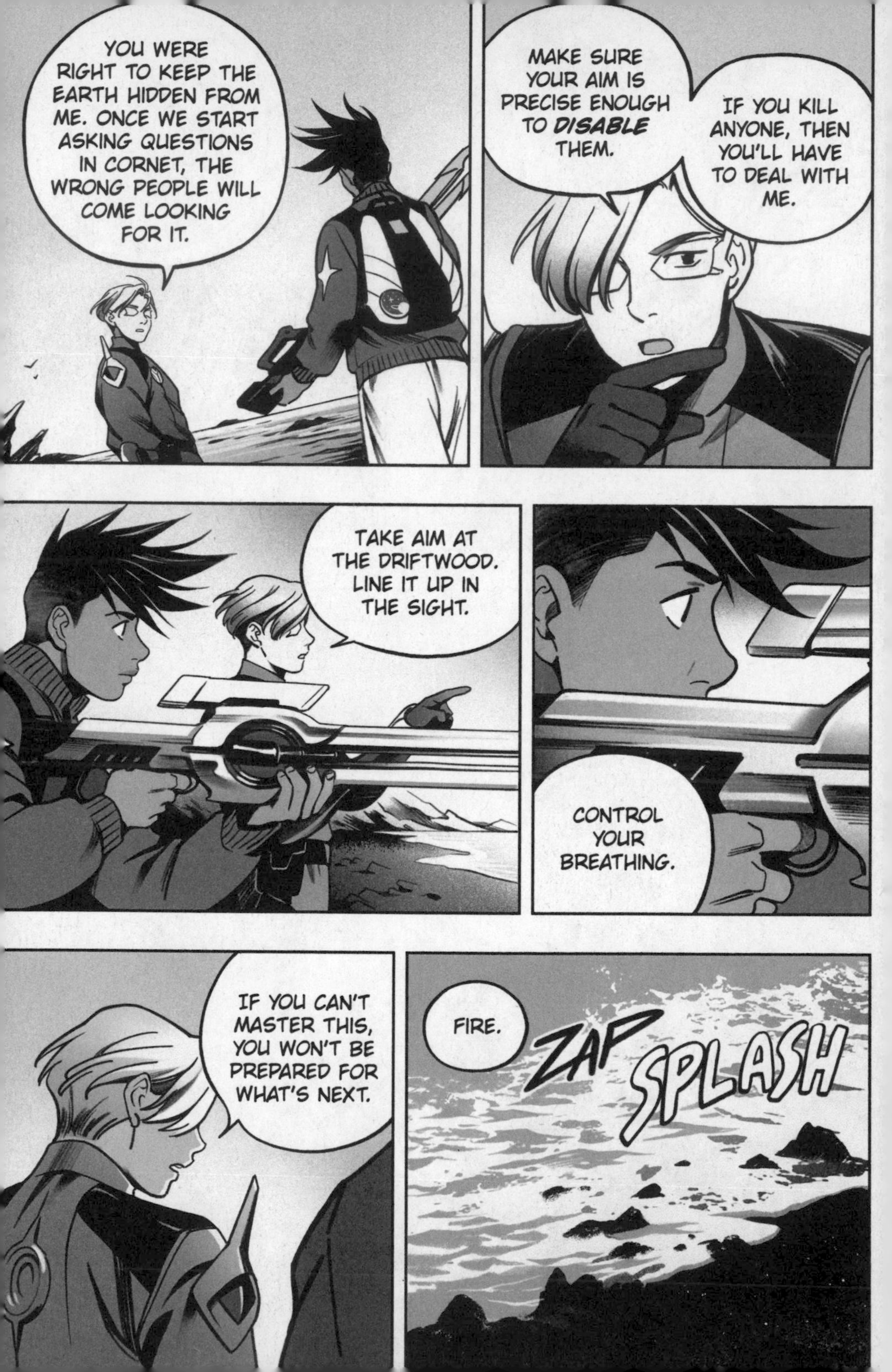
YOU WERE RIGHT TO KEEP THE EARTH HIDDEN FROM ME. ONCE WE START ASKING QUESTIONS IN CORNET, THE WRONG PEOPLE WILL COME LOOKING FOR IT.
MAKE SURE YOUR AIM IS PRECISE ENOUGH TO ***DISABLE*** THEM.
IF YOU KILL ANYONE, THEN YOU'LL HAVE TO DEAL WITH ME.
TAKE AIM AT THE DRIFTWOOD. LINE IT UP IN THE SIGHT.
CONTROL YOUR BREATHING.
IF YOU CAN'T MASTER THIS, YOU WON'T BE PREPARED FOR WHAT'S NEXT.
FIRE.
ZAP
SPLASH

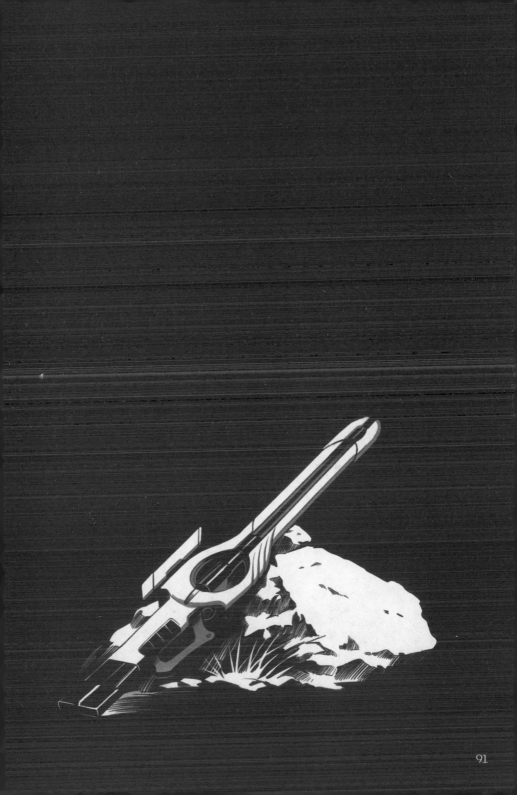

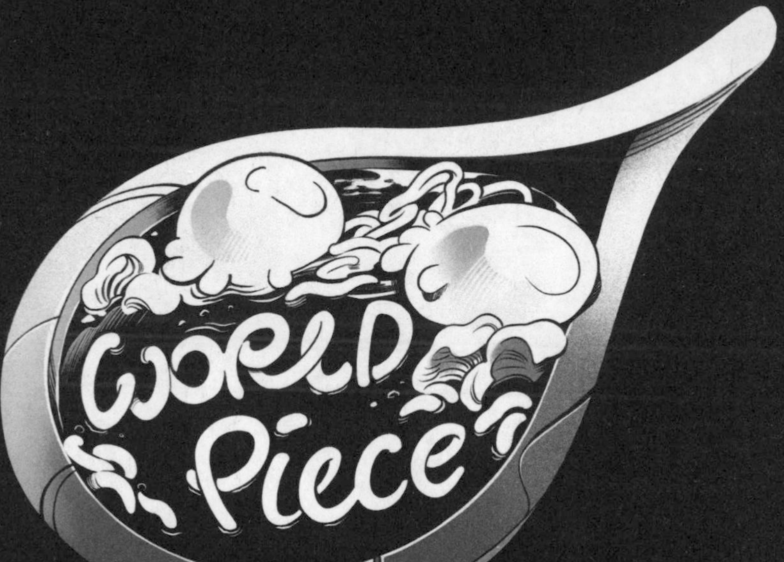
WORLD
PIECE

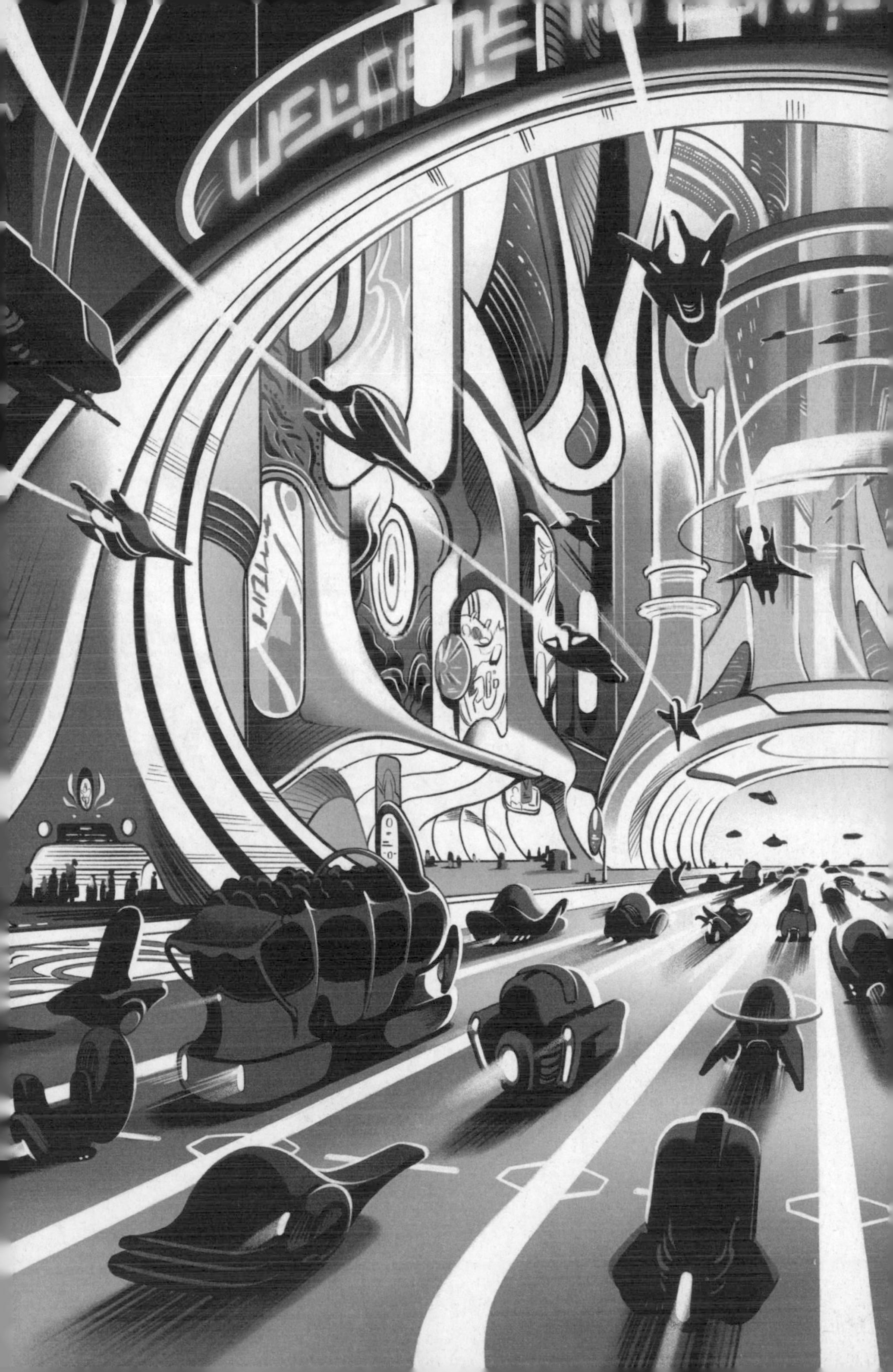

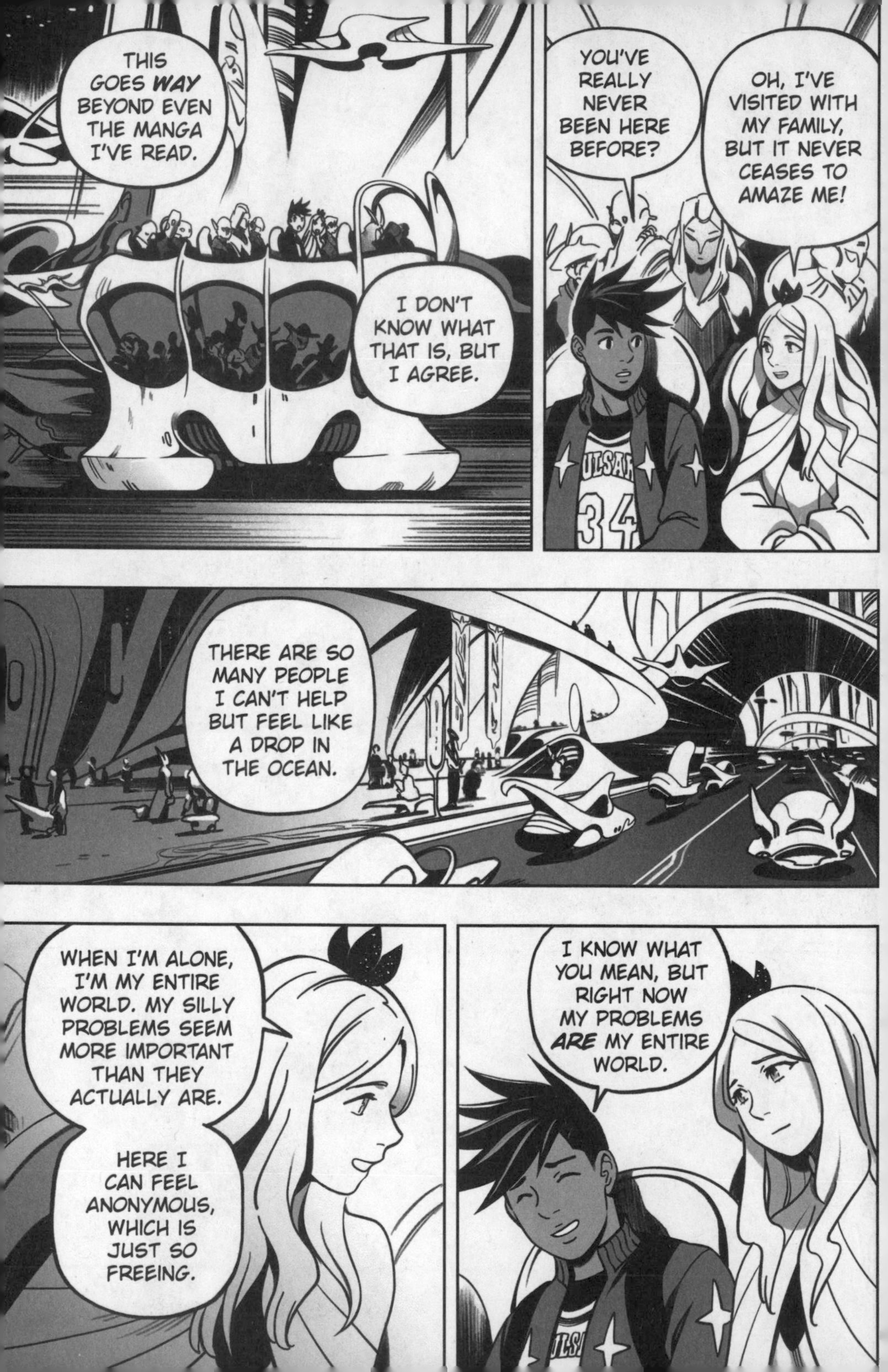
THIS GOES WAY BEYOND EVEN THE MANGA I'VE READ.
I DON'T KNOW WHAT THAT IS, BUT I AGREE.
YOU'VE REALLY NEVER BEEN HERE BEFORE?
OH, I'VE VISITED WITH MY FAMILY, BUT IT NEVER CEASES TO AMAZE ME!
THERE ARE SO MANY PEOPLE I CAN'T HELP BUT FEEL LIKE A DROP IN THE OCEAN.
WHEN I'M ALONE, I'M MY ENTIRE WORLD. MY SILLY PROBLEMS SEEM MORE IMPORTANT THAN THEY ACTUALLY ARE.
HERE I CAN FEEL ANONYMOUS, WHICH IS JUST SO FREEING.
I KNOW WHAT YOU MEAN, BUT RIGHT NOW MY PROBLEMS ARE MY ENTIRE WORLD.

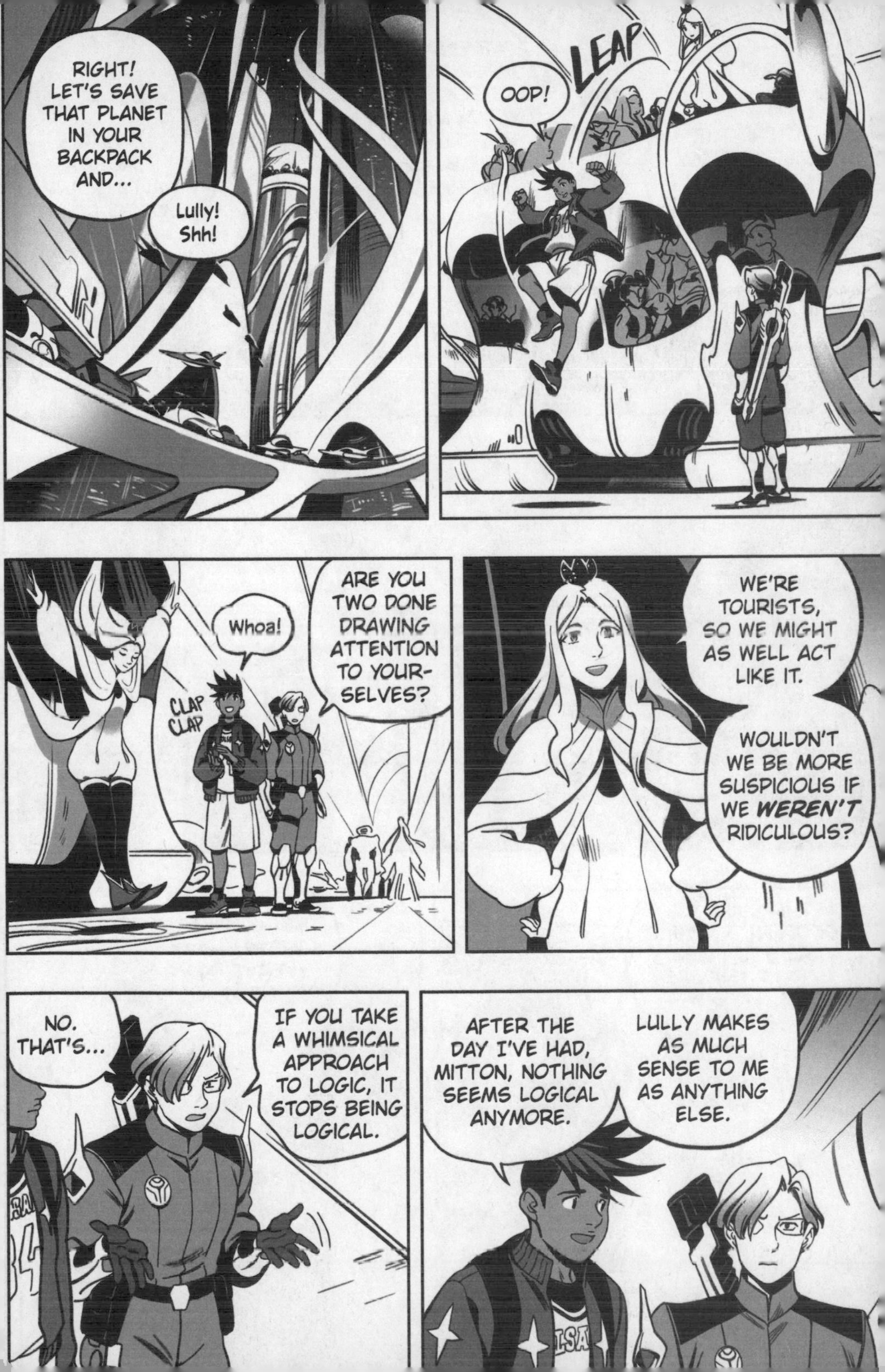
RIGHT! LET'S SAVE THAT PLANET IN YOUR BACKPACK AND...
Lully! Shh!
OOP!
LEAP
CLAP CLAP
Whoa!
ARE YOU TWO DONE DRAWING ATTENTION TO YOURSELVES?
WE'RE TOURISTS, SO WE MIGHT AS WELL ACT LIKE IT.
WOULDN'T WE BE MORE SUSPICIOUS IF WE *WEREN'T* RIDICULOUS?
NO. THAT'S...
IF YOU TAKE A WHIMSICAL APPROACH TO LOGIC, IT STOPS BEING LOGICAL.
AFTER THE DAY I'VE HAD, MITTON, NOTHING SEEMS LOGICAL ANYMORE.
LULLY MAKES AS MUCH SENSE TO ME AS ANYTHING ELSE.

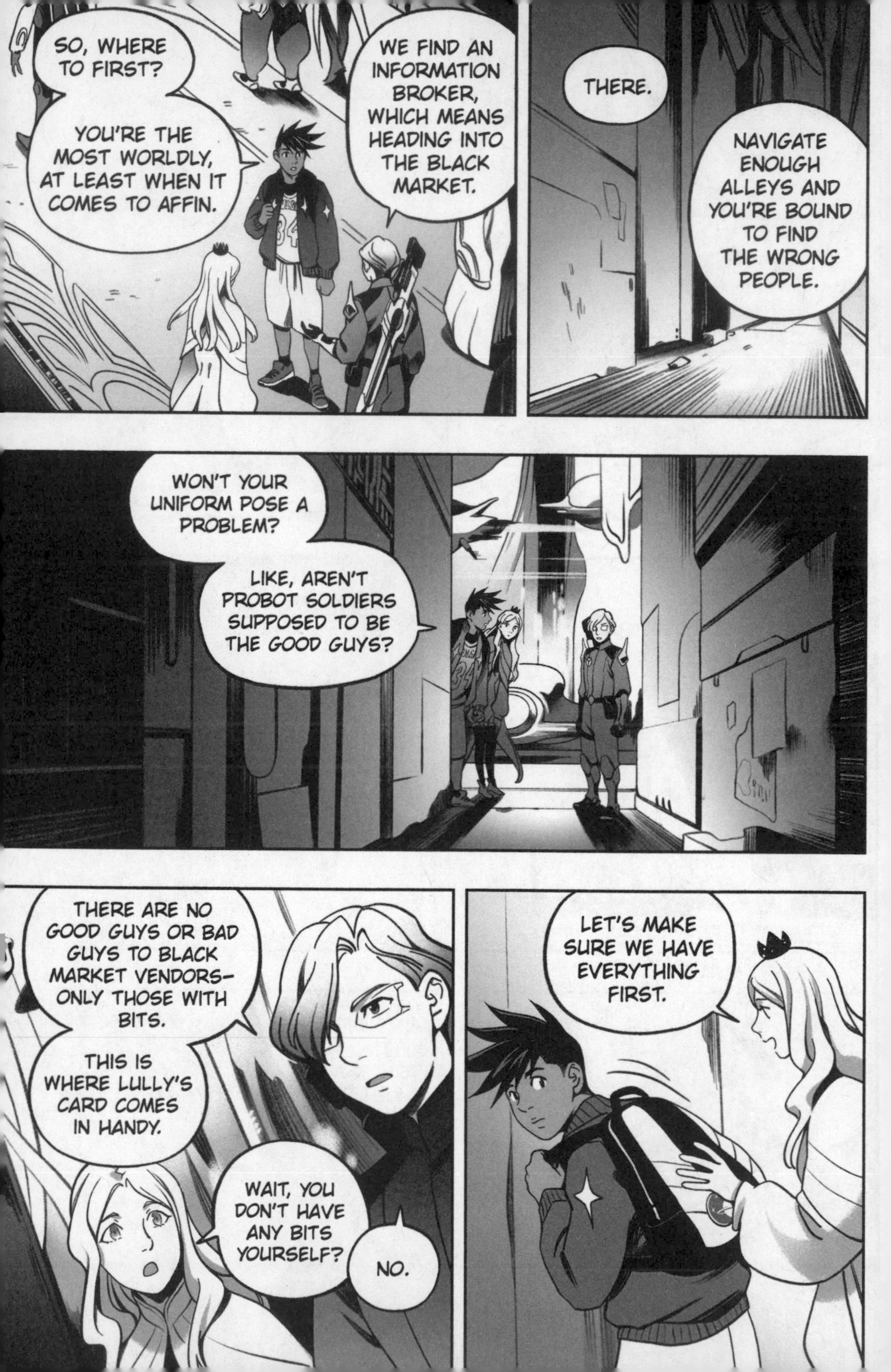
SO, WHERE TO FIRST?
YOU'RE THE MOST WORLDLY, AT LEAST WHEN IT COMES TO AFFIN.
WE FIND AN INFORMATION BROKER, WHICH MEANS HEADING INTO THE BLACK MARKET.
THERE.
NAVIGATE ENOUGH ALLEYS AND YOU'RE BOUND TO FIND THE WRONG PEOPLE.
WON'T YOUR UNIFORM POSE A PROBLEM?
LIKE, AREN'T PROBOT SOLDIERS SUPPOSED TO BE THE GOOD GUYS?
THERE ARE NO GOOD GUYS OR BAD GUYS TO BLACK MARKET VENDORS-ONLY THOSE WITH BITS.
THIS IS WHERE LULLY'S CARD COMES IN HANDY.
WAIT, YOU DON'T HAVE ANY BITS YOURSELF?
NO.
LET'S MAKE SURE WE HAVE EVERYTHING FIRST.

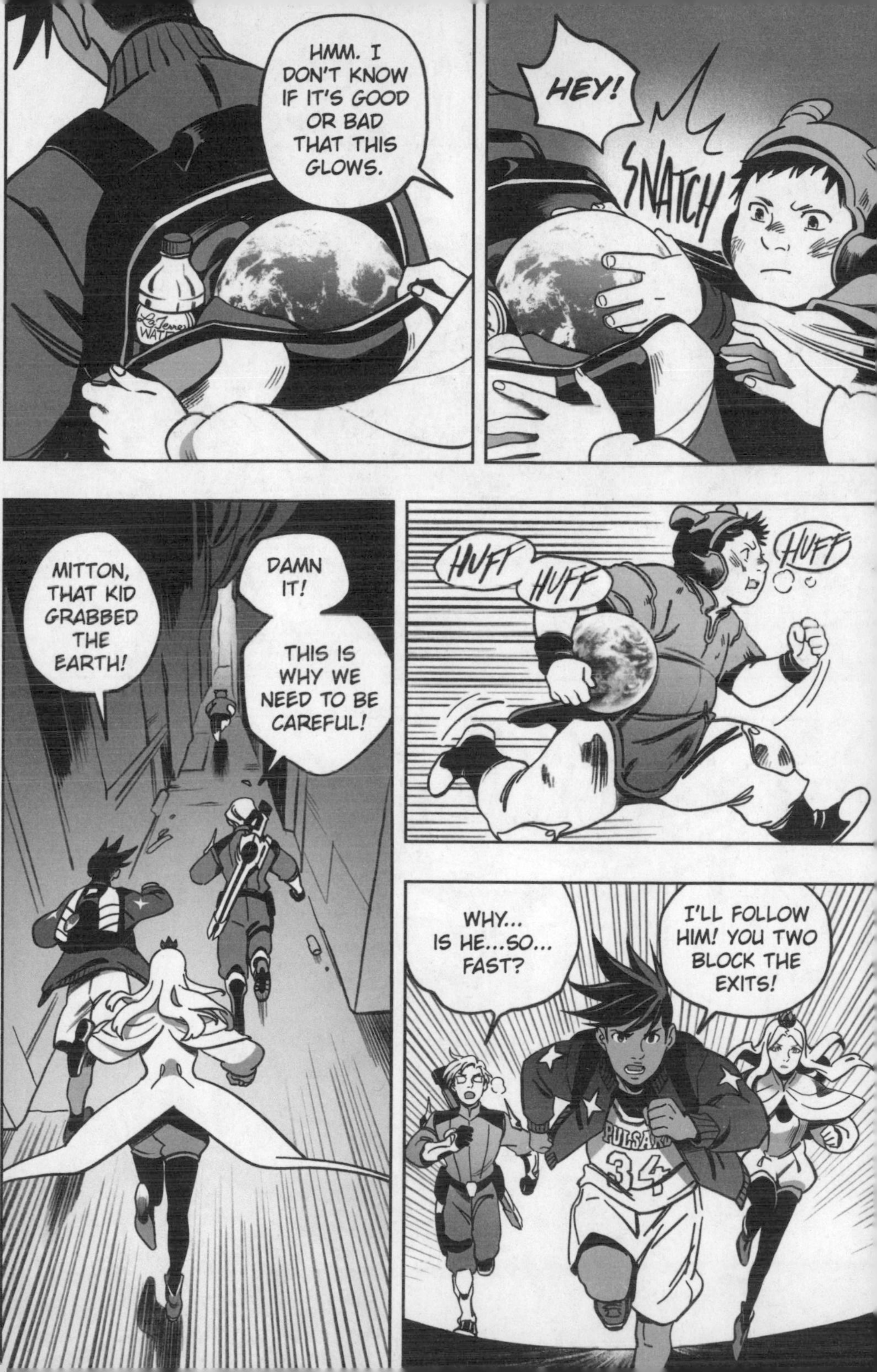
HMM. I DON'T KNOW IF IT'S GOOD OR BAD THAT THIS GLOWS.
HEY!
SNATCH
MITTON, THAT KID GRABBED THE EARTH!
DAMN IT!
THIS IS WHY WE NEED TO BE CAREFUL!
HUFF
HUFF
HUFF
WHY... IS HE...SO... FAST?
I'LL FOLLOW HIM! YOU TWO BLOCK THE EXITS!

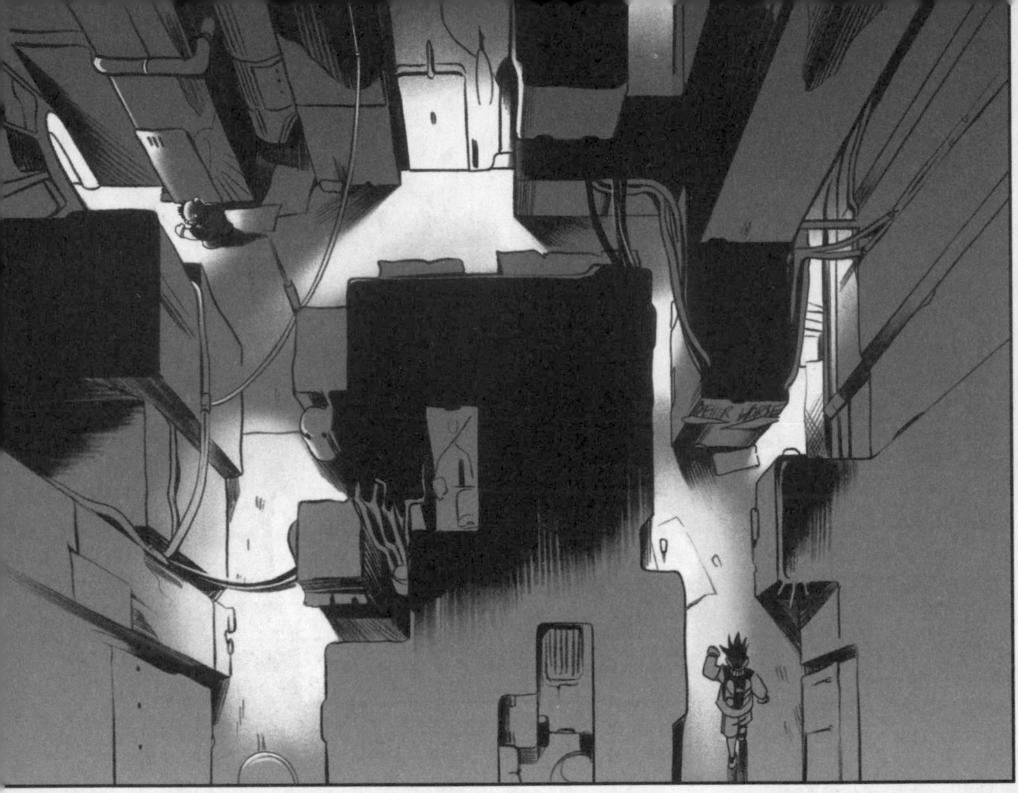

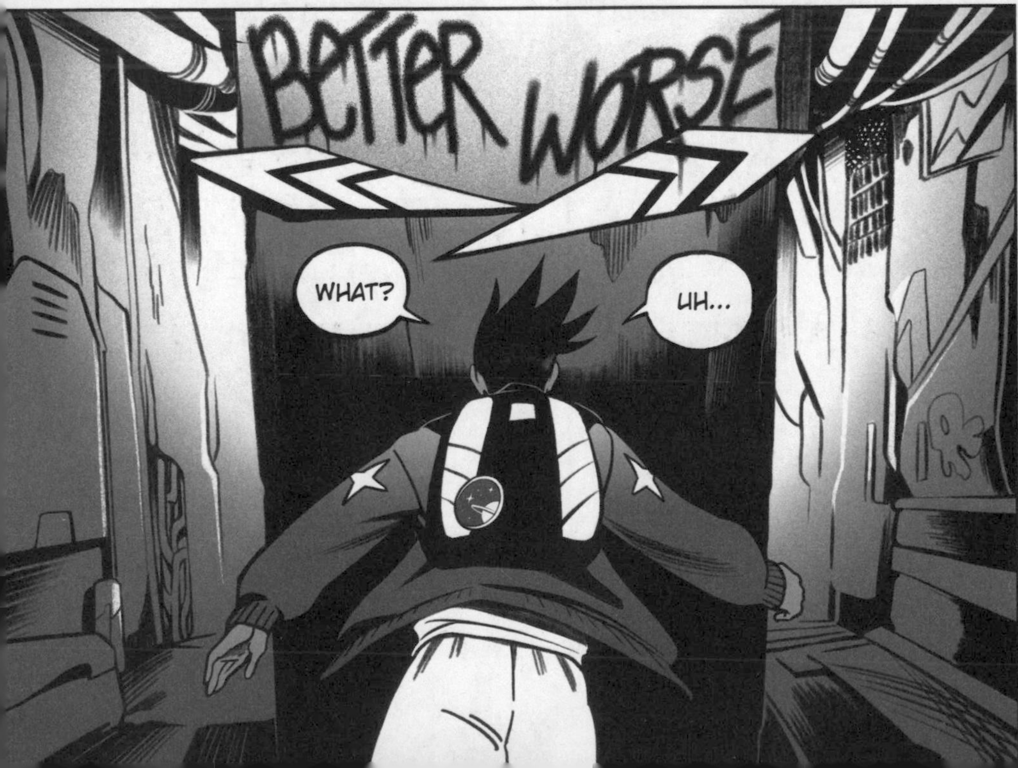
BETTER
WORSE
WHAT?
UH...

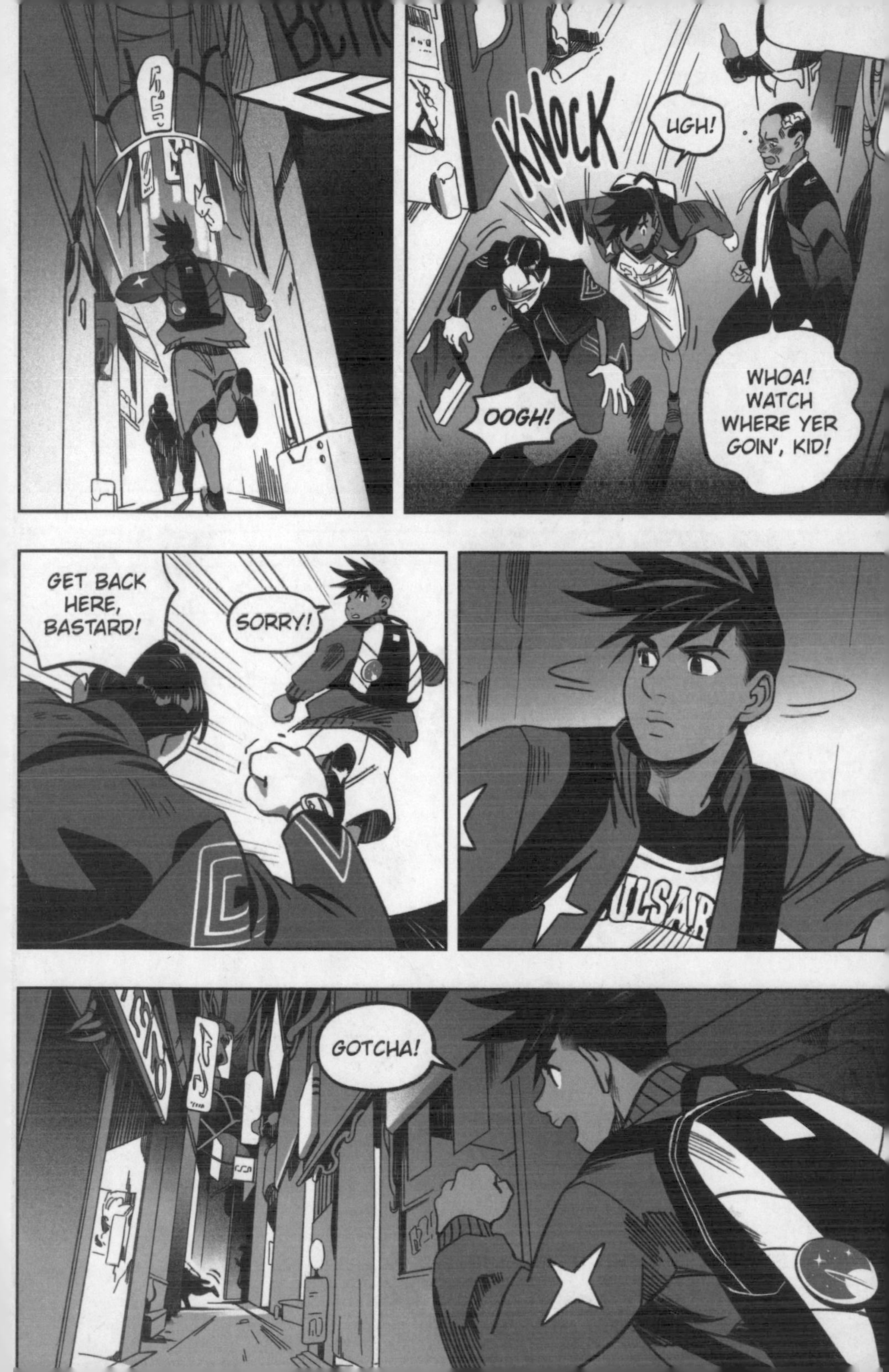
KNOCK
UGH!
OOGH!
WHOA! WATCH WHERE YER GOIN', KID!
GET BACK HERE, BASTARD!
SORRY!
GOTCHA!

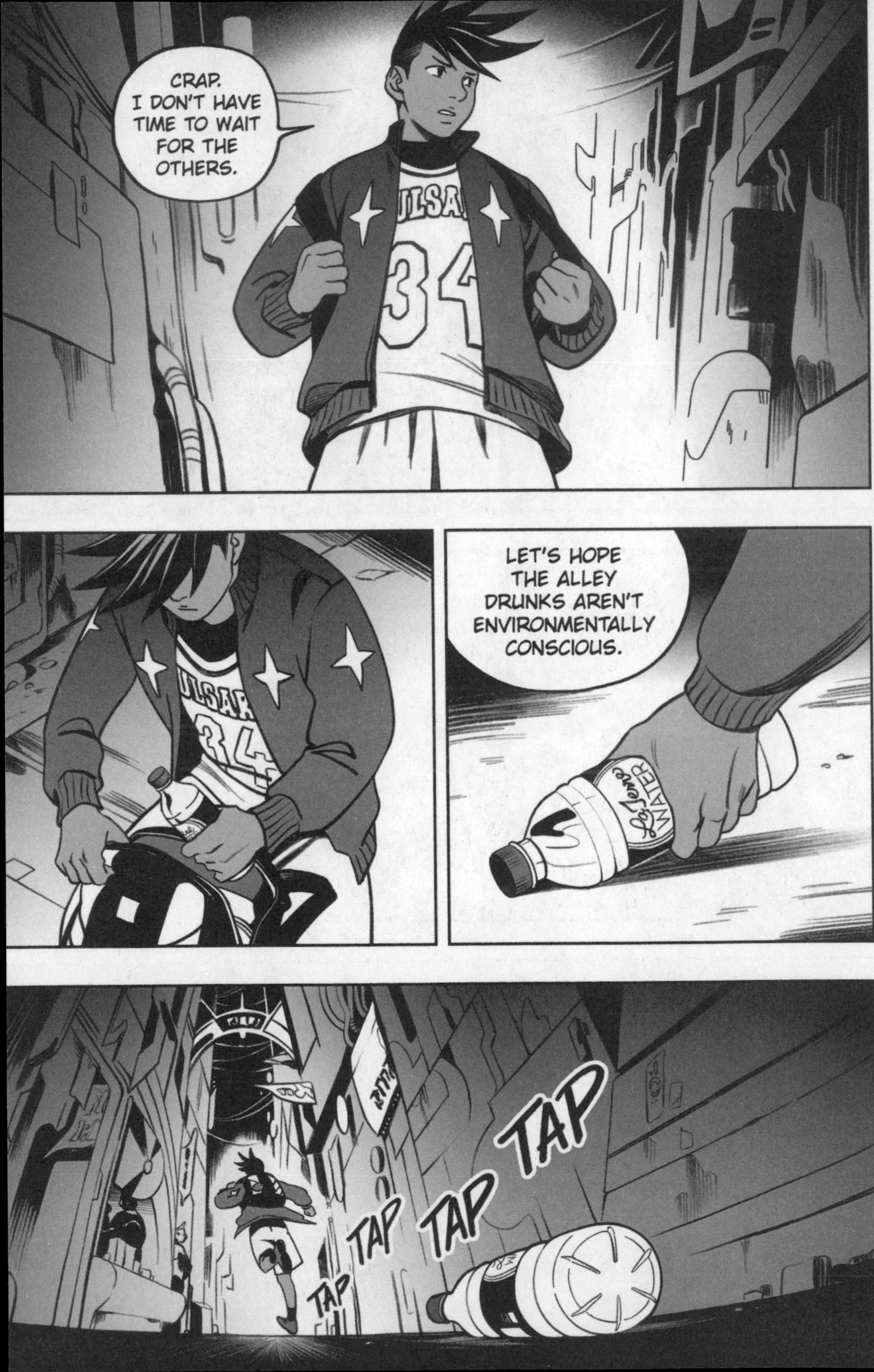
CRAP. I DON'T HAVE TIME TO WAIT FOR THE OTHERS.
LET'S HOPE THE ALLEY DRUNKS AREN'T ENVIRONMENTALLY CONSCIOUS.
WATER
TAP TAP TAP TAP

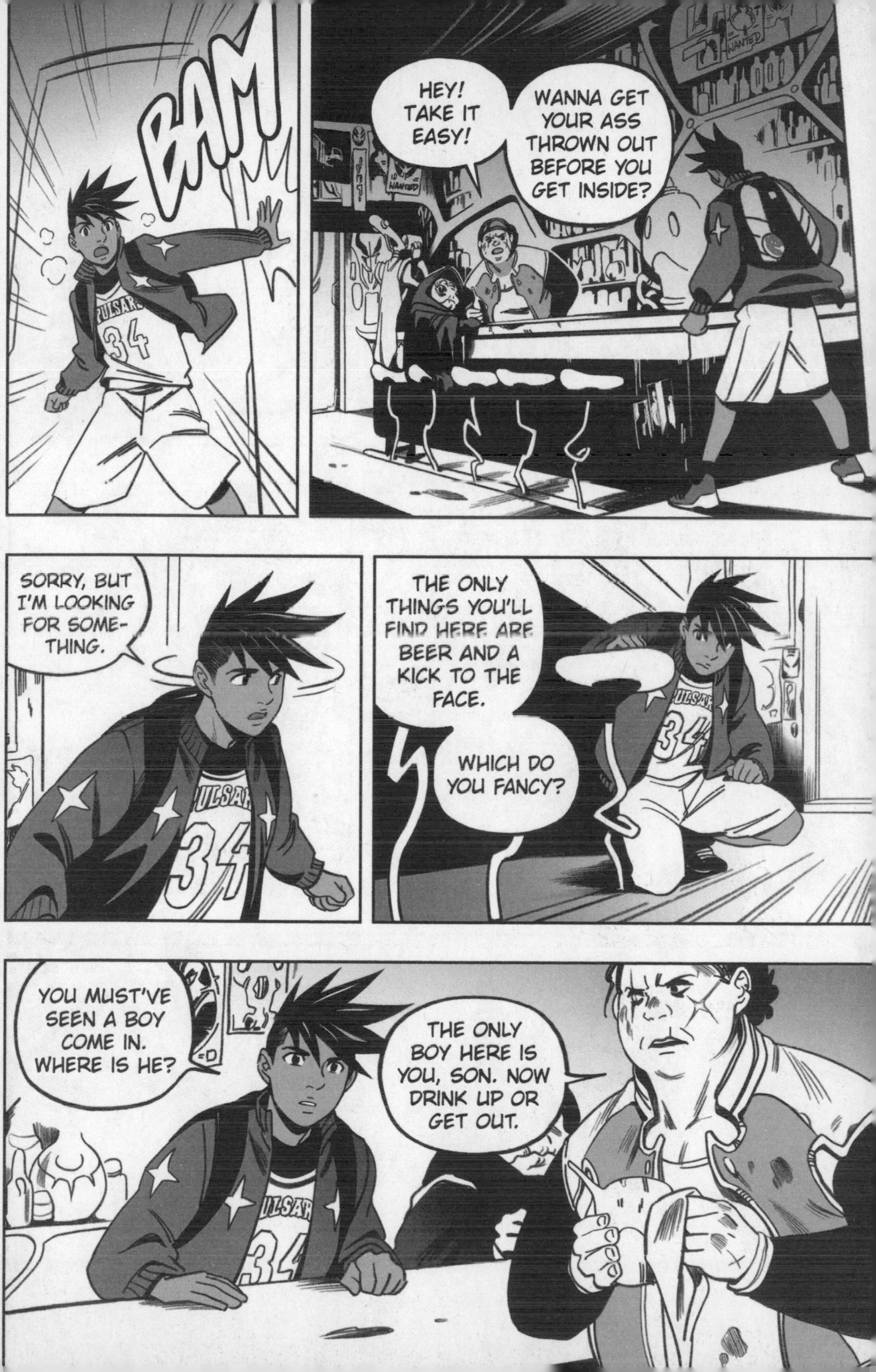
BAM
HEY! TAKE IT EASY!
WANNA GET YOUR ASS THROWN OUT BEFORE YOU GET INSIDE?
WANTED
WANTED
SORRY, BUT I'M LOOKING FOR SOME-THING.
THE ONLY THINGS YOU'LL FIND HERE ARE BEER AND A KICK TO THE FACE.
WHICH DO YOU FANCY?
YOU MUST'VE SEEN A BOY COME IN. WHERE IS HE?
THE ONLY BOY HERE IS YOU, SON. NOW DRINK UP OR GET OUT.

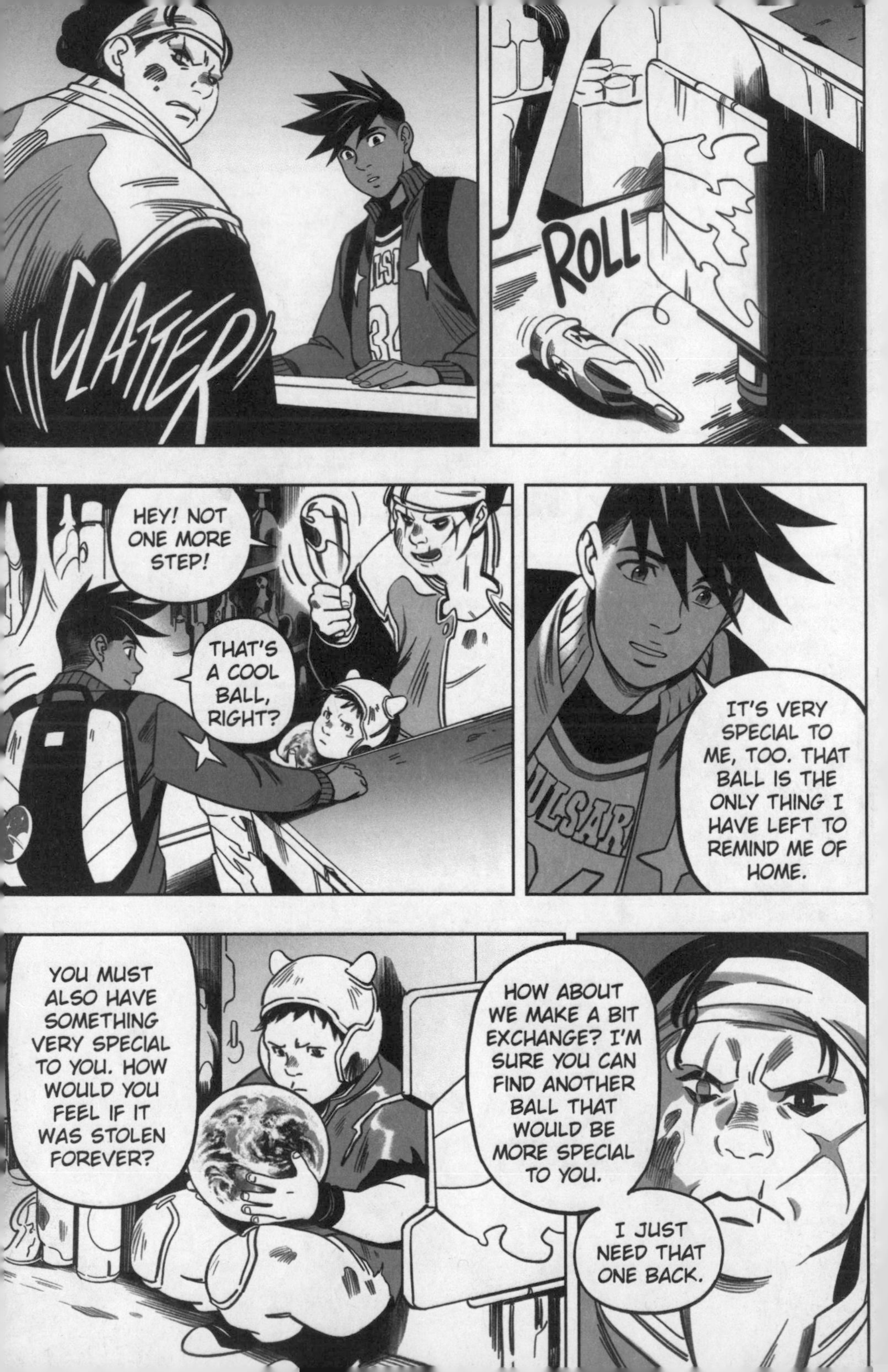
CLATTER
ROLL
HEY! NOT ONE MORE STEP!
THAT'S A COOL BALL, RIGHT?
IT'S VERY SPECIAL TO ME, TOO. THAT BALL IS THE ONLY THING I HAVE LEFT TO REMIND ME OF HOME.
YOU MUST ALSO HAVE SOMETHING VERY SPECIAL TO YOU. HOW WOULD YOU FEEL IF IT WAS STOLEN FOREVER?
HOW ABOUT WE MAKE A BIT EXCHANGE? I'M SURE YOU CAN FIND ANOTHER BALL THAT WOULD BE MORE SPECIAL TO YOU.
I JUST NEED THAT ONE BACK.

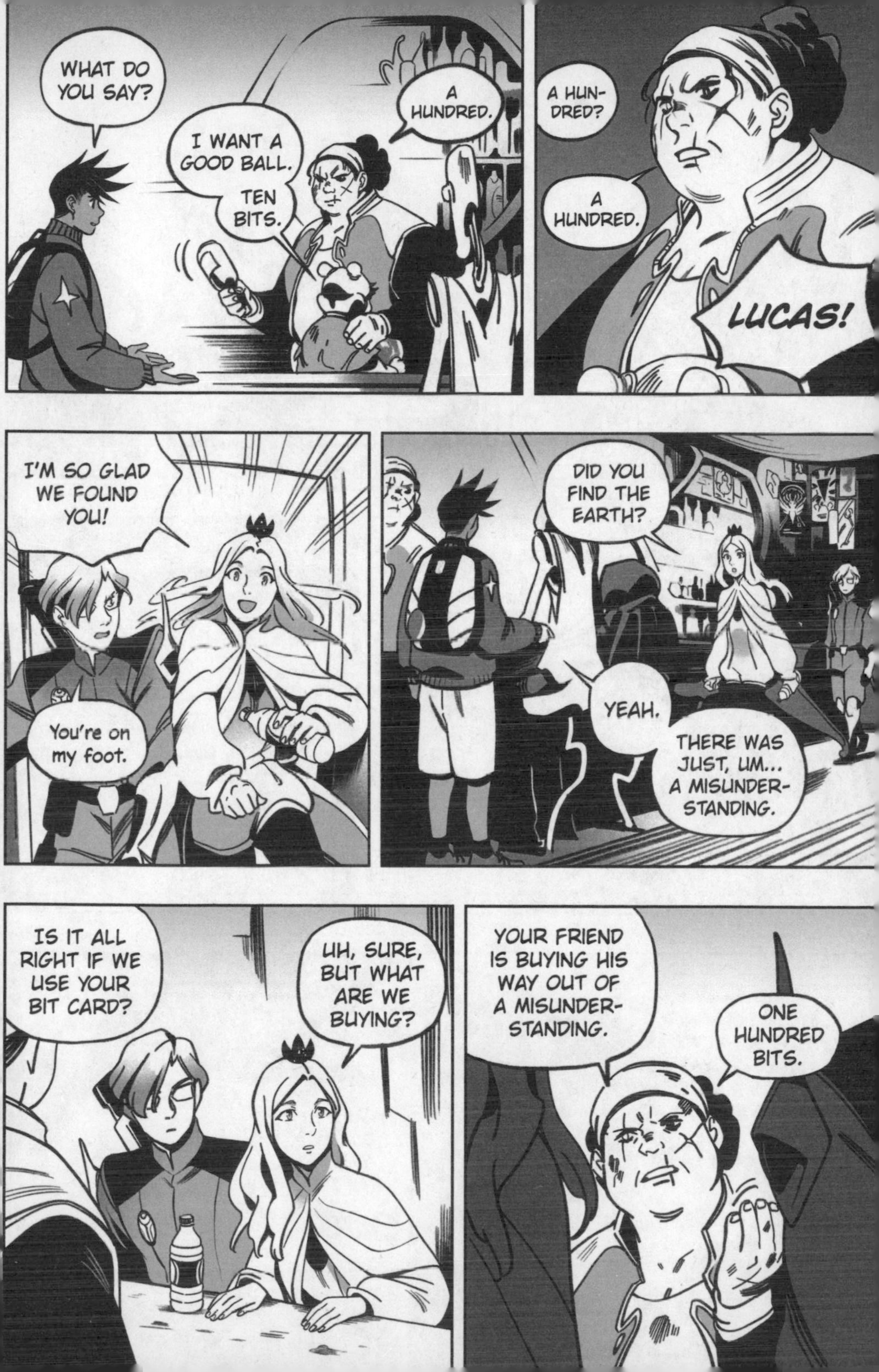
WHAT DO YOU SAY?
I WANT A GOOD BALL.
TEN BITS.
A HUNDRED.
A HUN-DRED?
A HUNDRED.
LUCAS!
I'M SO GLAD WE FOUND YOU!
You're on my foot.
DID YOU FIND THE EARTH?
YEAH.
THERE WAS JUST, UM... A MISUNDER-STANDING.
IS IT ALL RIGHT IF WE USE YOUR BIT CARD?
UH, SURE, BUT WHAT ARE WE BUYING?
YOUR FRIEND IS BUYING HIS WAY OUT OF A MISUNDER-STANDING.
ONE HUNDRED BITS.

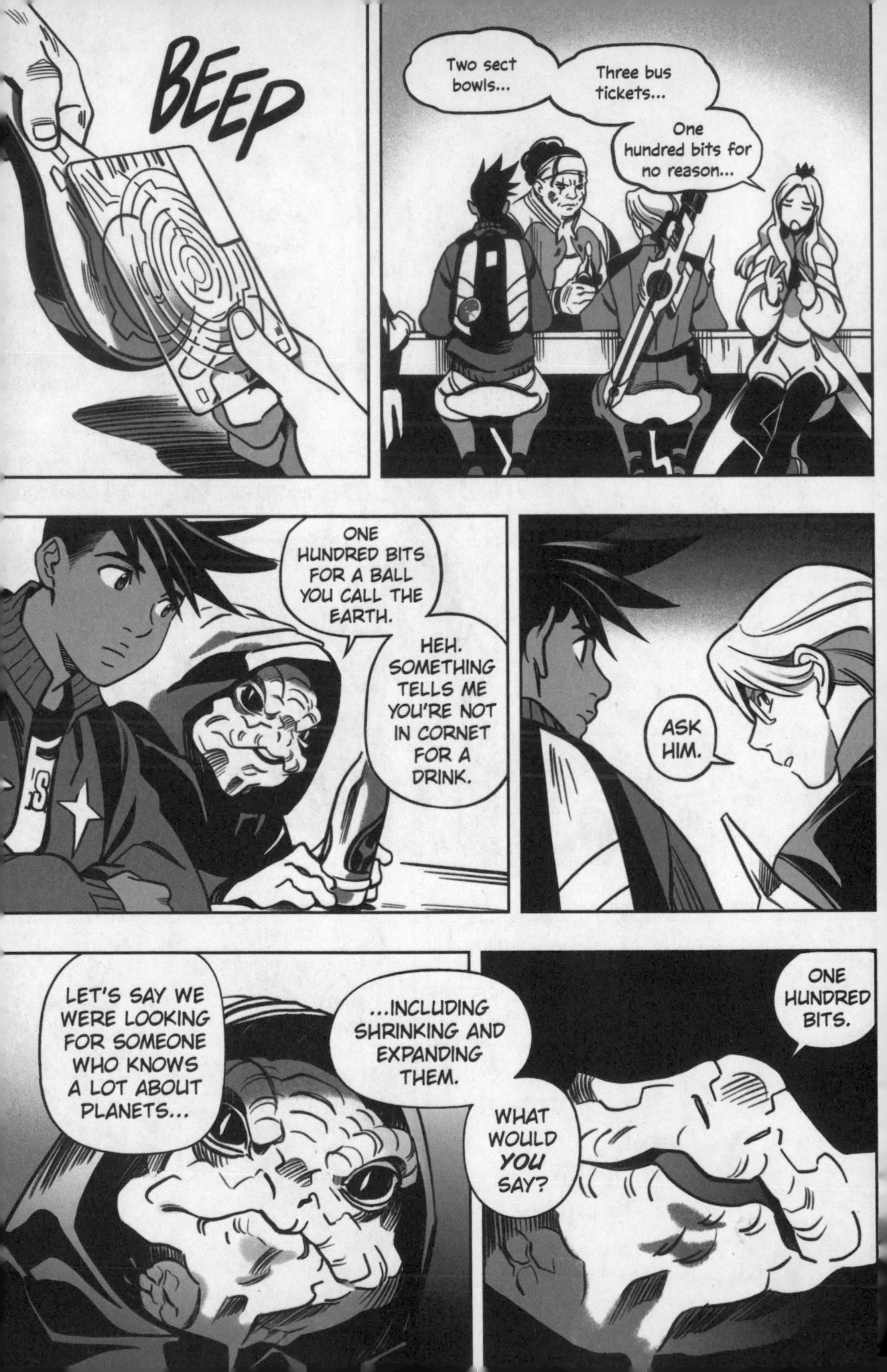
BEEP
Two sect bowls...
Three bus tickets...
One hundred bits for no reason...
ONE HUNDRED BITS FOR A BALL YOU CALL THE EARTH.
HEH. SOMETHING TELLS ME YOU'RE NOT IN CORNET FOR A DRINK.
ASK HIM.
LET'S SAY WE WERE LOOKING FOR SOMEONE WHO KNOWS A LOT ABOUT PLANETS...
...INCLUDING SHRINKING AND EXPANDING THEM.
WHAT WOULD *YOU* SAY?
ONE HUNDRED BITS.

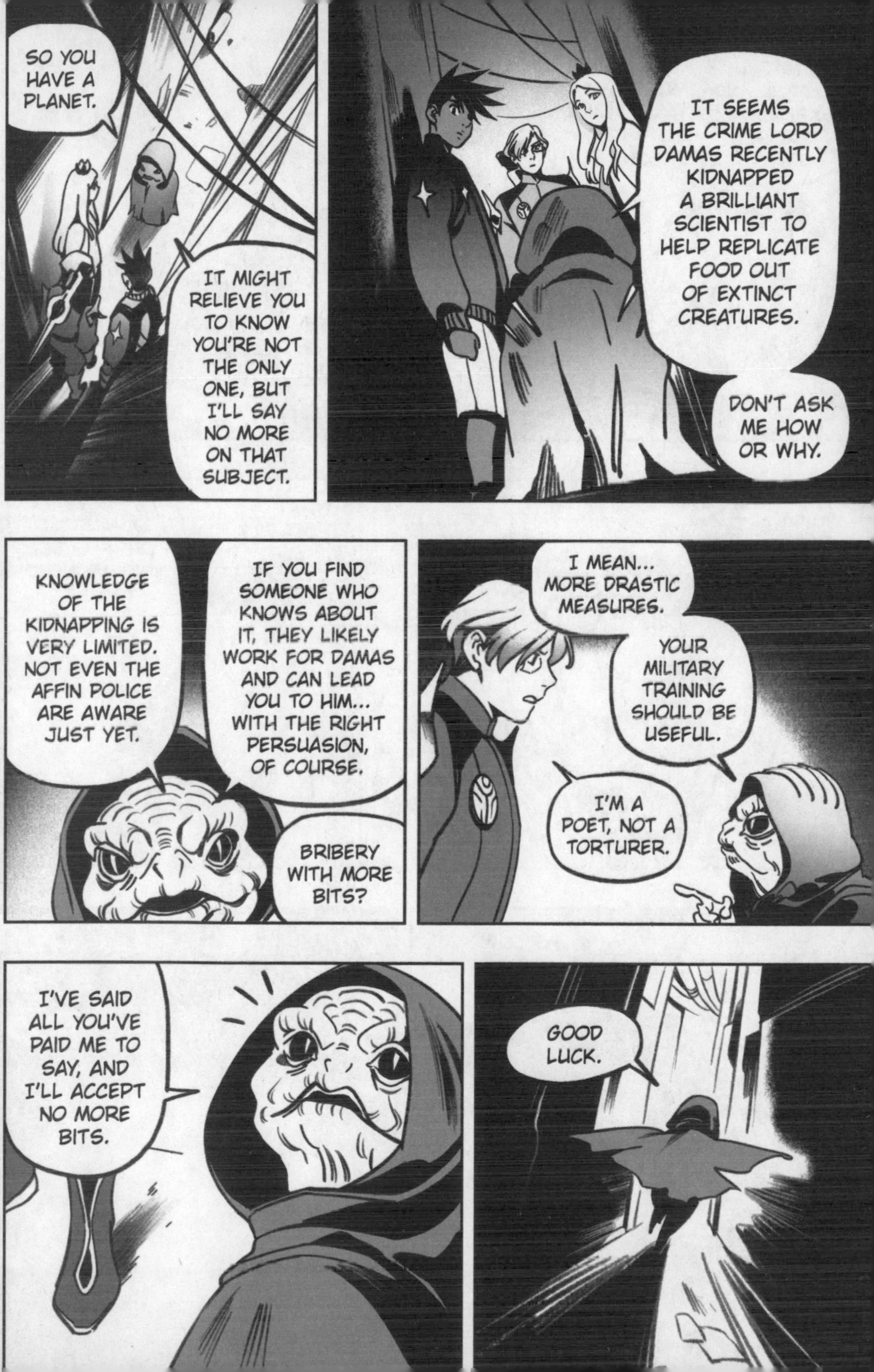
SO YOU HAVE A PLANET.
IT MIGHT RELIEVE YOU TO KNOW YOU'RE NOT THE ONLY ONE, BUT I'LL SAY NO MORE ON THAT SUBJECT.
IT SEEMS THE CRIME LORD DAMAS RECENTLY KIDNAPPED A BRILLIANT SCIENTIST TO HELP REPLICATE FOOD OUT OF EXTINCT CREATURES.
DON'T ASK ME HOW OR WHY.
KNOWLEDGE OF THE KIDNAPPING IS VERY LIMITED. NOT EVEN THE AFFIN POLICE ARE AWARE JUST YET.
IF YOU FIND SOMEONE WHO KNOWS ABOUT IT, THEY LIKELY WORK FOR DAMAS AND CAN LEAD YOU TO HIM... WITH THE RIGHT PERSUASION, OF COURSE.
BRIBERY WITH MORE BITS?
I MEAN... MORE DRASTIC MEASURES.
YOUR MILITARY TRAINING SHOULD BE USEFUL.
I'M A POET, NOT A TORTURER.
I'VE SAID ALL YOU'VE PAID ME TO SAY, AND I'LL ACCEPT NO MORE BITS.
GOOD LUCK.

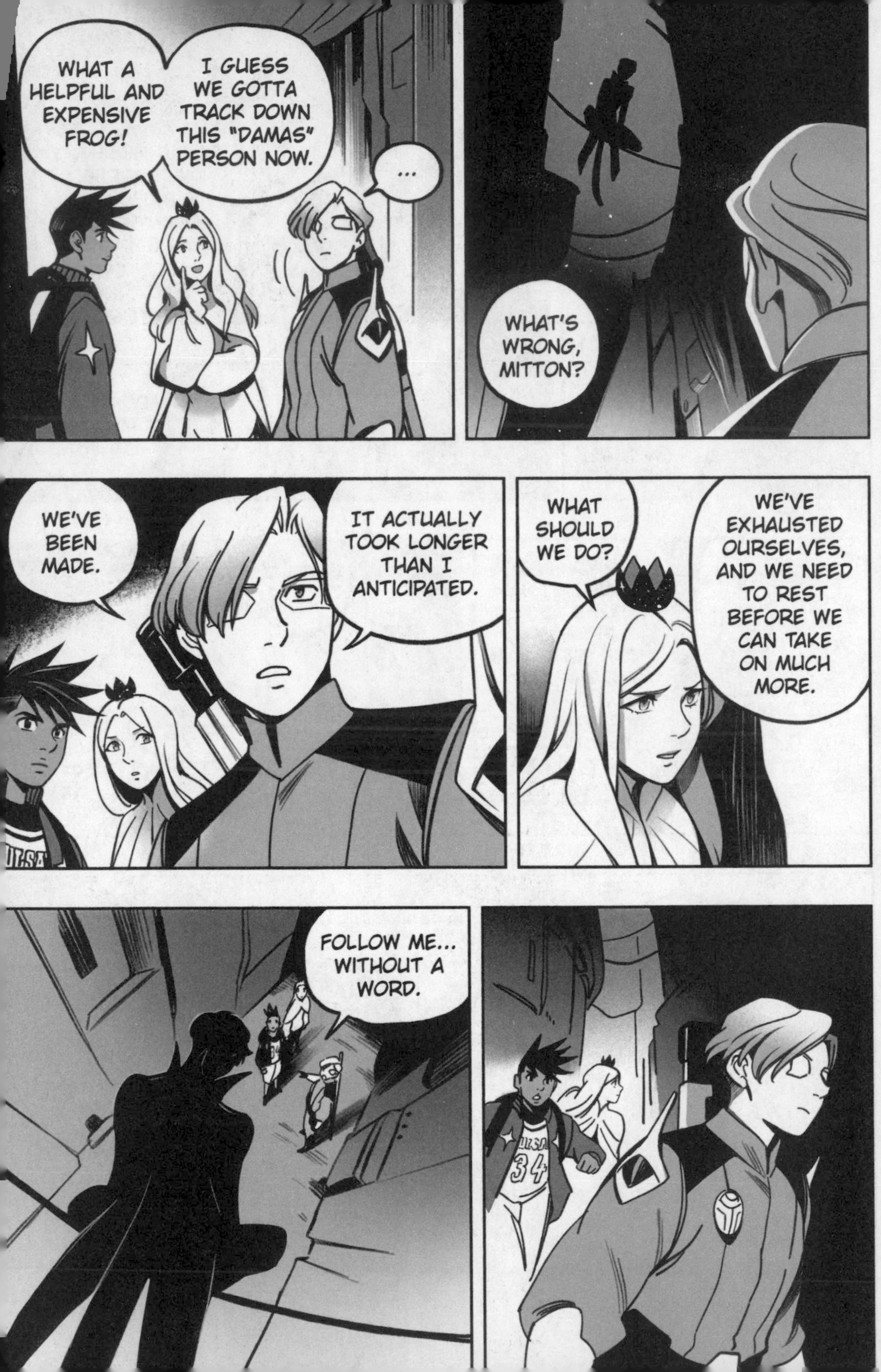
WHAT A HELPFUL AND EXPENSIVE FROG!
I GUESS WE GOTTA TRACK DOWN THIS "DAMAS" PERSON NOW.
...
WHAT'S WRONG, MITTON?
WE'VE BEEN MADE.
IT ACTUALLY TOOK LONGER THAN I ANTICIPATED.
WHAT SHOULD WE DO?
WE'VE EXHAUSTED OURSELVES, AND WE NEED TO REST BEFORE WE CAN TAKE ON MUCH MORE.
FOLLOW ME... WITHOUT A WORD.

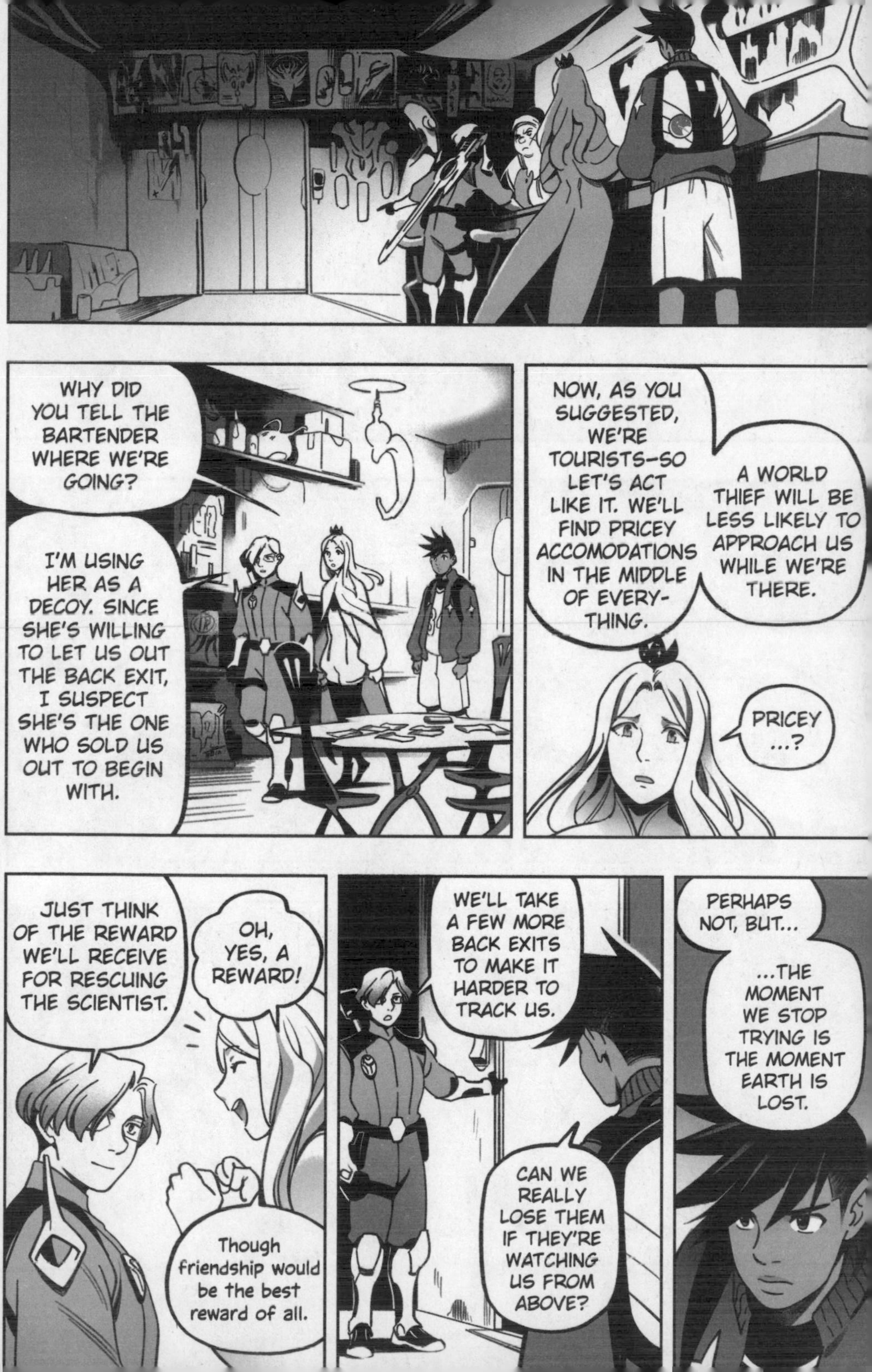
WHY DID YOU TELL THE BARTENDER WHERE WE'RE GOING?
I'M USING HER AS A DECOY. SINCE SHE'S WILLING TO LET US OUT THE BACK EXIT, I SUSPECT SHE'S THE ONE WHO SOLD US OUT TO BEGIN WITH.
NOW, AS YOU SUGGESTED, WE'RE TOURISTS—SO LET'S ACT LIKE IT. WE'LL FIND PRICEY ACCOMODATIONS IN THE MIDDLE OF EVERY-THING.
A WORLD THIEF WILL BE LESS LIKELY TO APPROACH US WHILE WE'RE THERE.
PRICEY ...?
JUST THINK OF THE REWARD WE'LL RECEIVE FOR RESCUING THE SCIENTIST.
OH, YES, A REWARD!
Though friendship would be the best reward of all.
WE'LL TAKE A FEW MORE BACK EXITS TO MAKE IT HARDER TO TRACK US.
CAN WE REALLY LOSE THEM IF THEY'RE WATCHING US FROM ABOVE?
PERHAPS NOT, BUT...
...THE MOMENT WE STOP TRYING IS THE MOMENT EARTH IS LOST.

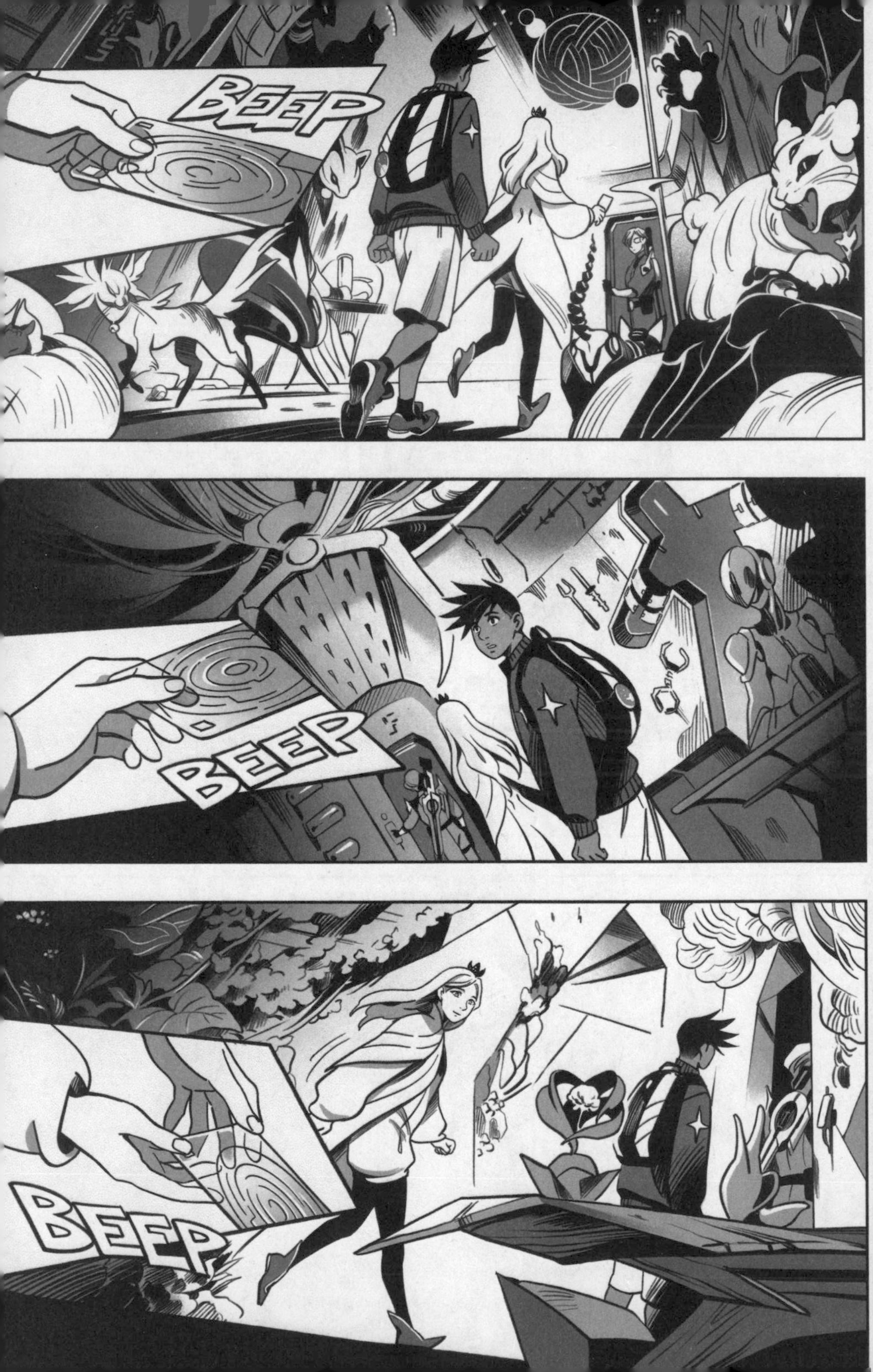
BEEP
BEEP
BEEP

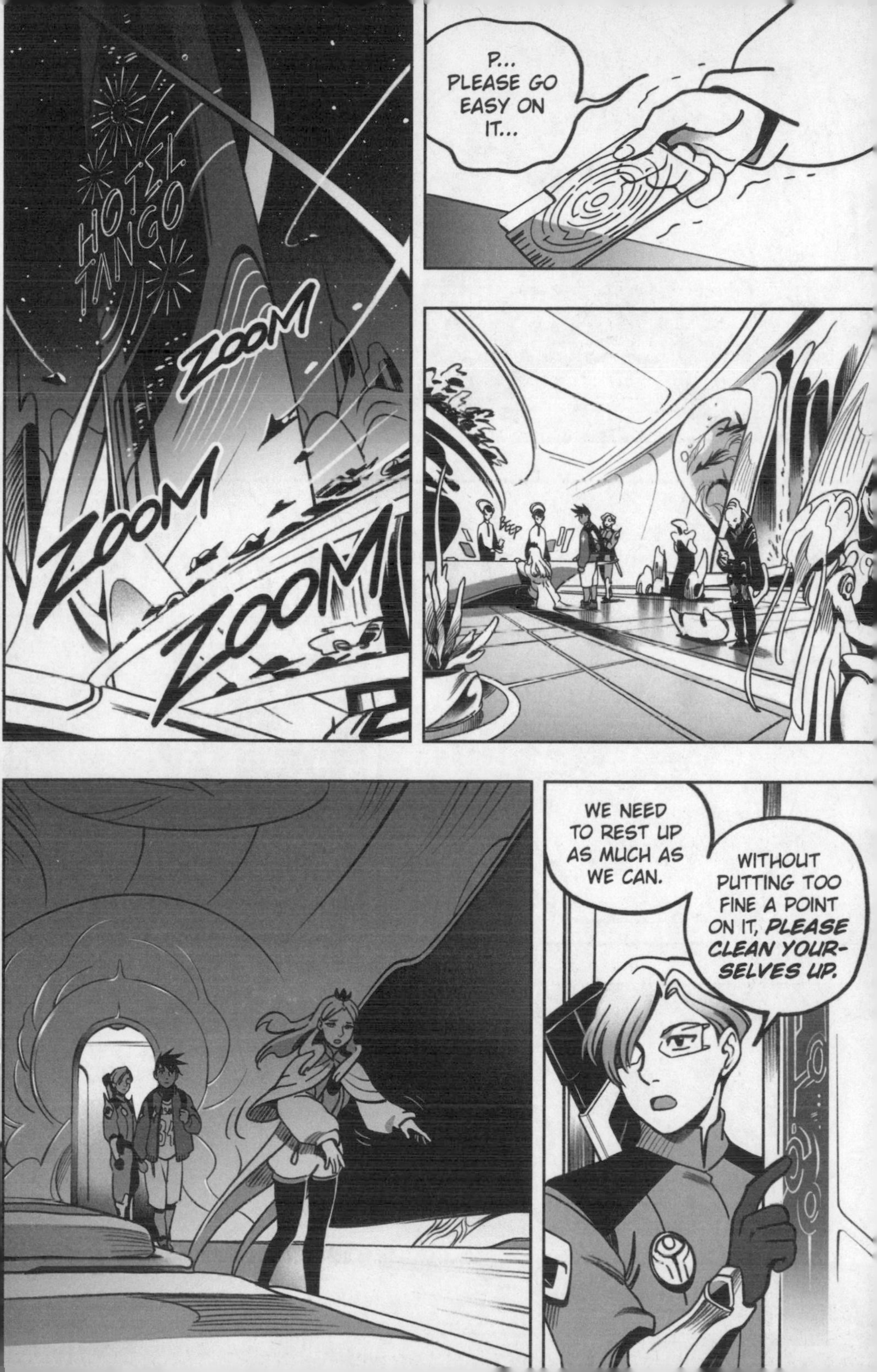
HOTEL TANGO
ZOOM
ZOOM
ZOOM
P... PLEASE GO EASY ON IT...
BEEP
WE NEED TO REST UP AS MUCH AS WE CAN.
WITHOUT PUTTING TOO FINE A POINT ON IT, ***PLEASE CLEAN YOURSELVES UP.***

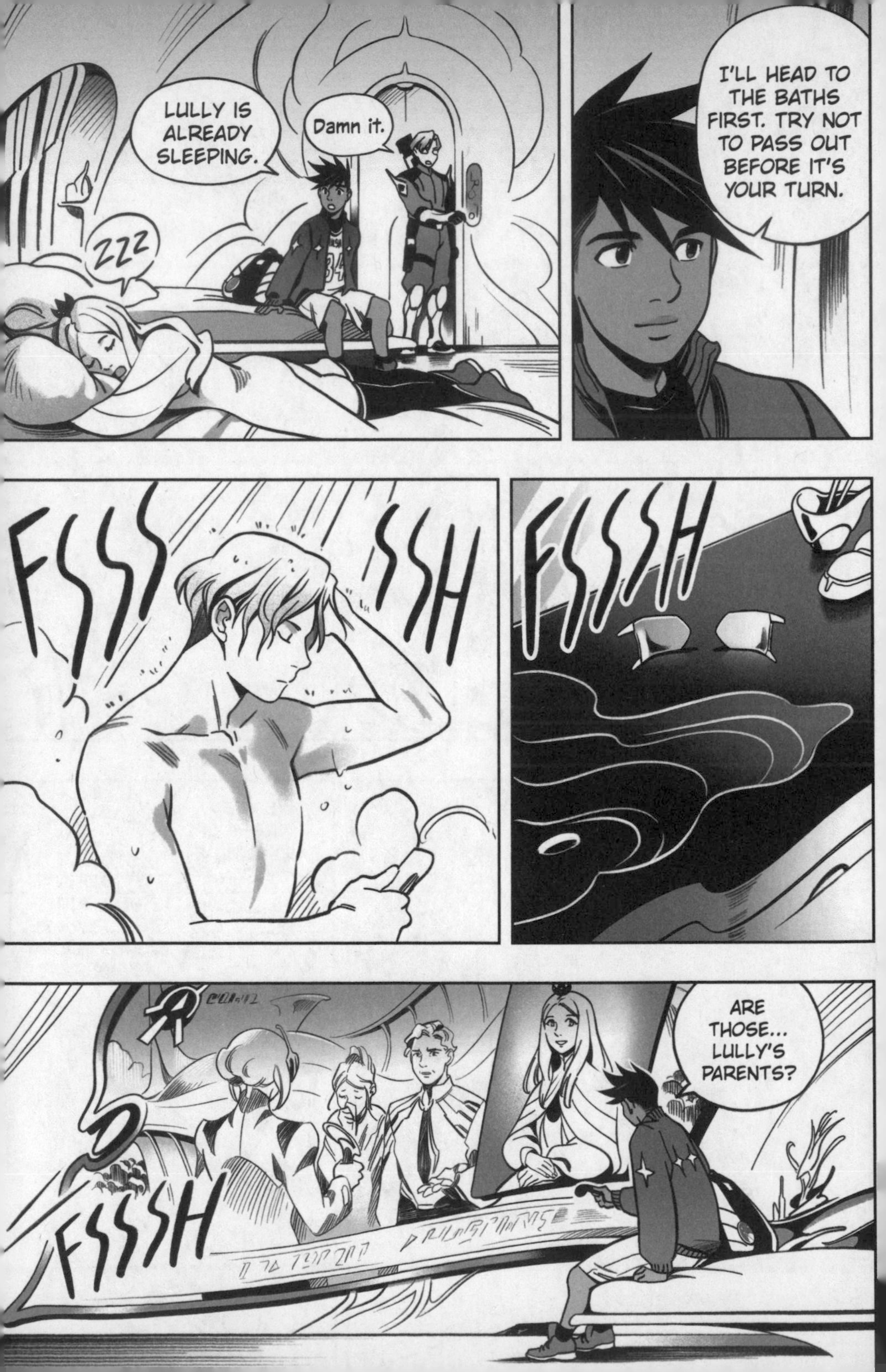
LULLY IS ALREADY SLEEPING.
Damn it.
ZZZ
I'LL HEAD TO THE BATHS FIRST. TRY NOT TO PASS OUT BEFORE IT'S YOUR TURN.
FSSS SSH
FSSSH
FSSSH
ARE THOSE... LULLY'S PARENTS?

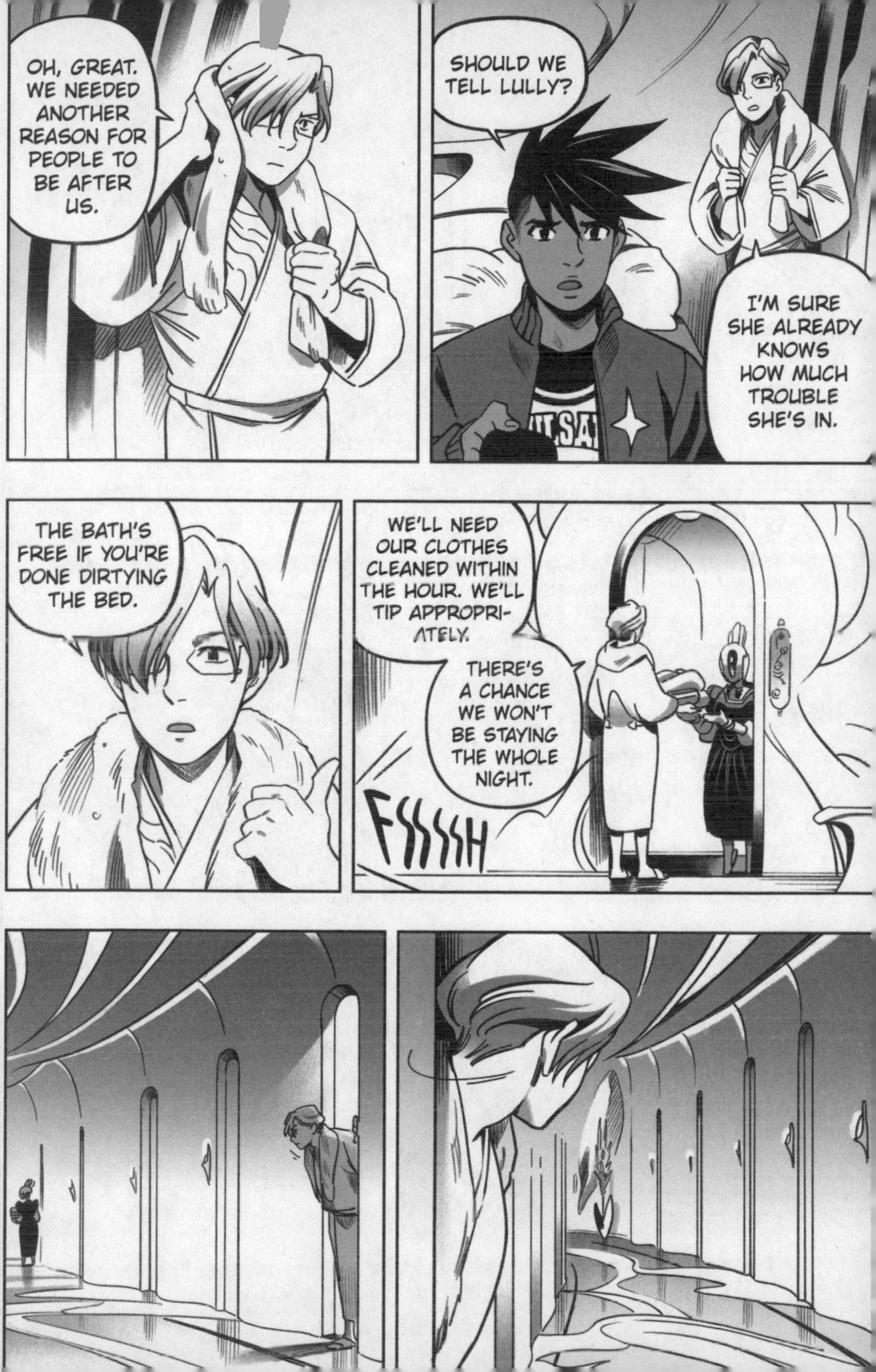
OH, GREAT. WE NEEDED ANOTHER REASON FOR PEOPLE TO BE AFTER US.
SHOULD WE TELL LULLY?
I'M SURE SHE ALREADY KNOWS HOW MUCH TROUBLE SHE'S IN.
THE BATH'S FREE IF YOU'RE DONE DIRTYING THE BED.
WE'LL NEED OUR CLOTHES CLEANED WITHIN THE HOUR. WE'LL TIP APPROPRI-ATELY.
THERE'S A CHANCE WE WON'T BE STAYING THE WHOLE NIGHT.
FSSSSH

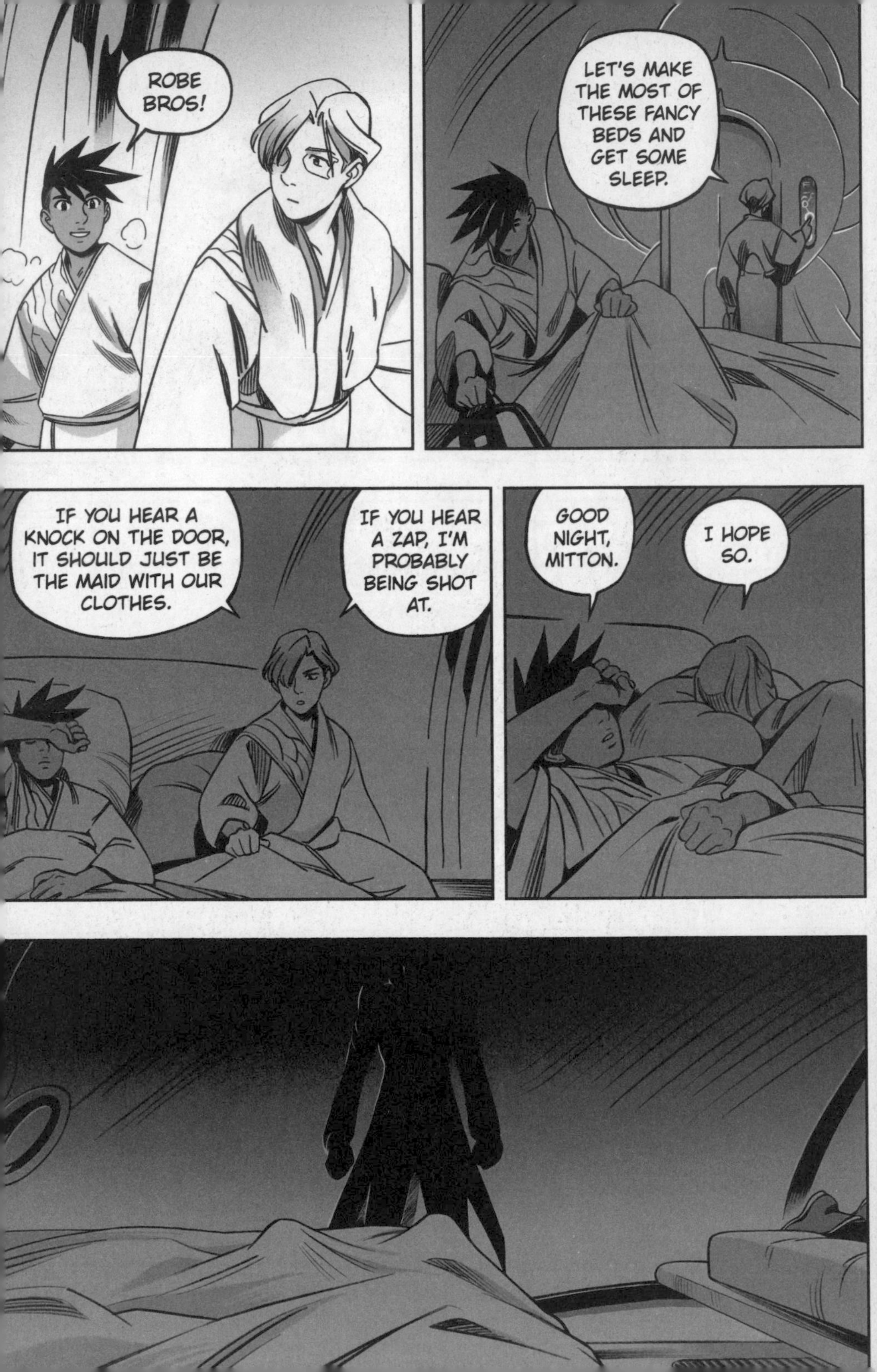
ROBE BROS!
LET'S MAKE THE MOST OF THESE FANCY BEDS AND GET SOME SLEEP.
IF YOU HEAR A KNOCK ON THE DOOR, IT SHOULD JUST BE THE MAID WITH OUR CLOTHES.
IF YOU HEAR A ZAP, I'M PROBABLY BEING SHOT AT.
GOOD NIGHT, MITTON.
I HOPE SO.

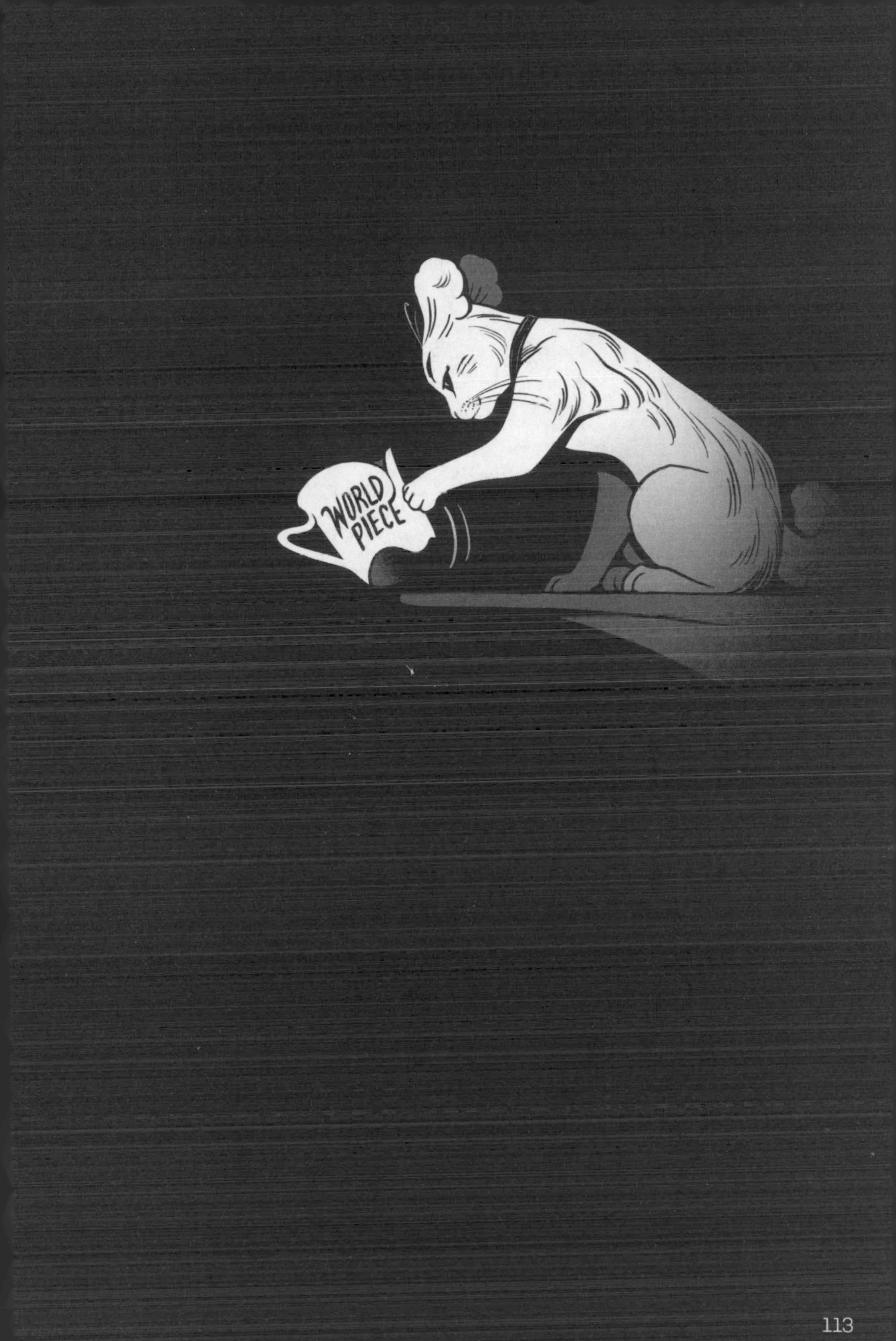
WORLD PIECE

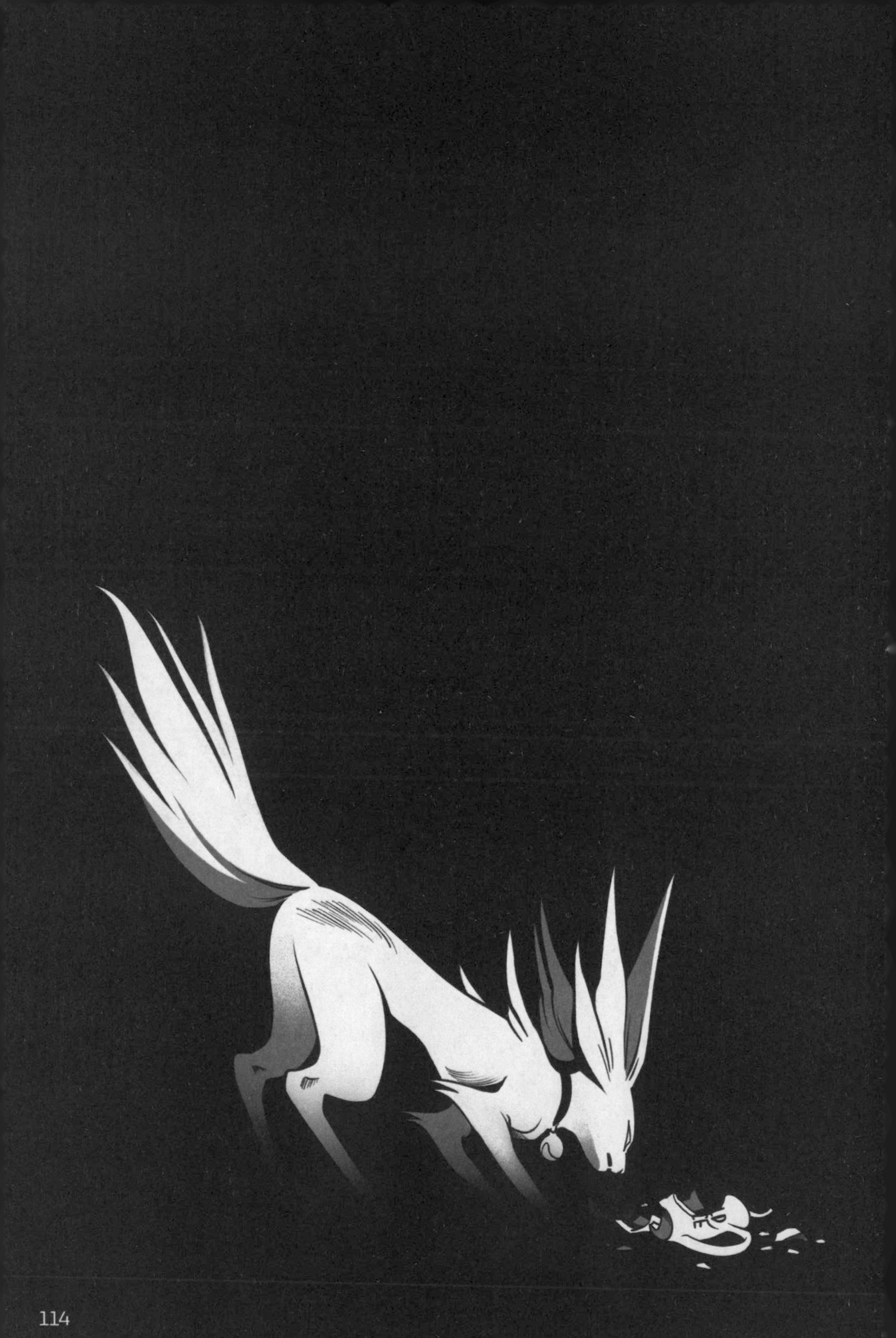

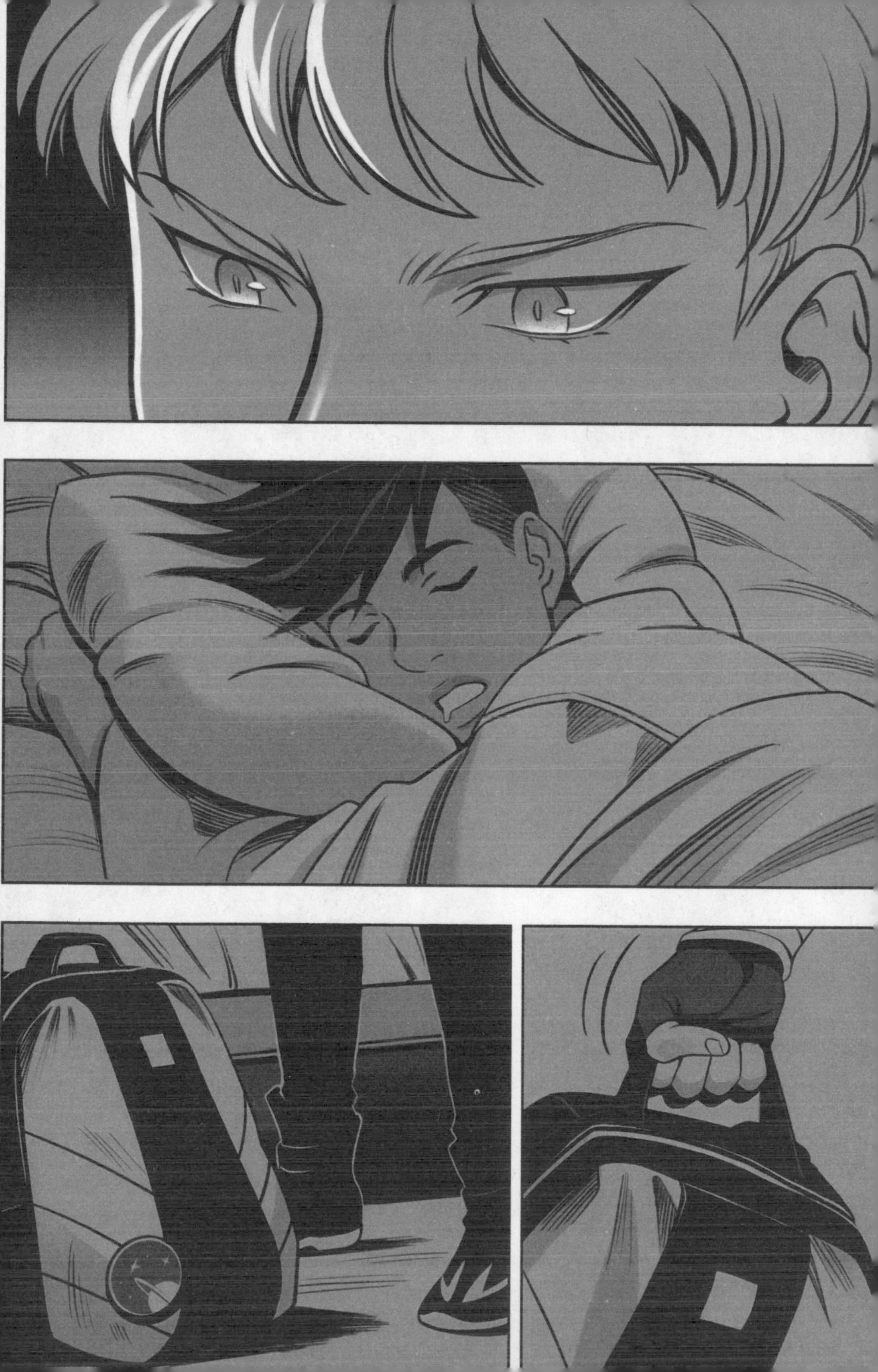

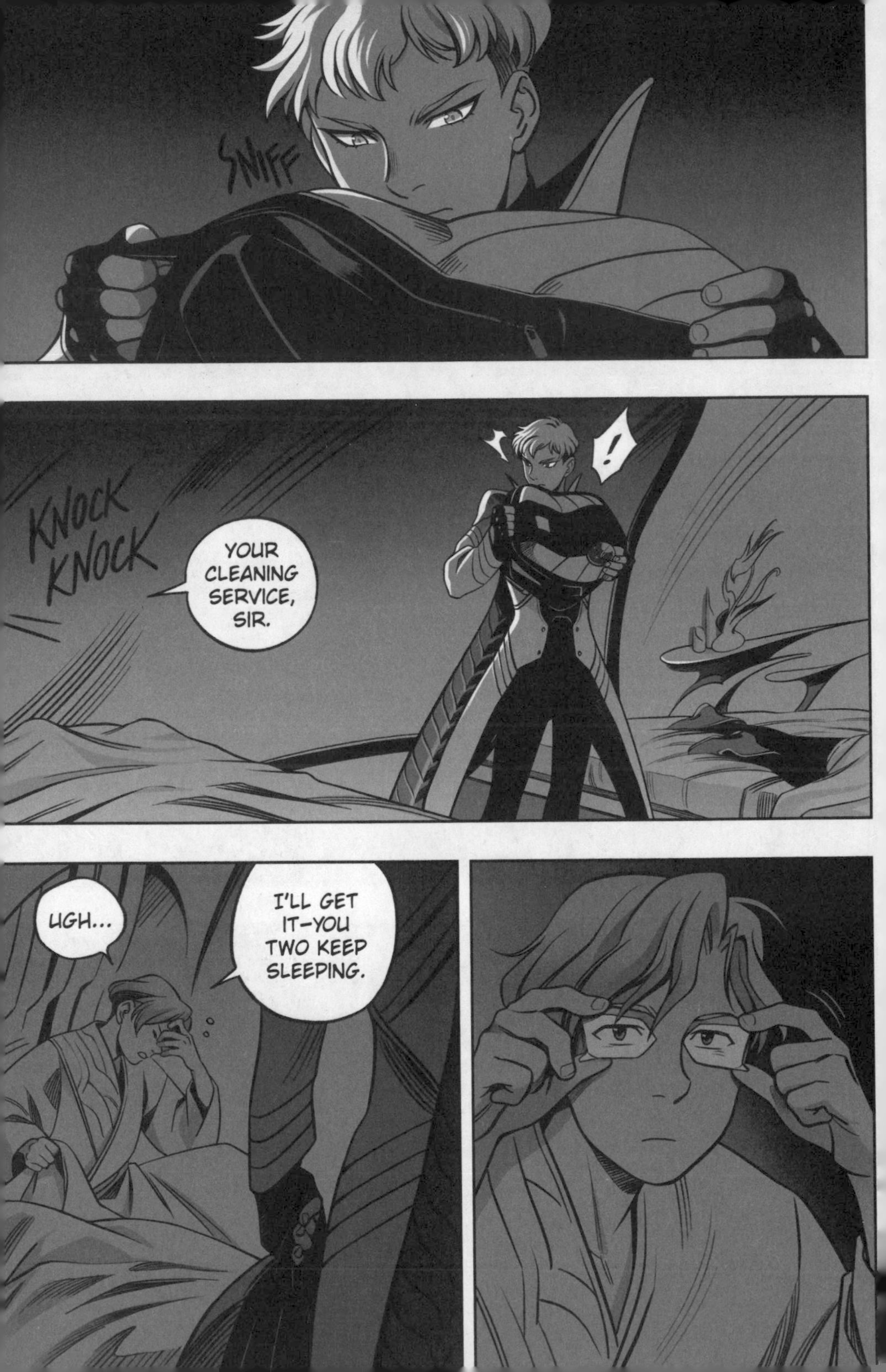
SNIFF
!
!
KNOCK KNOCK
YOUR CLEANING SERVICE, SIR.
UGH...
I'LL GET IT–YOU TWO KEEP SLEEPING.

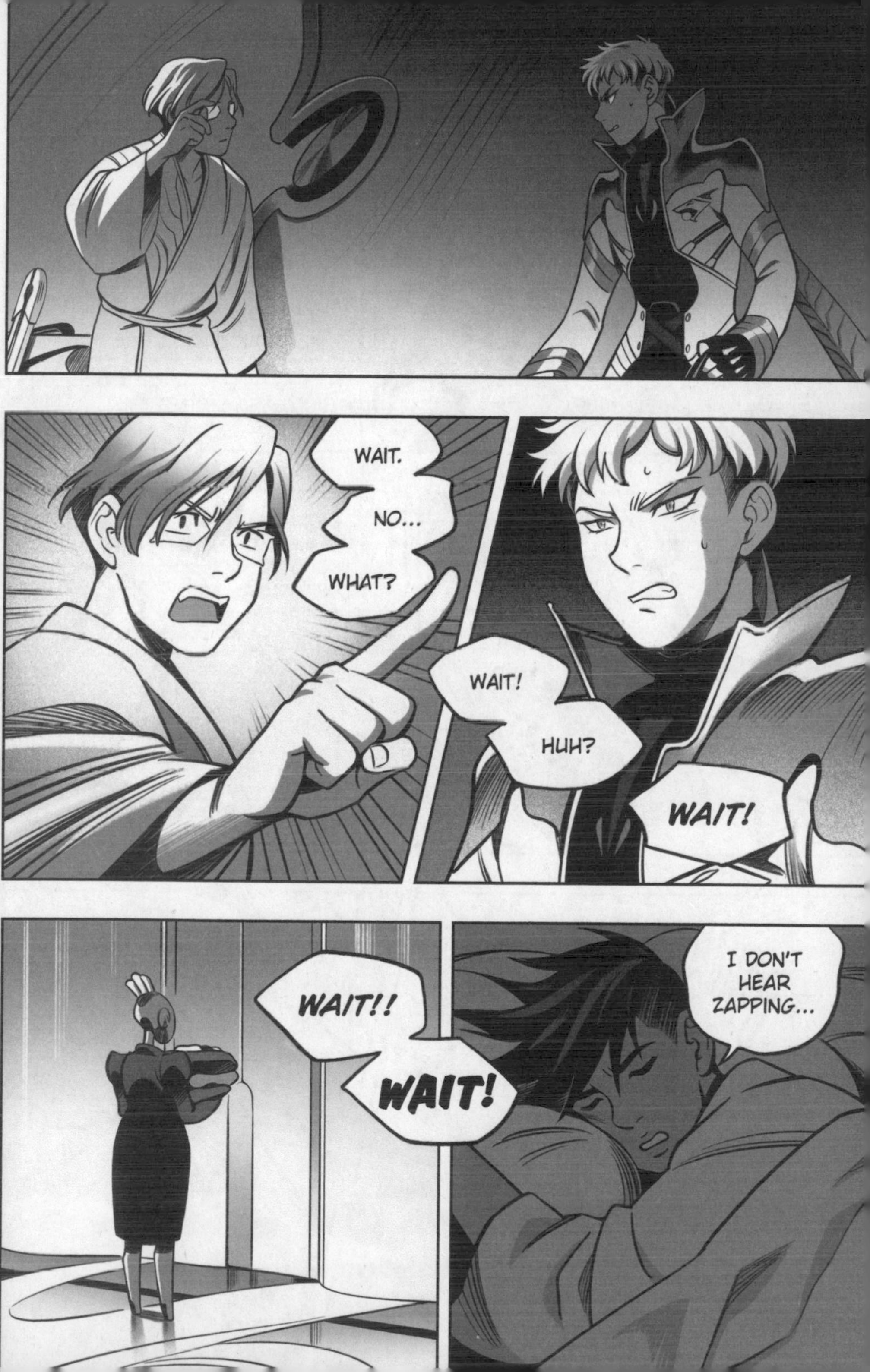
WAIT.
NO...
WHAT?
WAIT!
HUH?
WAIT!
WAIT!!
WAIT!
I DON'T HEAR ZAPPING...

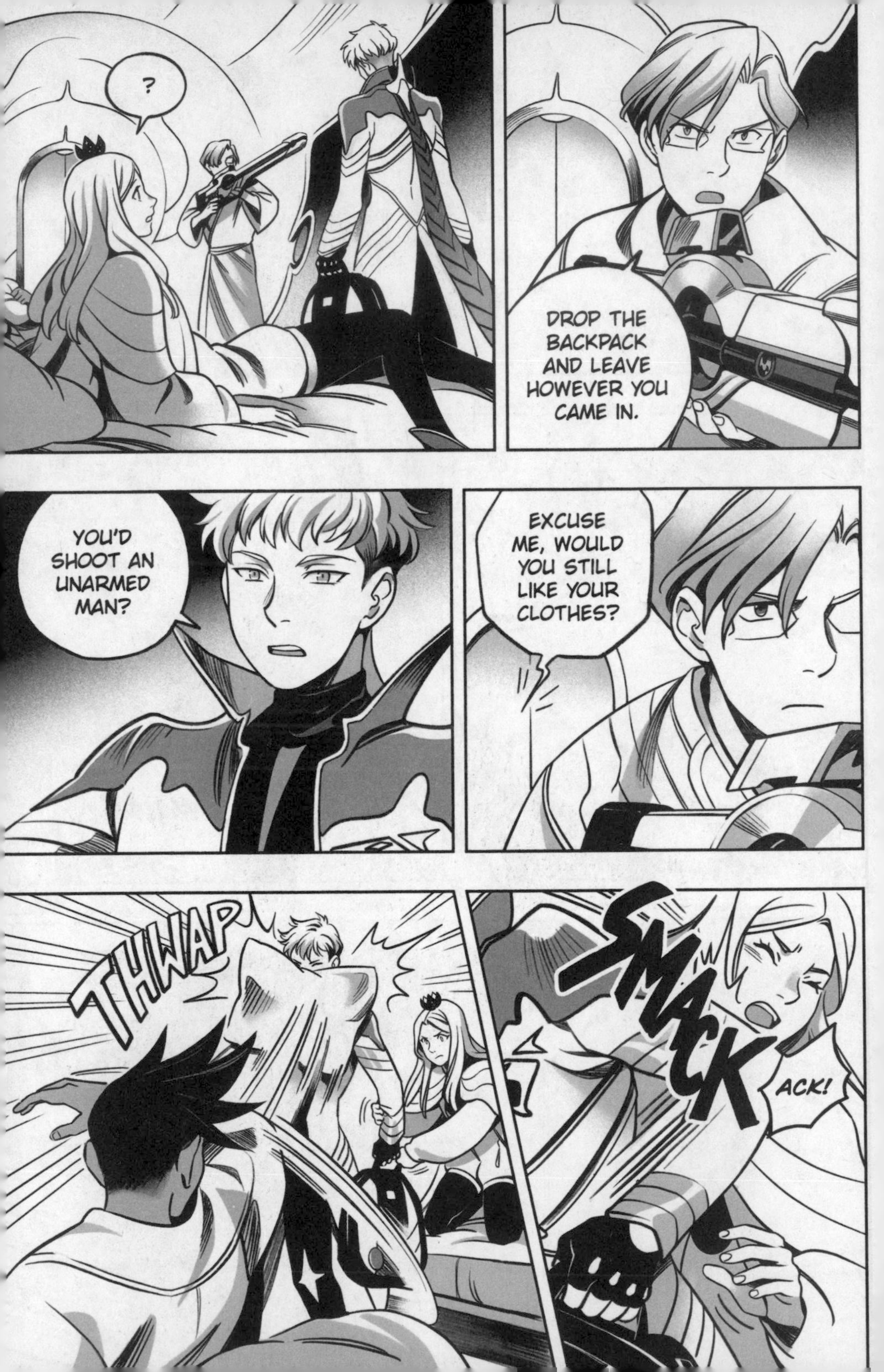
?
DROP THE BACKPACK AND LEAVE HOWEVER YOU CAME IN.
YOU'D SHOOT AN UNARMED MAN?
EXCUSE ME, WOULD YOU STILL LIKE YOUR CLOTHES?
THWAP
SMACK
ACK!

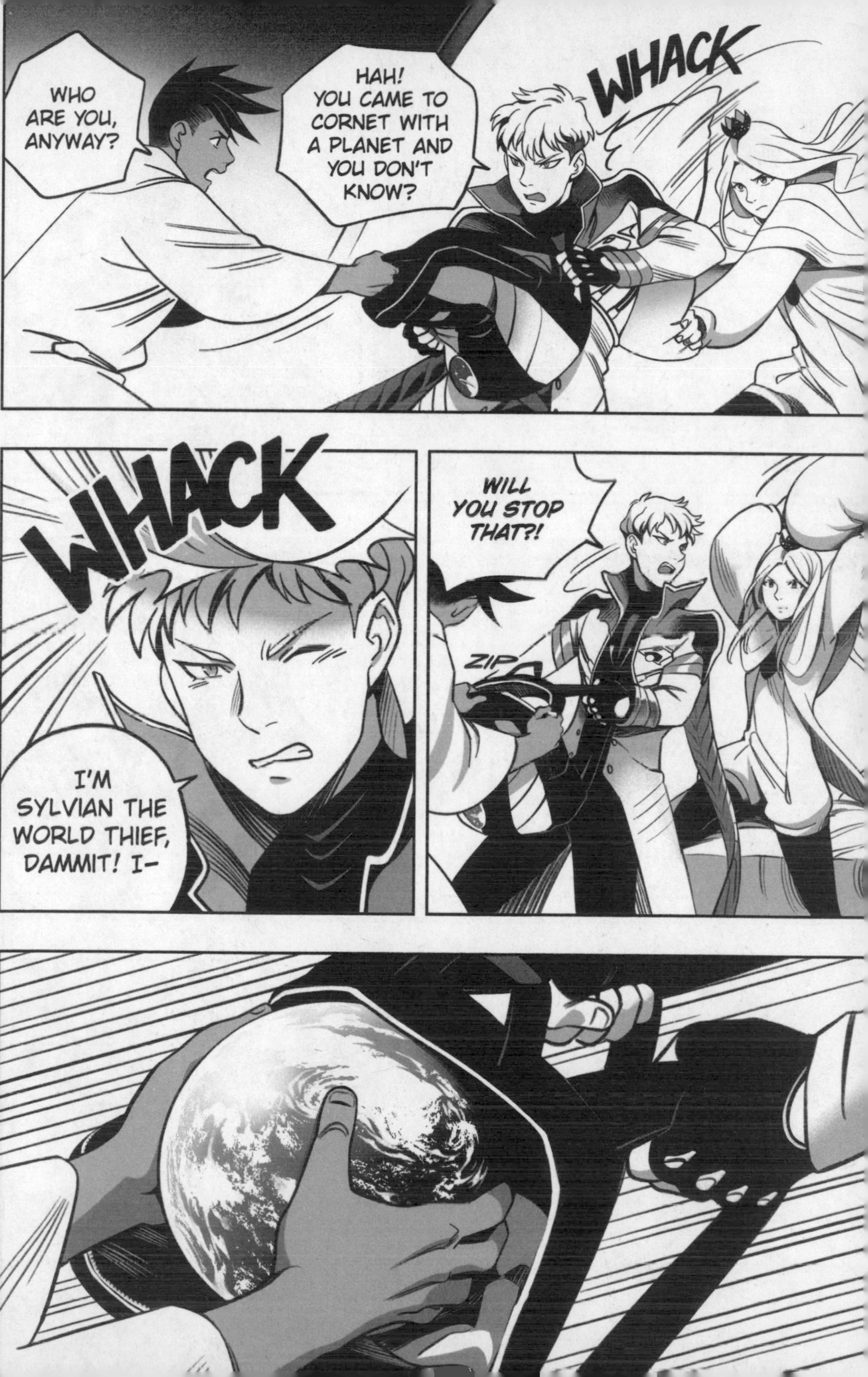
WHO ARE YOU, ANYWAY?
HAH! YOU CAME TO CORNET WITH A PLANET AND YOU DON'T KNOW?
WHACK
WHACK
I'M SYLVIAN THE WORLD THIEF, DAMMIT! I-
WILL YOU STOP THAT?!
ZIP

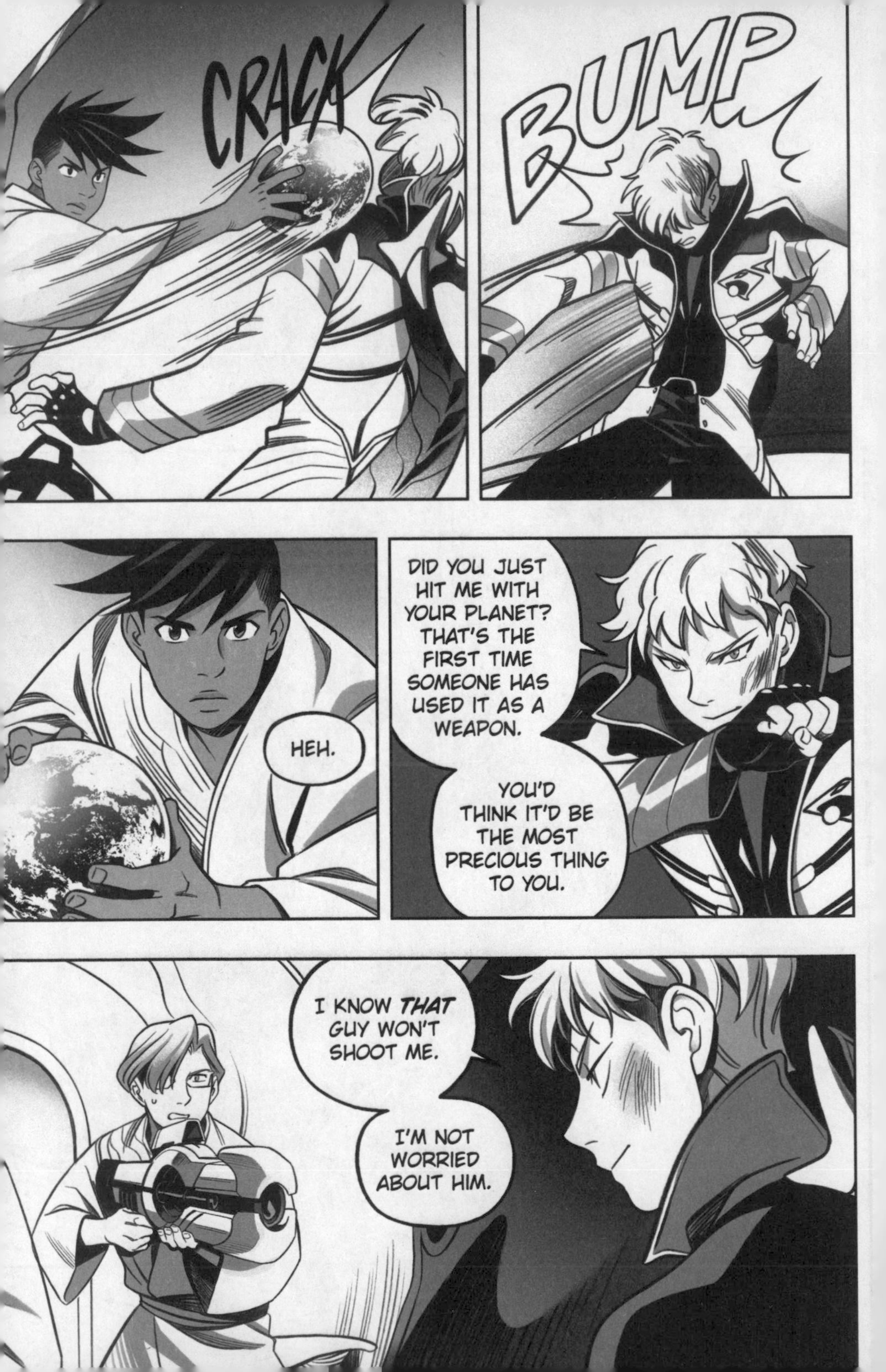
CRACK
BUMP
HEH.
DID YOU JUST HIT ME WITH YOUR PLANET? THAT'S THE FIRST TIME SOMEONE HAS USED IT AS A WEAPON.
YOU'D THINK IT'D BE THE MOST PRECIOUS THING TO YOU.
I KNOW *THAT* GUY WON'T SHOOT ME.
I'M NOT WORRIED ABOUT HIM.

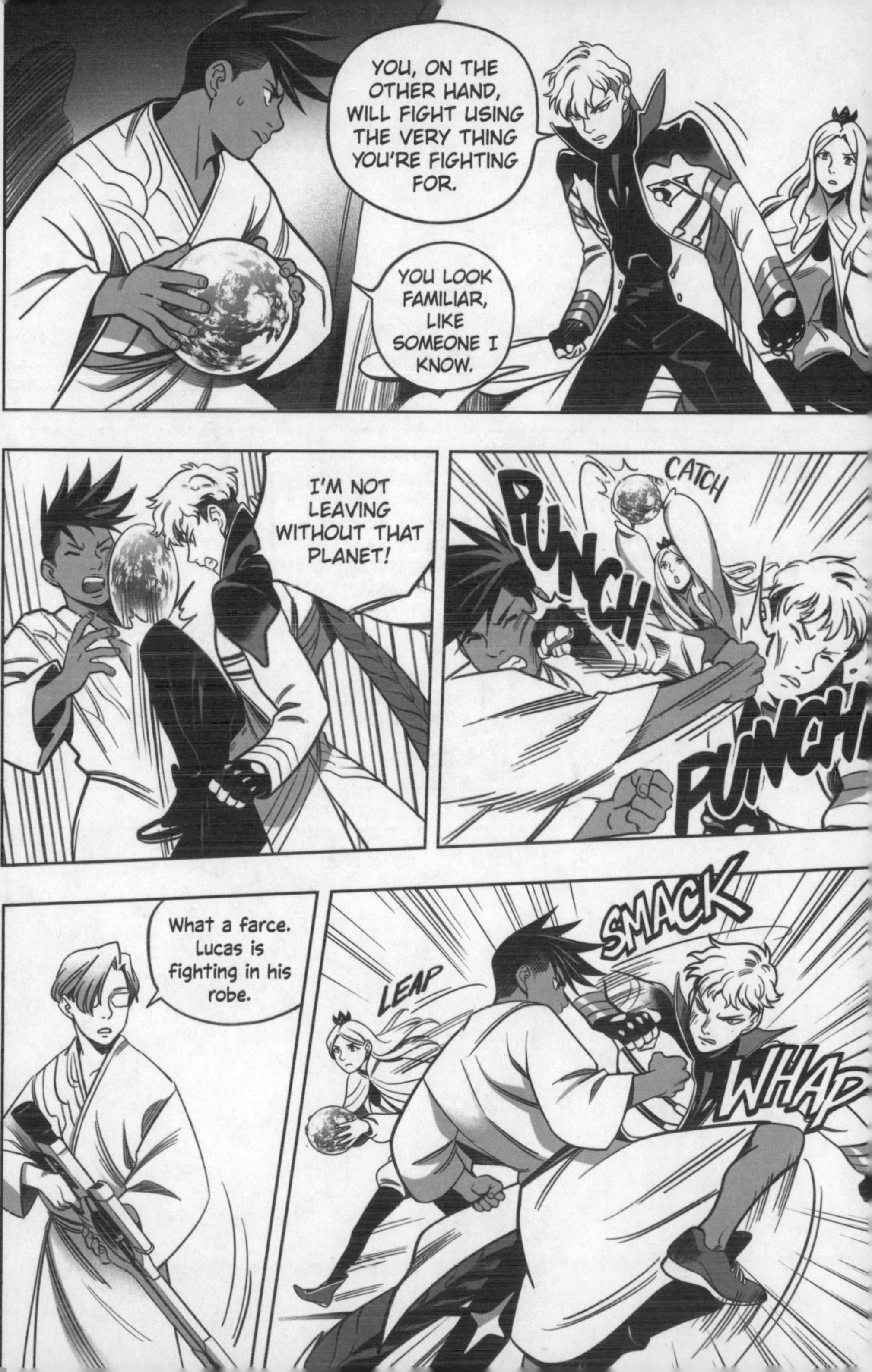
YOU, ON THE OTHER HAND, WILL FIGHT USING THE VERY THING YOU'RE FIGHTING FOR.
YOU LOOK FAMILIAR, LIKE SOMEONE I KNOW.
I'M NOT LEAVING WITHOUT THAT PLANET!
CATCH
PUNCH
PUNCH
What a farce. Lucas is fighting in his robe.
SMACK
LEAP
WHAP

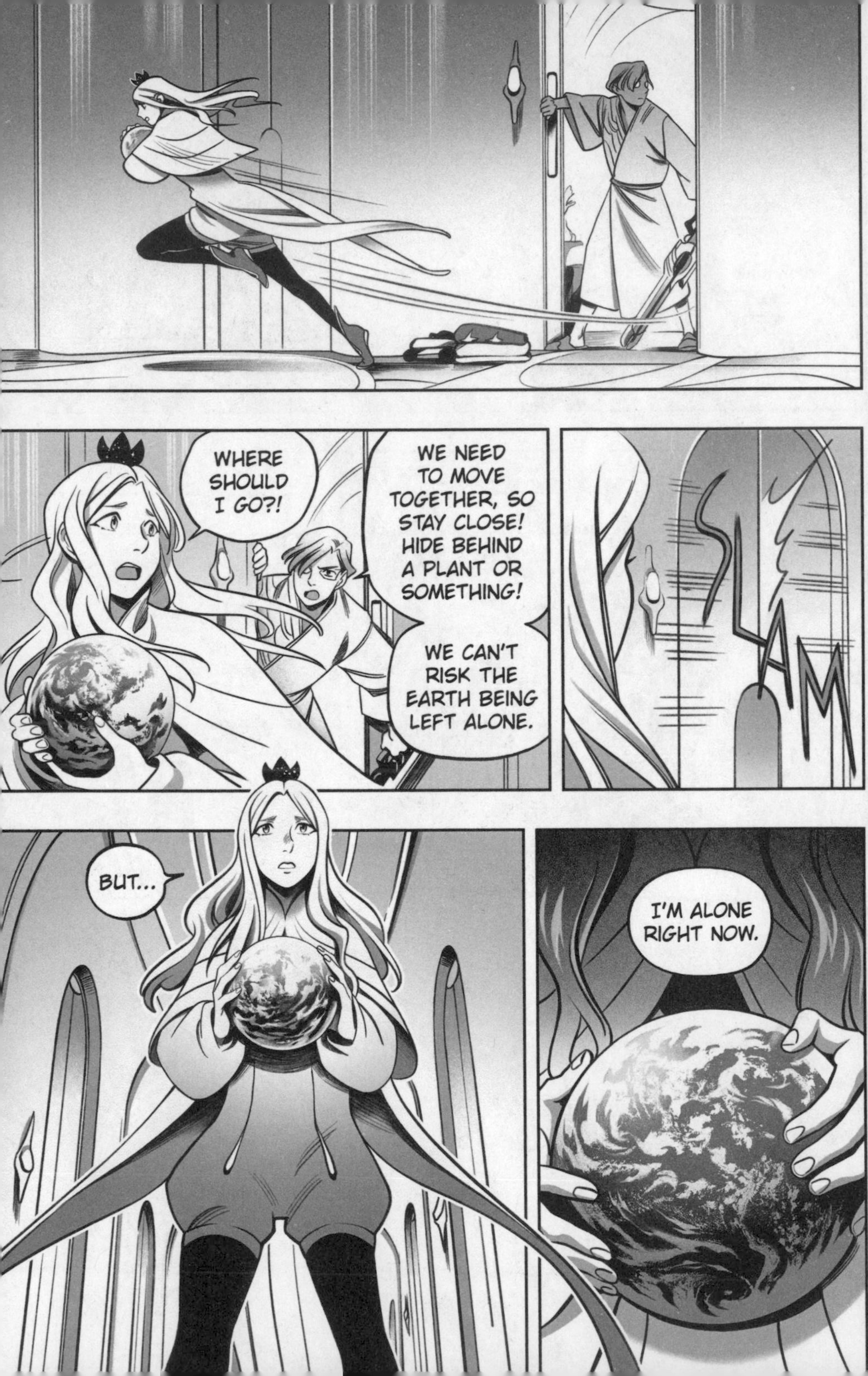
WHERE SHOULD I GO?!
WE NEED TO MOVE TOGETHER, SO STAY CLOSE! HIDE BEHIND A PLANT OR SOMETHING!
WE CAN'T RISK THE EARTH BEING LEFT ALONE.
SLAM
BUT...
I'M ALONE RIGHT NOW.

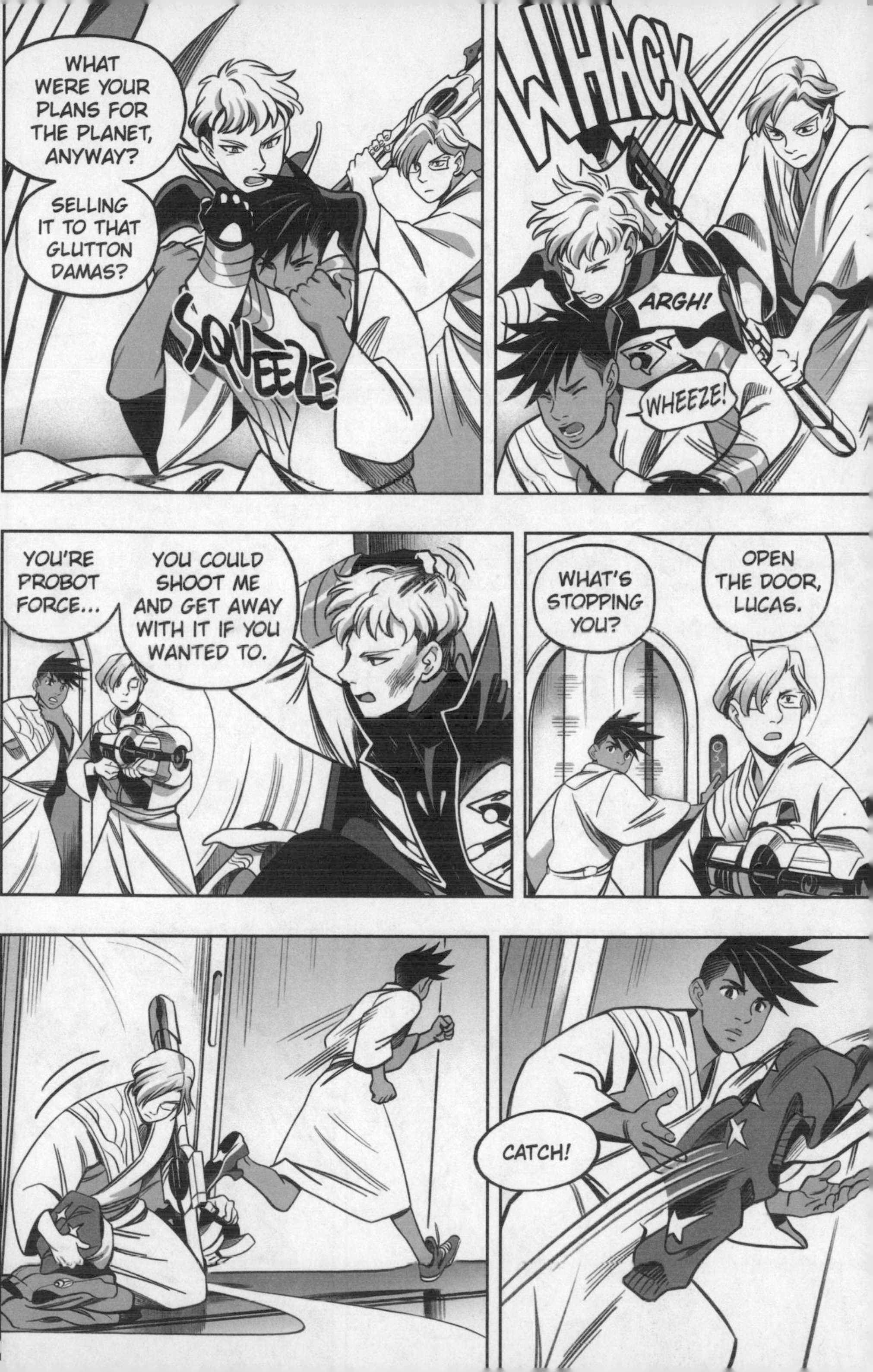
WHAT WERE YOUR PLANS FOR THE PLANET, ANYWAY?
SELLING IT TO THAT GLUTTON DAMAS?
SQUEEZE
WHACK
ARGH!
WHEEZE!
YOU'RE PROBOT FORCE...
YOU COULD SHOOT ME AND GET AWAY WITH IT IF YOU WANTED TO.
WHAT'S STOPPING YOU?
OPEN THE DOOR, LUCAS.
CATCH!

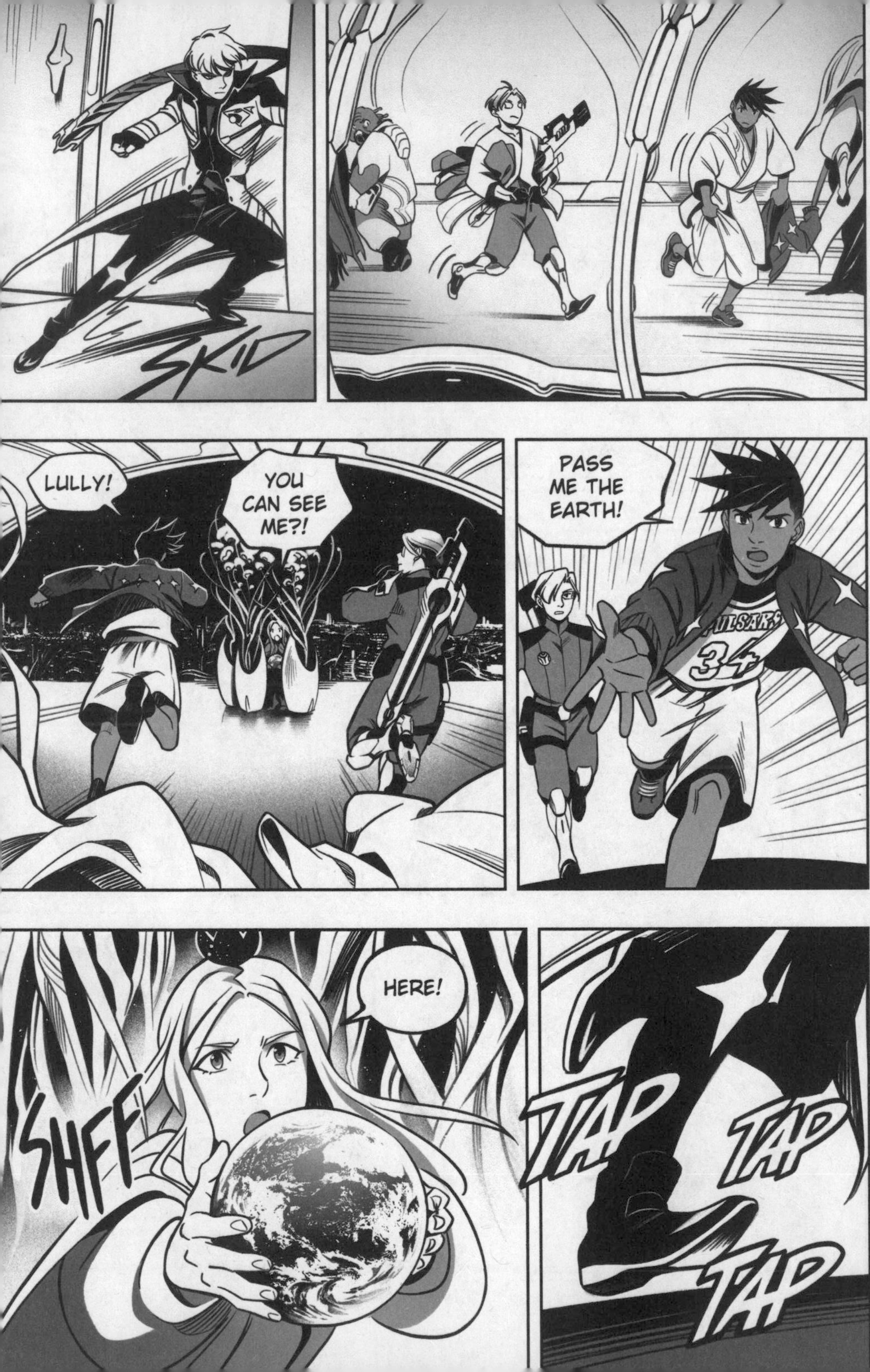
SKID
LULLY!
YOU CAN SEE ME?!
PASS ME THE EARTH!
PULSARS
34
SHFF
HERE!
TAP
TAP
TAP

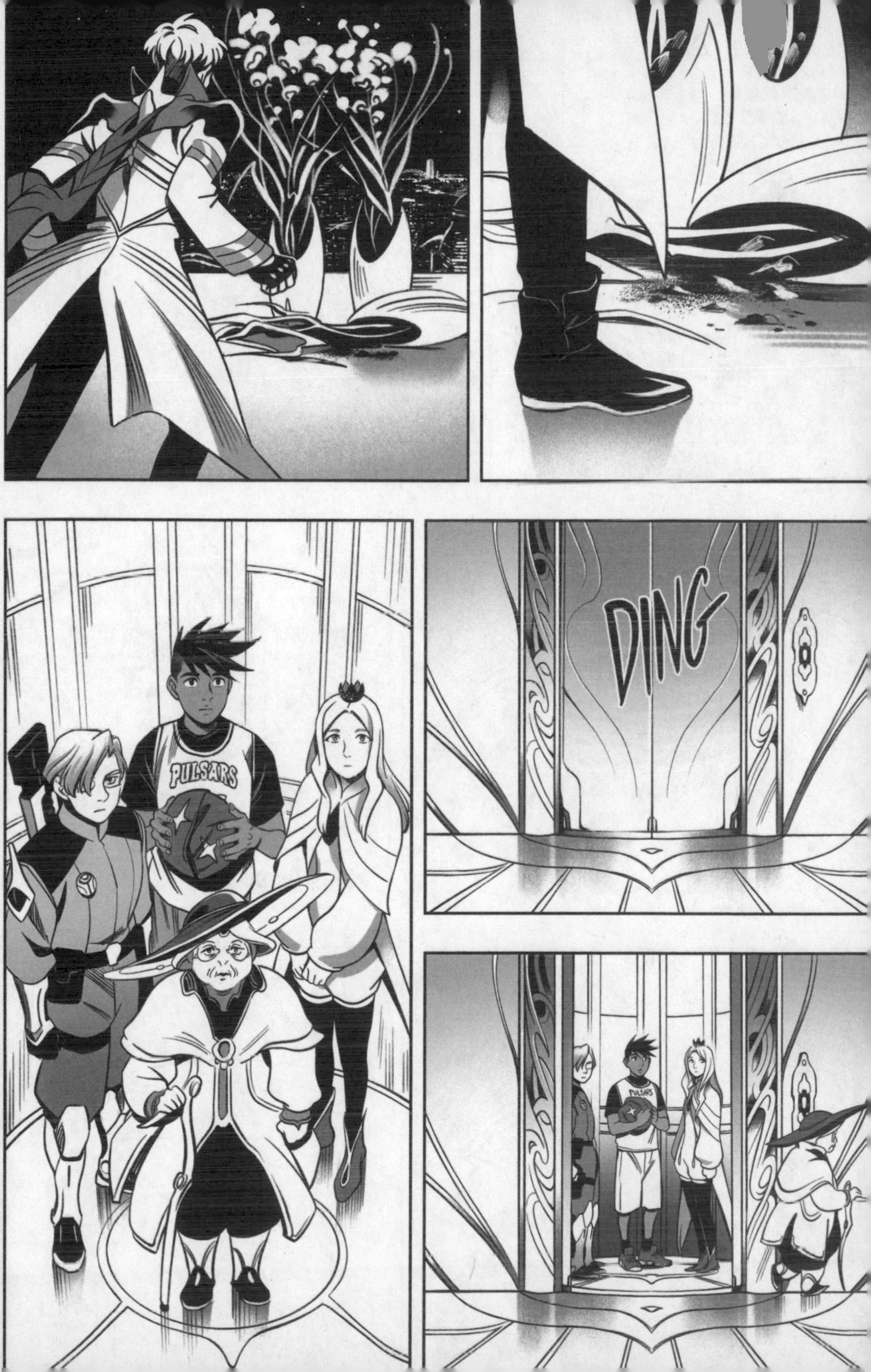
PULSARS
DING
PULSARS

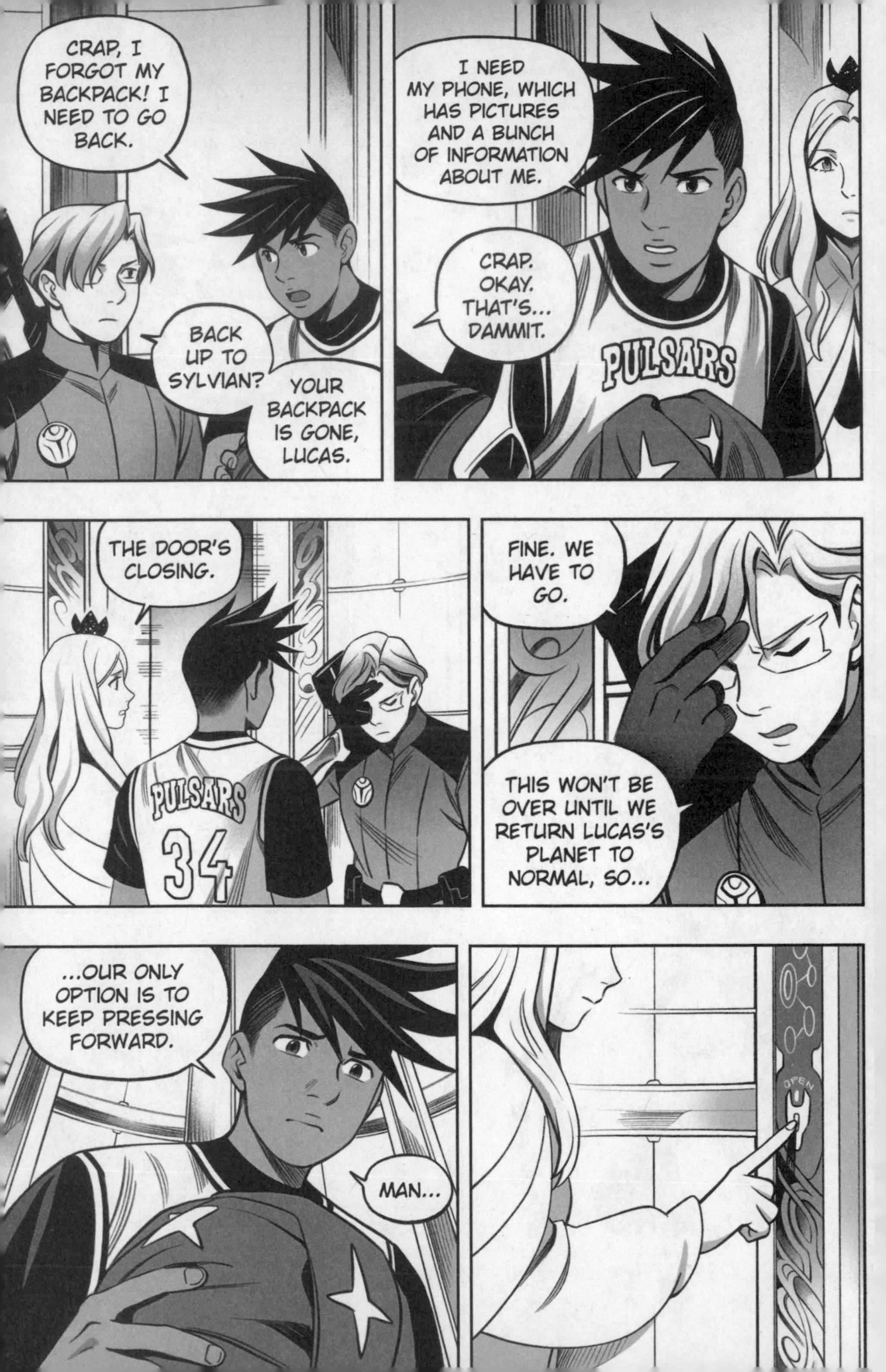
CRAP, I FORGOT MY BACKPACK! I NEED TO GO BACK.
BACK UP TO SYLVIAN?
YOUR BACKPACK IS GONE, LUCAS.
I NEED MY PHONE, WHICH HAS PICTURES AND A BUNCH OF INFORMATION ABOUT ME.
CRAP. OKAY. THAT'S... DAMMIT.
PULSARS
THE DOOR'S CLOSING.
PULSARS
34
FINE. WE HAVE TO GO.
THIS WON'T BE OVER UNTIL WE RETURN LUCAS'S PLANET TO NORMAL, SO...
...OUR ONLY OPTION IS TO KEEP PRESSING FORWARD.
MAN...
OPEN

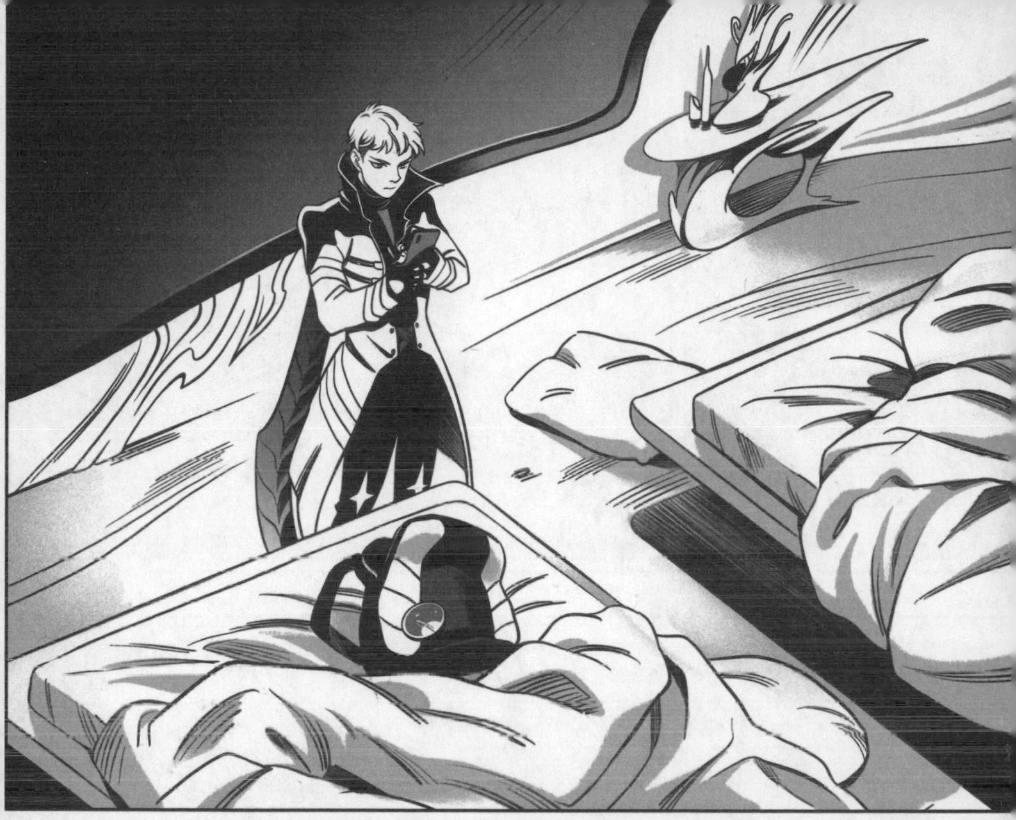

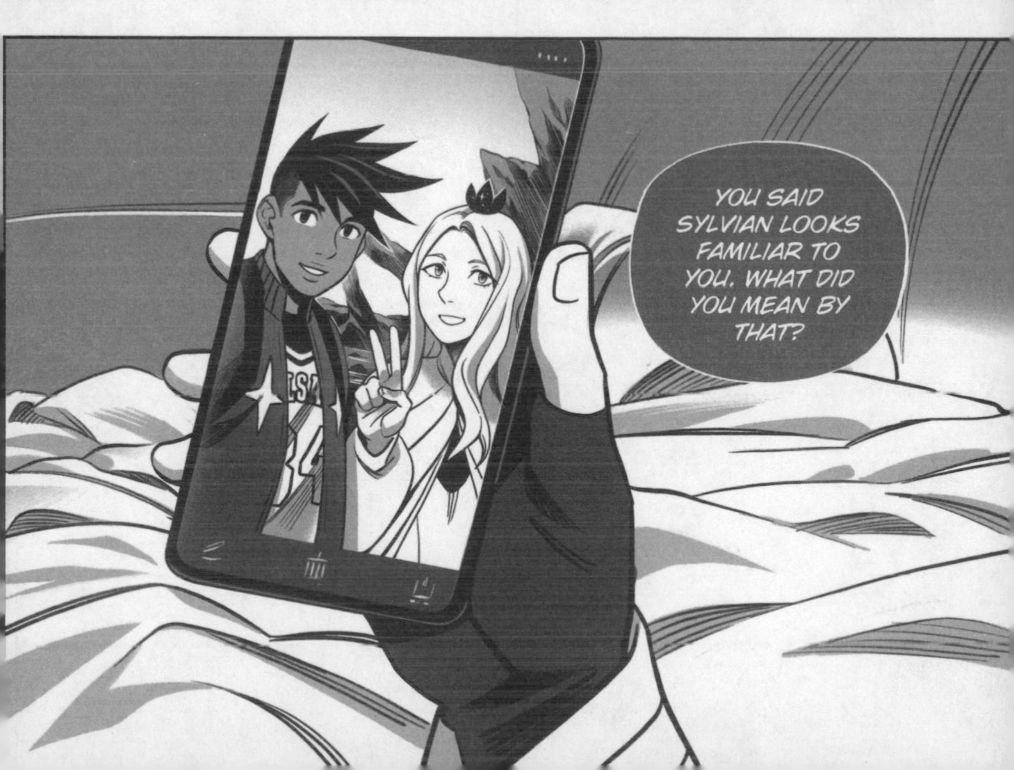
YOU SAID SYLVIAN LOOKS FAMILIAR TO YOU. WHAT DID YOU MEAN BY THAT?

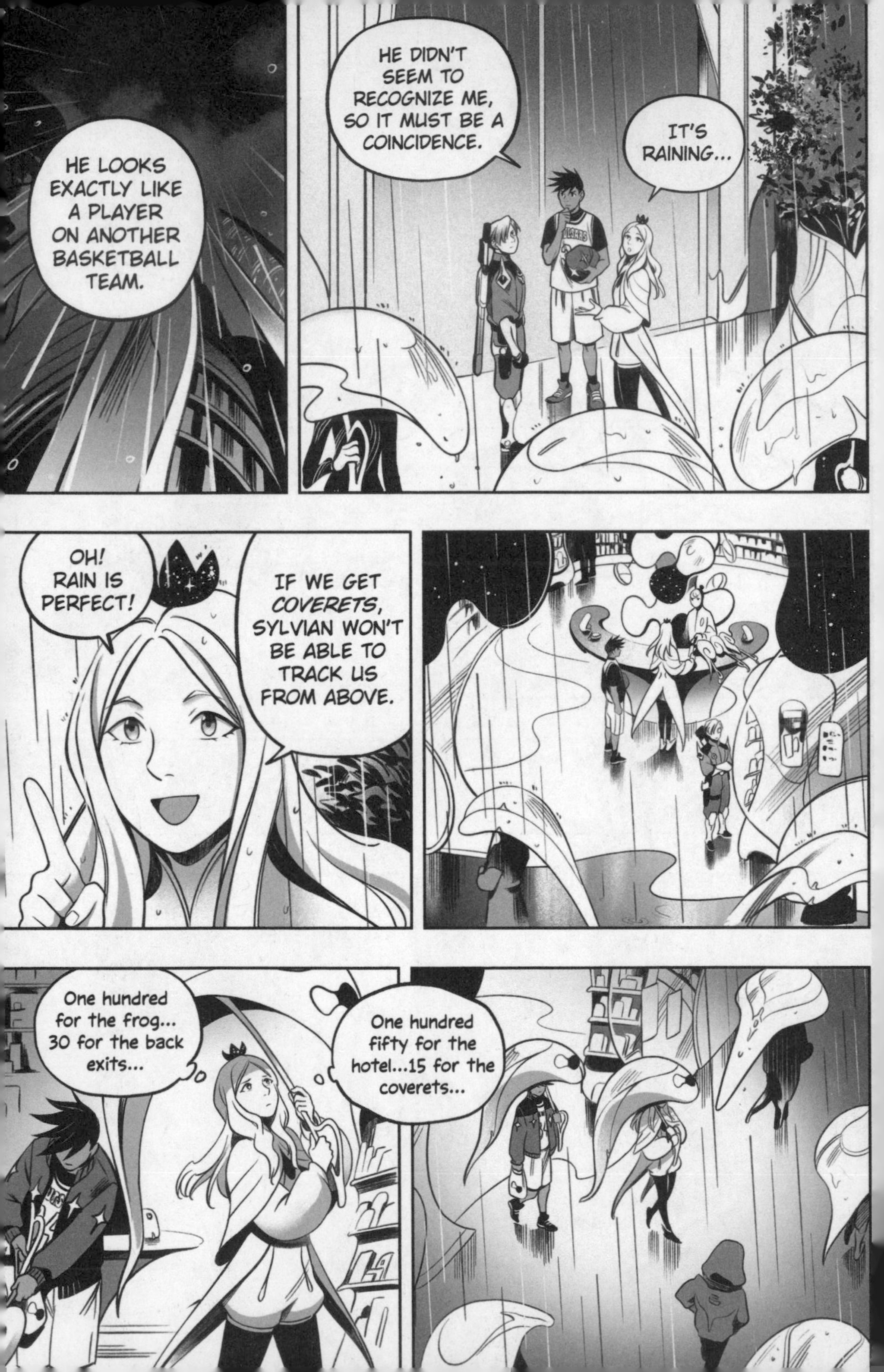
HE LOOKS EXACTLY LIKE A PLAYER ON ANOTHER BASKETBALL TEAM.
HE DIDN'T SEEM TO RECOGNIZE ME, SO IT MUST BE A COINCIDENCE.
IT'S RAINING...
OH! RAIN IS PERFECT!
IF WE GET *COVERETS*, SYLVIAN WON'T BE ABLE TO TRACK US FROM ABOVE.
One hundred for the frog... 30 for the back exits...
One hundred fifty for the hotel...15 for the coverets...

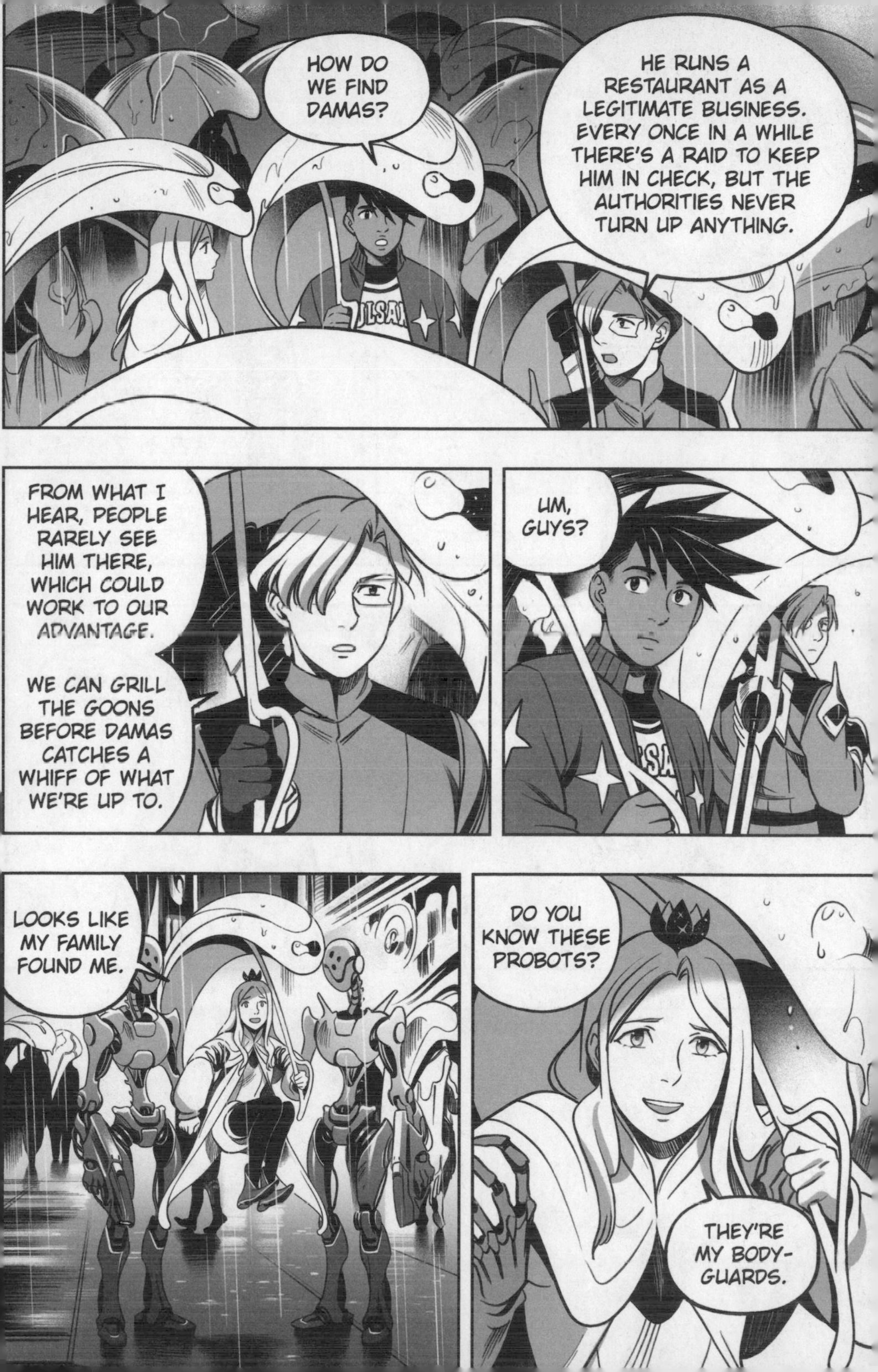
HOW DO WE FIND DAMAS?
HE RUNS A RESTAURANT AS A LEGITIMATE BUSINESS. EVERY ONCE IN A WHILE THERE'S A RAID TO KEEP HIM IN CHECK, BUT THE AUTHORITIES NEVER TURN UP ANYTHING.
FROM WHAT I HEAR, PEOPLE RARELY SEE HIM THERE, WHICH COULD WORK TO OUR ADVANTAGE.
WE CAN GRILL THE GOONS BEFORE DAMAS CATCHES A WHIFF OF WHAT WE'RE UP TO.
UM, GUYS?
LOOKS LIKE MY FAMILY FOUND ME.
DO YOU KNOW THESE PROBOTS?
THEY'RE MY BODY-GUARDS.

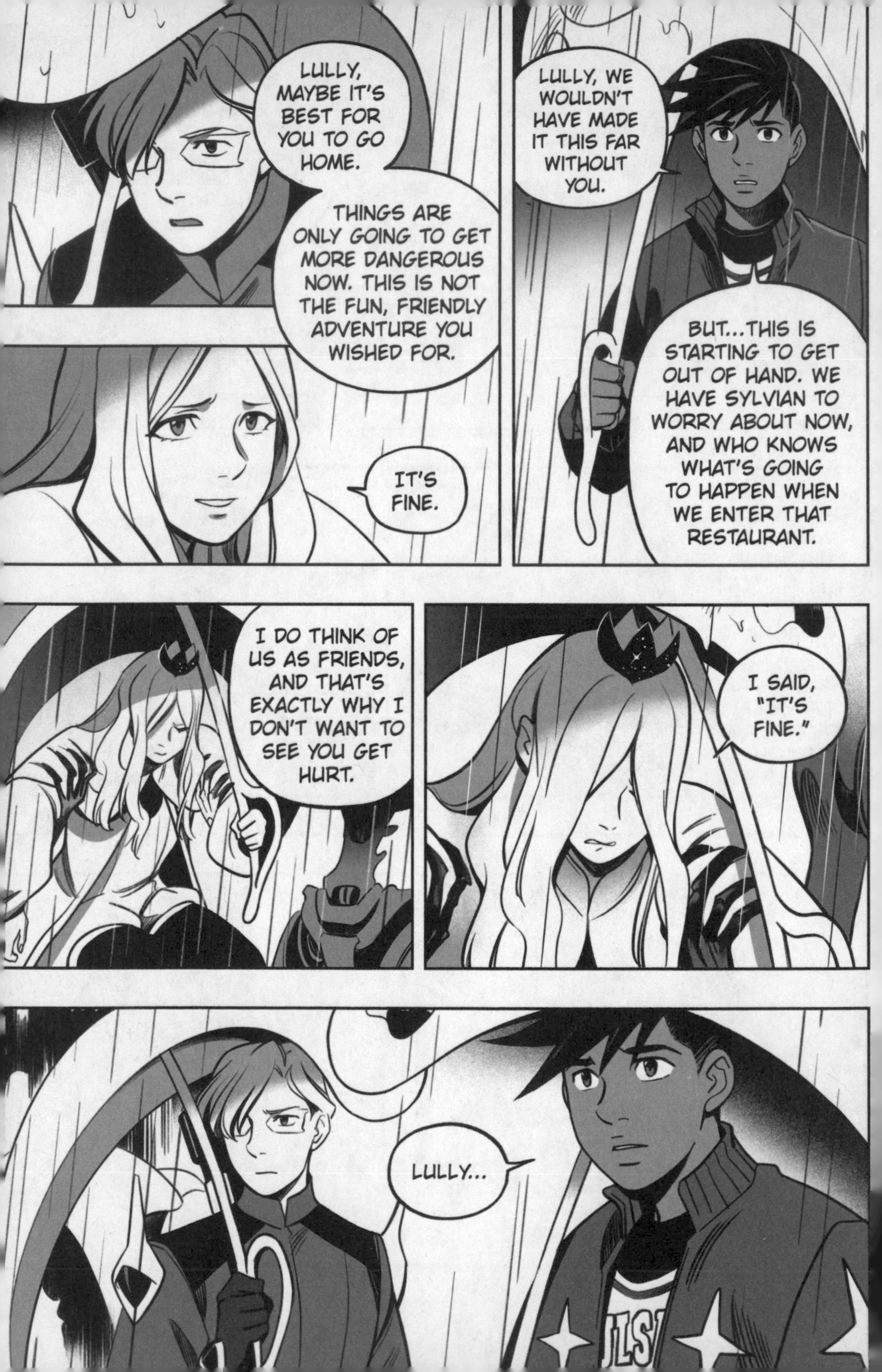
LULLY, MAYBE IT'S BEST FOR YOU TO GO HOME.
THINGS ARE ONLY GOING TO GET MORE DANGEROUS NOW. THIS IS NOT THE FUN, FRIENDLY ADVENTURE YOU WISHED FOR.
IT'S FINE.
LULLY, WE WOULDN'T HAVE MADE IT THIS FAR WITHOUT YOU.
BUT...THIS IS STARTING TO GET OUT OF HAND. WE HAVE SYLVIAN TO WORRY ABOUT NOW, AND WHO KNOWS WHAT'S GOING TO HAPPEN WHEN WE ENTER THAT RESTAURANT.
I DO THINK OF US AS FRIENDS, AND THAT'S EXACTLY WHY I DON'T WANT TO SEE YOU GET HURT.
I SAID, "IT'S FINE."
LULLY...

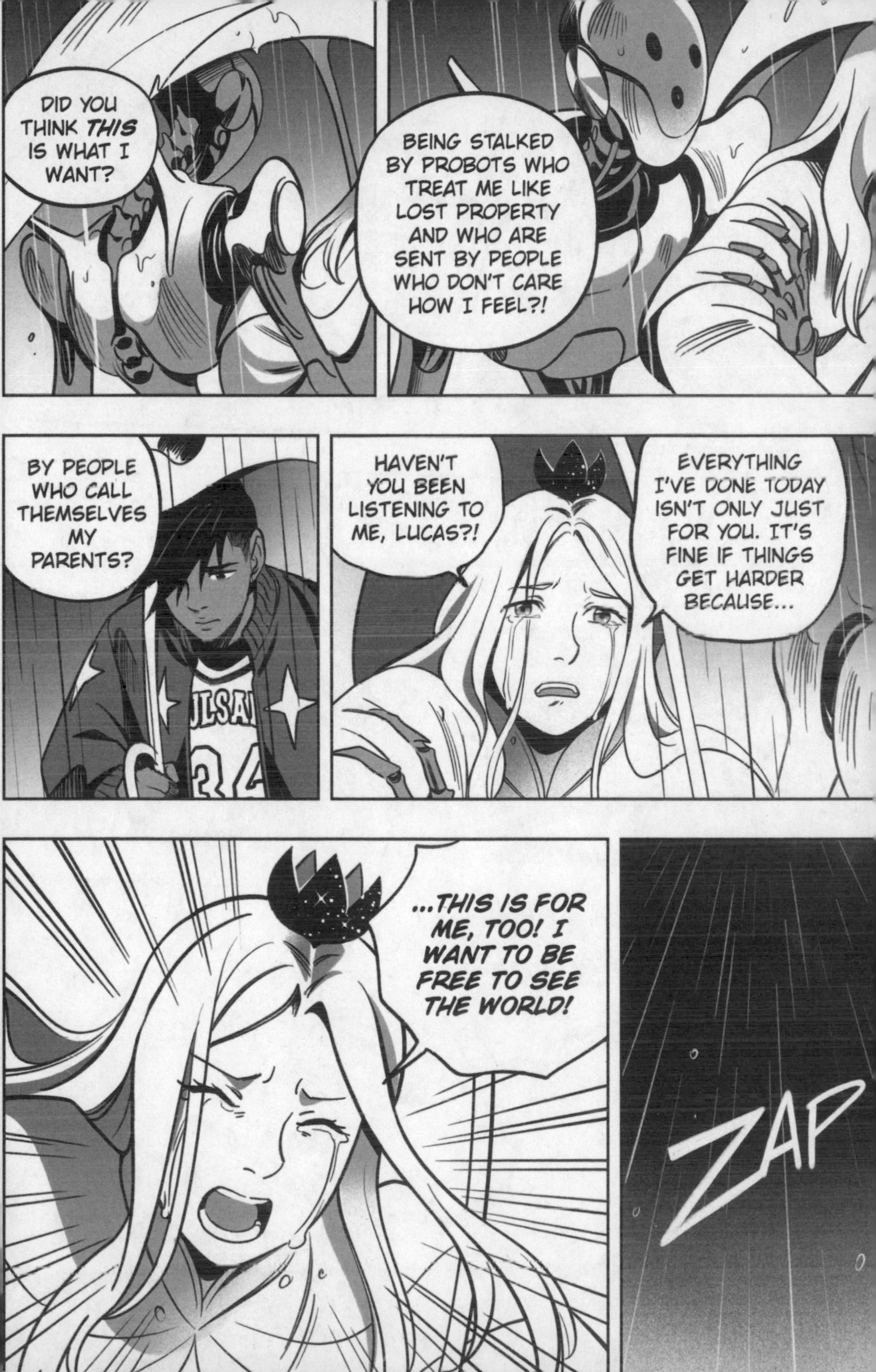
DID YOU THINK THIS IS WHAT I WANT?
BEING STALKED BY PROBOTS WHO TREAT ME LIKE LOST PROPERTY AND WHO ARE SENT BY PEOPLE WHO DON'T CARE HOW I FEEL?!
BY PEOPLE WHO CALL THEMSELVES MY PARENTS?
HAVEN'T YOU BEEN LISTENING TO ME, LUCAS?!
EVERYTHING I'VE DONE TODAY ISN'T ONLY JUST FOR YOU. IT'S FINE IF THINGS GET HARDER BECAUSE...
...THIS IS FOR ME, TOO! I WANT TO BE FREE TO SEE THE WORLD!
ZAP

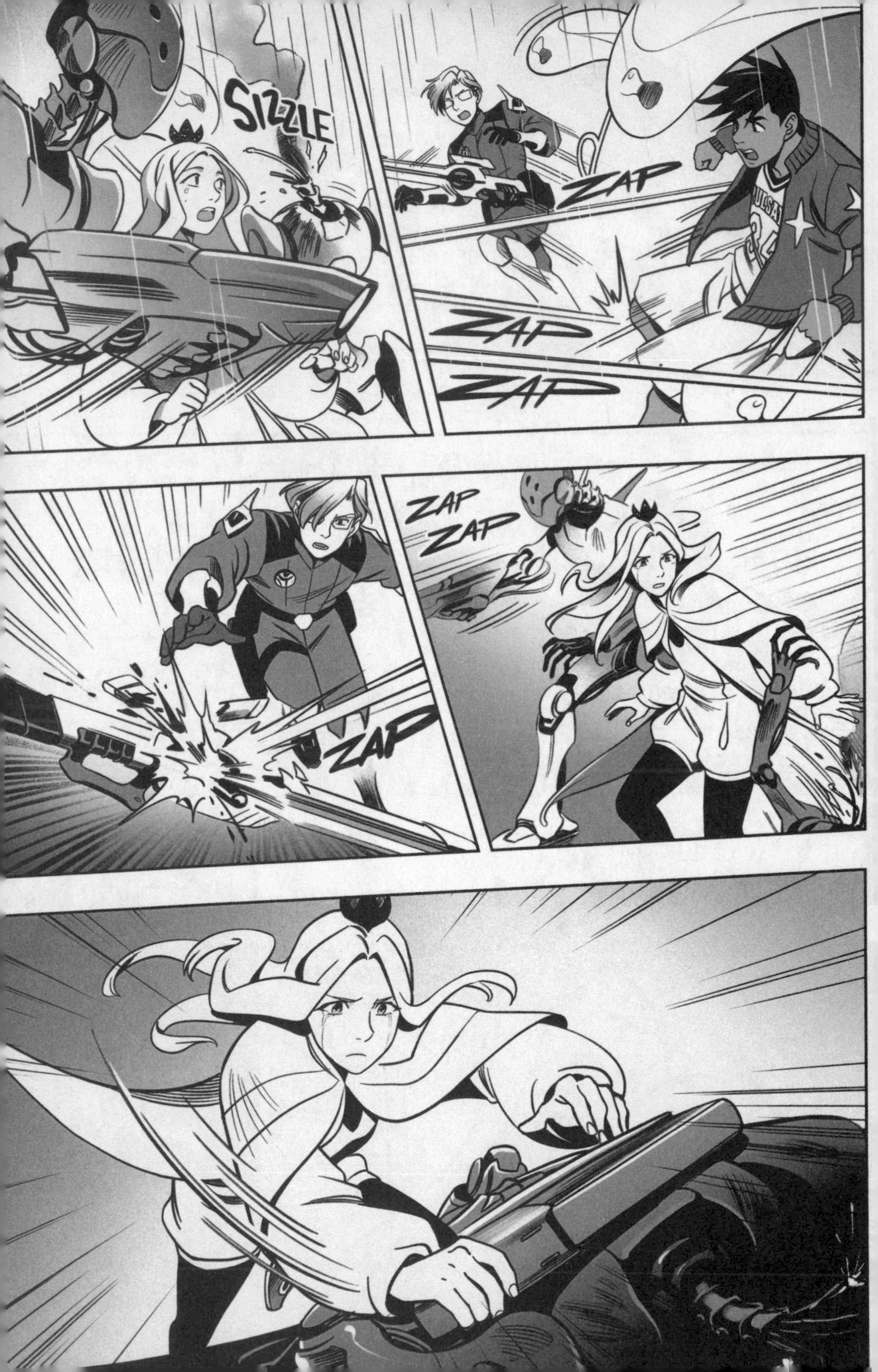
SIZZLE
ZAP
ZAP
ZAP
ZAP
ZAP
ZAP

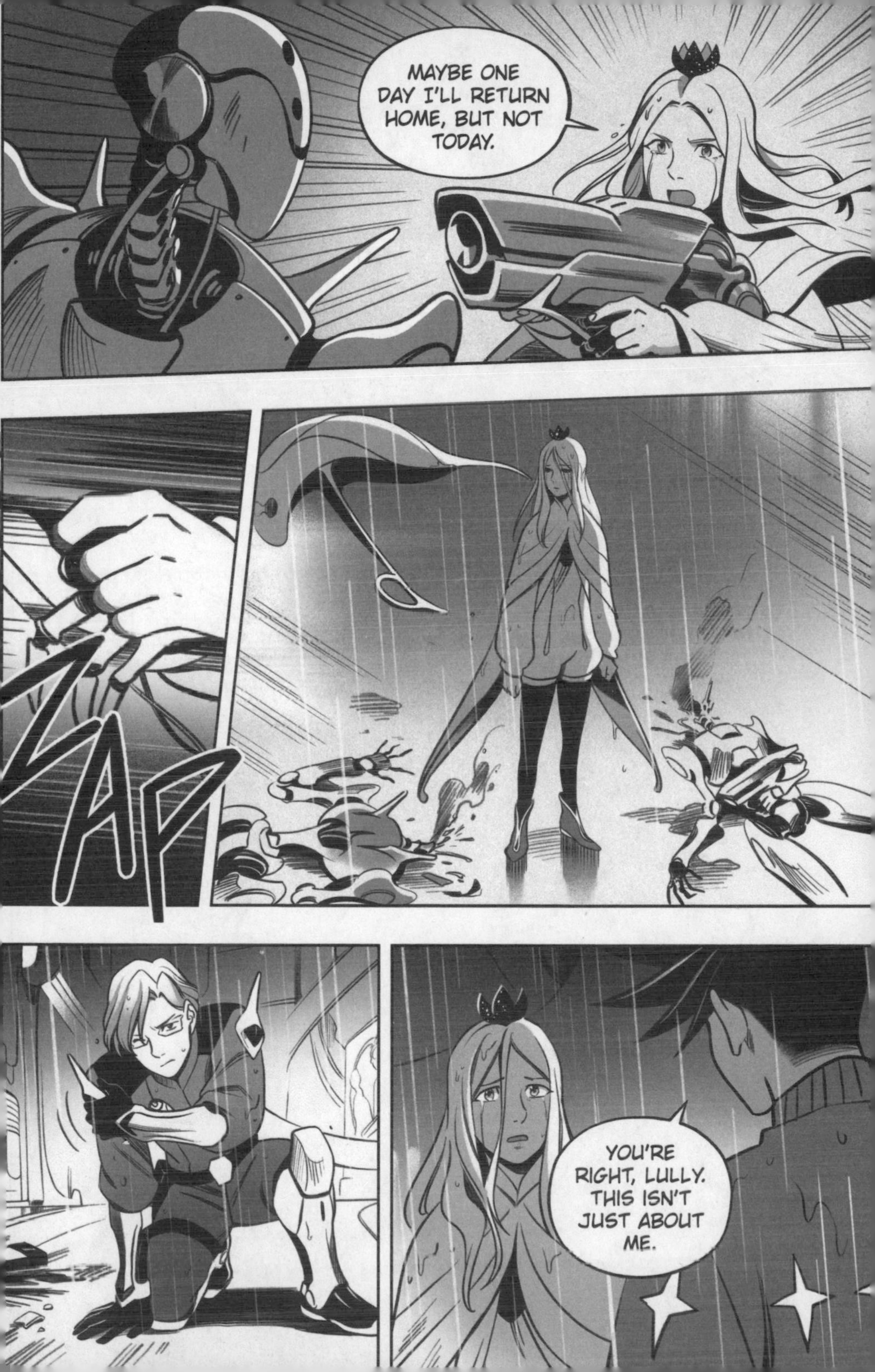
MAYBE ONE DAY I'LL RETURN HOME, BUT NOT TODAY.
ZAP
YOU'RE RIGHT, LULLY. THIS ISN'T JUST ABOUT ME.

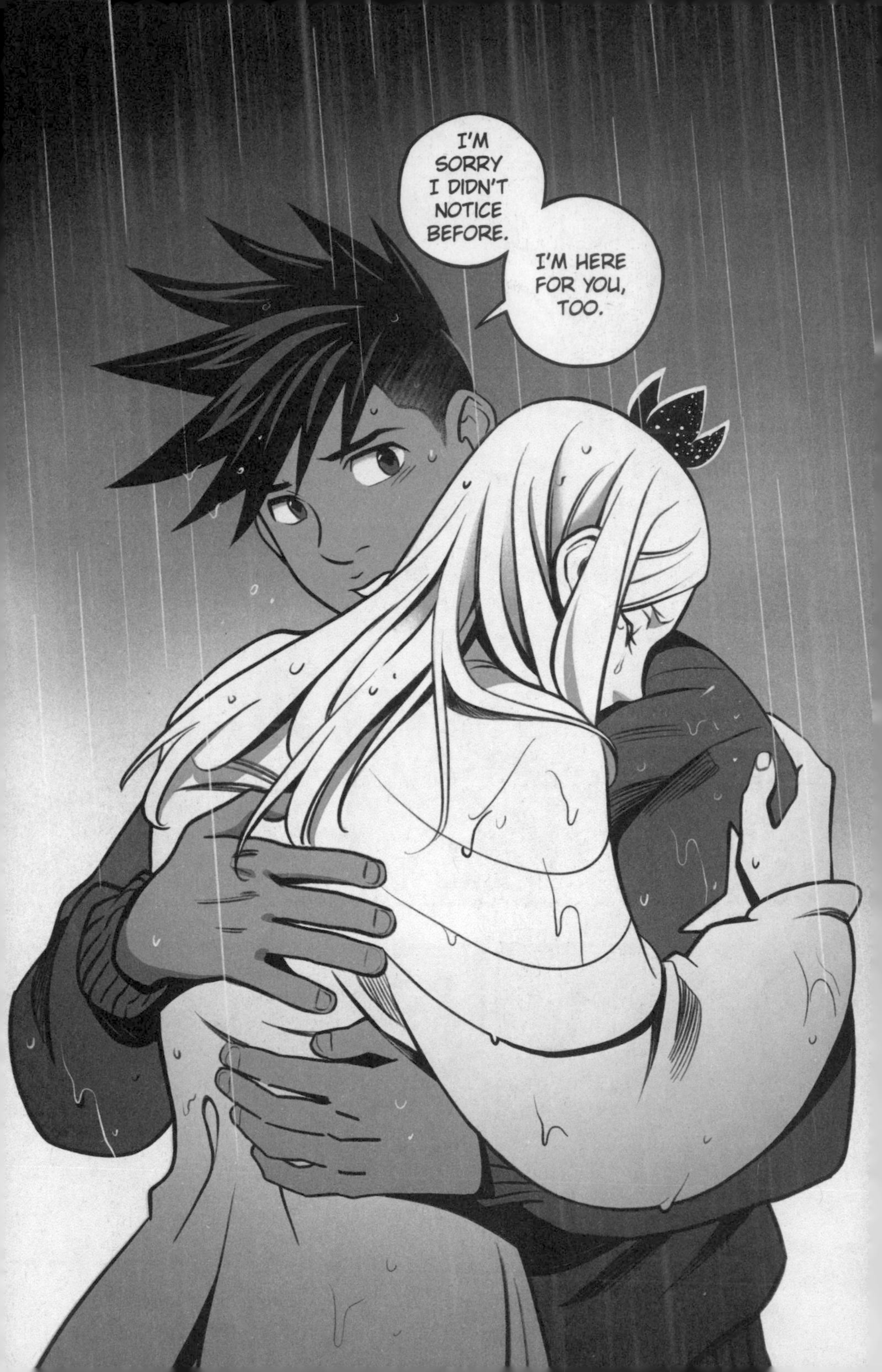
I'M SORRY I DIDN'T NOTICE BEFORE.
I'M HERE FOR YOU, TOO.

WORLD
PIECE

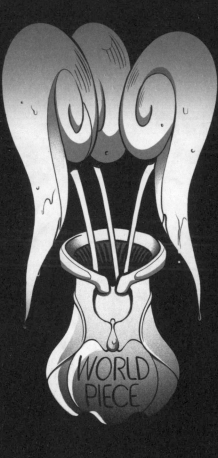

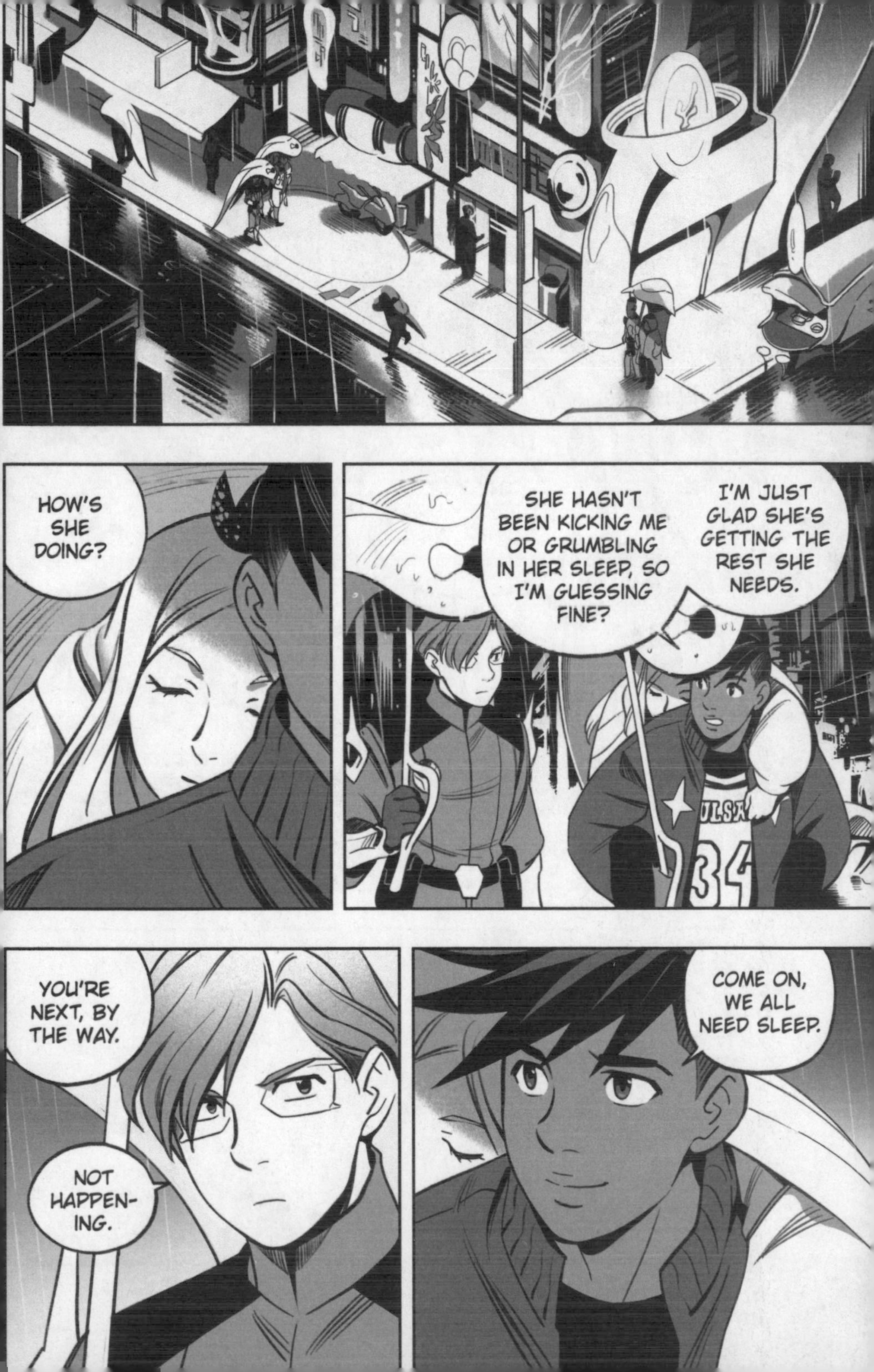
HOW'S SHE DOING?
SHE HASN'T BEEN KICKING ME OR GRUMBLING IN HER SLEEP, SO I'M GUESSING FINE?
I'M JUST GLAD SHE'S GETTING THE REST SHE NEEDS.
YOU'RE NEXT, BY THE WAY.
NOT HAPPEN-ING.
COME ON, WE ALL NEED SLEEP.

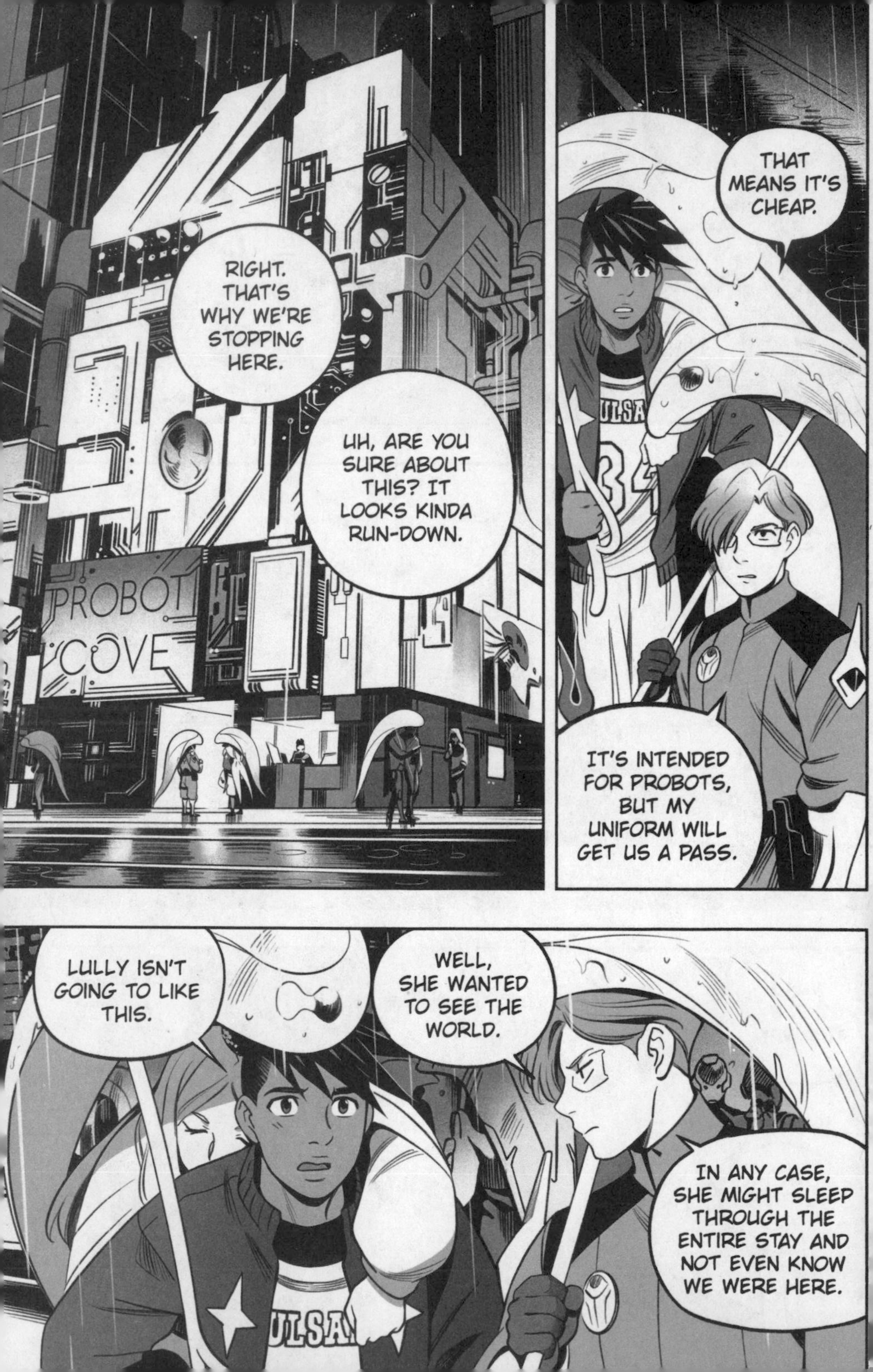
RIGHT. THAT'S WHY WE'RE STOPPING HERE.
UH, ARE YOU SURE ABOUT THIS? IT LOOKS KINDA RUN-DOWN.
PROBOT COVE
THAT MEANS IT'S CHEAP.
IT'S INTENDED FOR PROBOTS, BUT MY UNIFORM WILL GET US A PASS.
LULLY ISN'T GOING TO LIKE THIS.
WELL, SHE WANTED TO SEE THE WORLD.
IN ANY CASE, SHE MIGHT SLEEP THROUGH THE ENTIRE STAY AND NOT EVEN KNOW WE WERE HERE.

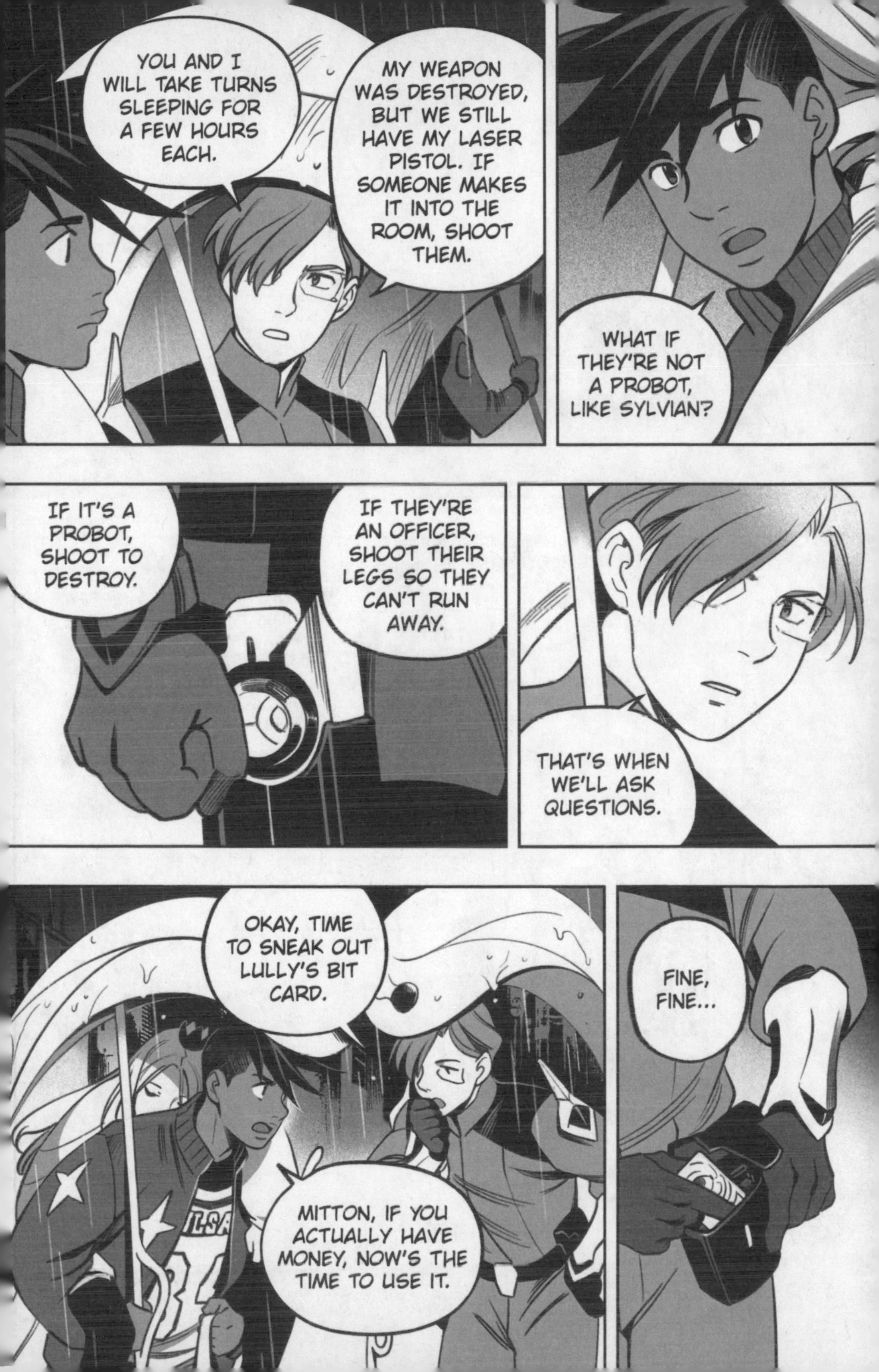
YOU AND I WILL TAKE TURNS SLEEPING FOR A FEW HOURS EACH.
MY WEAPON WAS DESTROYED, BUT WE STILL HAVE MY LASER PISTOL. IF SOMEONE MAKES IT INTO THE ROOM, SHOOT THEM.
WHAT IF THEY'RE NOT A PROBOT, LIKE SYLVIAN?
IF IT'S A PROBOT, SHOOT TO DESTROY.
IF THEY'RE AN OFFICER, SHOOT THEIR LEGS SO THEY CAN'T RUN AWAY.
THAT'S WHEN WE'LL ASK QUESTIONS.
OKAY, TIME TO SNEAK OUT LULLY'S BIT CARD.
MITTON, IF YOU ACTUALLY HAVE MONEY, NOW'S THE TIME TO USE IT.
FINE, FINE...

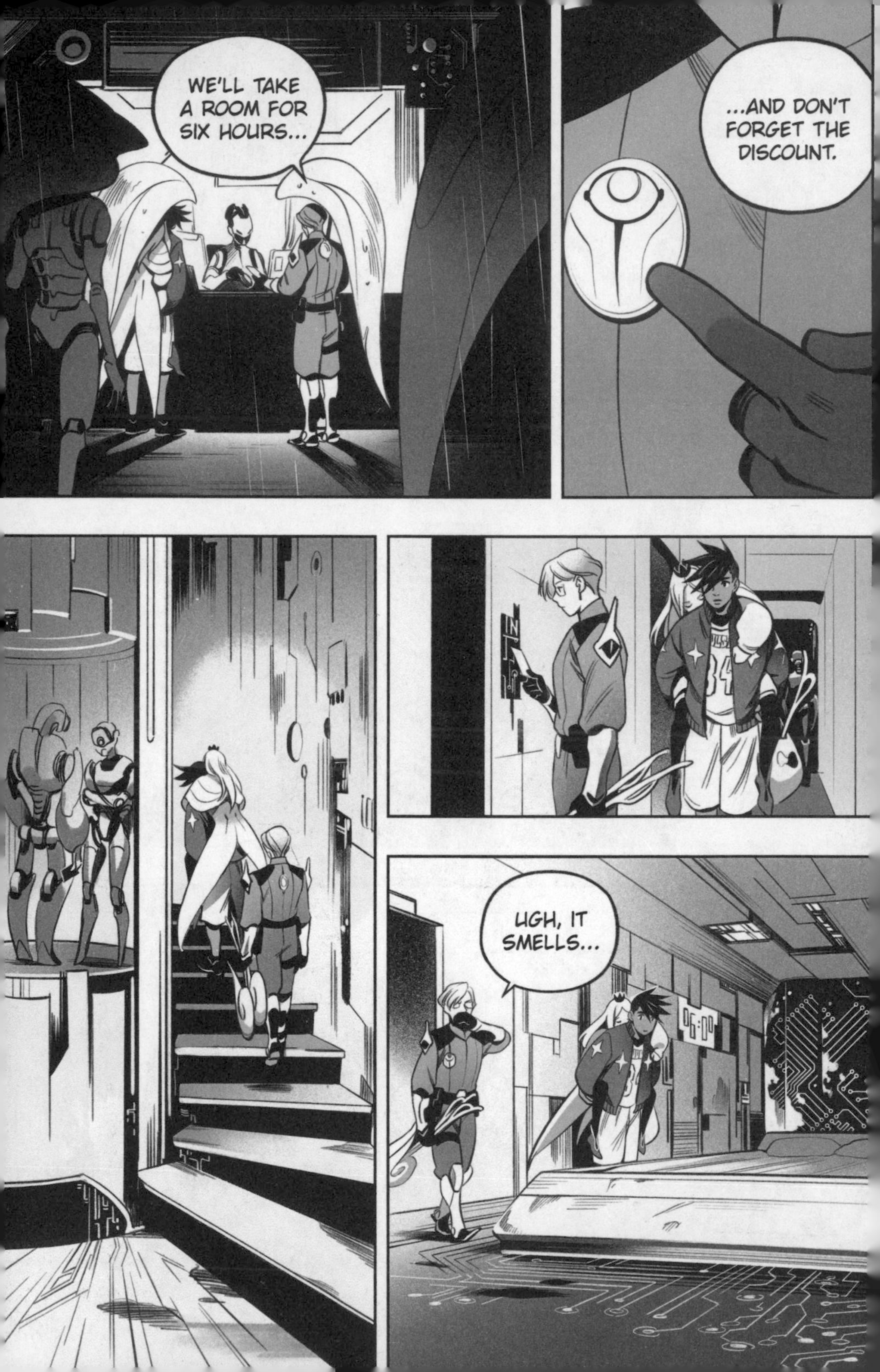
WE'LL TAKE A ROOM FOR SIX HOURS...
...AND DON'T FORGET THE DISCOUNT.
UGH, IT SMELLS...

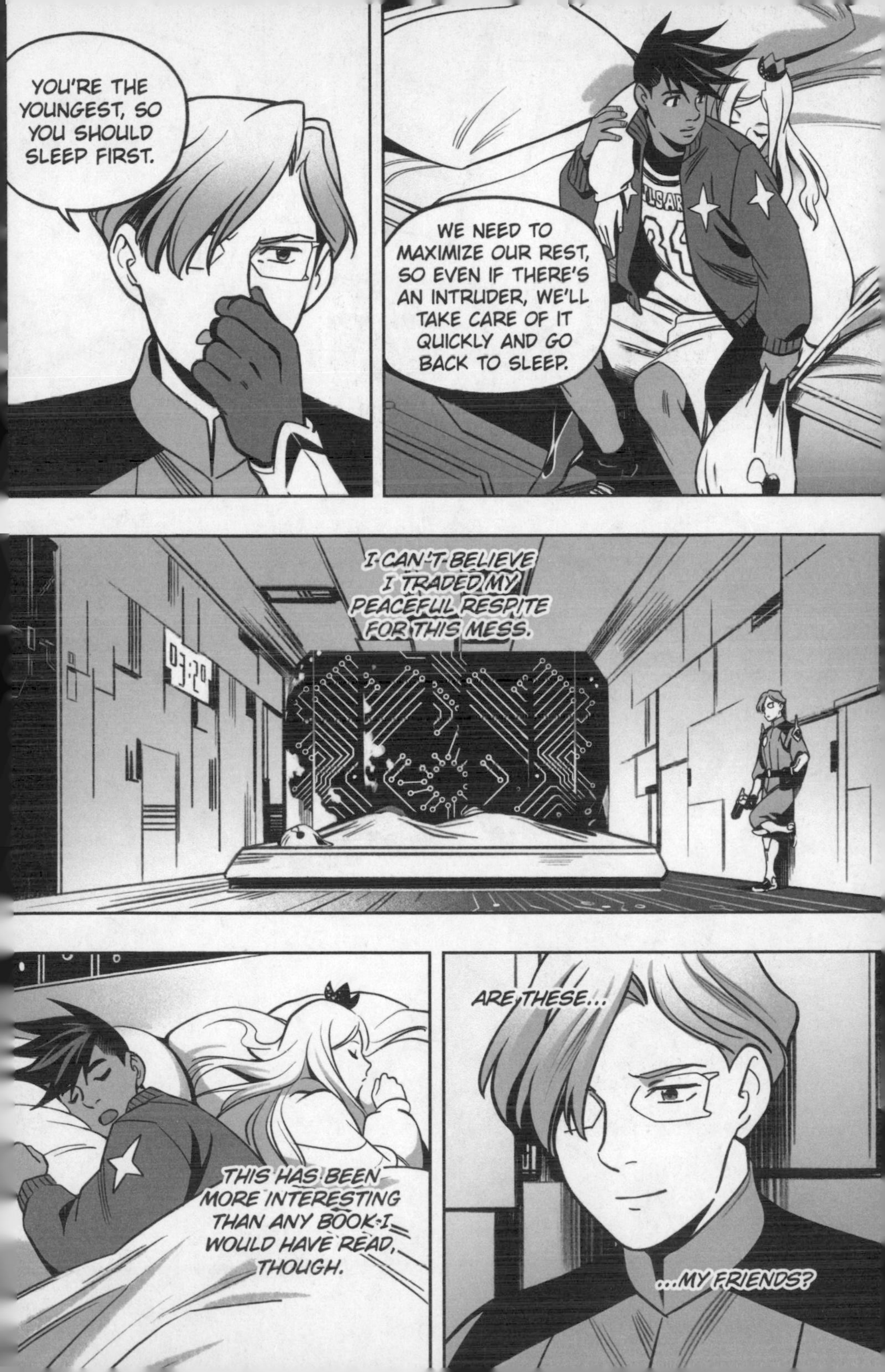
YOU'RE THE YOUNGEST, SO YOU SHOULD SLEEP FIRST.
WE NEED TO MAXIMIZE OUR REST, SO EVEN IF THERE'S AN INTRUDER, WE'LL TAKE CARE OF IT QUICKLY AND GO BACK TO SLEEP.
03:20
I CAN'T BELIEVE I TRADED MY PEACEFUL RESPITE FOR THIS MESS.
THIS HAS BEEN MORE INTERESTING THAN ANY BOOK I WOULD HAVE READ, THOUGH.
ARE THESE...
...MY FRIENDS?

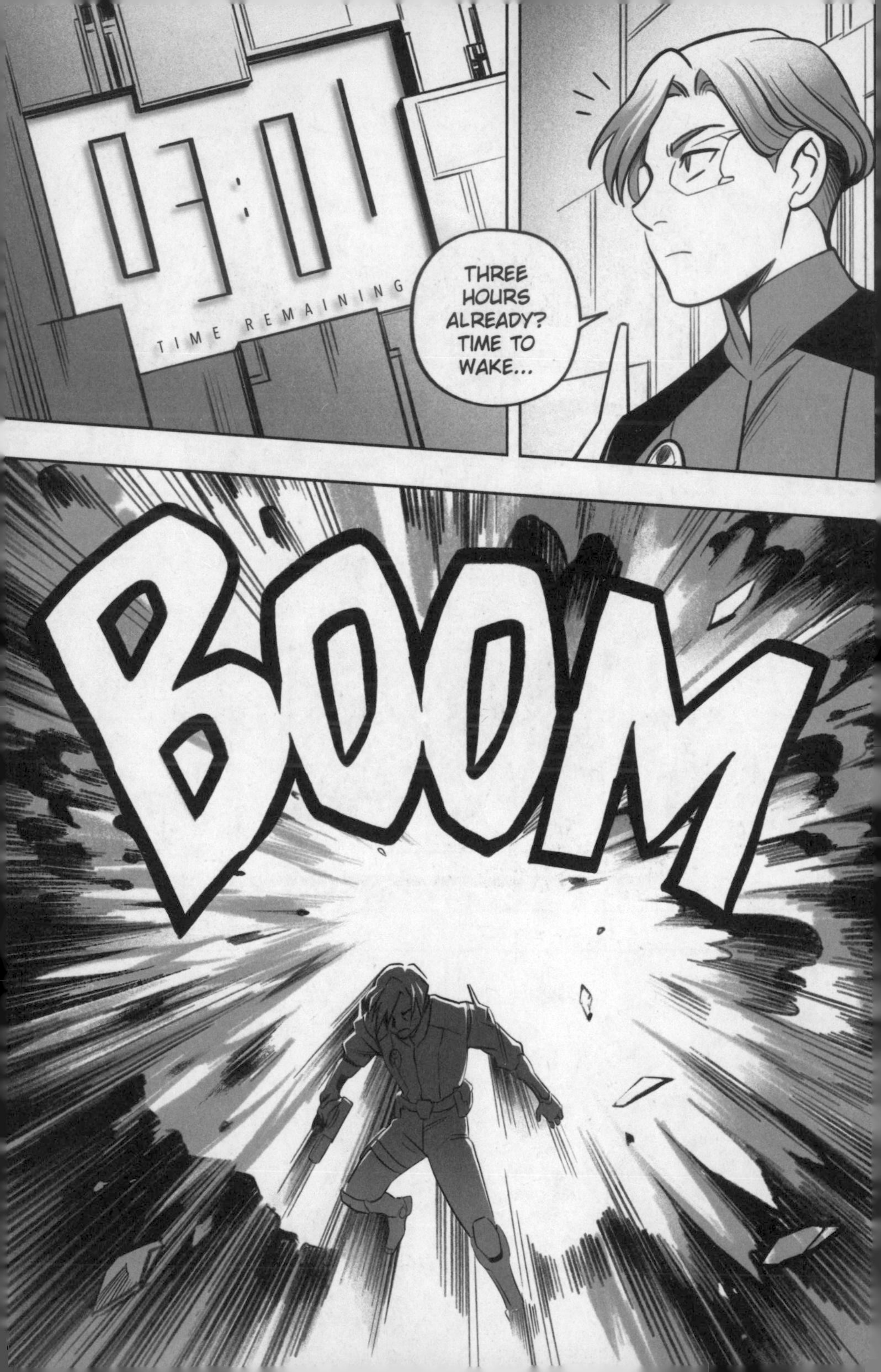
3:01
TIME REMAINING
THREE HOURS ALREADY? TIME TO WAKE...
BOOM

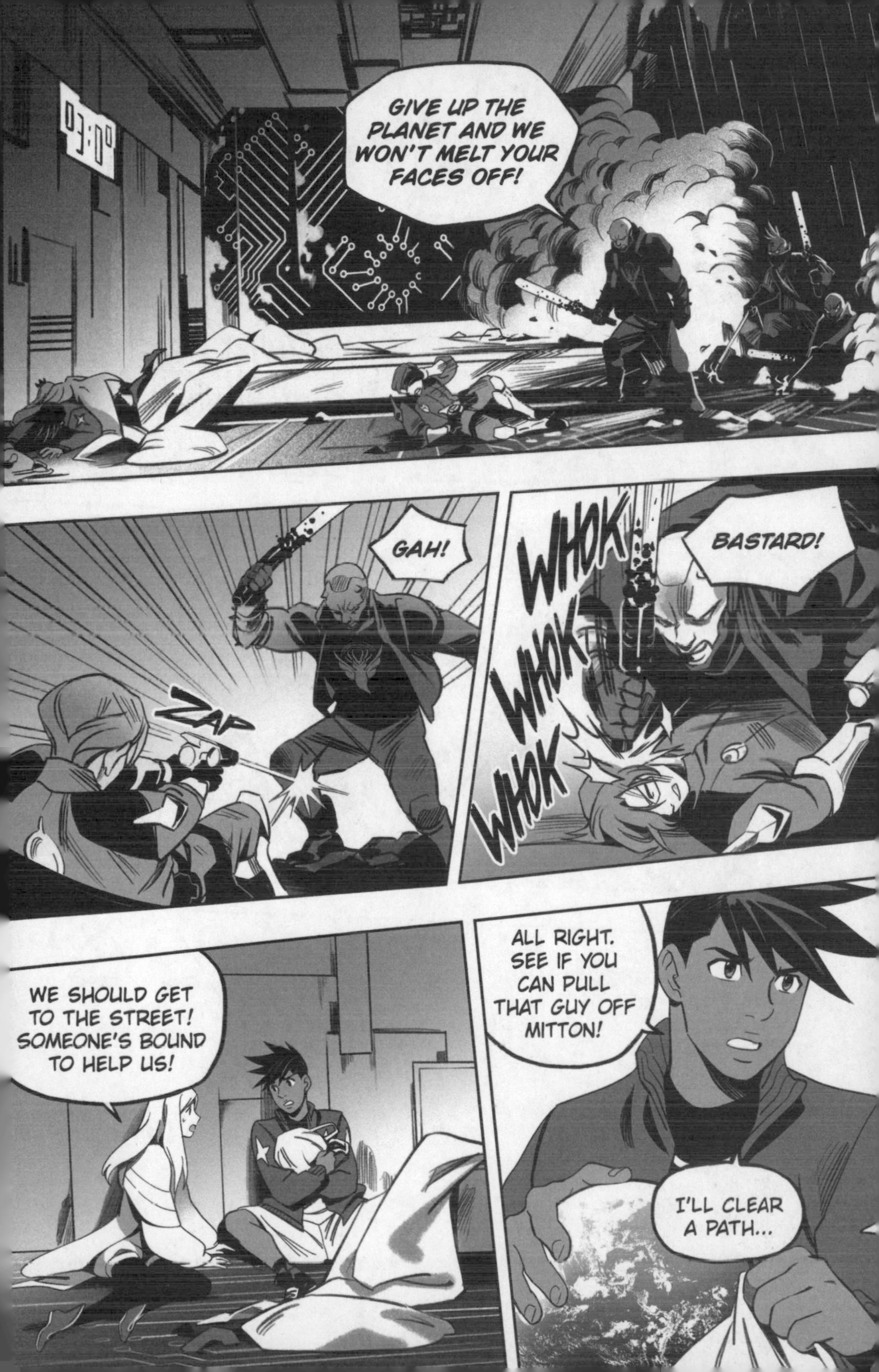
03:00
GIVE UP THE PLANET AND WE WON'T MELT YOUR FACES OFF!
GAH!
ZAP
WHOK WHOK WHOK
BASTARD!
WE SHOULD GET TO THE STREET! SOMEONE'S BOUND TO HELP US!
ALL RIGHT. SEE IF YOU CAN PULL THAT GUY OFF MITTON!
I'LL CLEAR A PATH...

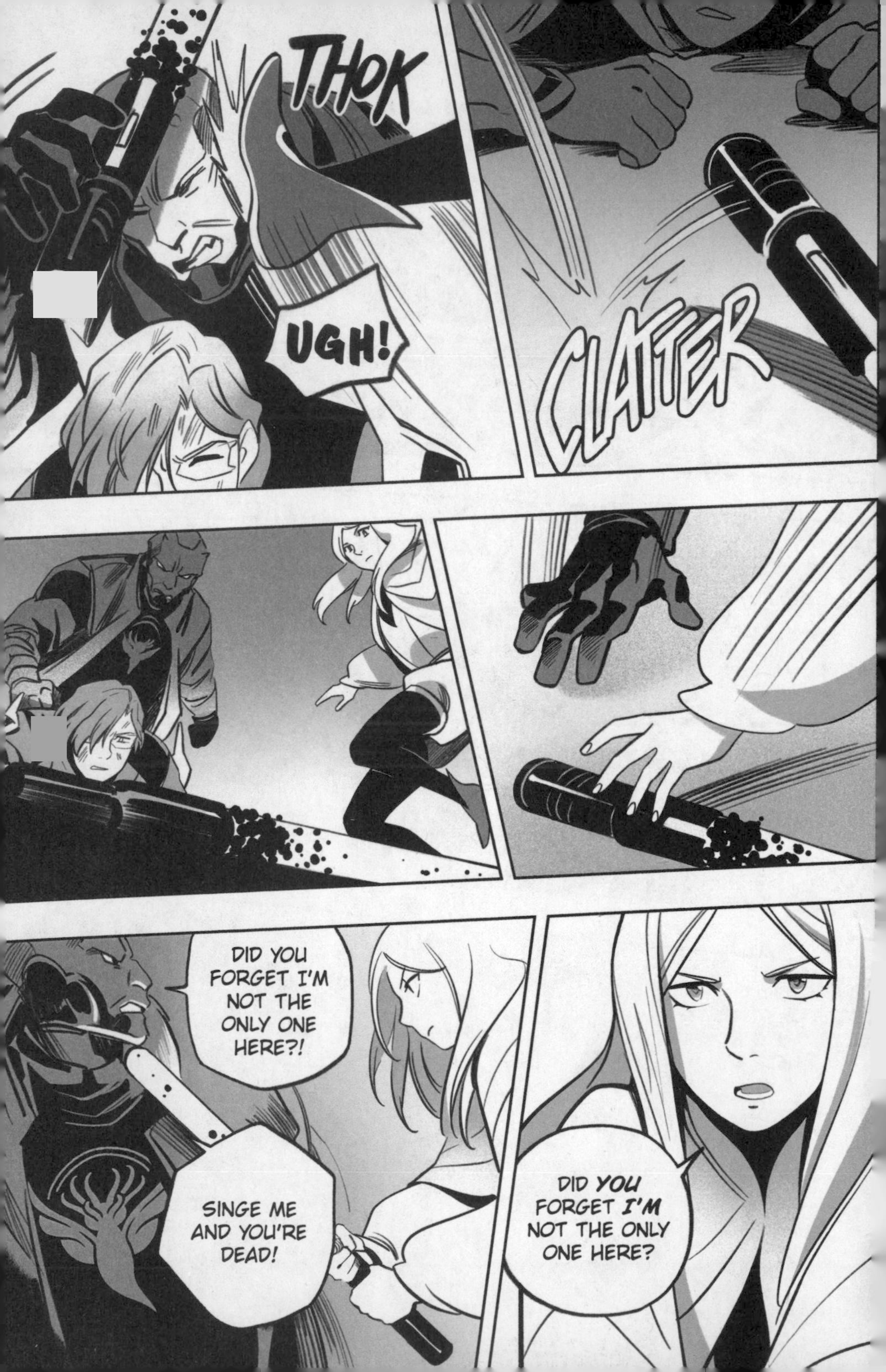
THOK
UGH!
CLATTER
DID YOU FORGET I'M NOT THE ONLY ONE HERE?!
SINGE ME AND YOU'RE DEAD!
DID *YOU* FORGET *I'M* NOT THE ONLY ONE HERE?

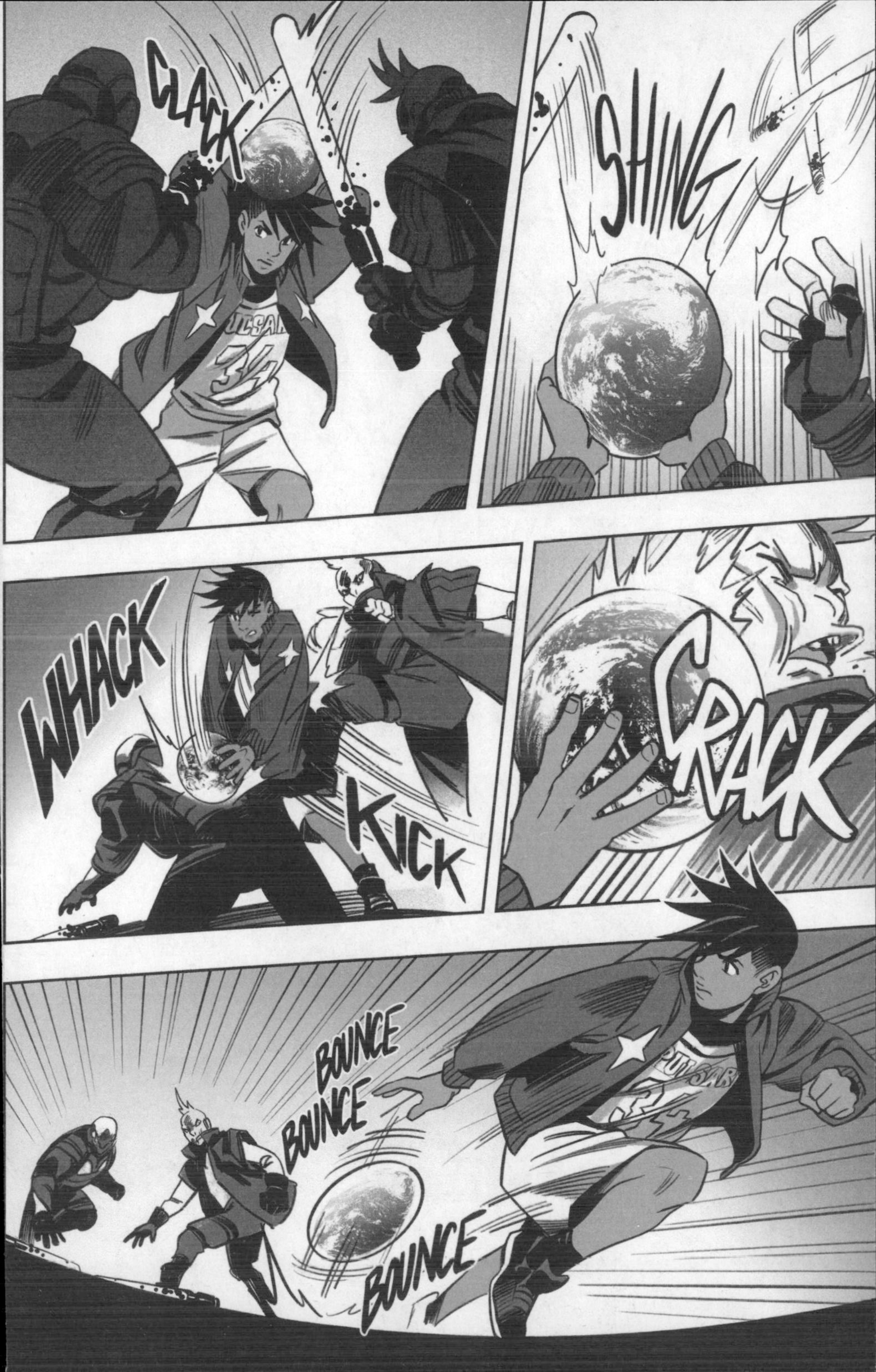
CLACK
SHING
WHACK
KICK
CRACK
BOUNCE
BOUNCE
BOUNCE

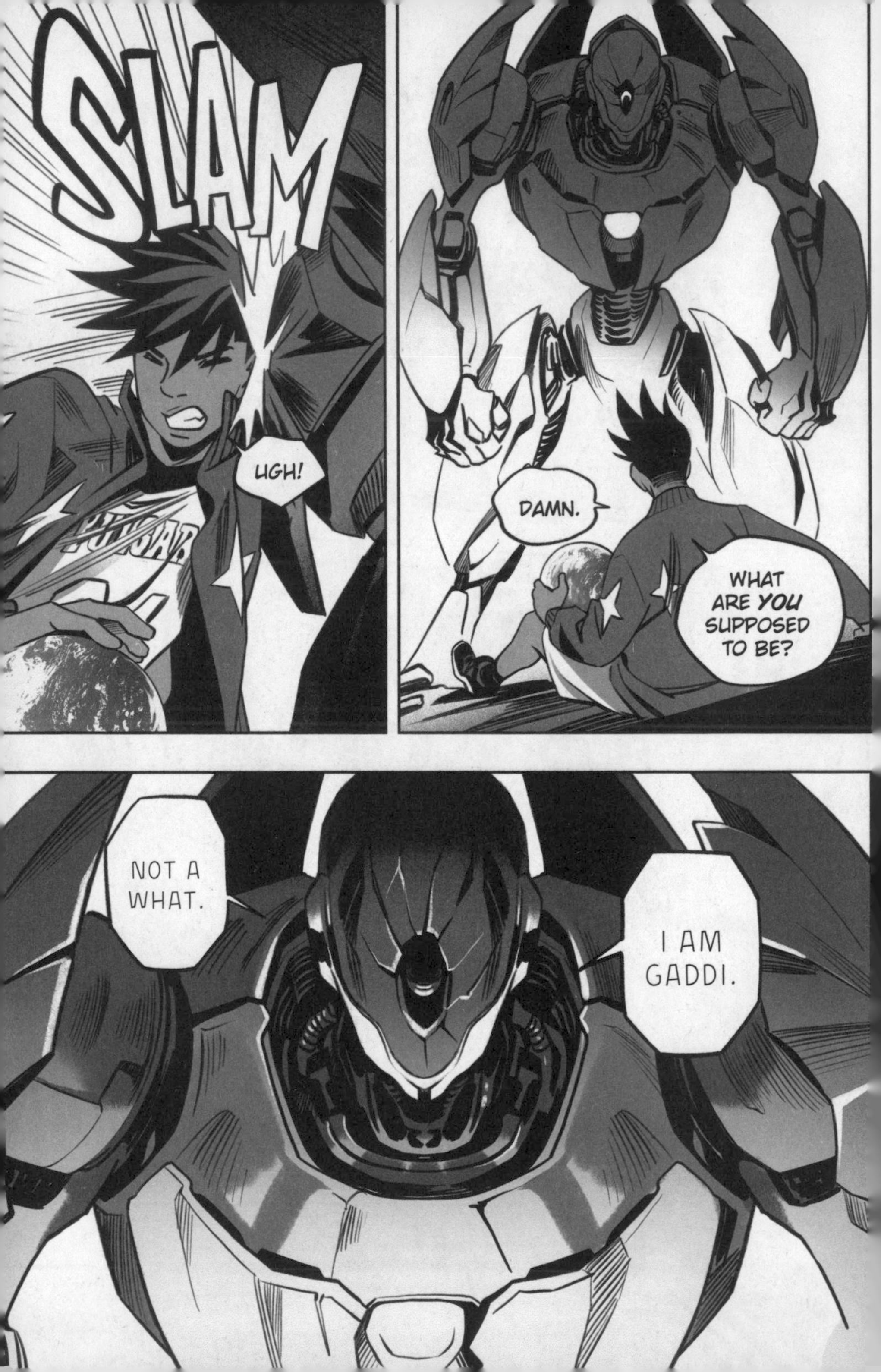
SLAM
UGH!
DAMN.
WHAT ARE *YOU* SUPPOSED TO BE?
NOT A WHAT.
I AM GADDI.

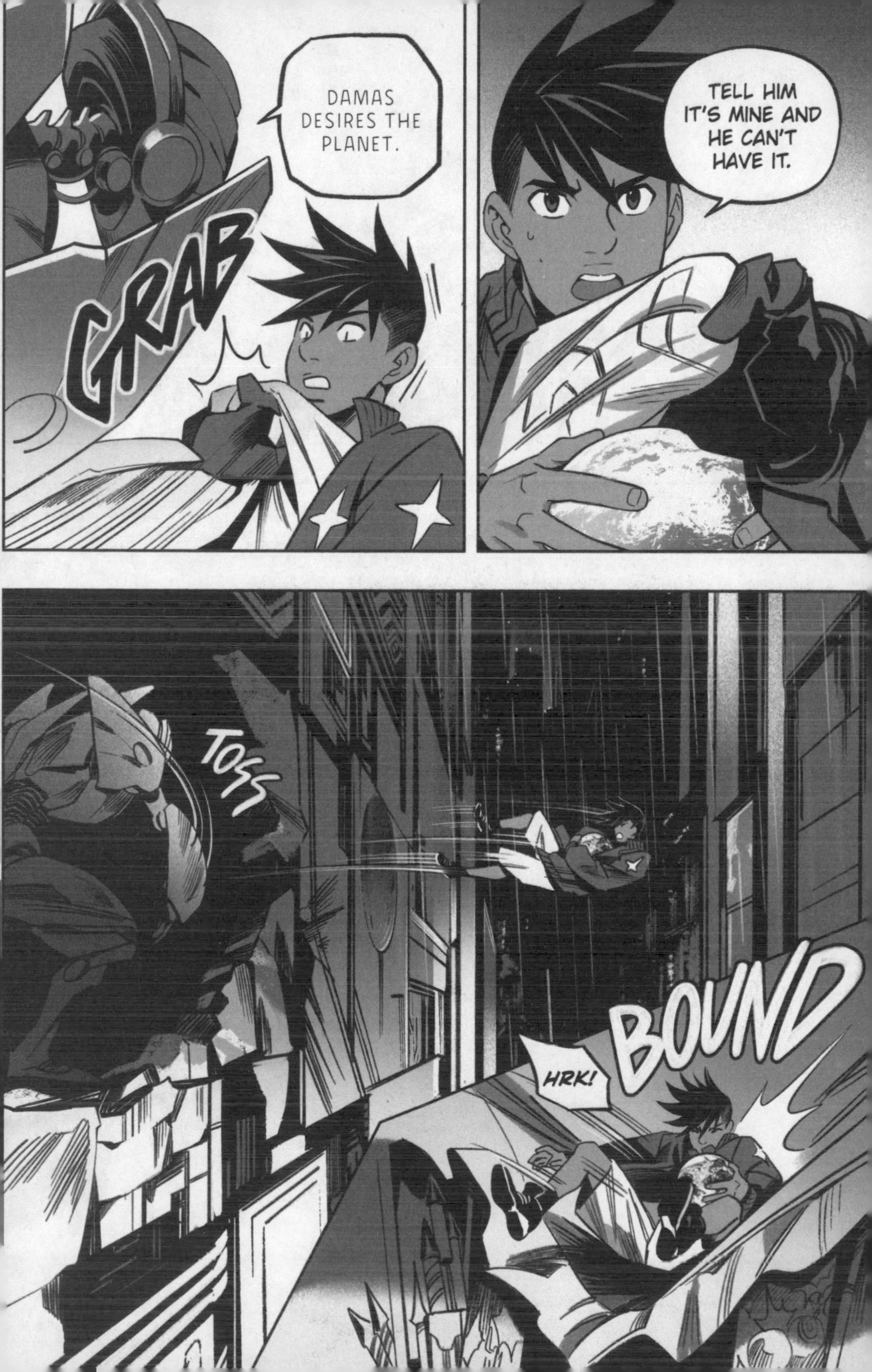
DAMAS DESIRES THE PLANET.
GRAB
TELL HIM IT'S MINE AND HE CAN'T HAVE IT.
TOSS
HRK!
BOUND

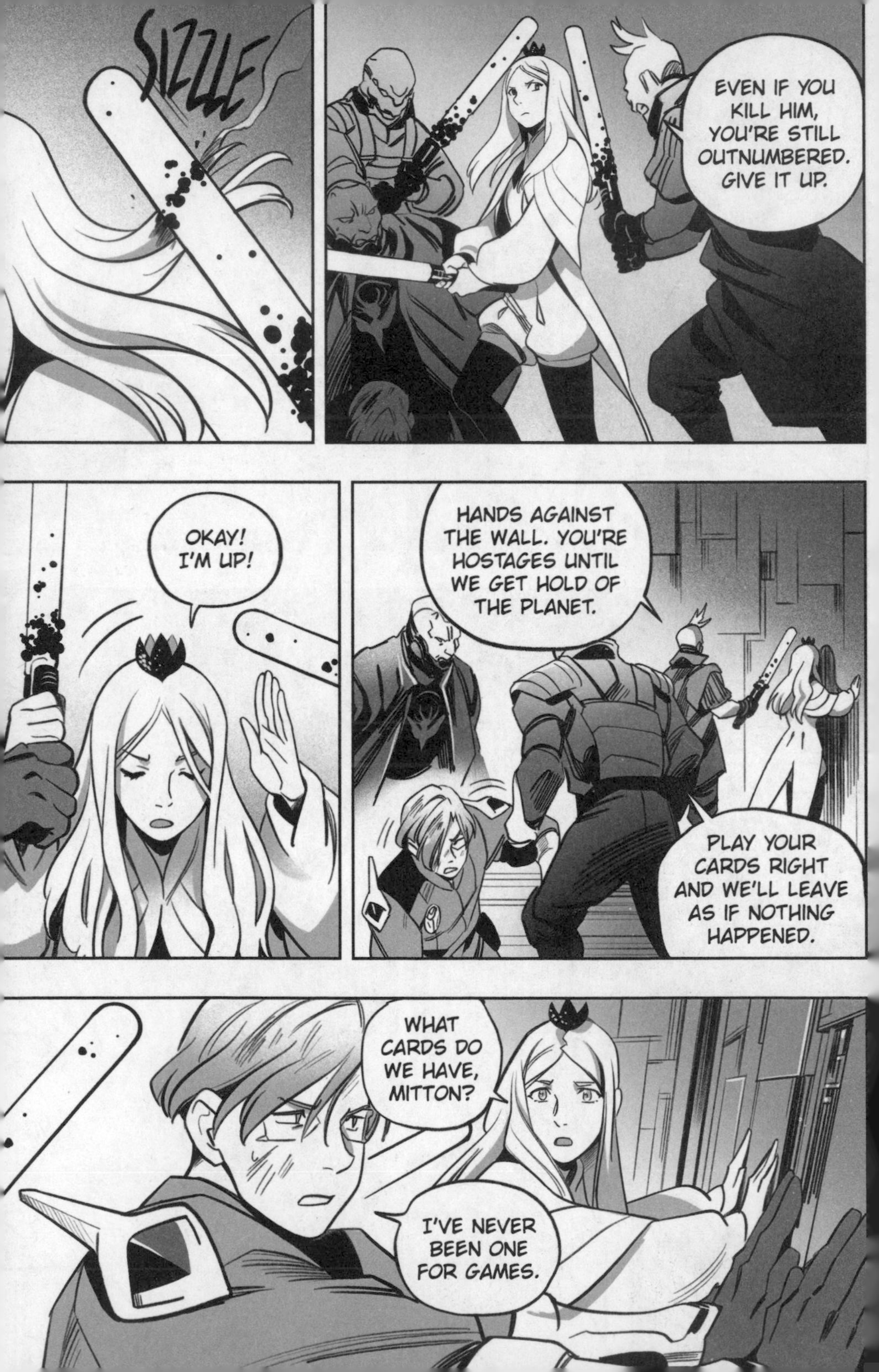
SIZZLE
EVEN IF YOU KILL HIM, YOU'RE STILL OUTNUMBERED. GIVE IT UP.
OKAY! I'M UP!
HANDS AGAINST THE WALL. YOU'RE HOSTAGES UNTIL WE GET HOLD OF THE PLANET.
PLAY YOUR CARDS RIGHT AND WE'LL LEAVE AS IF NOTHING HAPPENED.
WHAT CARDS DO WE HAVE, MITTON?
I'VE NEVER BEEN ONE FOR GAMES.

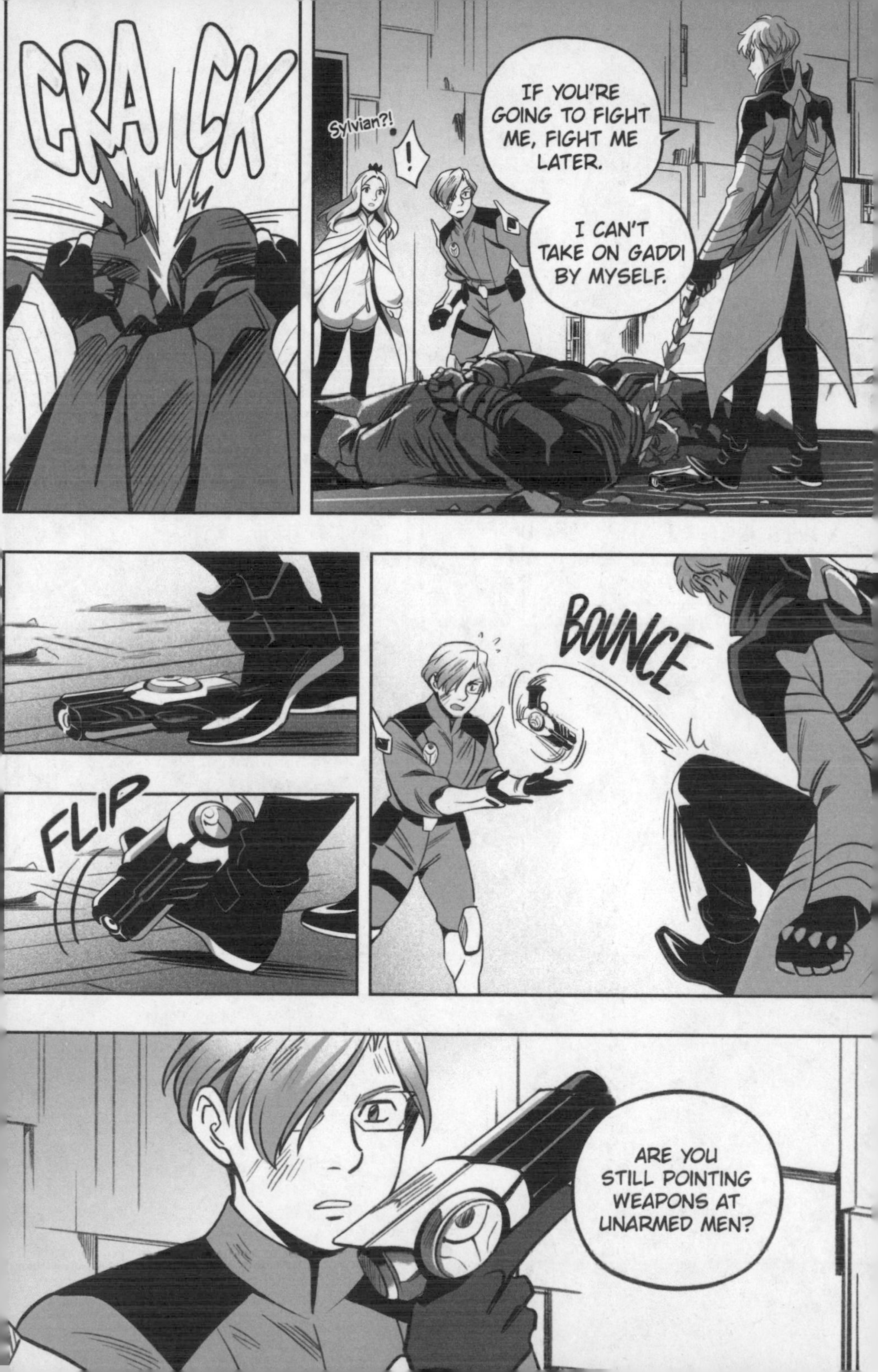
CRACK
Sylvian?!
!
IF YOU'RE GOING TO FIGHT ME, FIGHT ME LATER.
I CAN'T TAKE ON GADDI BY MYSELF.
FLIP
BOUNCE
ARE YOU STILL POINTING WEAPONS AT UNARMED MEN?

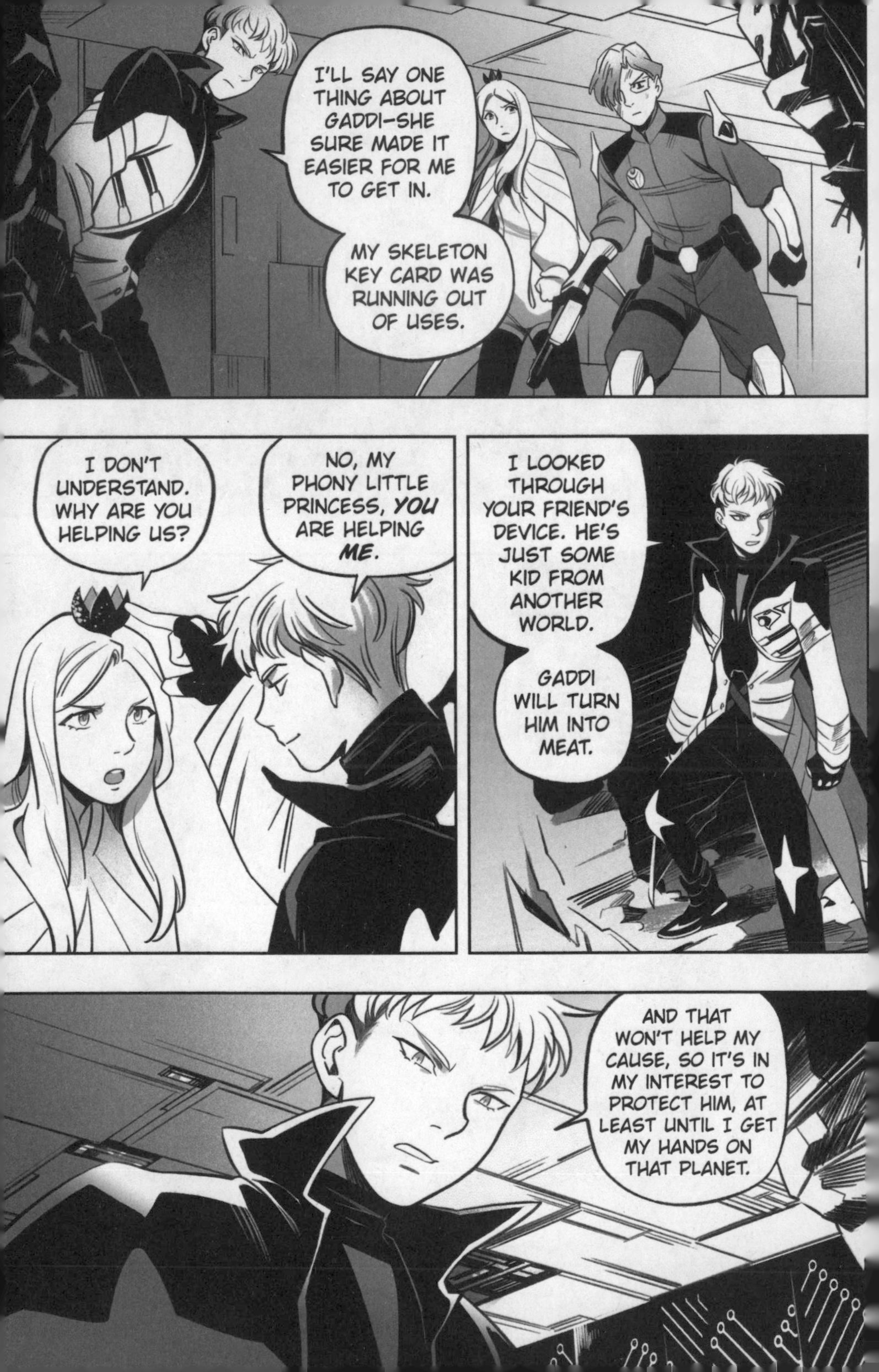
I'LL SAY ONE THING ABOUT GADDI—SHE SURE MADE IT EASIER FOR ME TO GET IN.
MY SKELETON KEY CARD WAS RUNNING OUT OF USES.
I DON'T UNDERSTAND. WHY ARE YOU HELPING US?
NO, MY PHONY LITTLE PRINCESS, *YOU* ARE HELPING ***ME***.
I LOOKED THROUGH YOUR FRIEND'S DEVICE. HE'S JUST SOME KID FROM ANOTHER WORLD.
GADDI WILL TURN HIM INTO MEAT.
AND THAT WON'T HELP MY CAUSE, SO IT'S IN MY INTEREST TO PROTECT HIM, AT LEAST UNTIL I GET MY HANDS ON THAT PLANET.

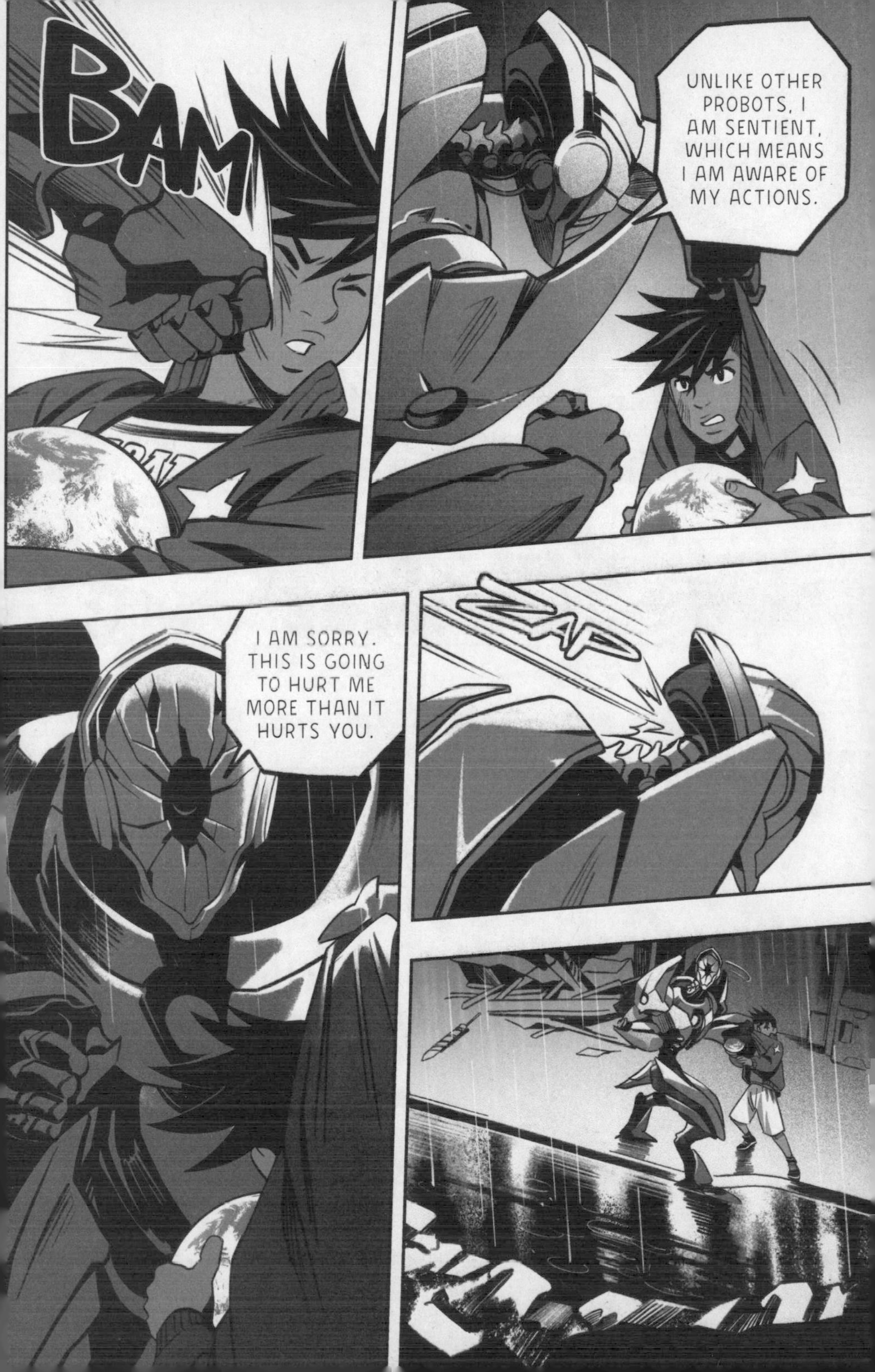
BAM
UNLIKE OTHER PROBOTS, I AM SENTIENT, WHICH MEANS I AM AWARE OF MY ACTIONS.
I AM SORRY. THIS IS GOING TO HURT ME MORE THAN IT HURTS YOU.
ZAP

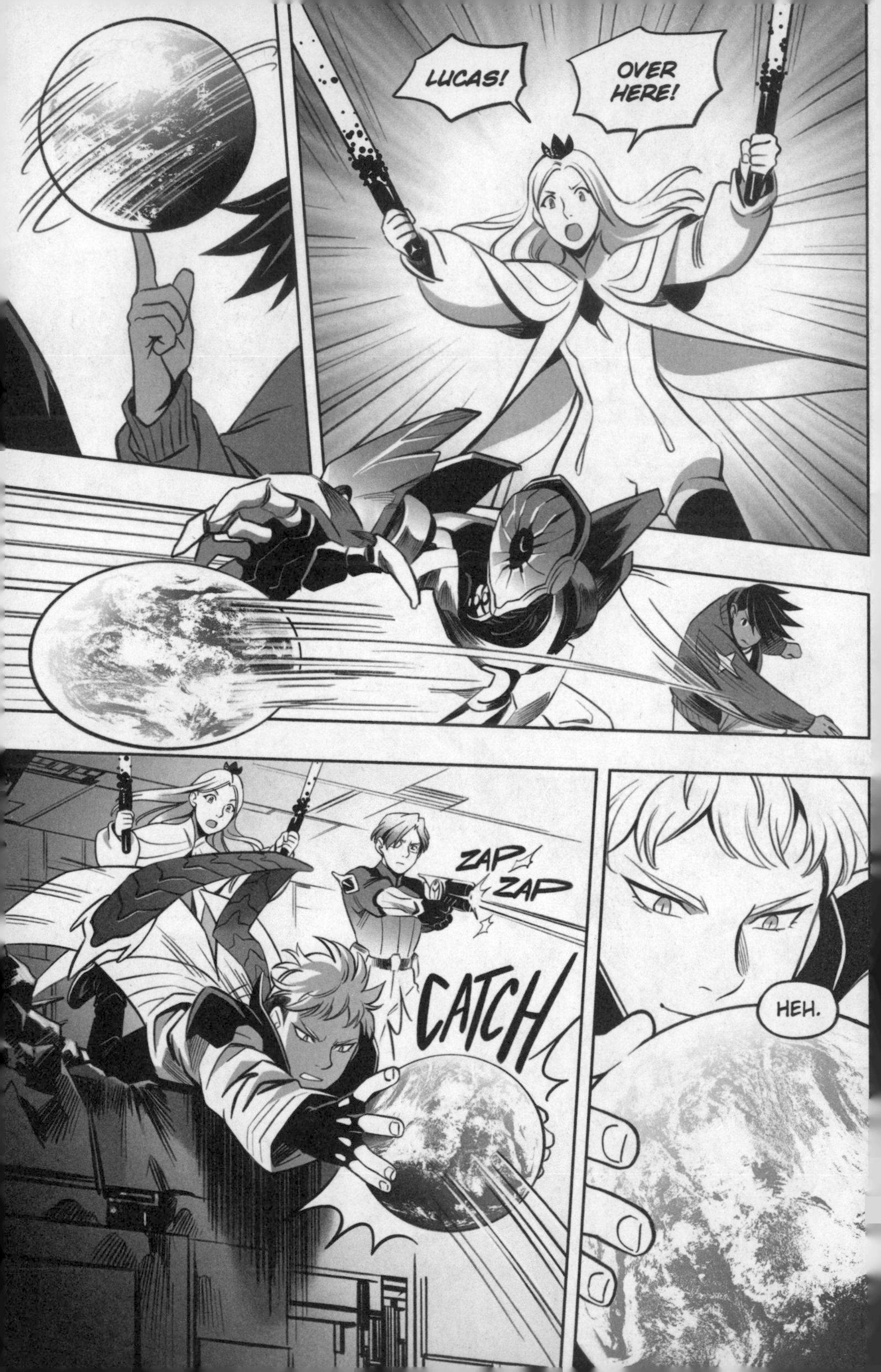
LUCAS!
OVER HERE!
ZAP
ZAP
CATCH
HEH.

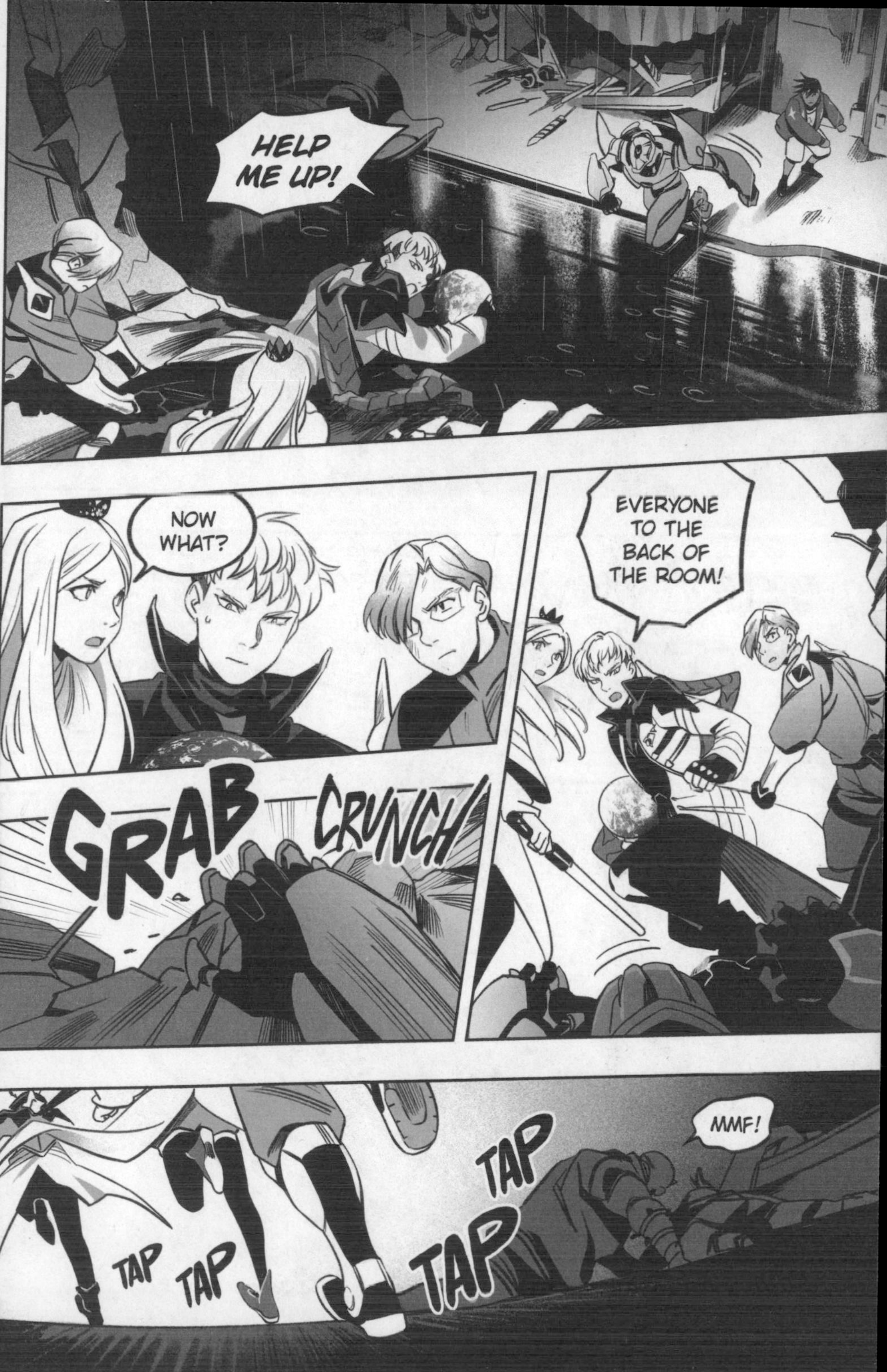
HELP ME UP!
NOW WHAT?
GRAB
CRUNCH
EVERYONE TO THE BACK OF THE ROOM!
TAP
TAP
TAP
TAP
MMF!

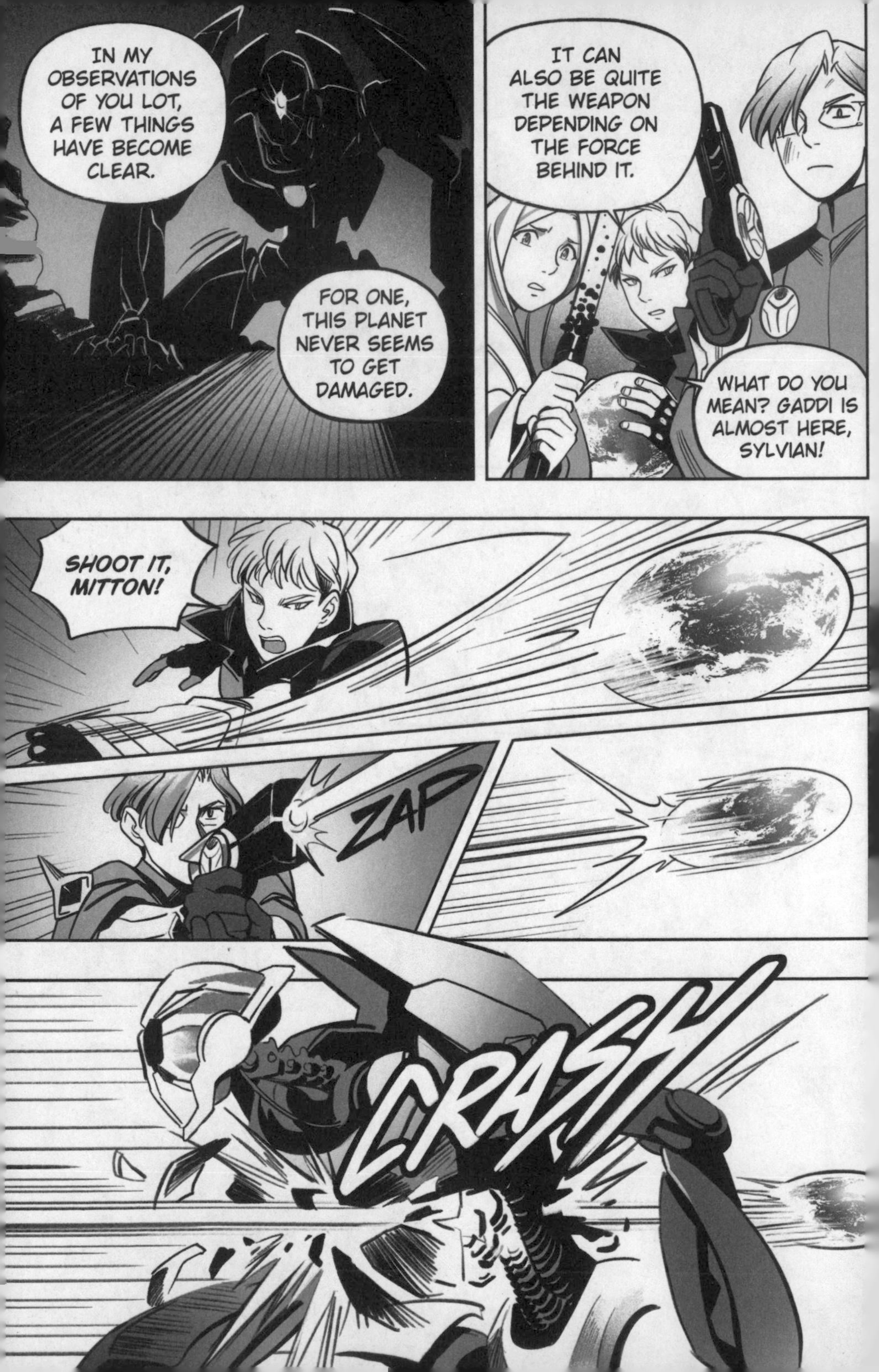
IN MY OBSERVATIONS OF YOU LOT, A FEW THINGS HAVE BECOME CLEAR.
FOR ONE, THIS PLANET NEVER SEEMS TO GET DAMAGED.
IT CAN ALSO BE QUITE THE WEAPON DEPENDING ON THE FORCE BEHIND IT.
WHAT DO YOU MEAN? GADDI IS ALMOST HERE, SYLVIAN!
SHOOT IT, MITTON!
ZAP
CRASH

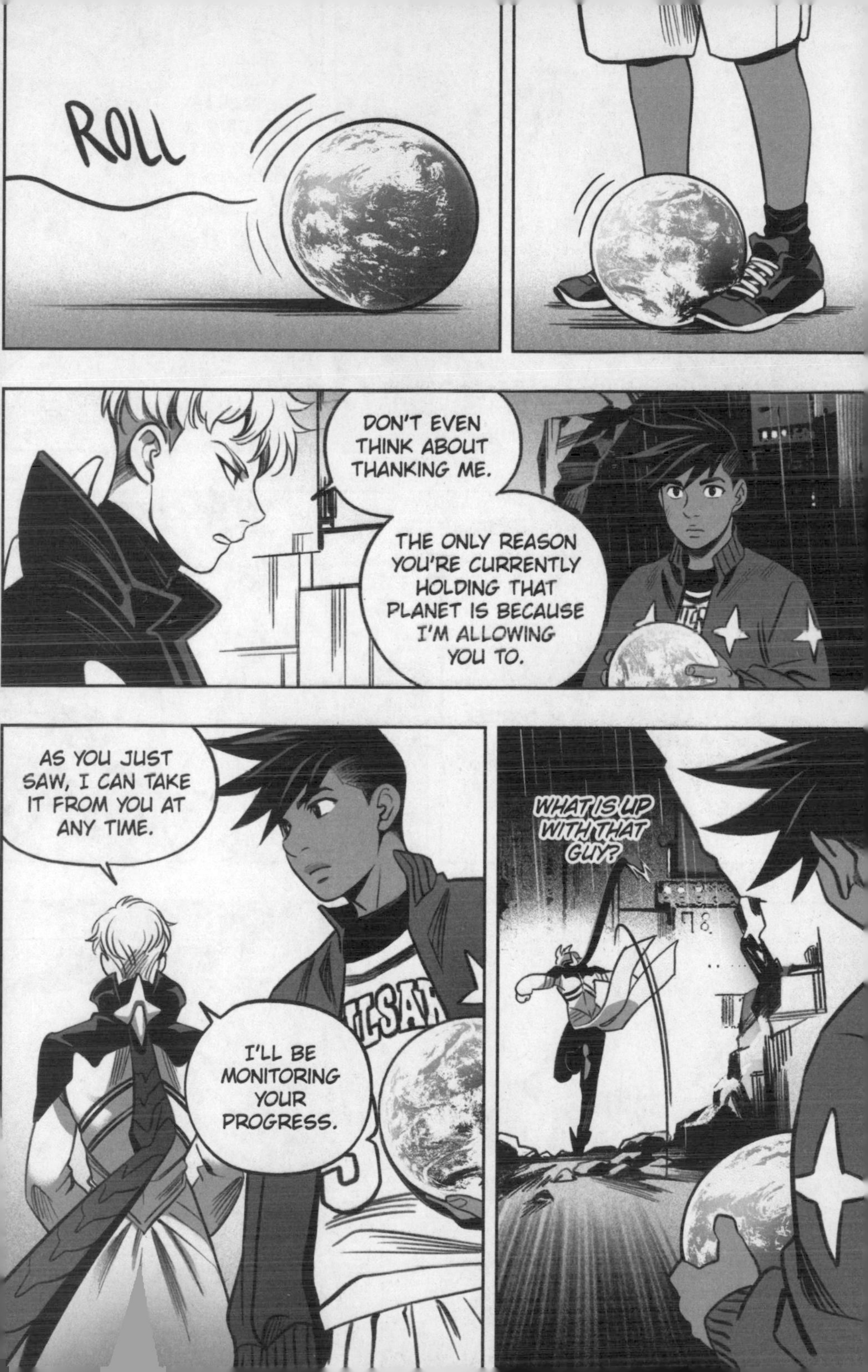
ROLL
DON'T EVEN THINK ABOUT THANKING ME.
THE ONLY REASON YOU'RE CURRENTLY HOLDING THAT PLANET IS BECAUSE I'M ALLOWING YOU TO.
AS YOU JUST SAW, I CAN TAKE IT FROM YOU AT ANY TIME.
I'LL BE MONITORING YOUR PROGRESS.
WHAT IS UP WITH THAT GUY?

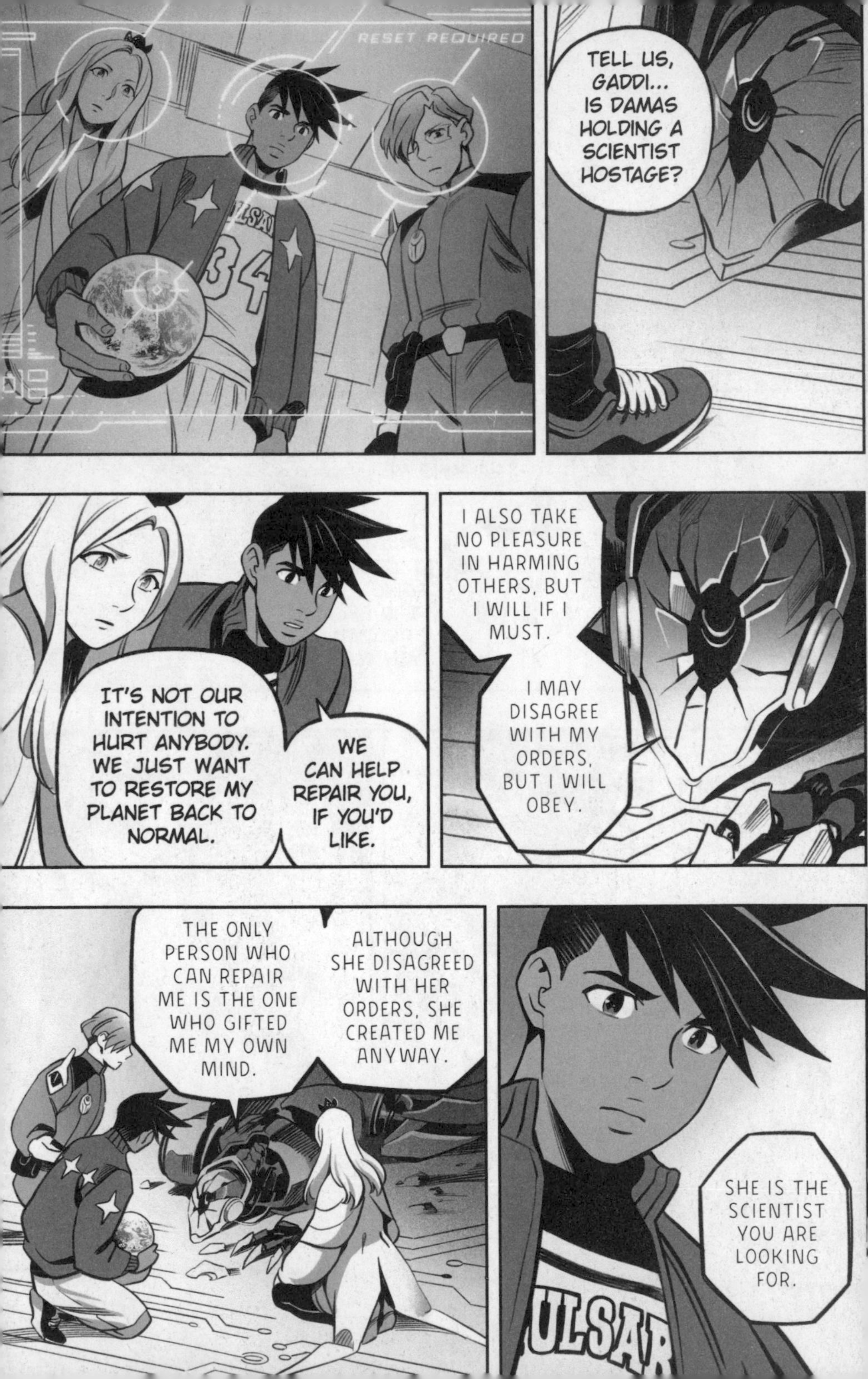
RESET REQUIRED
TELL US, GADDI... IS DAMAS HOLDING A SCIENTIST HOSTAGE?
IT'S NOT OUR INTENTION TO HURT ANYBODY. WE JUST WANT TO RESTORE MY PLANET BACK TO NORMAL.
WE CAN HELP REPAIR YOU, IF YOU'D LIKE.
I ALSO TAKE NO PLEASURE IN HARMING OTHERS, BUT I WILL IF I MUST.
I MAY DISAGREE WITH MY ORDERS, BUT I WILL OBEY.
THE ONLY PERSON WHO CAN REPAIR ME IS THE ONE WHO GIFTED ME MY OWN MIND.
ALTHOUGH SHE DISAGREED WITH HER ORDERS, SHE CREATED ME ANYWAY.
SHE IS THE SCIENTIST YOU ARE LOOKING FOR.

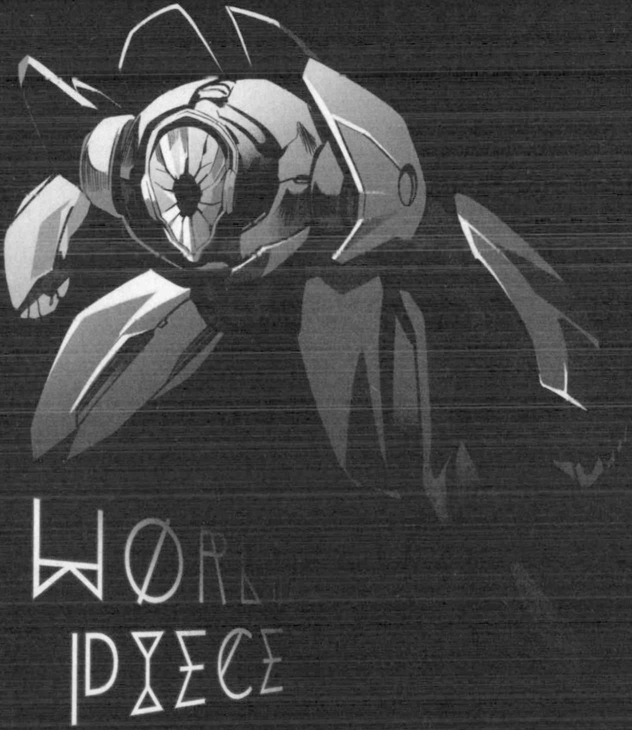
WØRL
PIECE

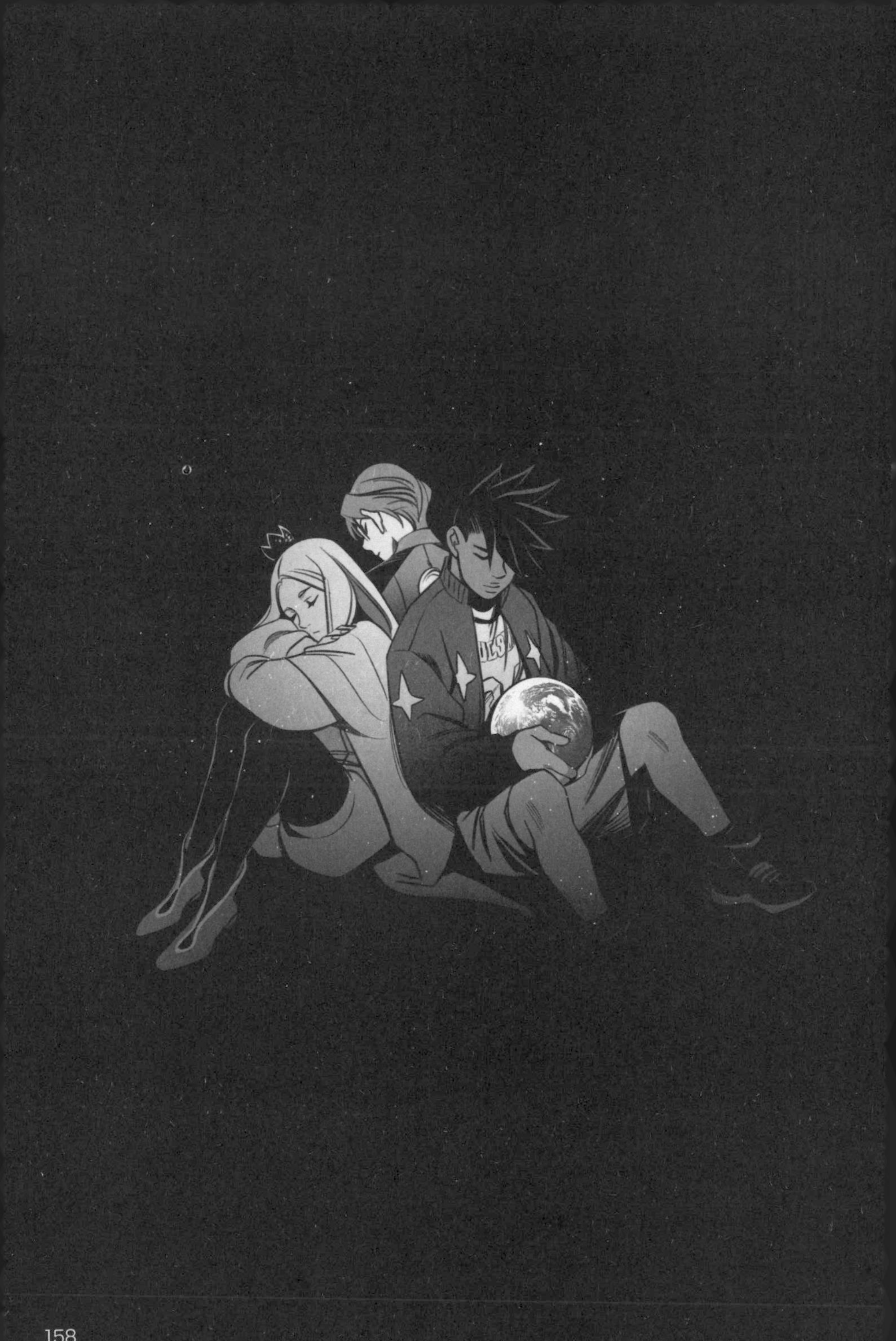

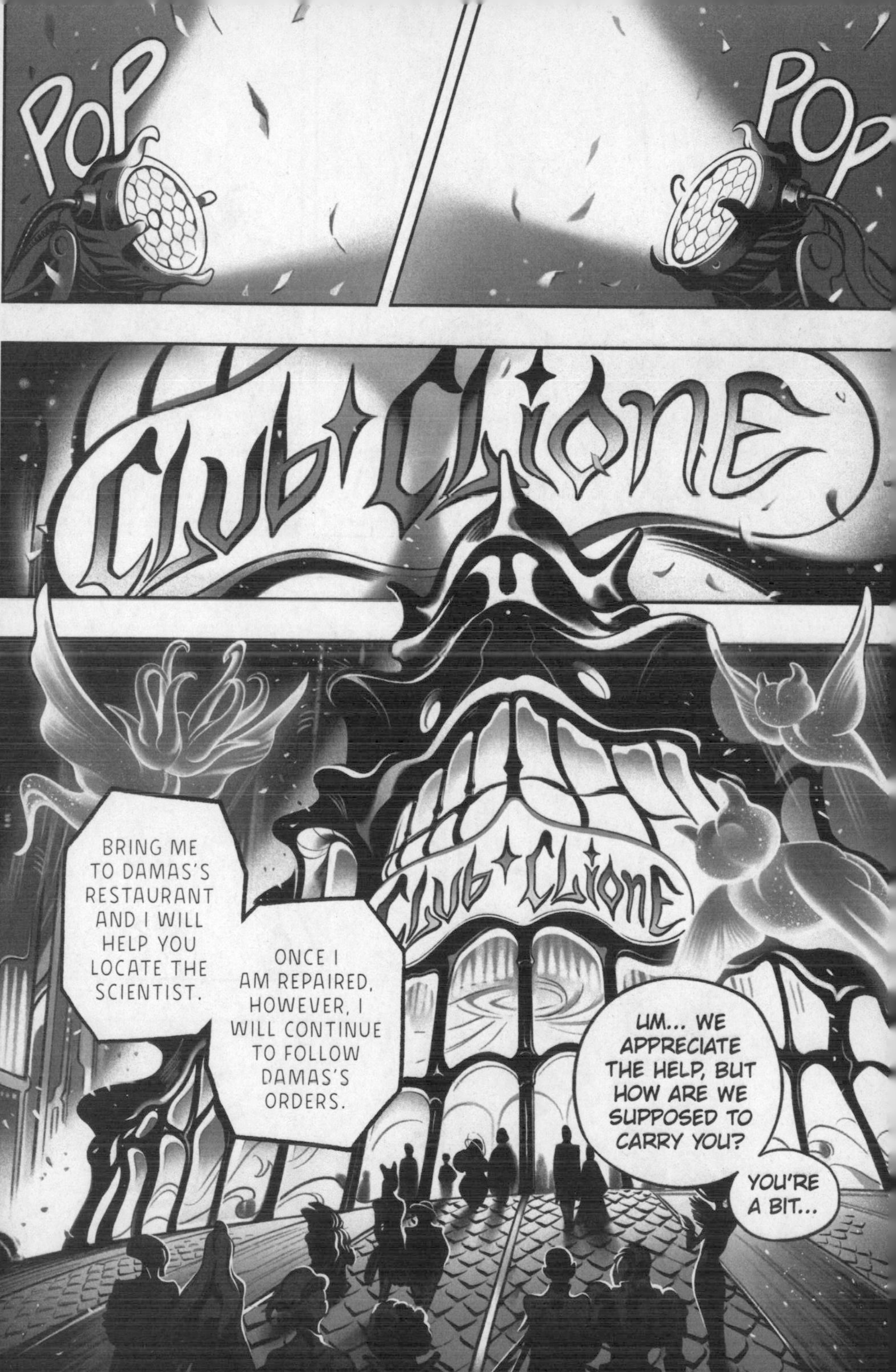
POP
POP
CLUB CLIONE
CLUB CLIONE
BRING ME TO DAMAS'S RESTAURANT AND I WILL HELP YOU LOCATE THE SCIENTIST.
ONCE I AM REPAIRED, HOWEVER, I WILL CONTINUE TO FOLLOW DAMAS'S ORDERS.
UM... WE APPRECIATE THE HELP, BUT HOW ARE WE SUPPOSED TO CARRY YOU?
YOU'RE A BIT...

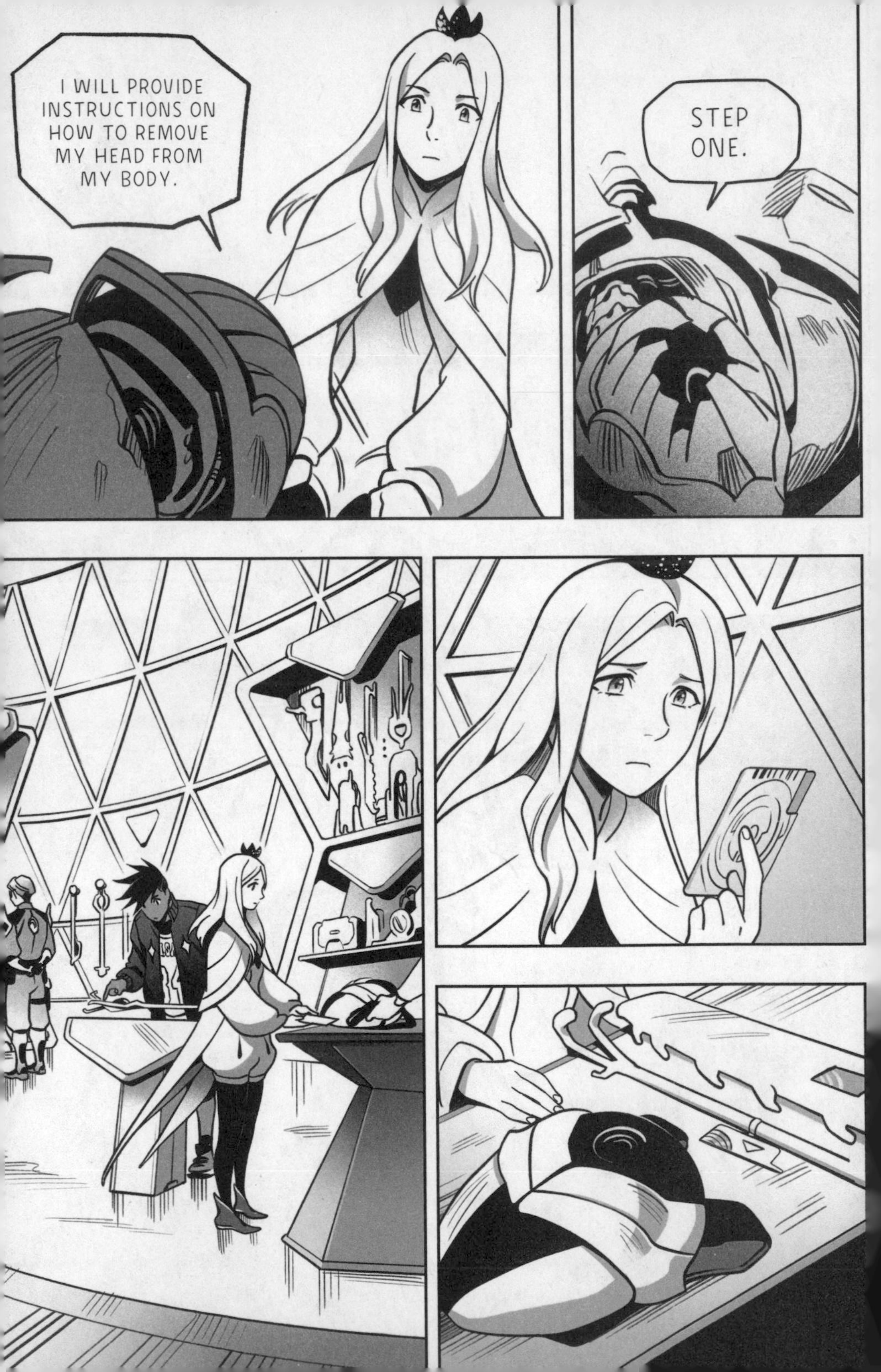
I WILL PROVIDE INSTRUCTIONS ON HOW TO REMOVE MY HEAD FROM MY BODY.
STEP ONE.

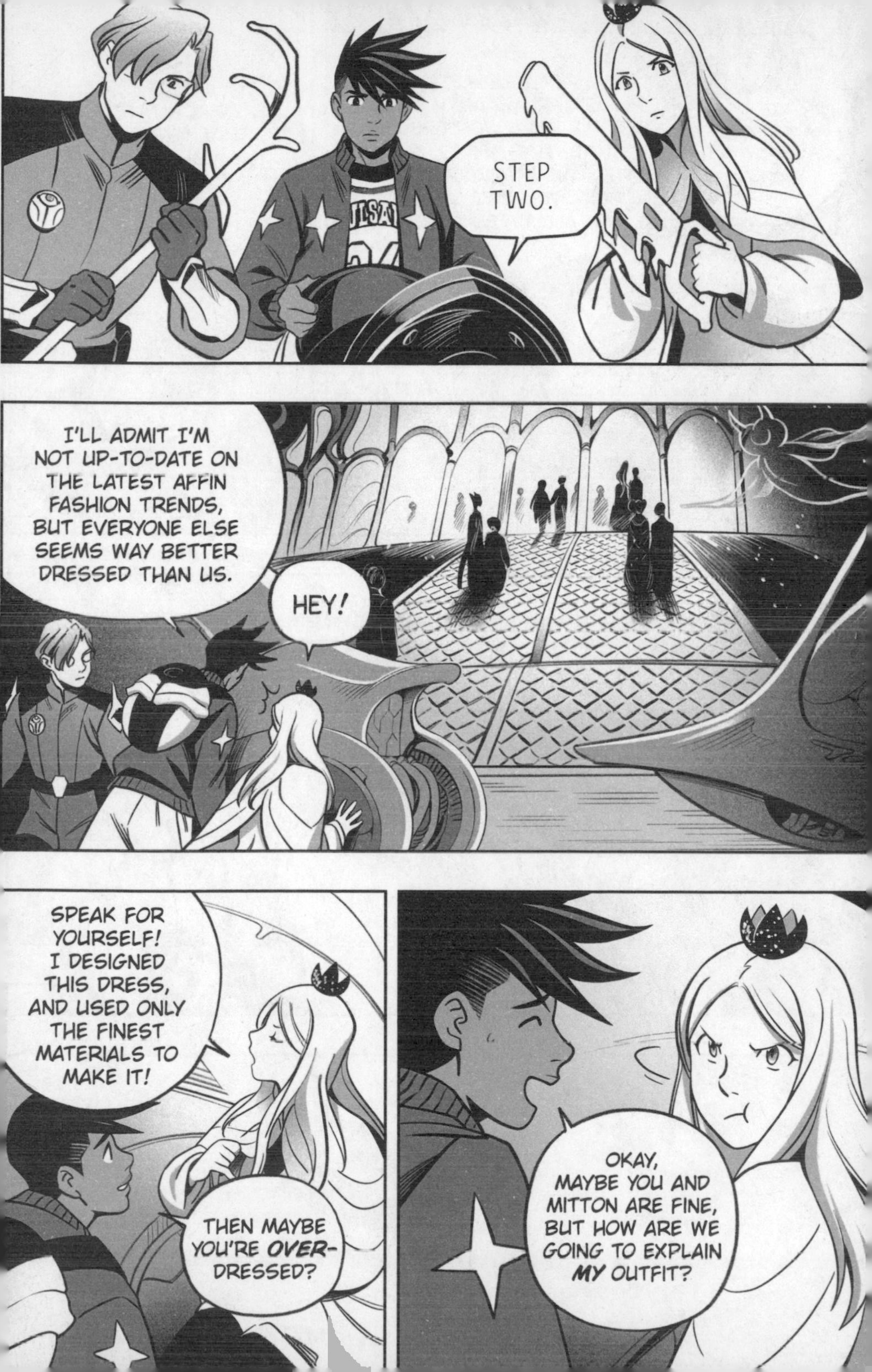
STEP TWO.
I'LL ADMIT I'M NOT UP-TO-DATE ON THE LATEST AFFIN FASHION TRENDS, BUT EVERYONE ELSE SEEMS WAY BETTER DRESSED THAN US.
HEY!
SPEAK FOR YOURSELF! I DESIGNED THIS DRESS, AND USED ONLY THE FINEST MATERIALS TO MAKE IT!
THEN MAYBE YOU'RE *OVER*-DRESSED?
OKAY, MAYBE YOU AND MITTON ARE FINE, BUT HOW ARE WE GOING TO EXPLAIN *MY* OUTFIT?

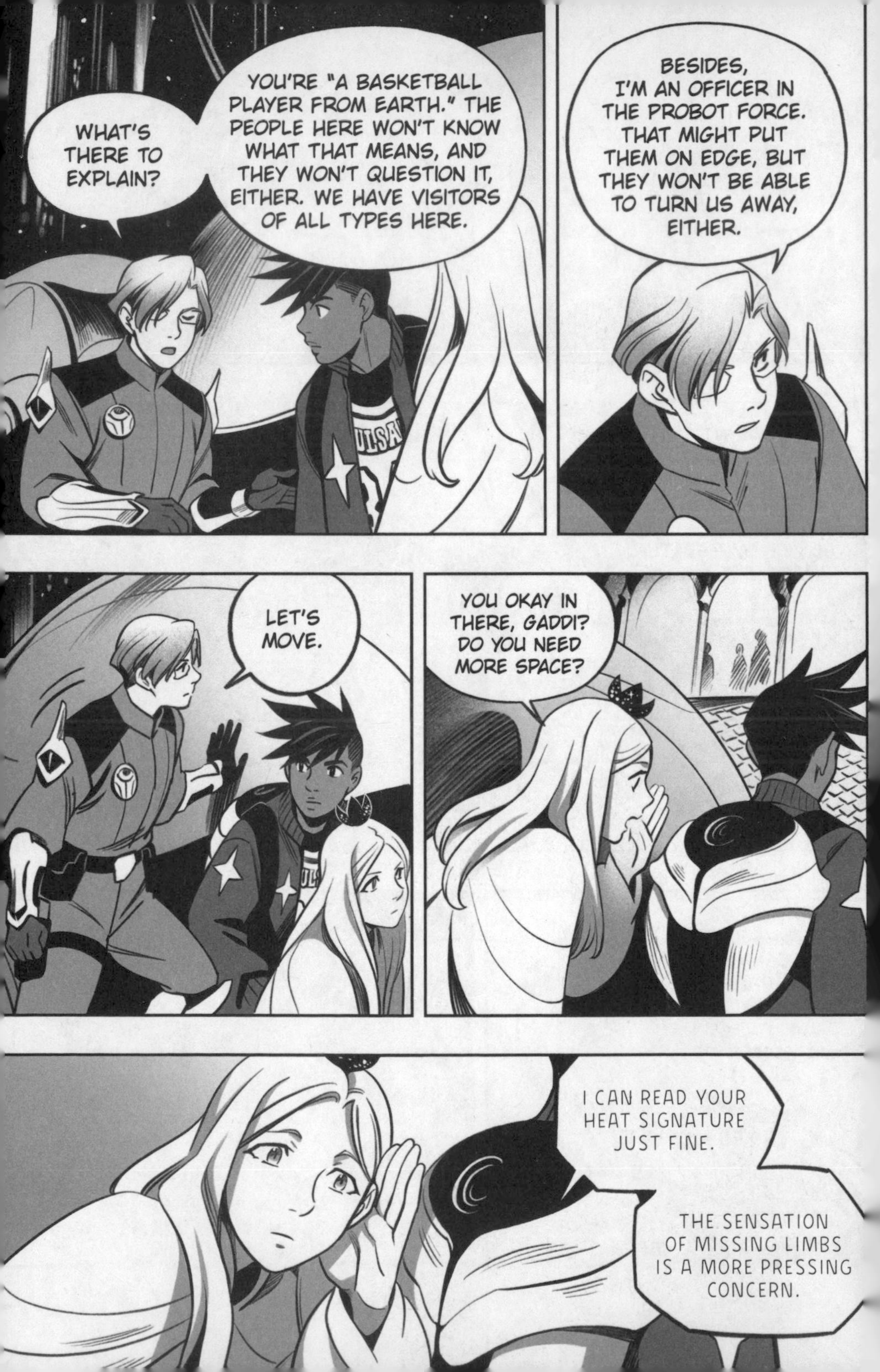
WHAT'S THERE TO EXPLAIN?
YOU'RE "A BASKETBALL PLAYER FROM EARTH." THE PEOPLE HERE WON'T KNOW WHAT THAT MEANS, AND THEY WON'T QUESTION IT, EITHER. WE HAVE VISITORS OF ALL TYPES HERE.
BESIDES, I'M AN OFFICER IN THE PROBOT FORCE. THAT MIGHT PUT THEM ON EDGE, BUT THEY WON'T BE ABLE TO TURN US AWAY, EITHER.
LET'S MOVE.
YOU OKAY IN THERE, GADDI? DO YOU NEED MORE SPACE?
I CAN READ YOUR HEAT SIGNATURE JUST FINE.
THE SENSATION OF MISSING LIMBS IS A MORE PRESSING CONCERN.

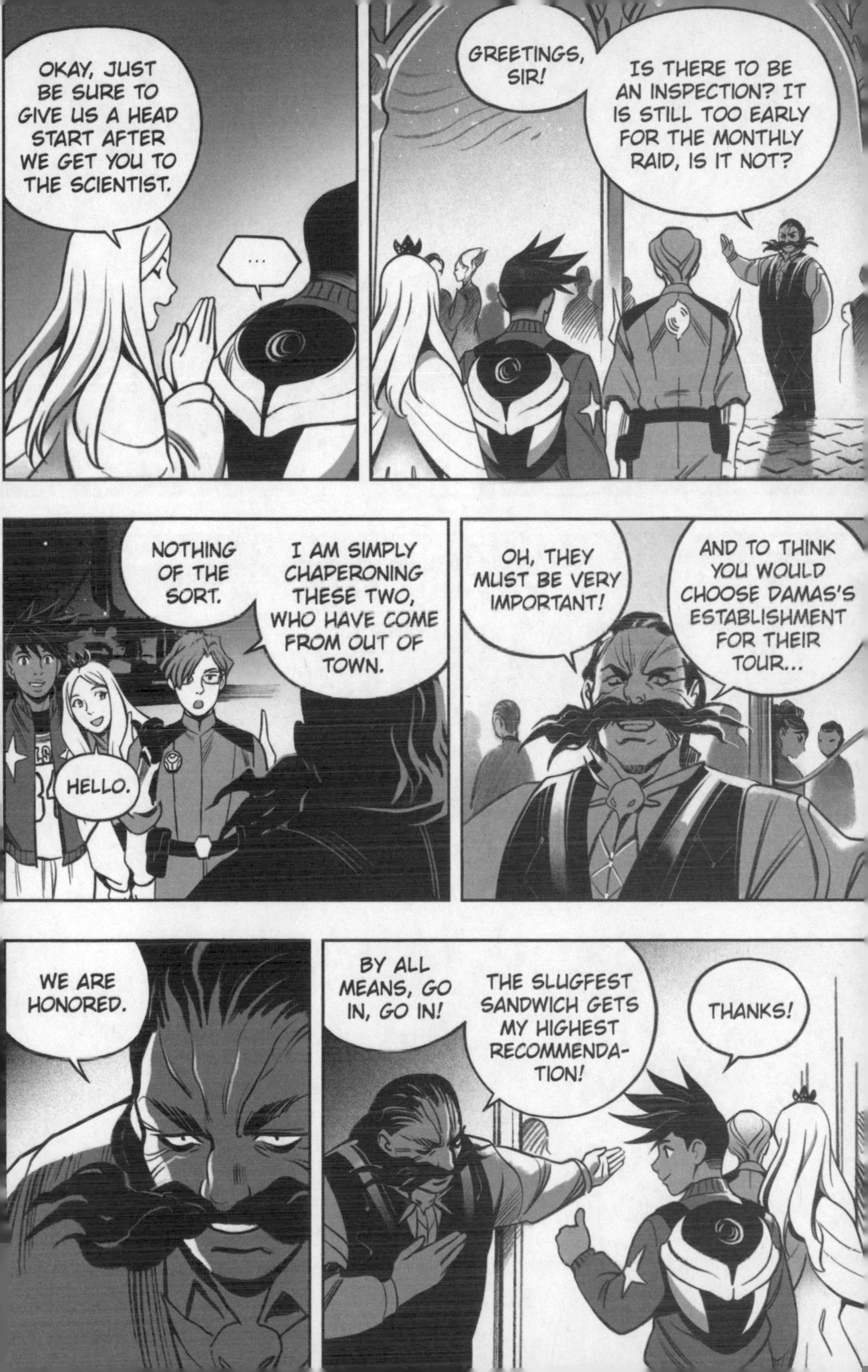
OKAY, JUST BE SURE TO GIVE US A HEAD START AFTER WE GET YOU TO THE SCIENTIST.
...
GREETINGS, SIR!
IS THERE TO BE AN INSPECTION? IT IS STILL TOO EARLY FOR THE MONTHLY RAID, IS IT NOT?
NOTHING OF THE SORT.
I AM SIMPLY CHAPERONING THESE TWO, WHO HAVE COME FROM OUT OF TOWN.
HELLO.
OH, THEY MUST BE VERY IMPORTANT!
AND TO THINK YOU WOULD CHOOSE DAMAS'S ESTABLISHMENT FOR THEIR TOUR...
WE ARE HONORED.
BY ALL MEANS, GO IN, GO IN!
THE SLUGFEST SANDWICH GETS MY HIGHEST RECOMMENDA-TION!
THANKS!

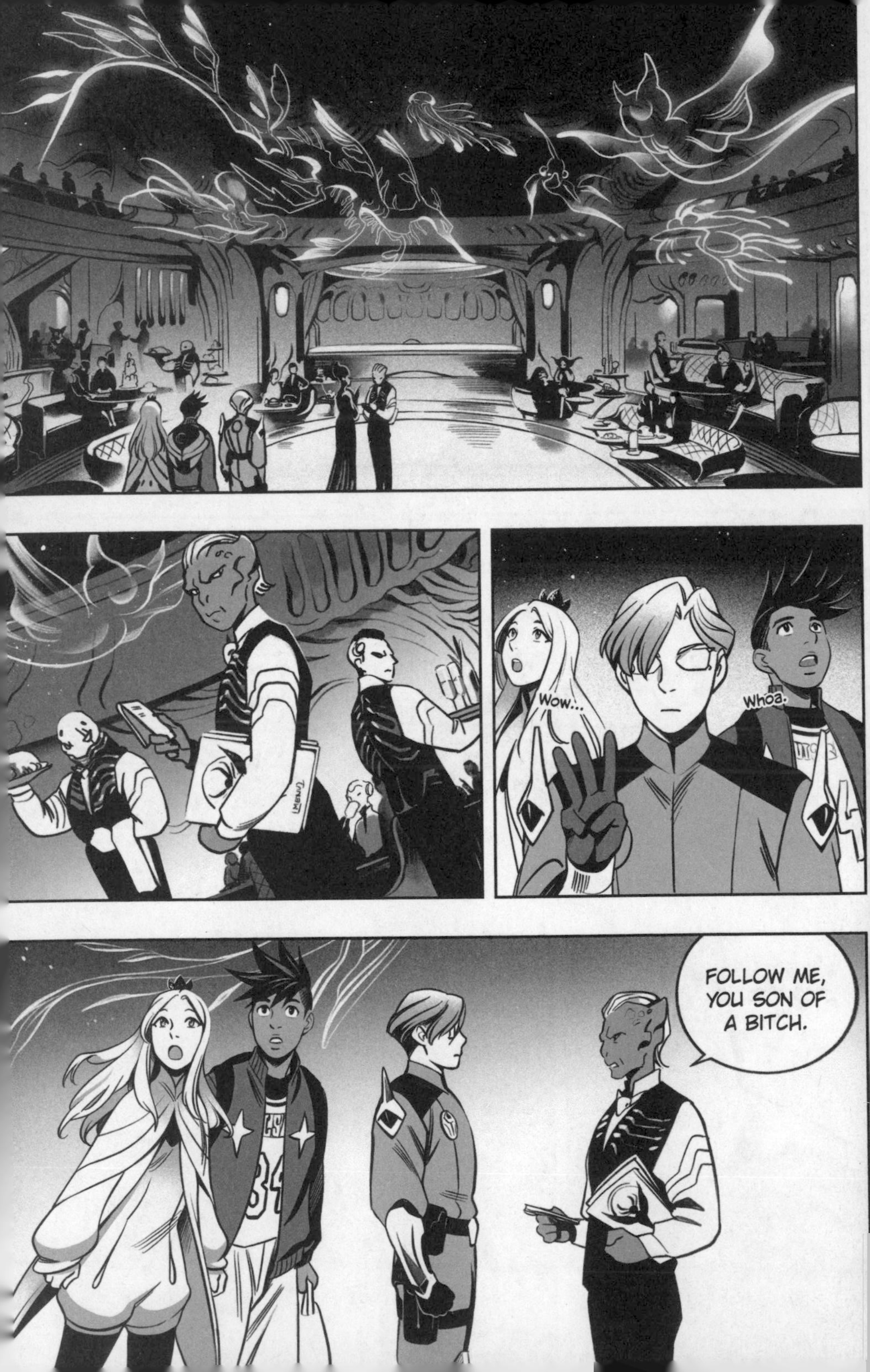
Wow...
Whoa.
FOLLOW ME, YOU SON OF A BITCH.

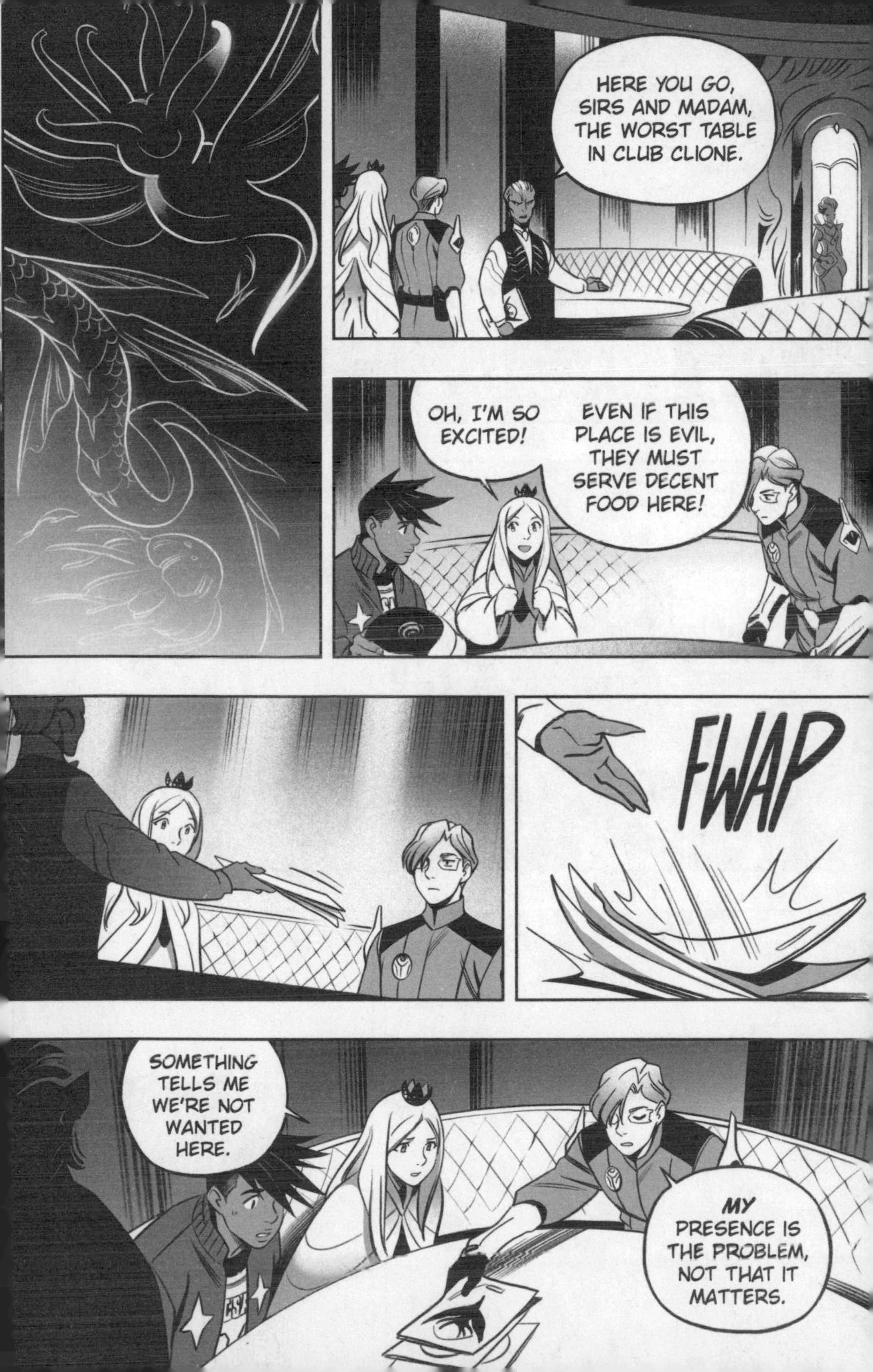
HERE YOU GO, SIRS AND MADAM, THE WORST TABLE IN CLUB CLIONE.
OH, I'M SO EXCITED!
EVEN IF THIS PLACE IS EVIL, THEY MUST SERVE DECENT FOOD HERE!
FWAP
SOMETHING TELLS ME WE'RE NOT WANTED HERE.
MY PRESENCE IS THE PROBLEM, NOT THAT IT MATTERS.

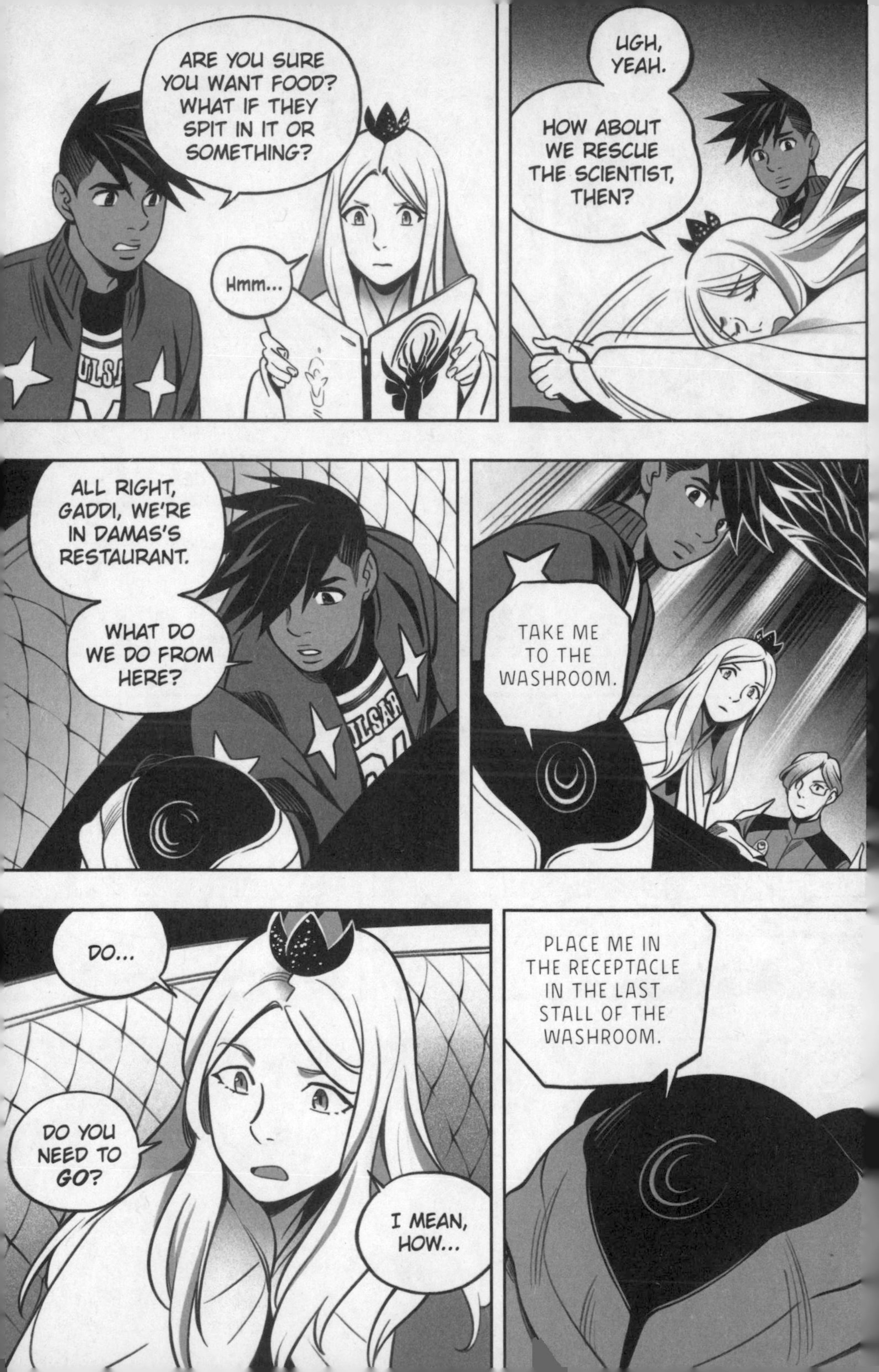
ARE YOU SURE YOU WANT FOOD? WHAT IF THEY SPIT IN IT OR SOMETHING?
HMM...
UGH, YEAH.
HOW ABOUT WE RESCUE THE SCIENTIST, THEN?
ALL RIGHT, GADDI, WE'RE IN DAMAS'S RESTAURANT.
WHAT DO WE DO FROM HERE?
TAKE ME TO THE WASHROOM.
DO...
DO YOU NEED TO GO?
I MEAN, HOW...
PLACE ME IN THE RECEPTACLE IN THE LAST STALL OF THE WASHROOM.

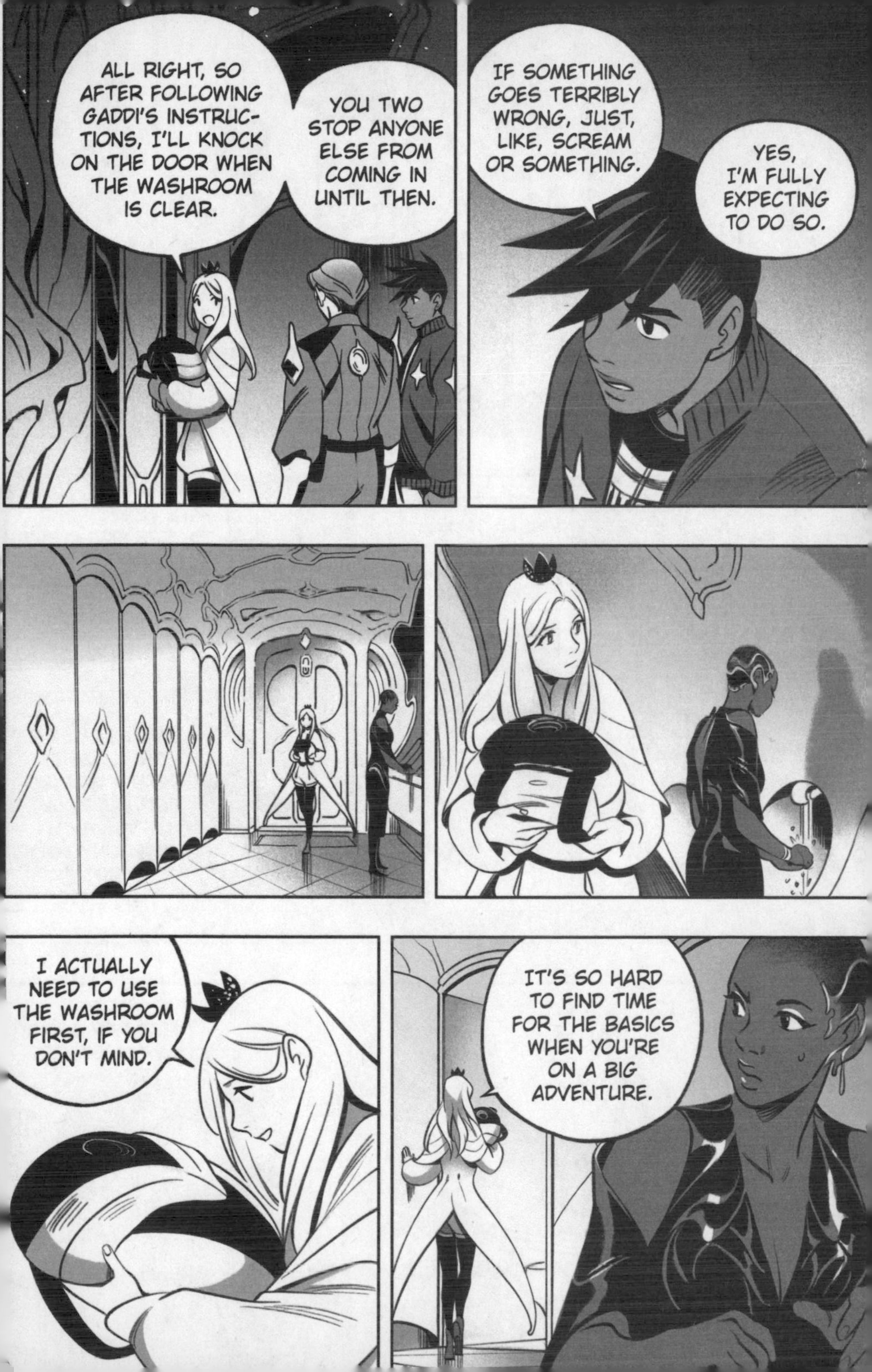
ALL RIGHT, SO AFTER FOLLOWING GADDI'S INSTRUC-TIONS, I'LL KNOCK ON THE DOOR WHEN THE WASHROOM IS CLEAR.
YOU TWO STOP ANYONE ELSE FROM COMING IN UNTIL THEN.
IF SOMETHING GOES TERRIBLY WRONG, JUST, LIKE, SCREAM OR SOMETHING.
YES, I'M FULLY EXPECTING TO DO SO.
I ACTUALLY NEED TO USE THE WASHROOM FIRST, IF YOU DON'T MIND.
IT'S SO HARD TO FIND TIME FOR THE BASICS WHEN YOU'RE ON A BIG ADVENTURE.

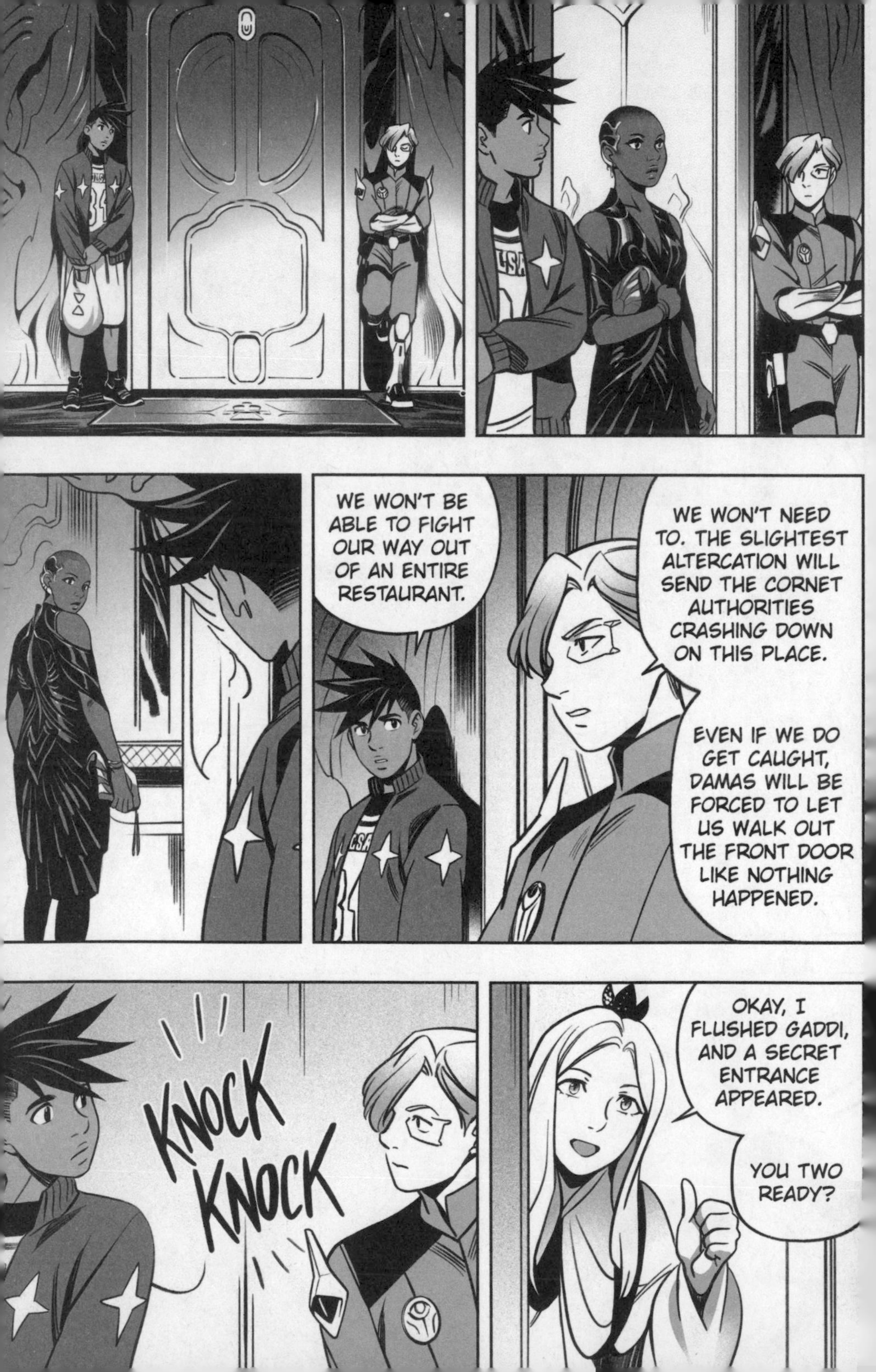
WE WON'T BE ABLE TO FIGHT OUR WAY OUT OF AN ENTIRE RESTAURANT.
WE WON'T NEED TO. THE SLIGHTEST ALTERCATION WILL SEND THE CORNET AUTHORITIES CRASHING DOWN ON THIS PLACE.
EVEN IF WE DO GET CAUGHT, DAMAS WILL BE FORCED TO LET US WALK OUT THE FRONT DOOR LIKE NOTHING HAPPENED.
KNOCK KNOCK
OKAY, I FLUSHED GADDI, AND A SECRET ENTRANCE APPEARED.
YOU TWO READY?

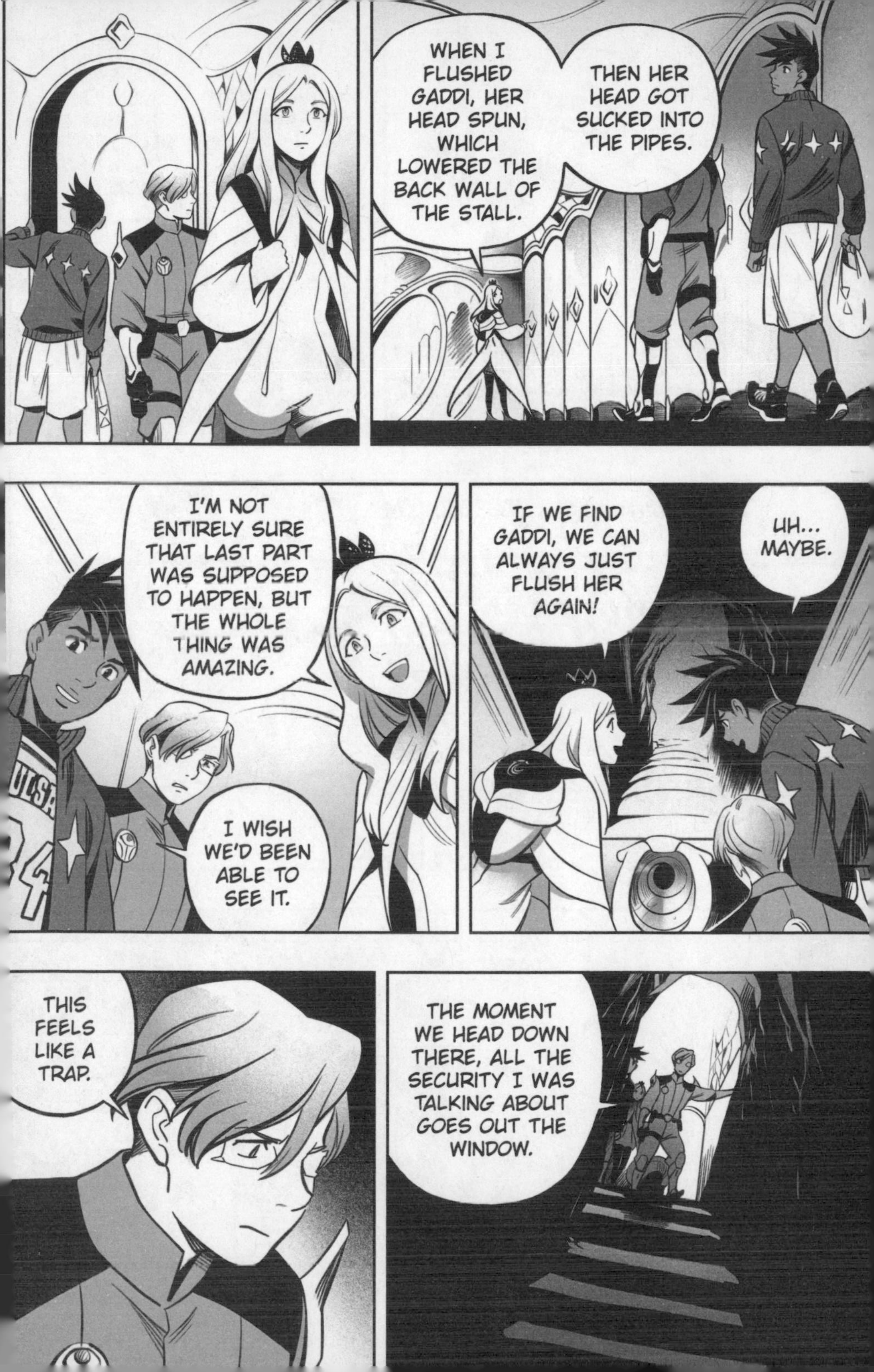
WHEN I FLUSHED GADDI, HER HEAD SPUN, WHICH LOWERED THE BACK WALL OF THE STALL.
THEN HER HEAD GOT SUCKED INTO THE PIPES.
I'M NOT ENTIRELY SURE THAT LAST PART WAS SUPPOSED TO HAPPEN, BUT THE WHOLE THING WAS AMAZING.
I WISH WE'D BEEN ABLE TO SEE IT.
IF WE FIND GADDI, WE CAN ALWAYS JUST FLUSH HER AGAIN!
UH... MAYBE.
THIS FEELS LIKE A TRAP.
THE MOMENT WE HEAD DOWN THERE, ALL THE SECURITY I WAS TALKING ABOUT GOES OUT THE WINDOW.

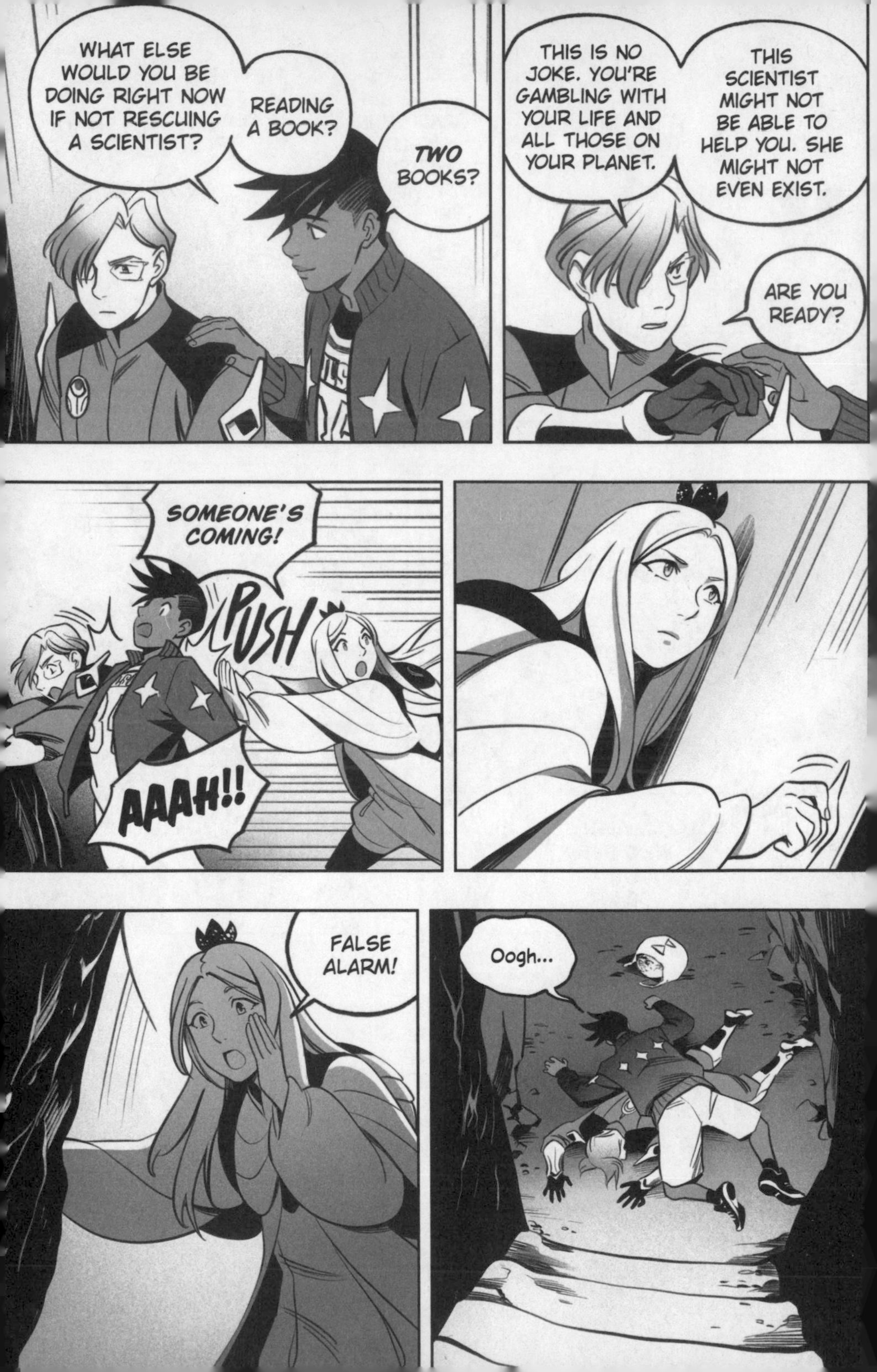
WHAT ELSE WOULD YOU BE DOING RIGHT NOW IF NOT RESCUING A SCIENTIST?
READING A BOOK?
TWO BOOKS?
THIS IS NO JOKE. YOU'RE GAMBLING WITH YOUR LIFE AND ALL THOSE ON YOUR PLANET.
THIS SCIENTIST MIGHT NOT BE ABLE TO HELP YOU. SHE MIGHT NOT EVEN EXIST.
ARE YOU READY?
SOMEONE'S COMING!
PUSH
AAAH!!
FALSE ALARM!
Oogh...

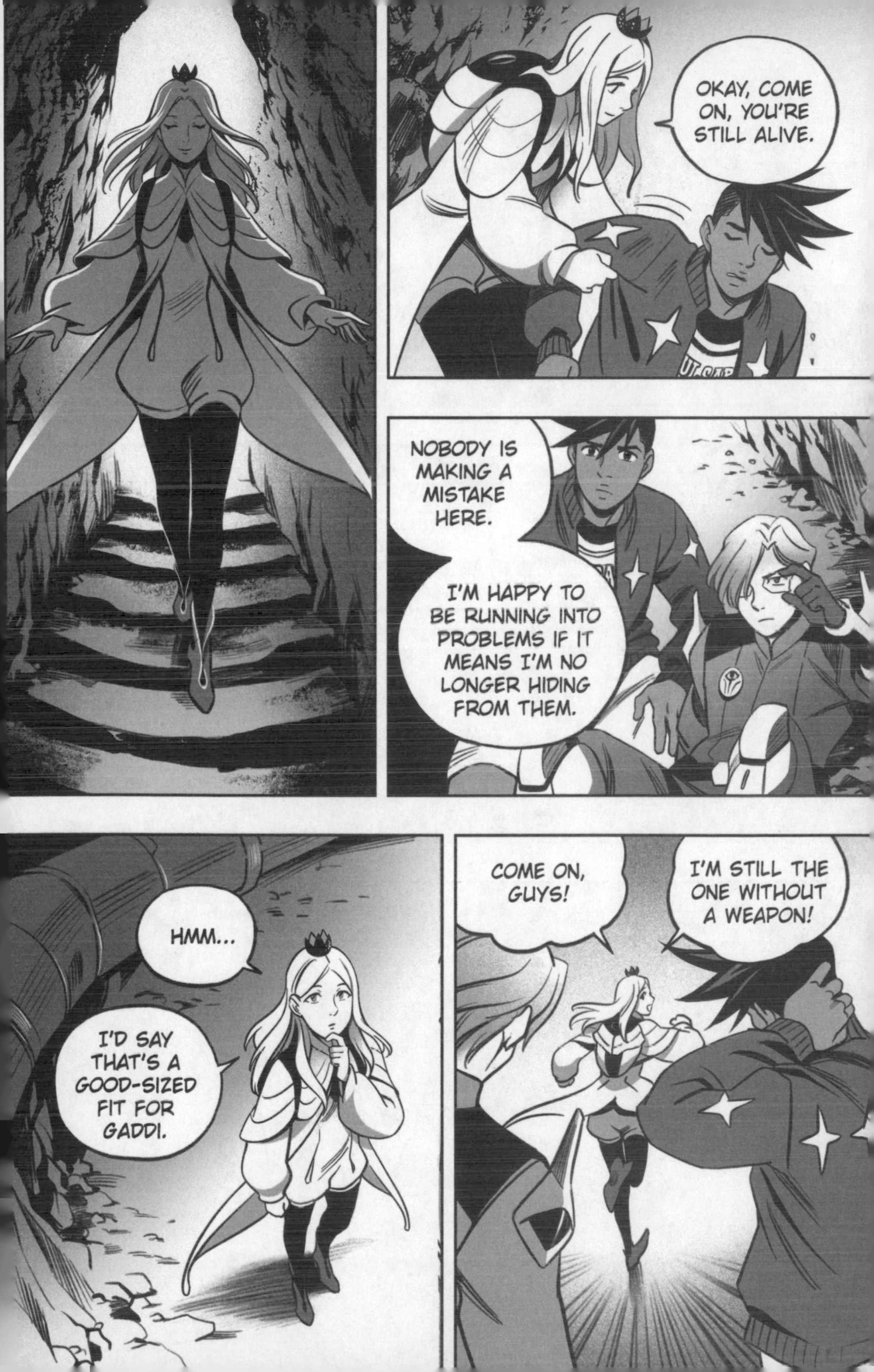
OKAY, COME ON, YOU'RE STILL ALIVE.
NOBODY IS MAKING A MISTAKE HERE.
I'M HAPPY TO BE RUNNING INTO PROBLEMS IF IT MEANS I'M NO LONGER HIDING FROM THEM.
HMM...
I'D SAY THAT'S A GOOD-SIZED FIT FOR GADDI.
COME ON, GUYS!
I'M STILL THE ONE WITHOUT A WEAPON!

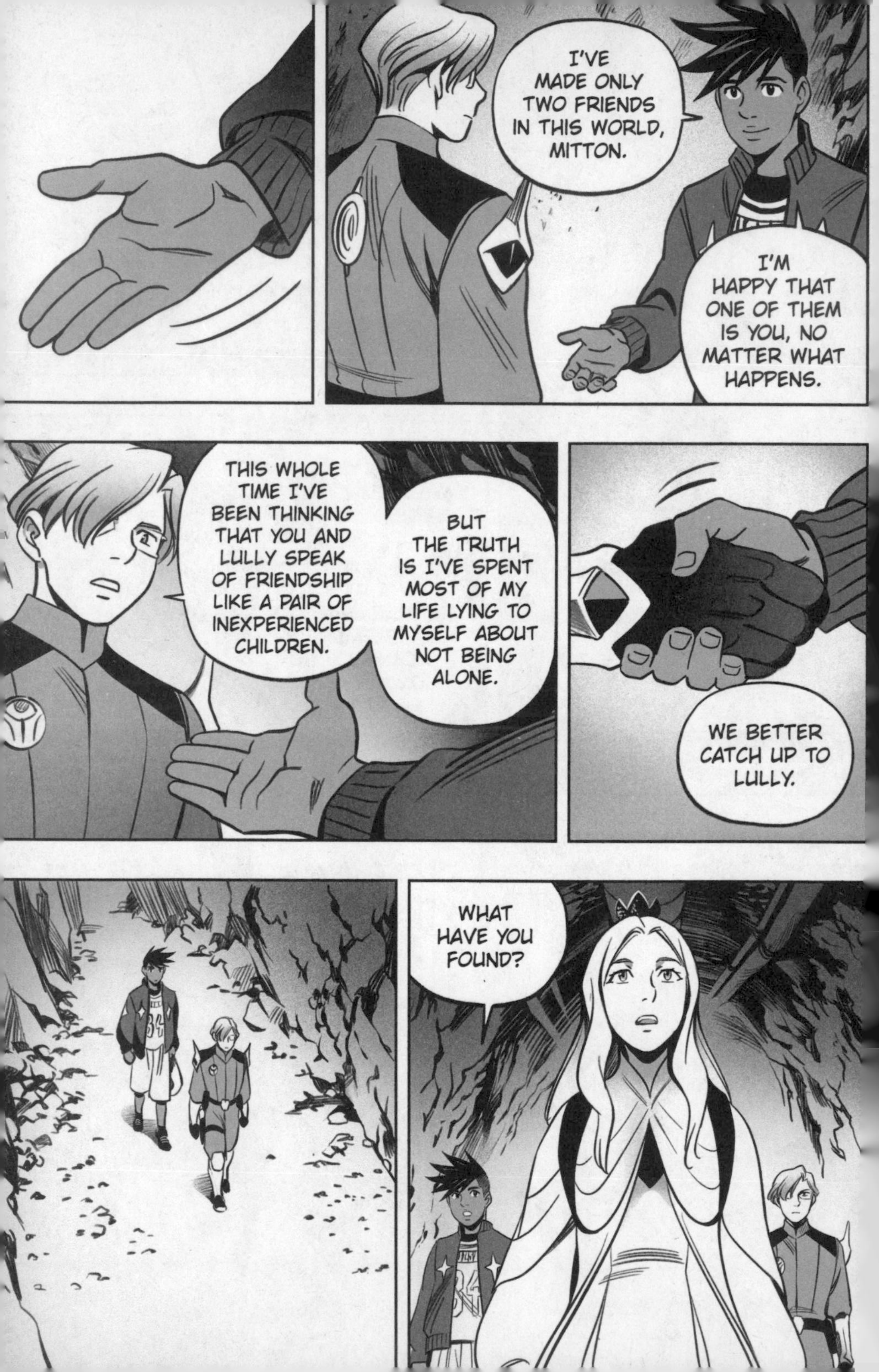
I'VE MADE ONLY TWO FRIENDS IN THIS WORLD, MITTON.
I'M HAPPY THAT ONE OF THEM IS YOU, NO MATTER WHAT HAPPENS.
THIS WHOLE TIME I'VE BEEN THINKING THAT YOU AND LULLY SPEAK OF FRIENDSHIP LIKE A PAIR OF INEXPERIENCED CHILDREN.
BUT THE TRUTH IS I'VE SPENT MOST OF MY LIFE LYING TO MYSELF ABOUT NOT BEING ALONE.
WE BETTER CATCH UP TO LULLY.
WHAT HAVE YOU FOUND?

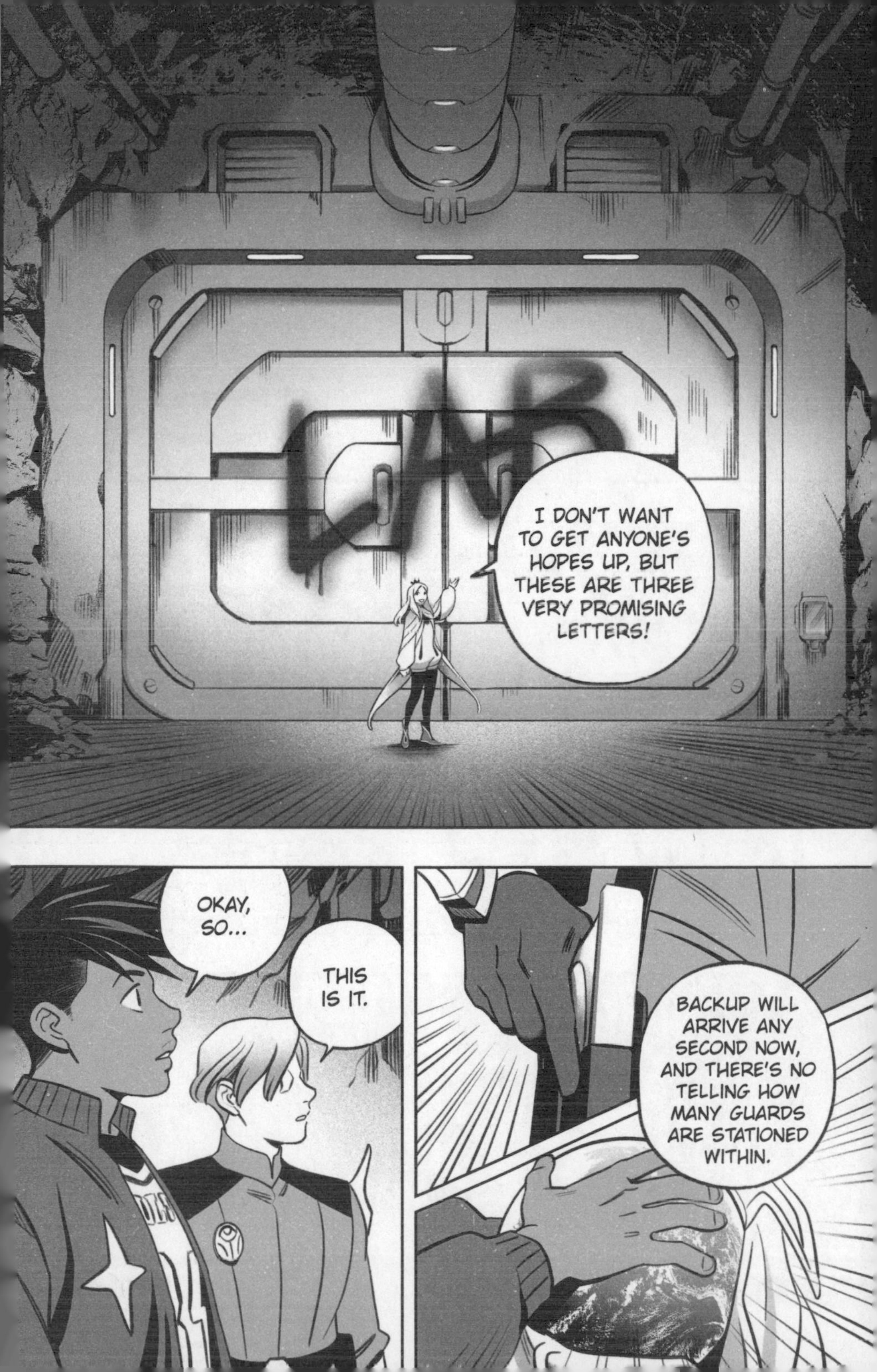
I DON'T WANT TO GET ANYONE'S HOPES UP, BUT THESE ARE THREE VERY PROMISING LETTERS!
OKAY, SO...
THIS IS IT.
BACKUP WILL ARRIVE ANY SECOND NOW, AND THERE'S NO TELLING HOW MANY GUARDS ARE STATIONED WITHIN.

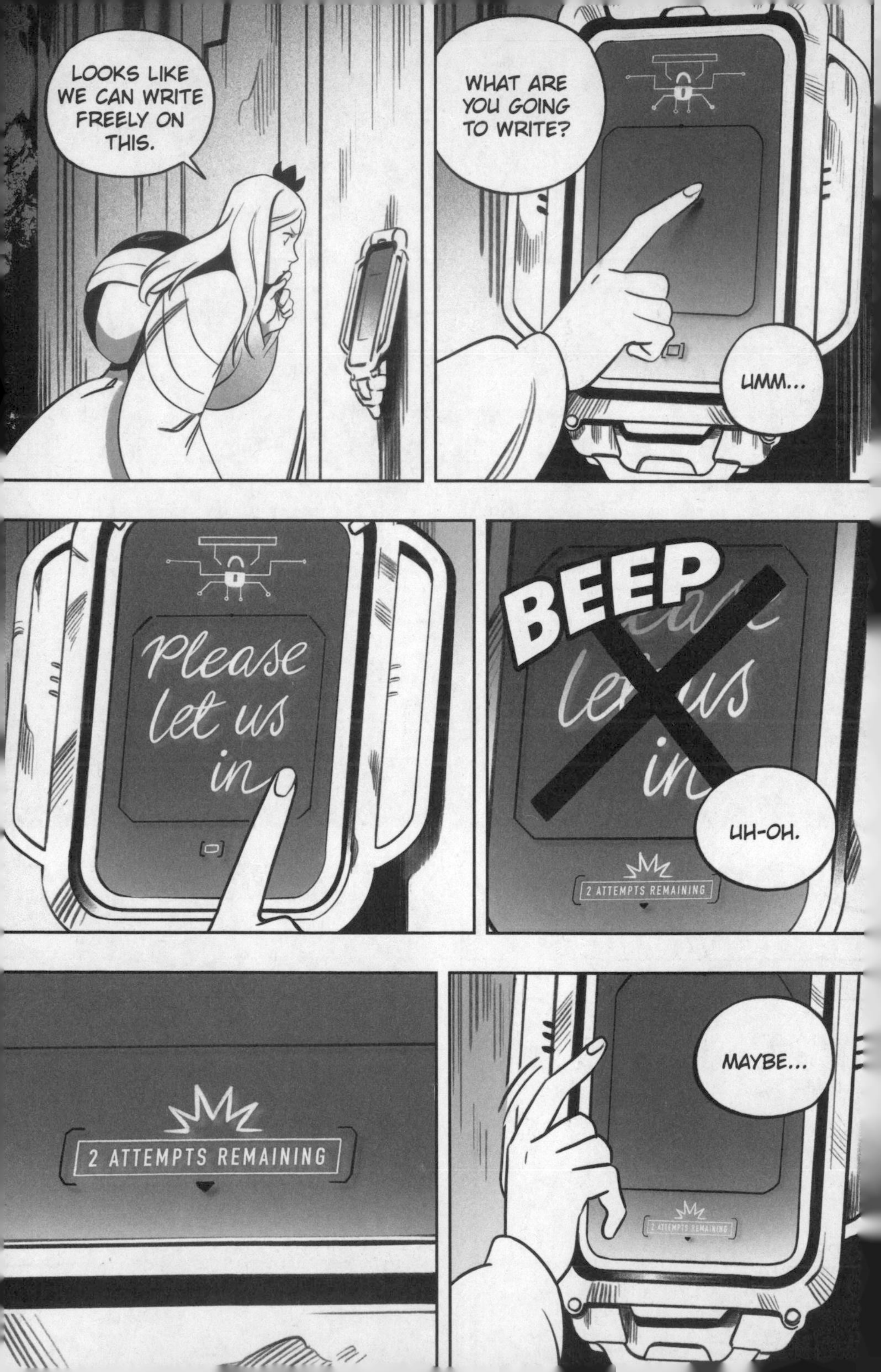
LOOKS LIKE WE CAN WRITE FREELY ON THIS.
WHAT ARE YOU GOING TO WRITE?
UMM...
Please let us in
BEEP
UH-OH.
2 ATTEMPTS REMAINING
2 ATTEMPTS REMAINING
MAYBE...

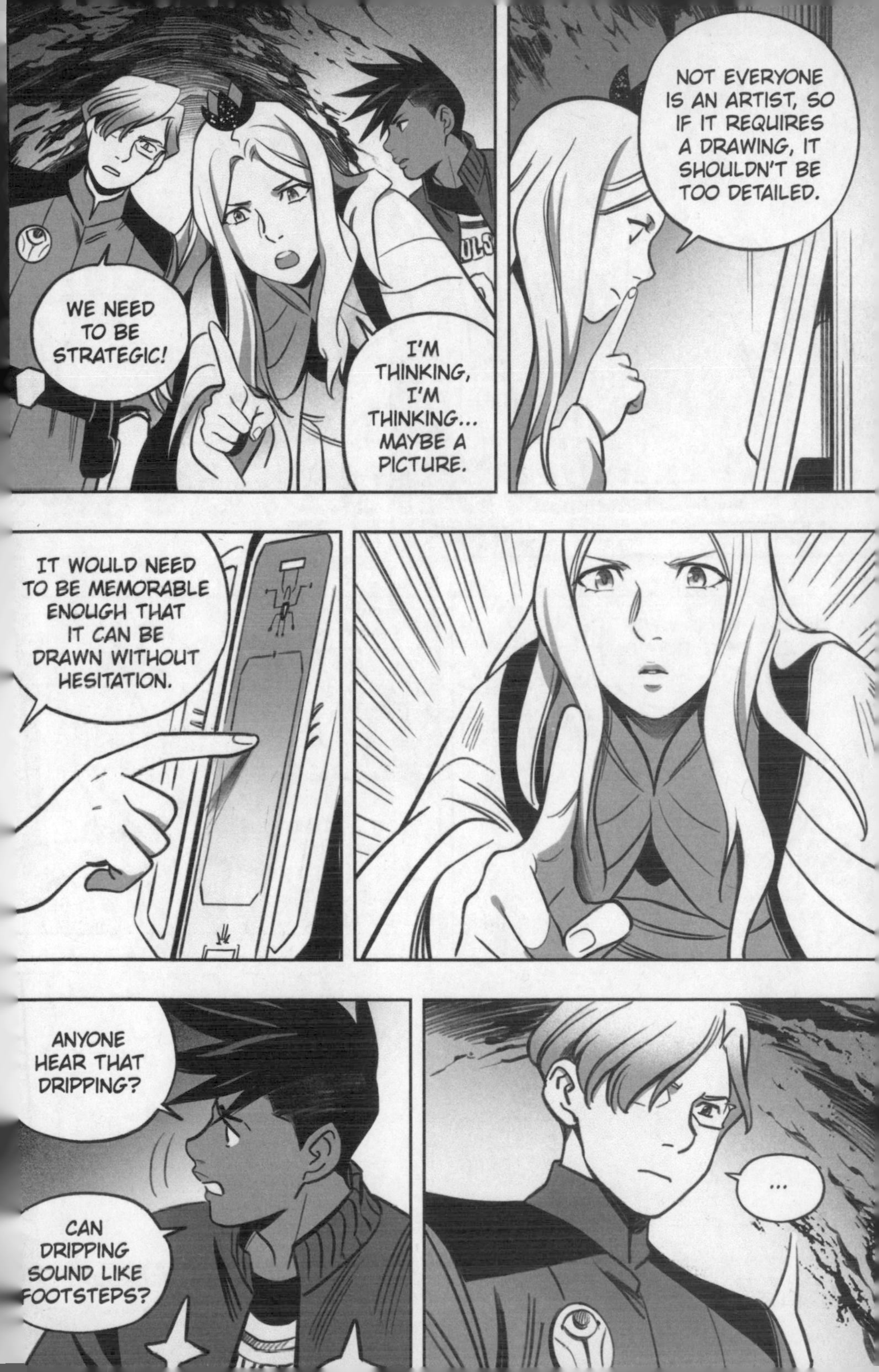
WE NEED TO BE STRATEGIC!
I'M THINKING, I'M THINKING... MAYBE A PICTURE.
NOT EVERYONE IS AN ARTIST, SO IF IT REQUIRES A DRAWING, IT SHOULDN'T BE TOO DETAILED.
IT WOULD NEED TO BE MEMORABLE ENOUGH THAT IT CAN BE DRAWN WITHOUT HESITATION.
ANYONE HEAR THAT DRIPPING?
CAN DRIPPING SOUND LIKE FOOTSTEPS?
...

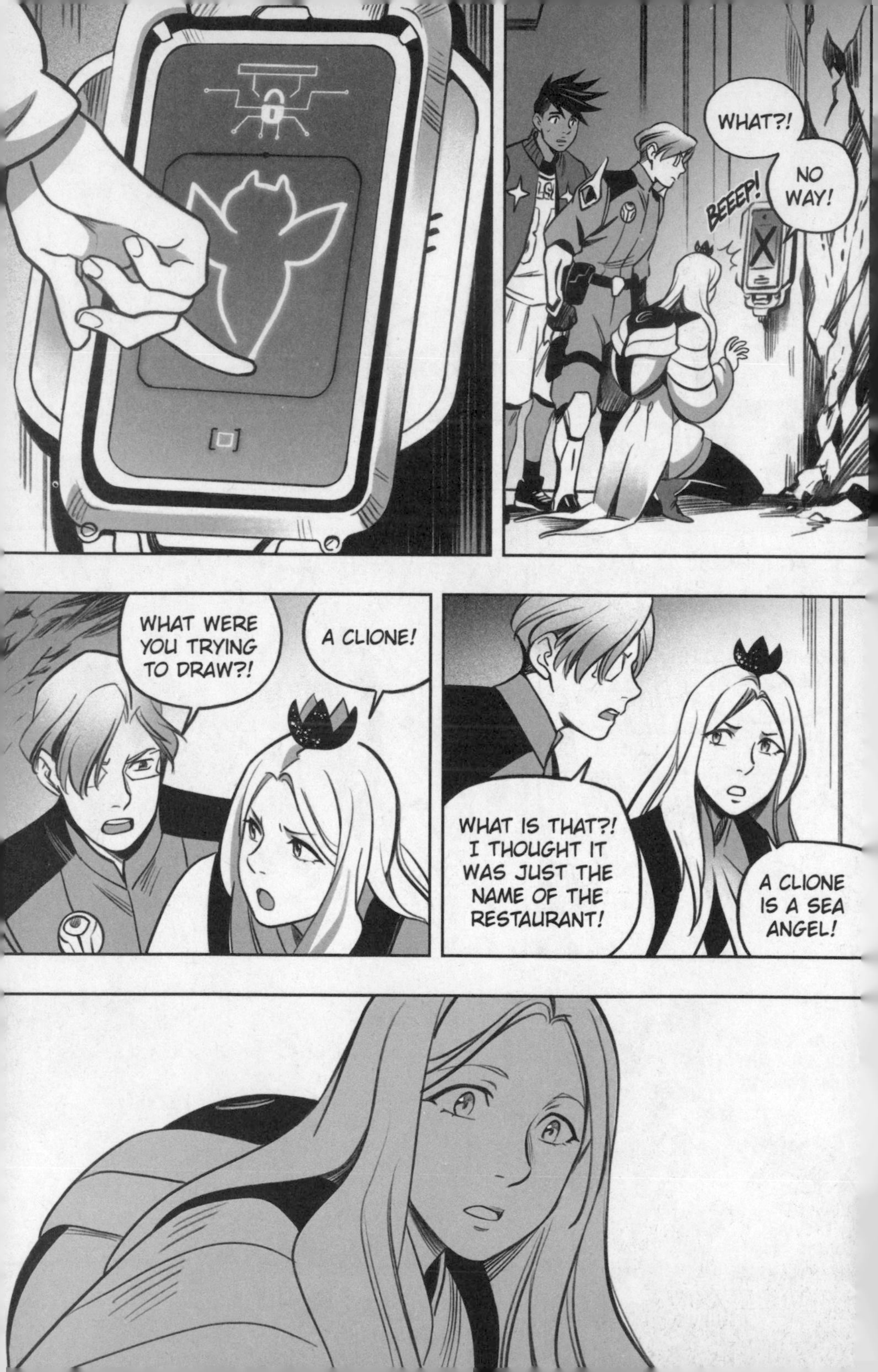
WHAT?!
NO WAY!
BEEEP!
WHAT WERE YOU TRYING TO DRAW?!
A CLIONE!
WHAT IS THAT?! I THOUGHT IT WAS JUST THE NAME OF THE RESTAURANT!
A CLIONE IS A SEA ANGEL!

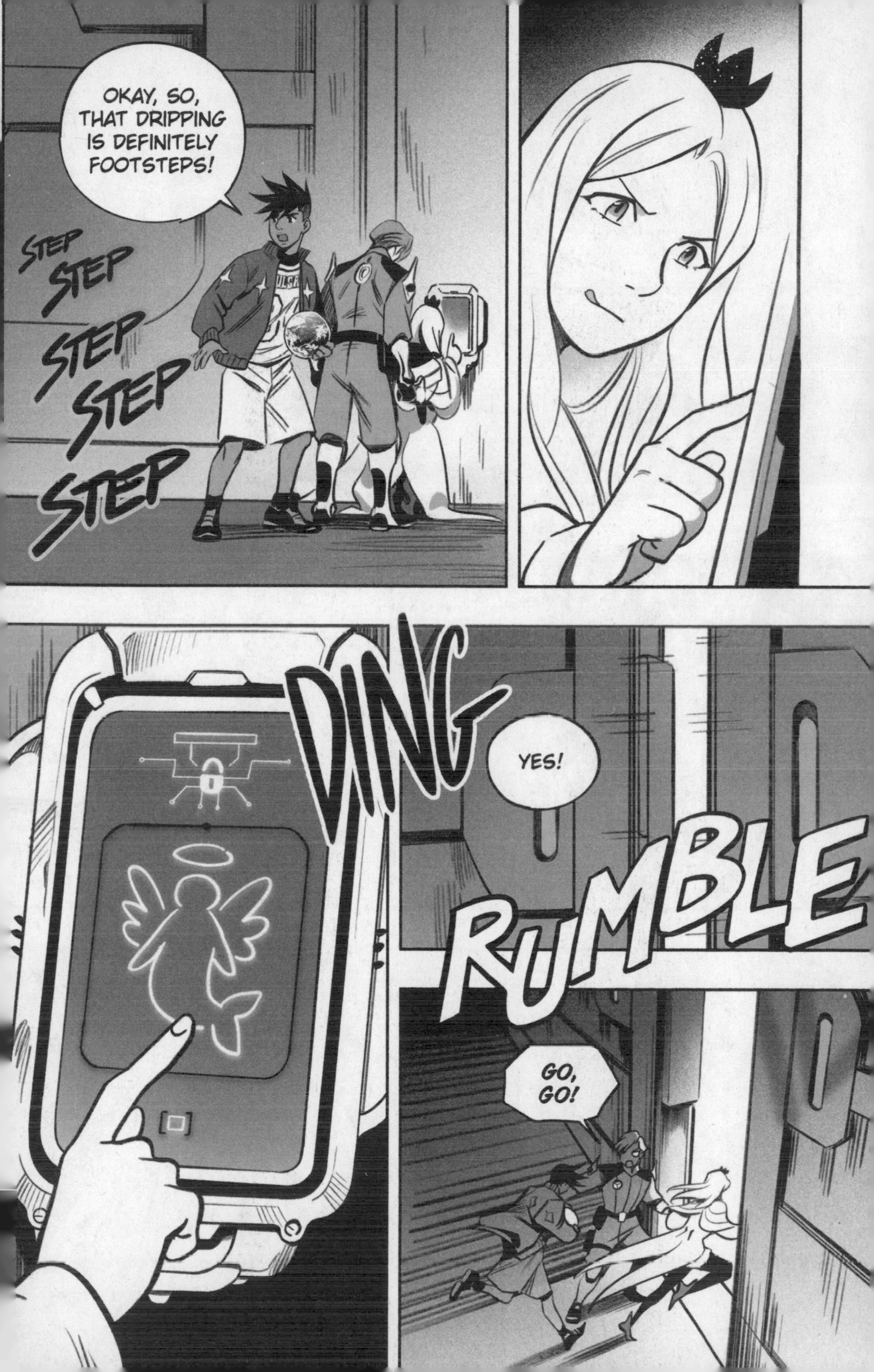
OKAY, SO, THAT DRIPPING IS DEFINITELY FOOTSTEPS!
STEP STEP STEP STEP STEP
DING
YES!
RUMBLE
GO, GO!

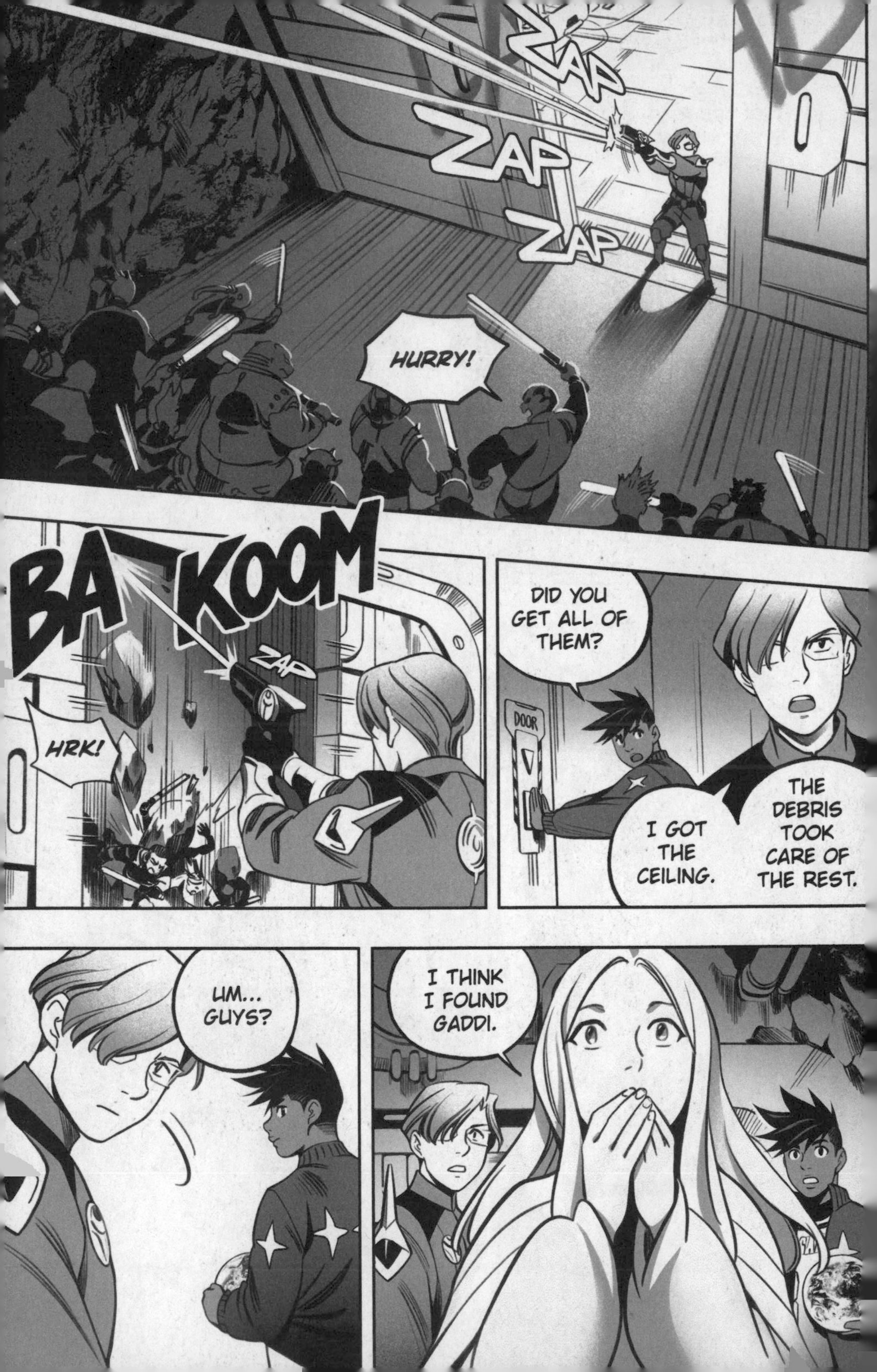
ZAP
ZAP
ZAP
HURRY!
BA-KOOM
ZAP
HRK!
DID YOU GET ALL OF THEM?
I GOT THE CEILING.
THE DEBRIS TOOK CARE OF THE REST.
UM... GUYS?
I THINK I FOUND GADDI.

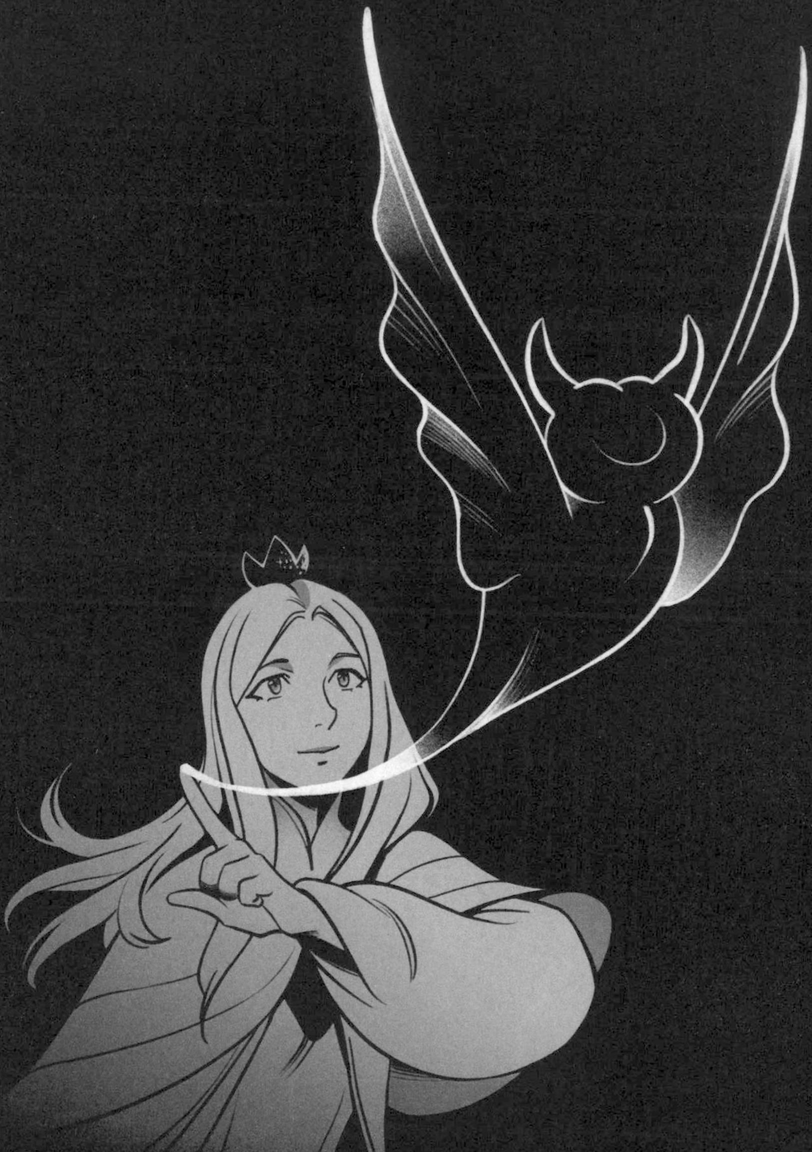

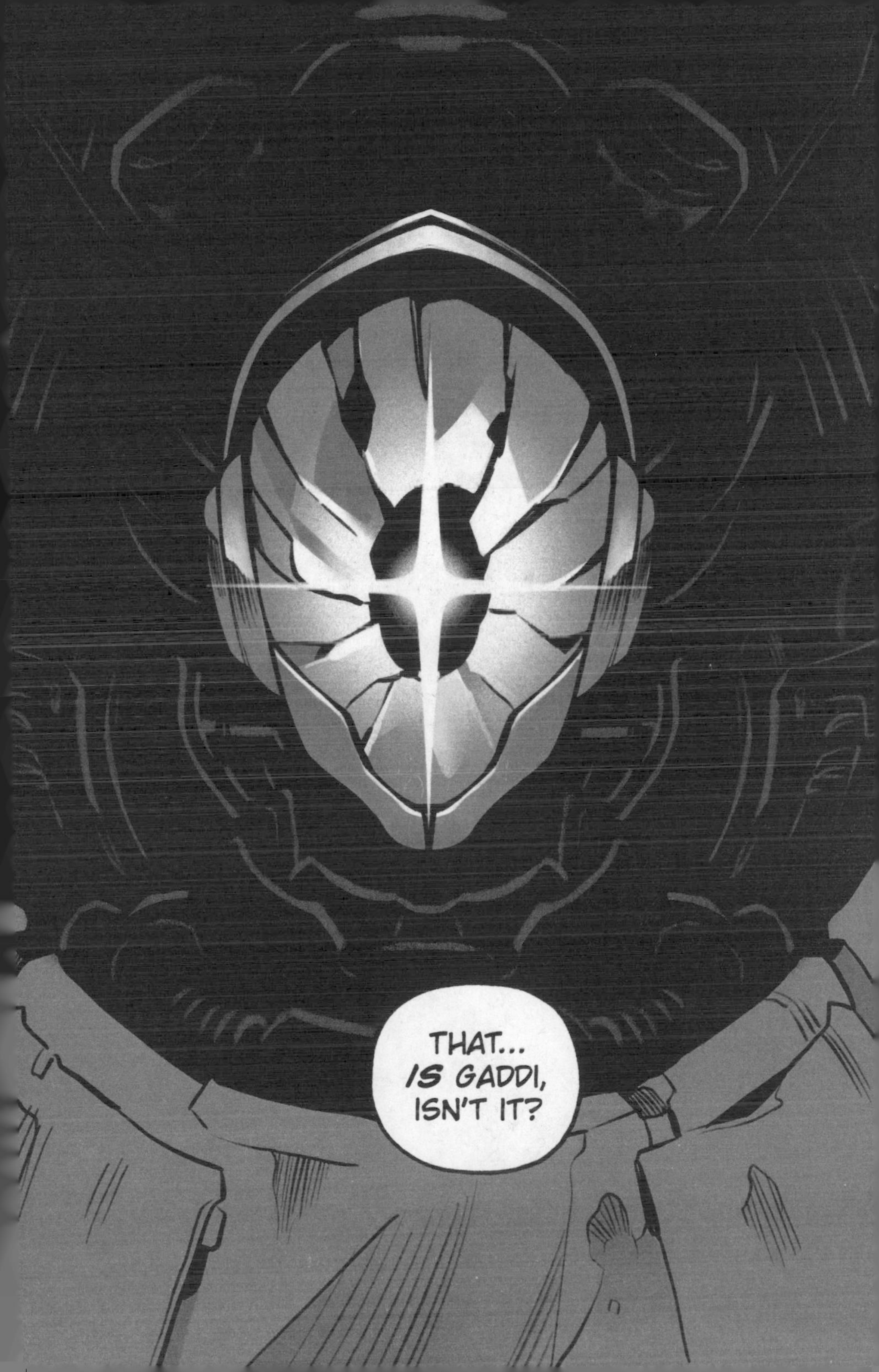
THAT... *IS* GADDI, ISN'T IT?

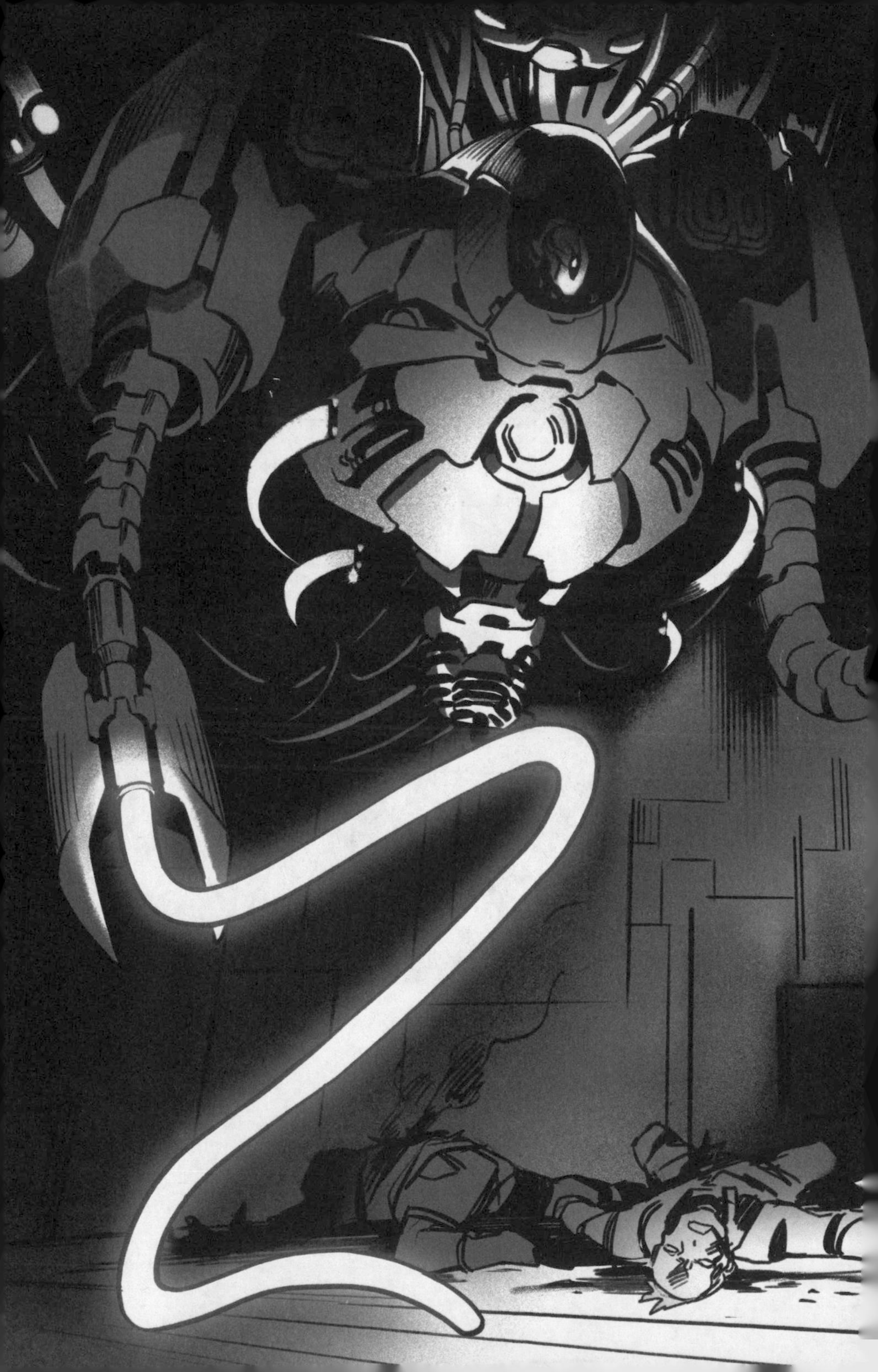

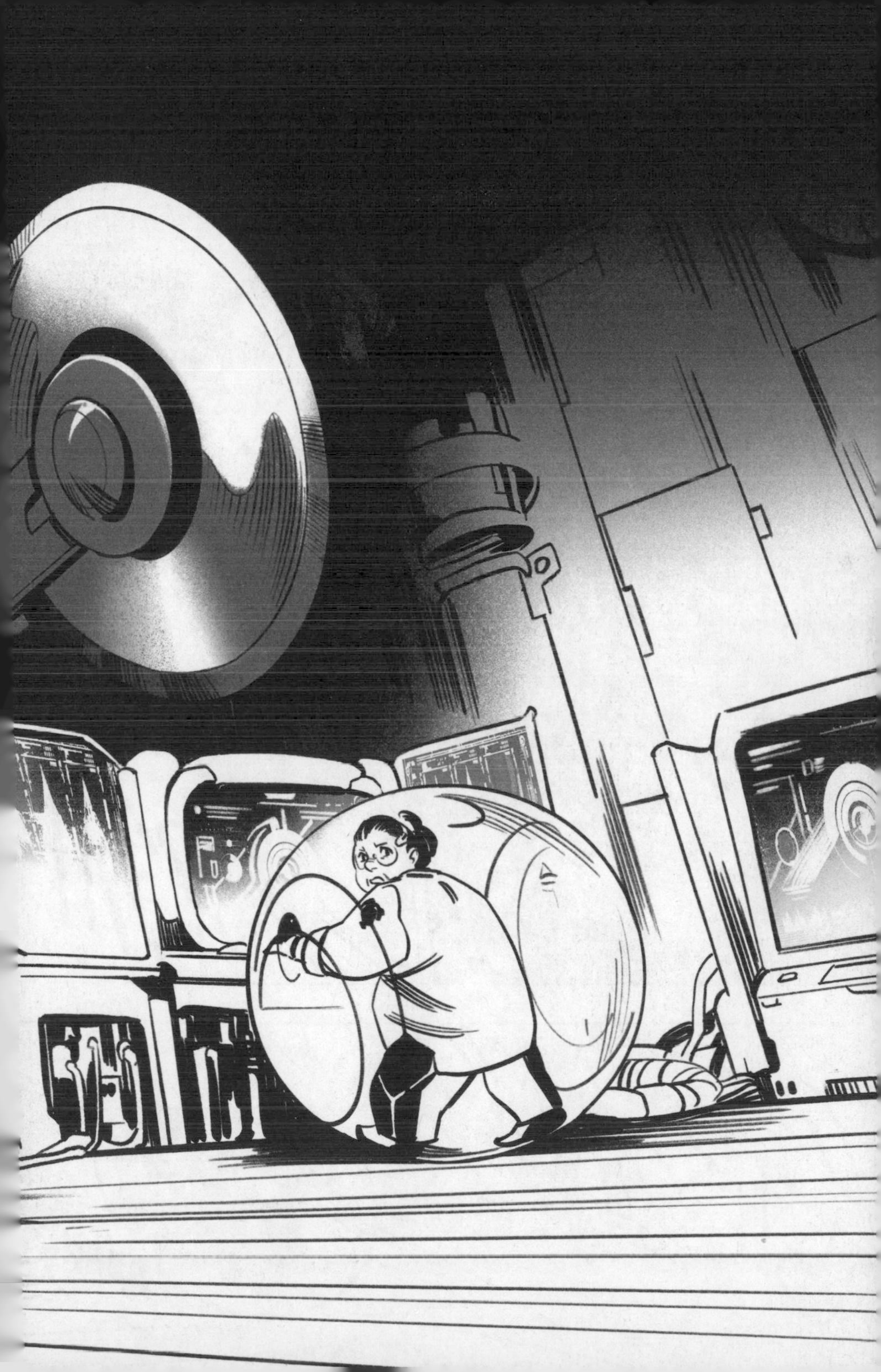

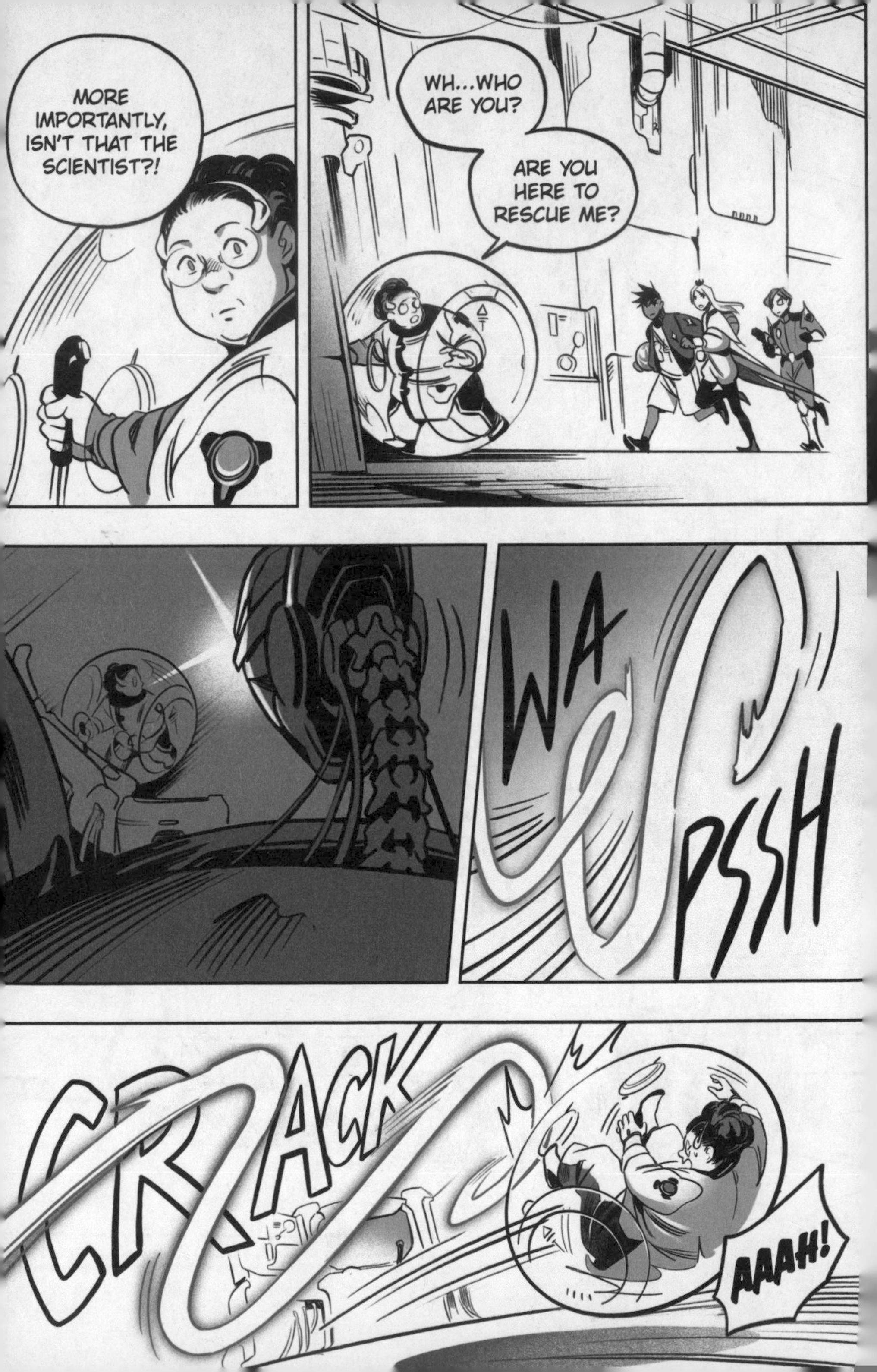
MORE IMPORTANTLY, ISN'T THAT THE SCIENTIST?!
WH...WHO ARE YOU?
ARE YOU HERE TO RESCUE ME?
WA
PSSH
CRACK
AAAH!

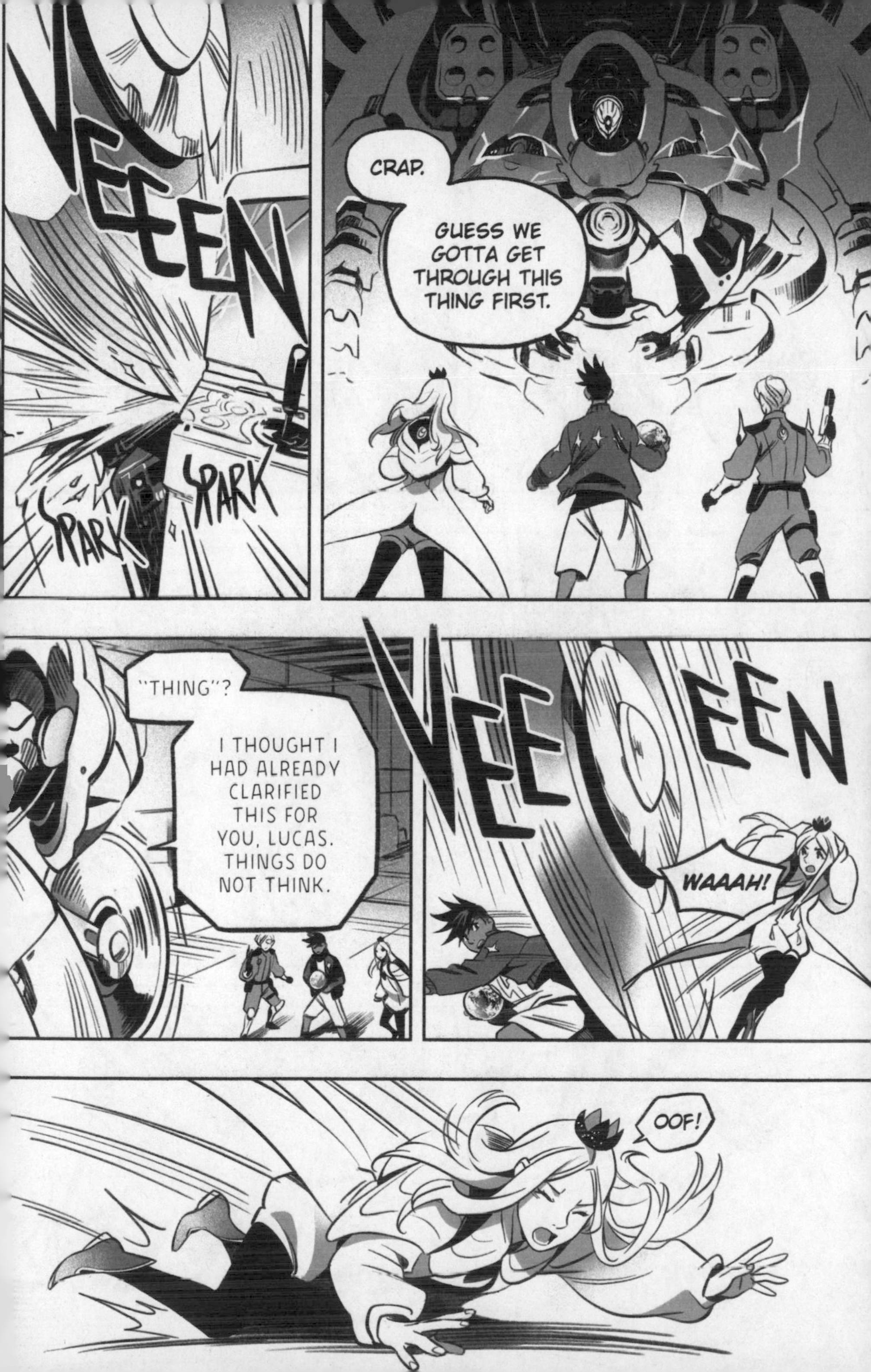
VEEEN
SPARK
SPARK
CRAP.
GUESS WE GOTTA GET THROUGH THIS THING FIRST.
"THING"?
I THOUGHT I HAD ALREADY CLARIFIED THIS FOR YOU, LUCAS. THINGS DO NOT THINK.
VEEEEN
WAAAH!
OOF!

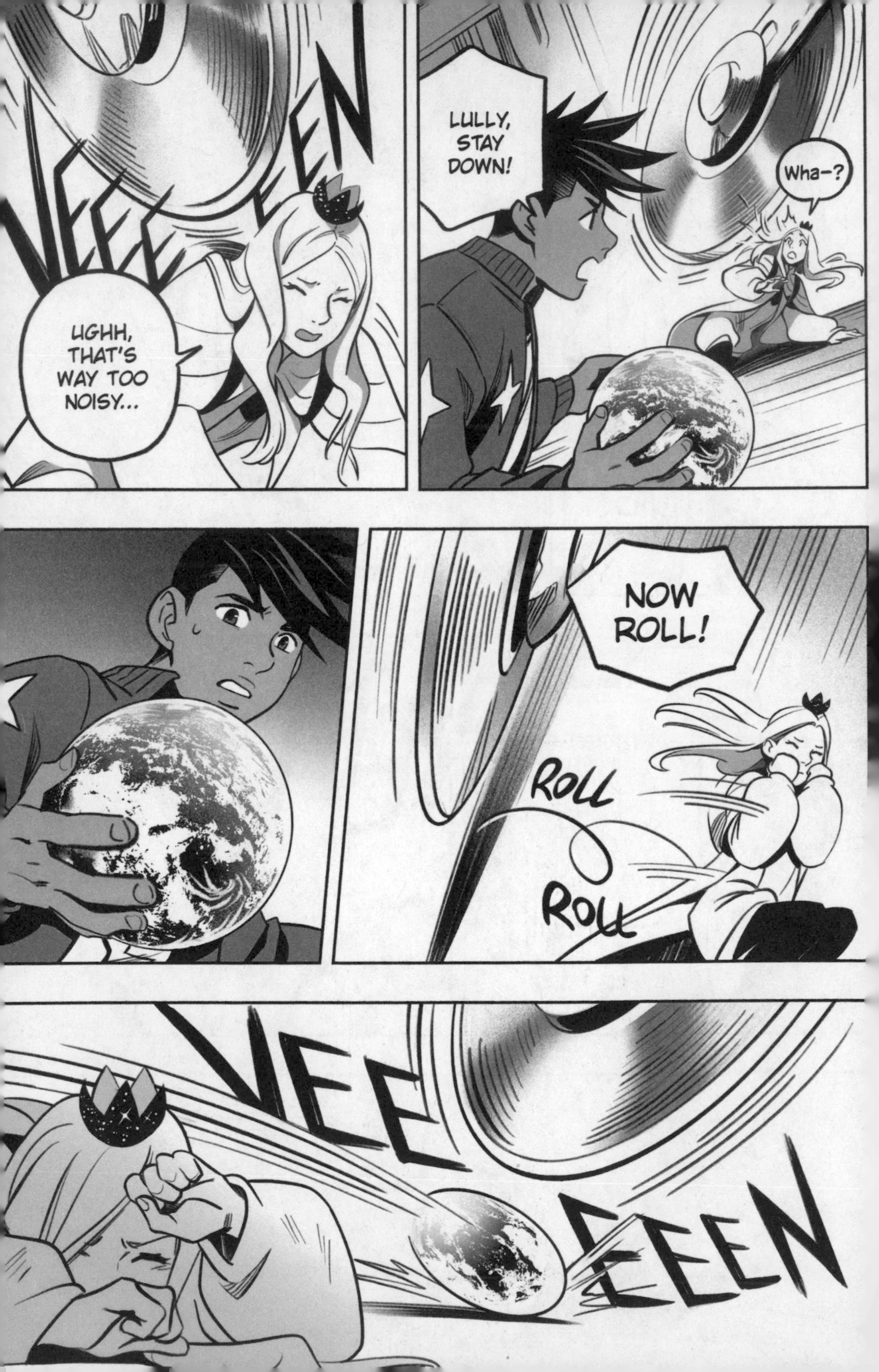
VEEEEEN
UGHH, THAT'S WAY TOO NOISY...
LULLY, STAY DOWN!
Wha-?
NOW ROLL!
ROLL
ROLL
VEEEEEEN

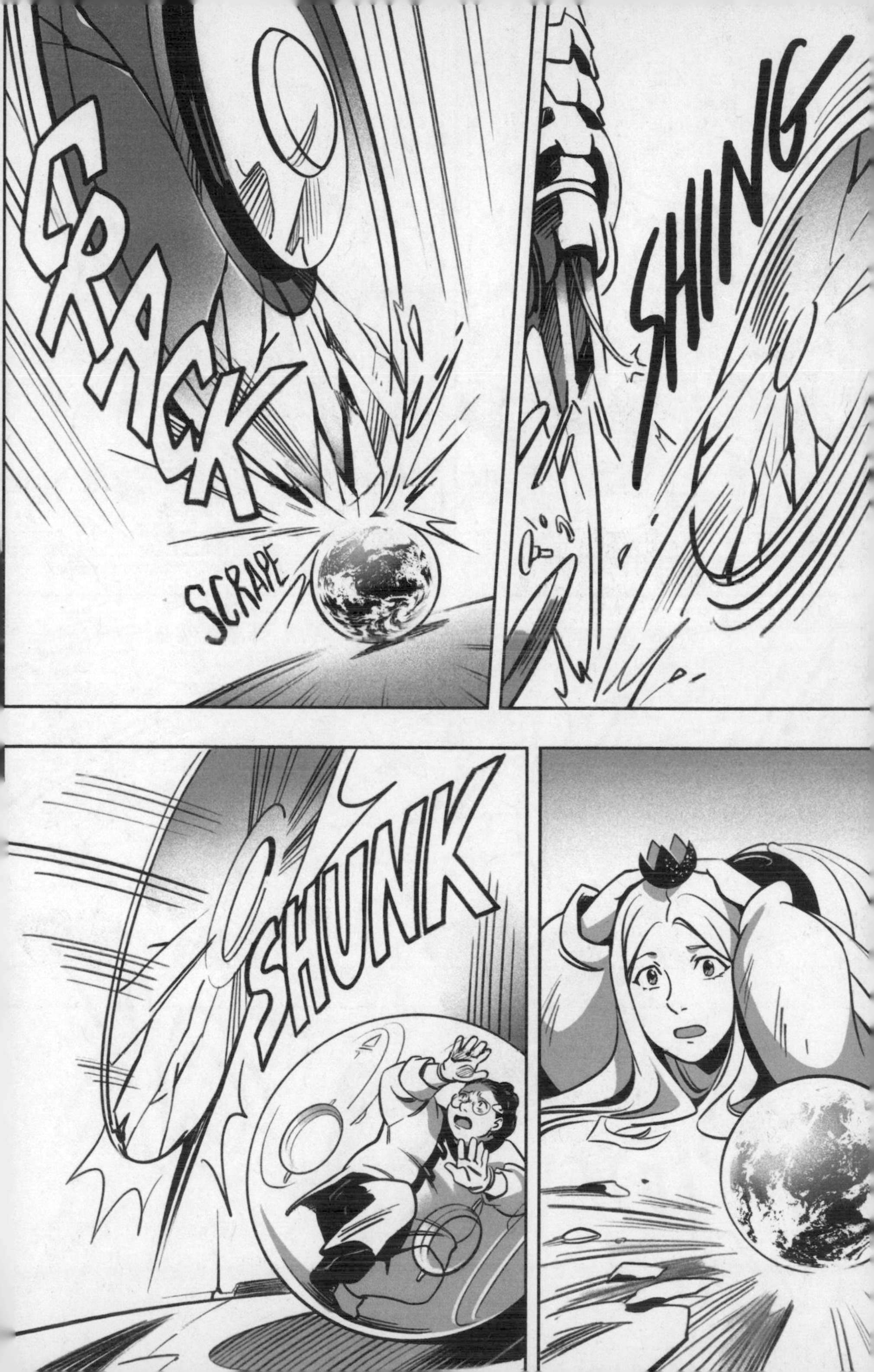
CRACK
SCRAPE
SHING
SHUNK

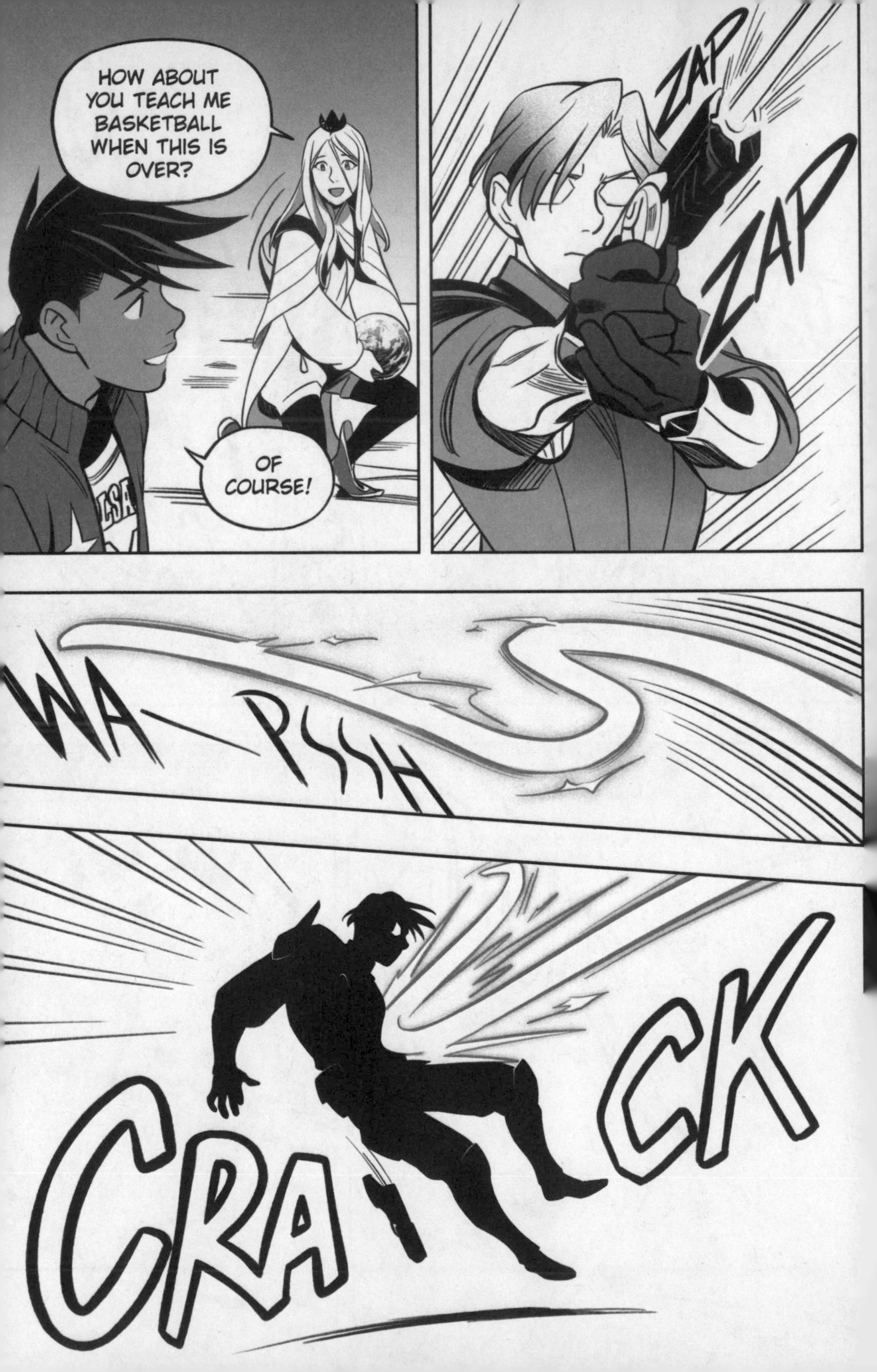
HOW ABOUT YOU TEACH ME BASKETBALL WHEN THIS IS OVER?
OF COURSE!
ZAP
ZAP
WA—PSSSH
CRA CK

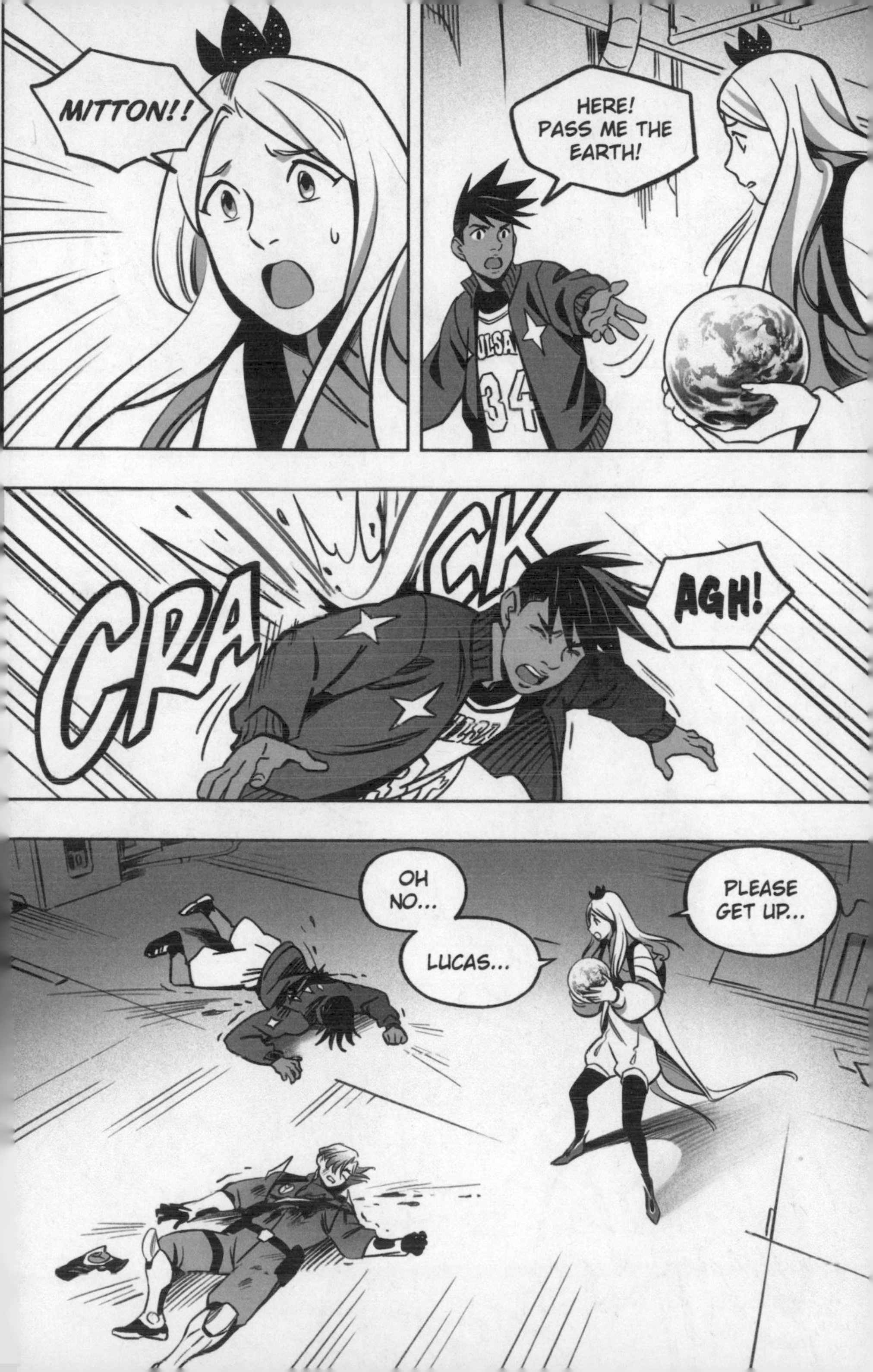
MITTON!!
HERE! PASS ME THE EARTH!
34
CRACK
AGH!
OH NO...
LUCAS...
PLEASE GET UP...

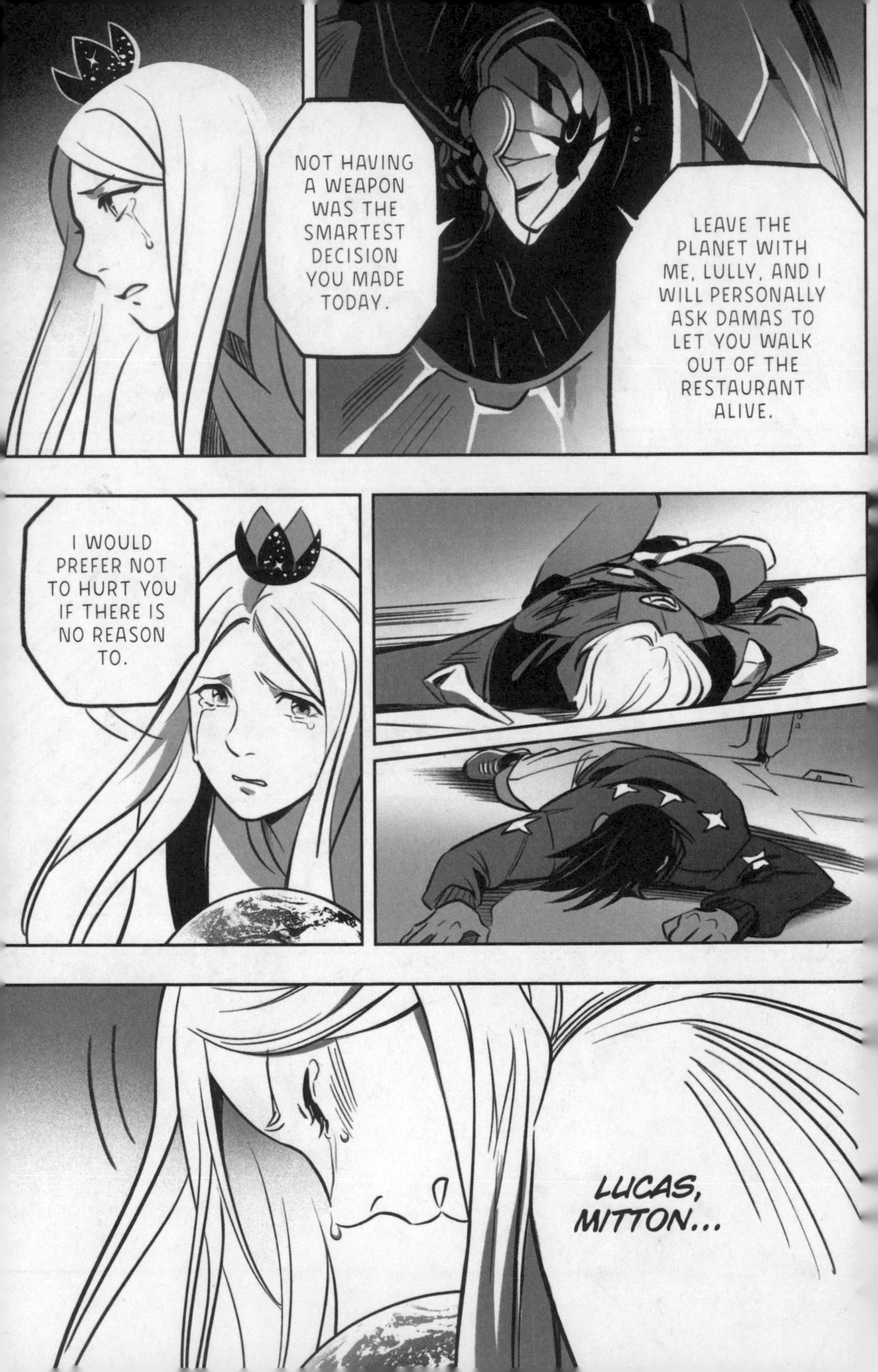
NOT HAVING A WEAPON WAS THE SMARTEST DECISION YOU MADE TODAY.
LEAVE THE PLANET WITH ME, LULLY, AND I WILL PERSONALLY ASK DAMAS TO LET YOU WALK OUT OF THE RESTAURANT ALIVE.
I WOULD PREFER NOT TO HURT YOU IF THERE IS NO REASON TO.
LUCAS, MITTON...

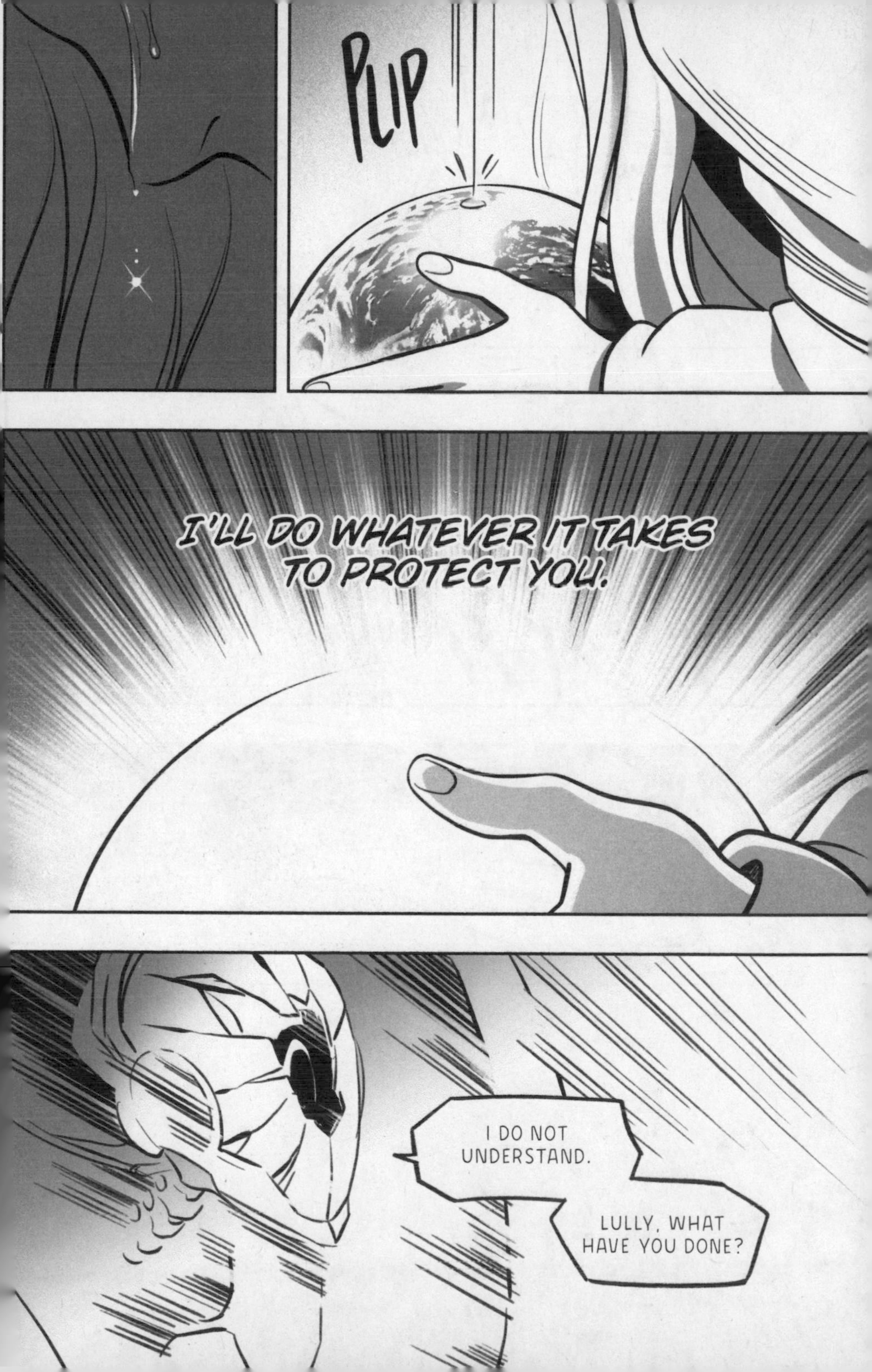
PLIP
I'LL DO WHATEVER IT TAKES TO PROTECT YOU.
I DO NOT UNDERSTAND.
LULLY, WHAT HAVE YOU DONE?

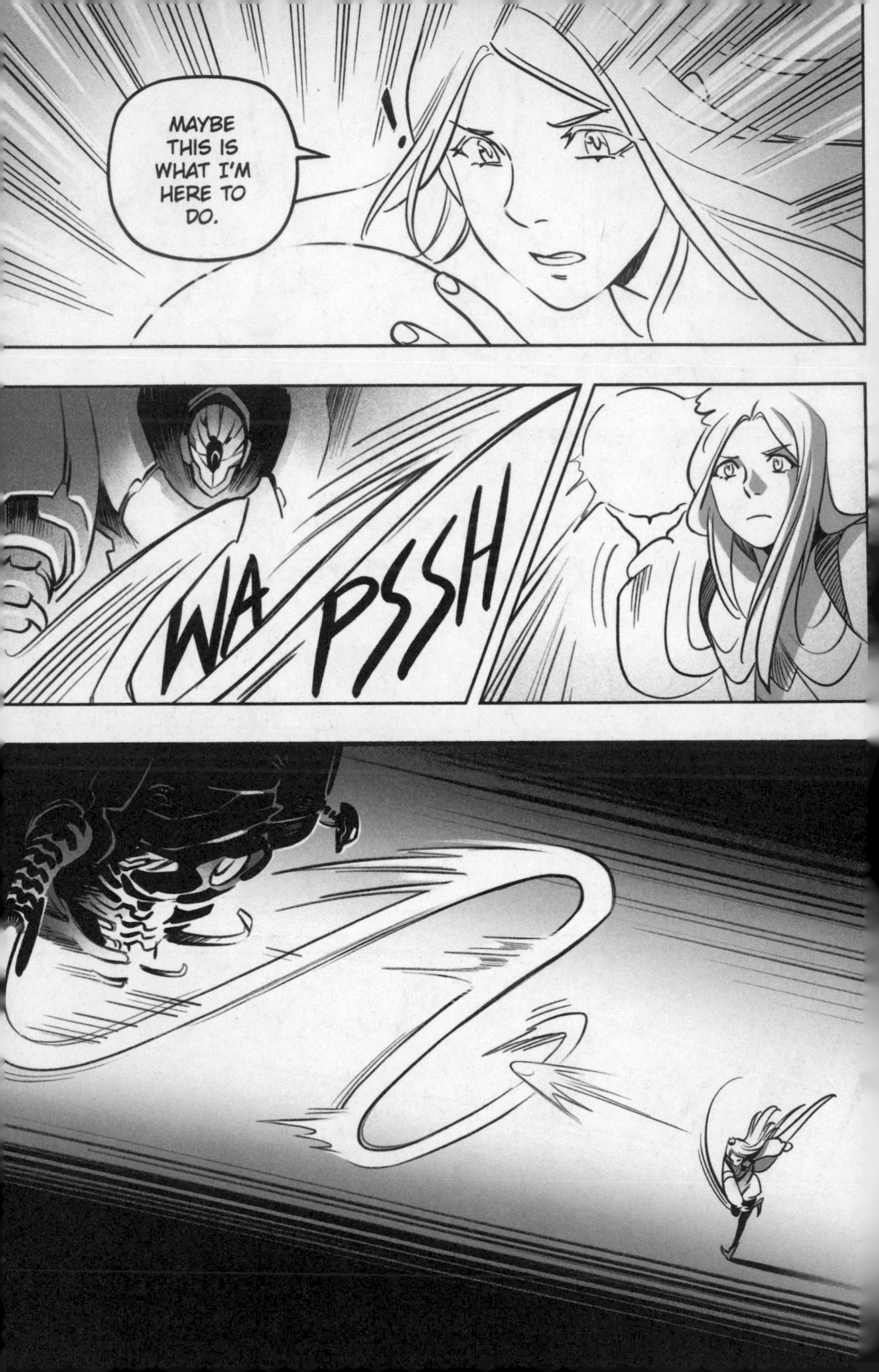
MAYBE THIS IS WHAT I'M HERE TO DO.
!
WA PSSH

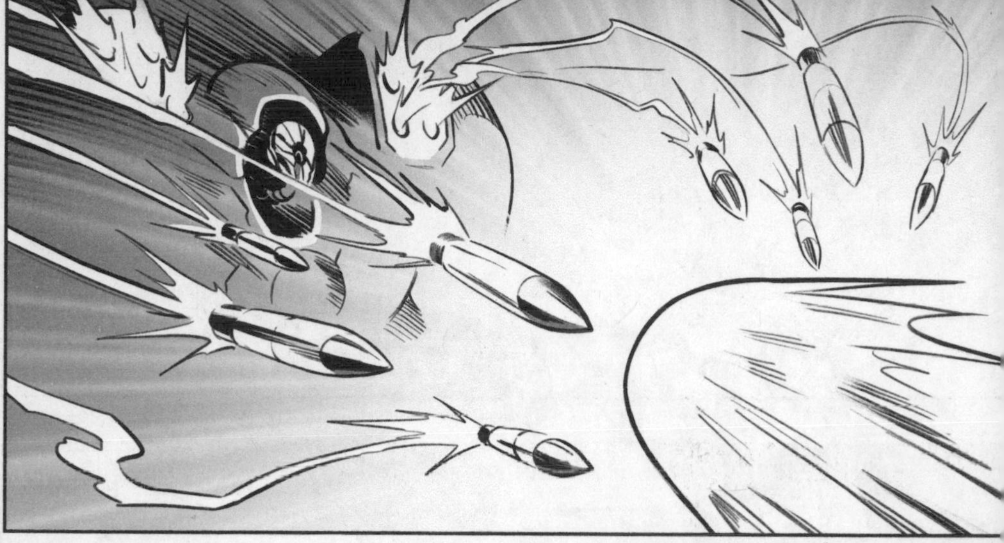

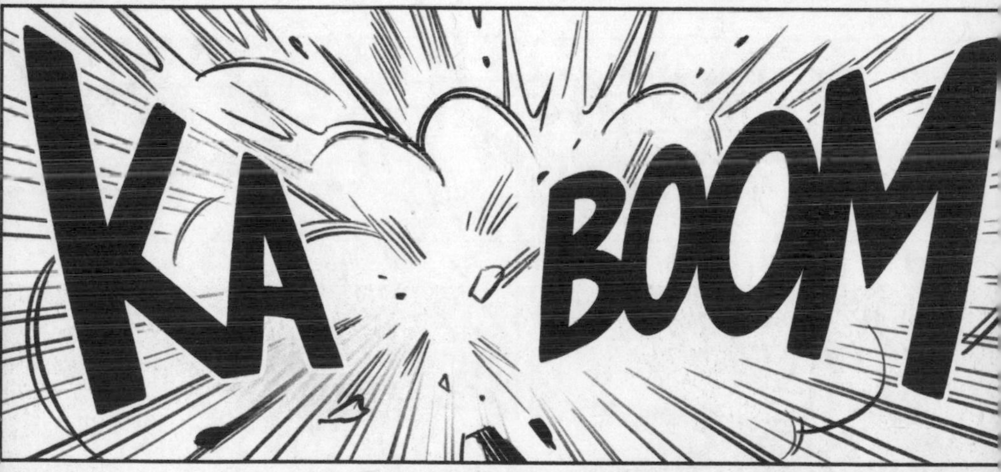
KA BOOM

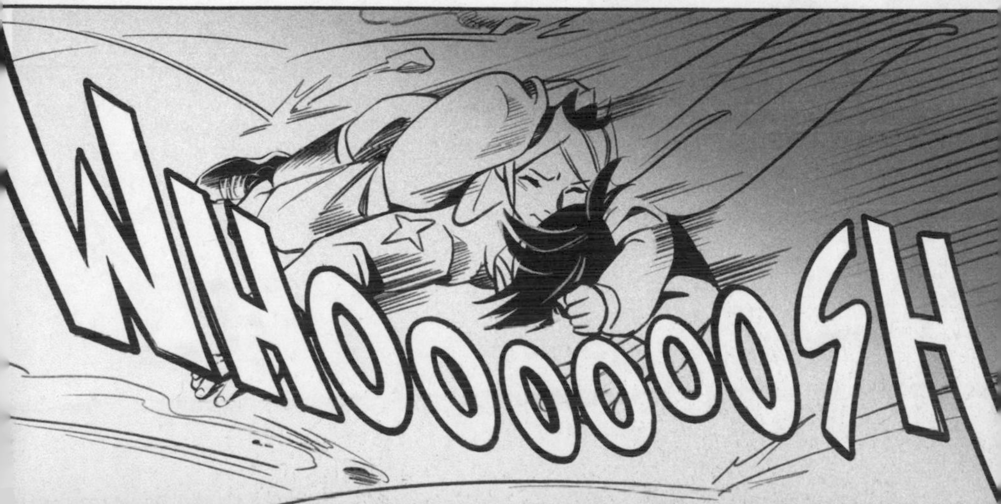
WHOOOOOOSH

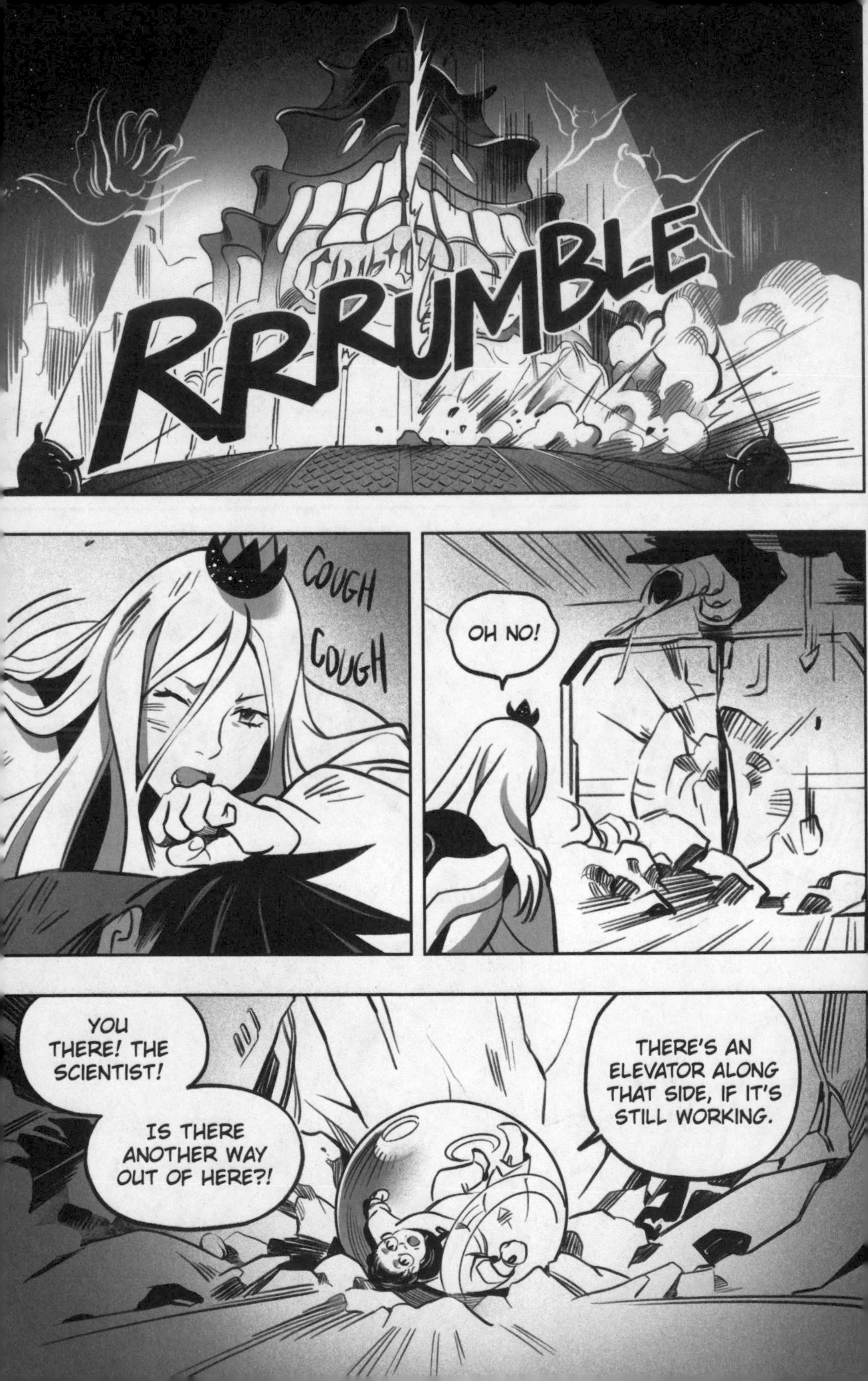
RRRUMBLE
COUGH
COUGH
OH NO!
YOU THERE! THE SCIENTIST!
IS THERE ANOTHER WAY OUT OF HERE?!
THERE'S AN ELEVATOR ALONG THAT SIDE, IF IT'S STILL WORKING.

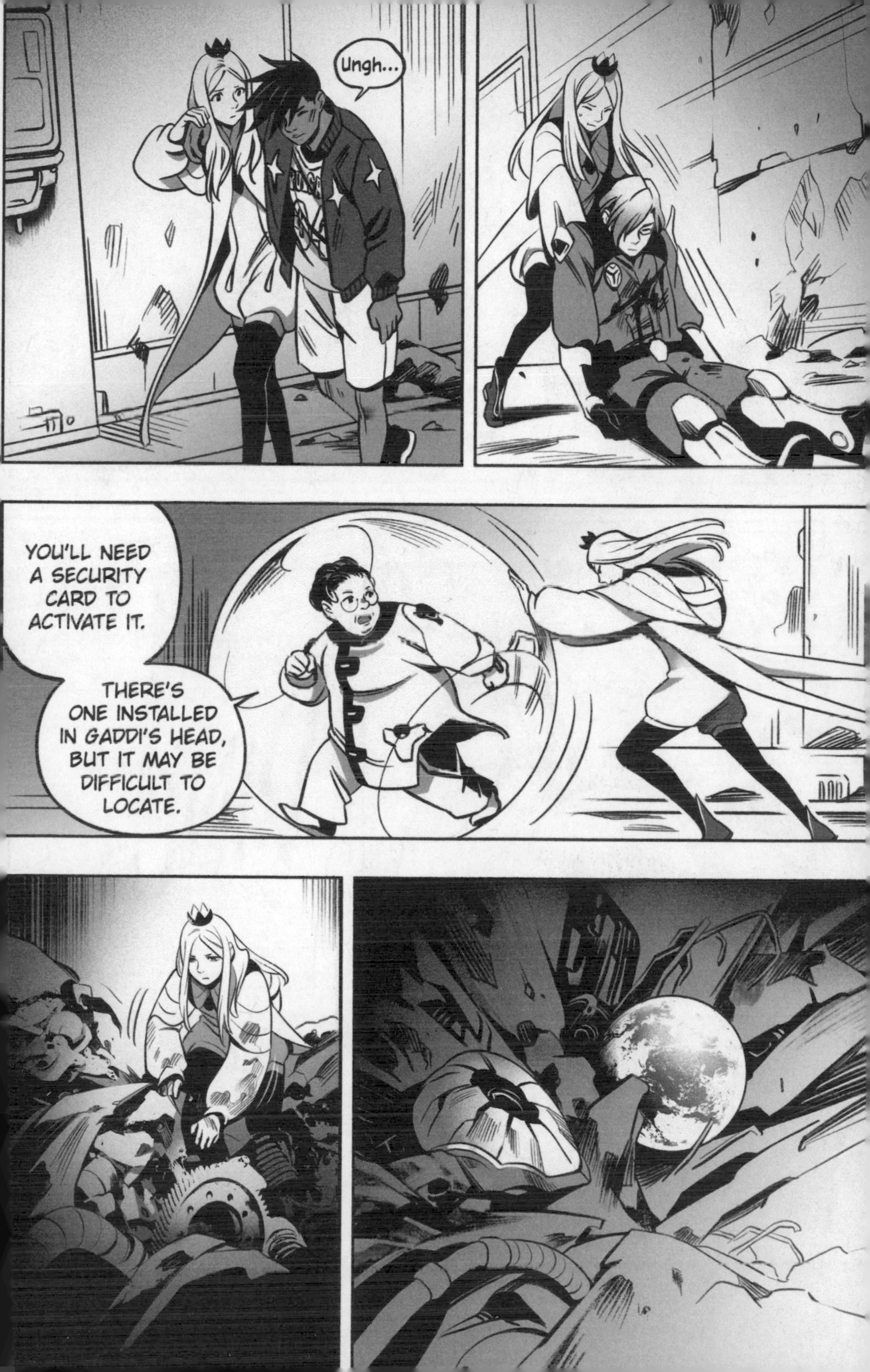
Ungh...
YOU'LL NEED A SECURITY CARD TO ACTIVATE IT.
THERE'S ONE INSTALLED IN GADDI'S HEAD, BUT IT MAY BE DIFFICULT TO LOCATE.

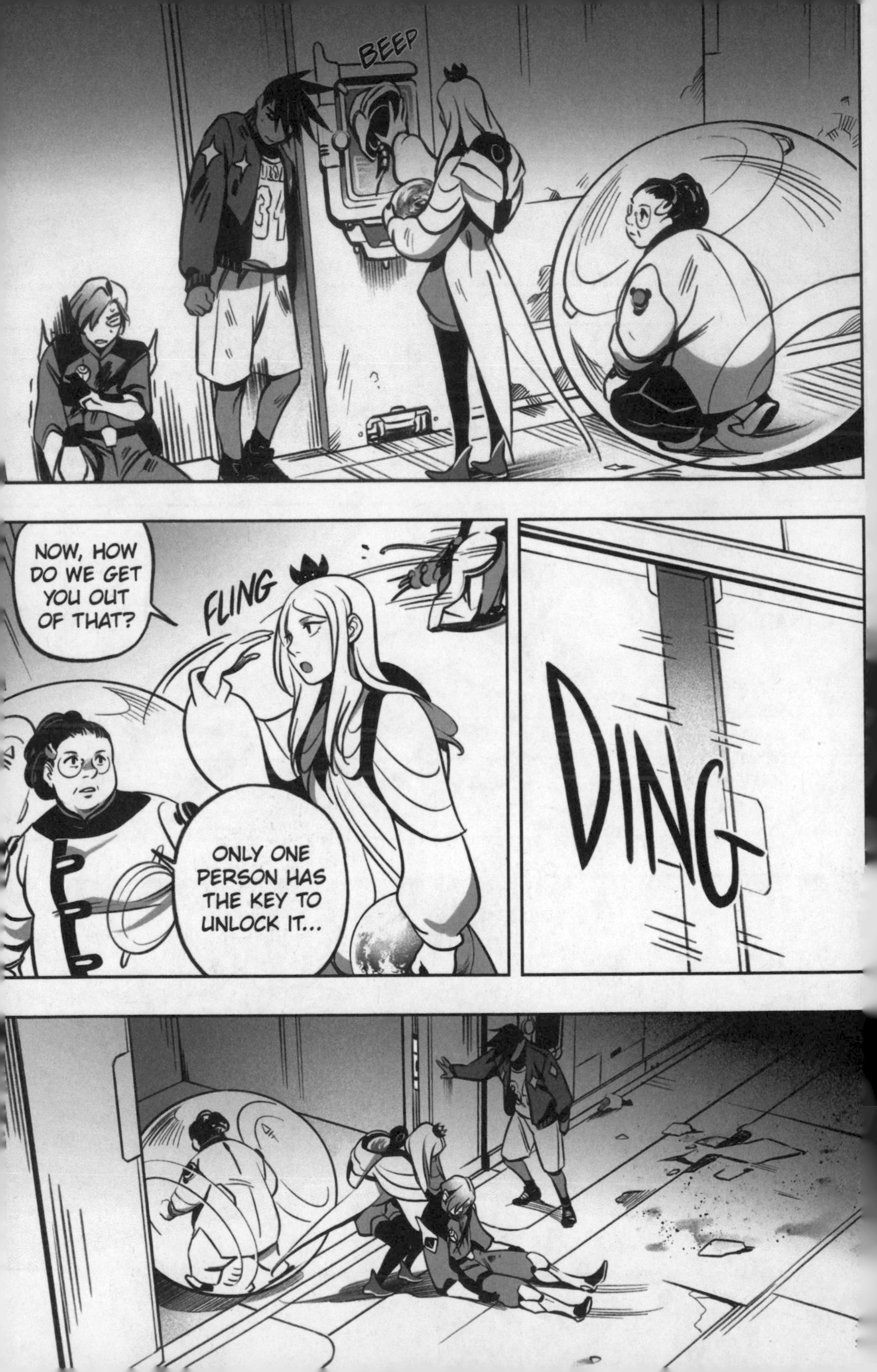
BEEP
NOW, HOW DO WE GET YOU OUT OF THAT?
FLING
ONLY ONE PERSON HAS THE KEY TO UNLOCK IT...
DING

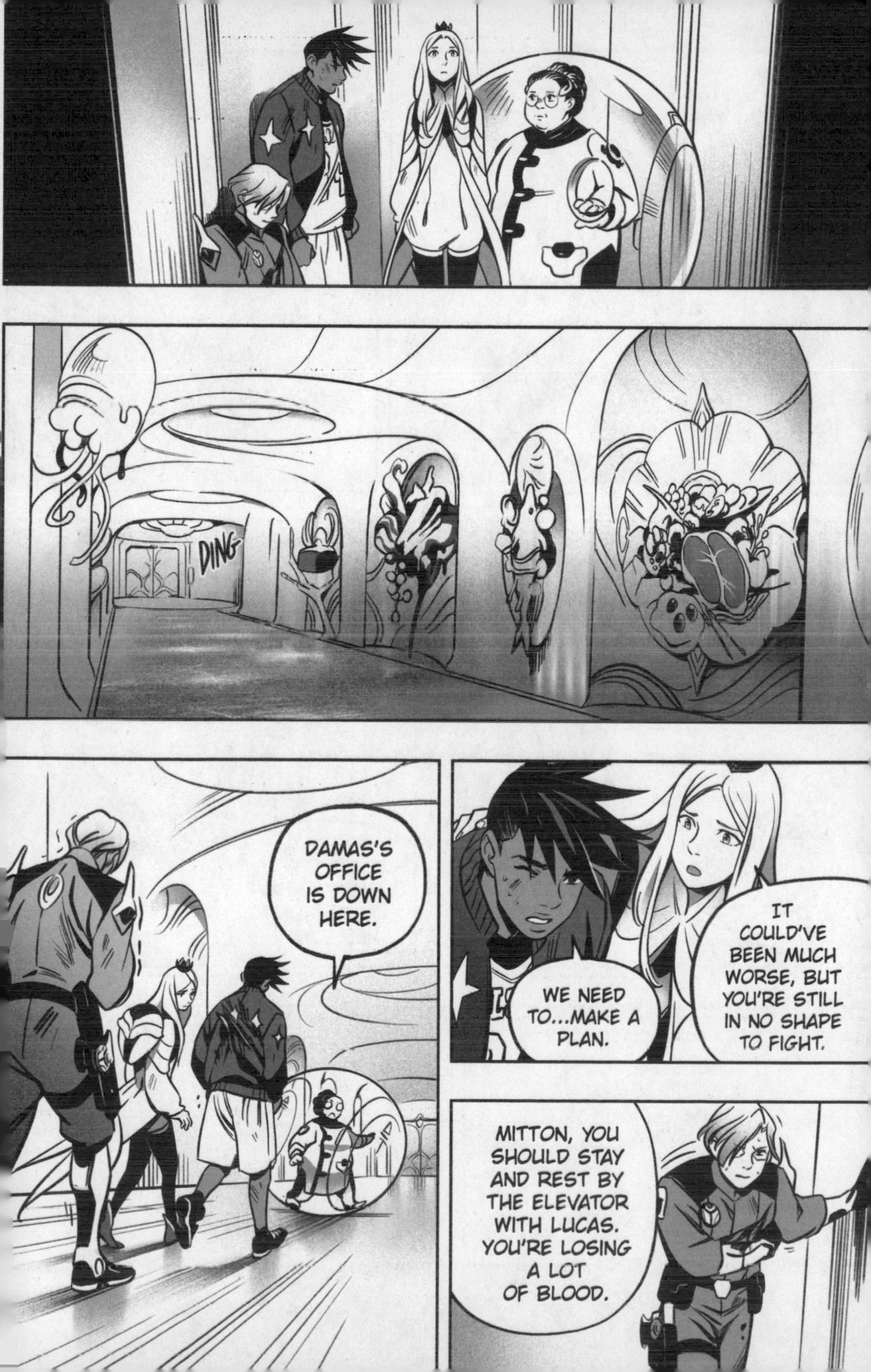
DING
DAMAS'S OFFICE IS DOWN HERE.
WE NEED TO...MAKE A PLAN.
IT COULD'VE BEEN MUCH WORSE, BUT YOU'RE STILL IN NO SHAPE TO FIGHT.
MITTON, YOU SHOULD STAY AND REST BY THE ELEVATOR WITH LUCAS. YOU'RE LOSING A LOT OF BLOOD.

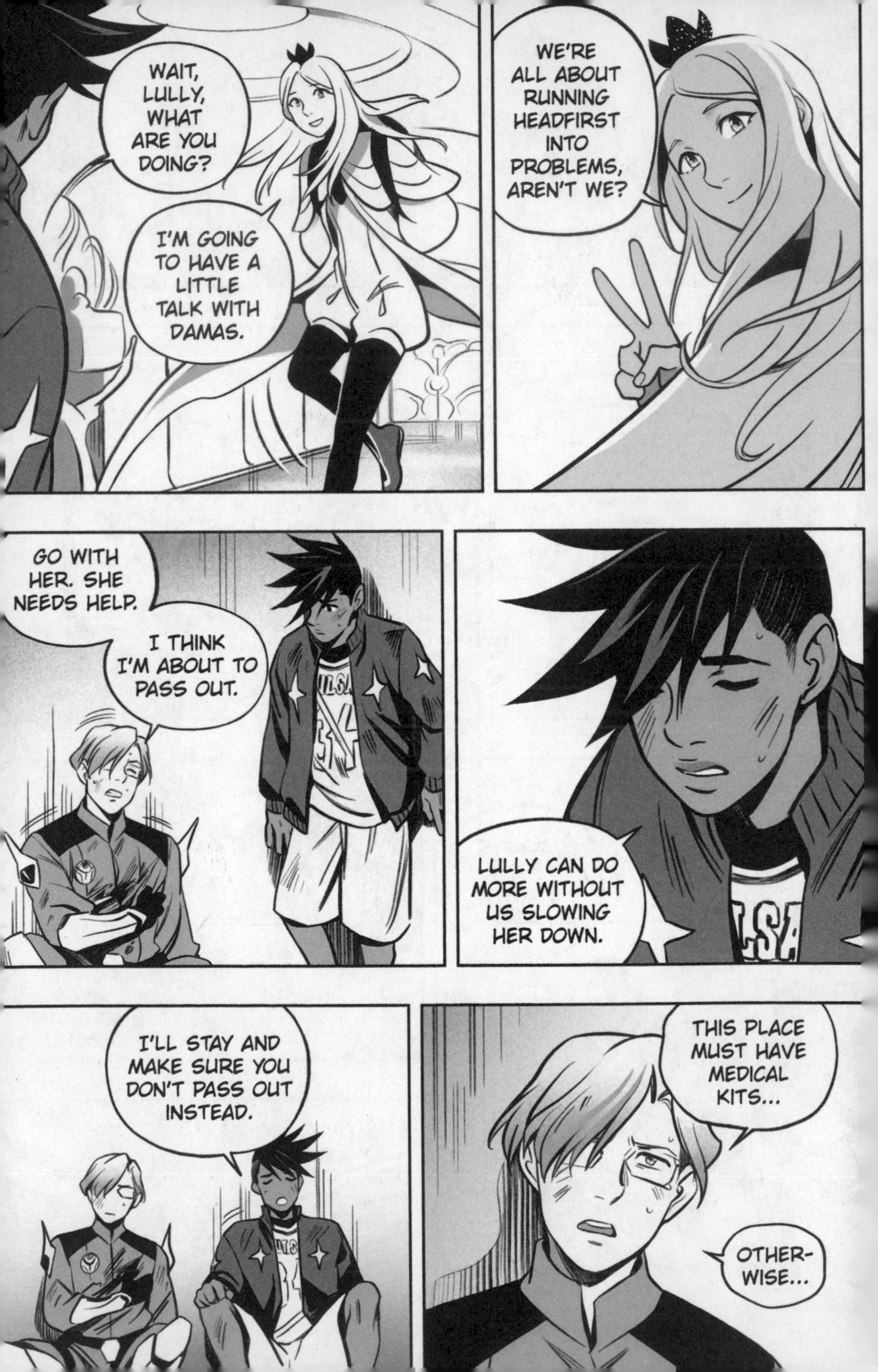
WAIT, LULLY, WHAT ARE YOU DOING?
I'M GOING TO HAVE A LITTLE TALK WITH DAMAS.
WE'RE ALL ABOUT RUNNING HEADFIRST INTO PROBLEMS, AREN'T WE?
GO WITH HER. SHE NEEDS HELP.
I THINK I'M ABOUT TO PASS OUT.
LULLY CAN DO MORE WITHOUT US SLOWING HER DOWN.
I'LL STAY AND MAKE SURE YOU DON'T PASS OUT INSTEAD.
THIS PLACE MUST HAVE MEDICAL KITS...
OTHER-WISE...

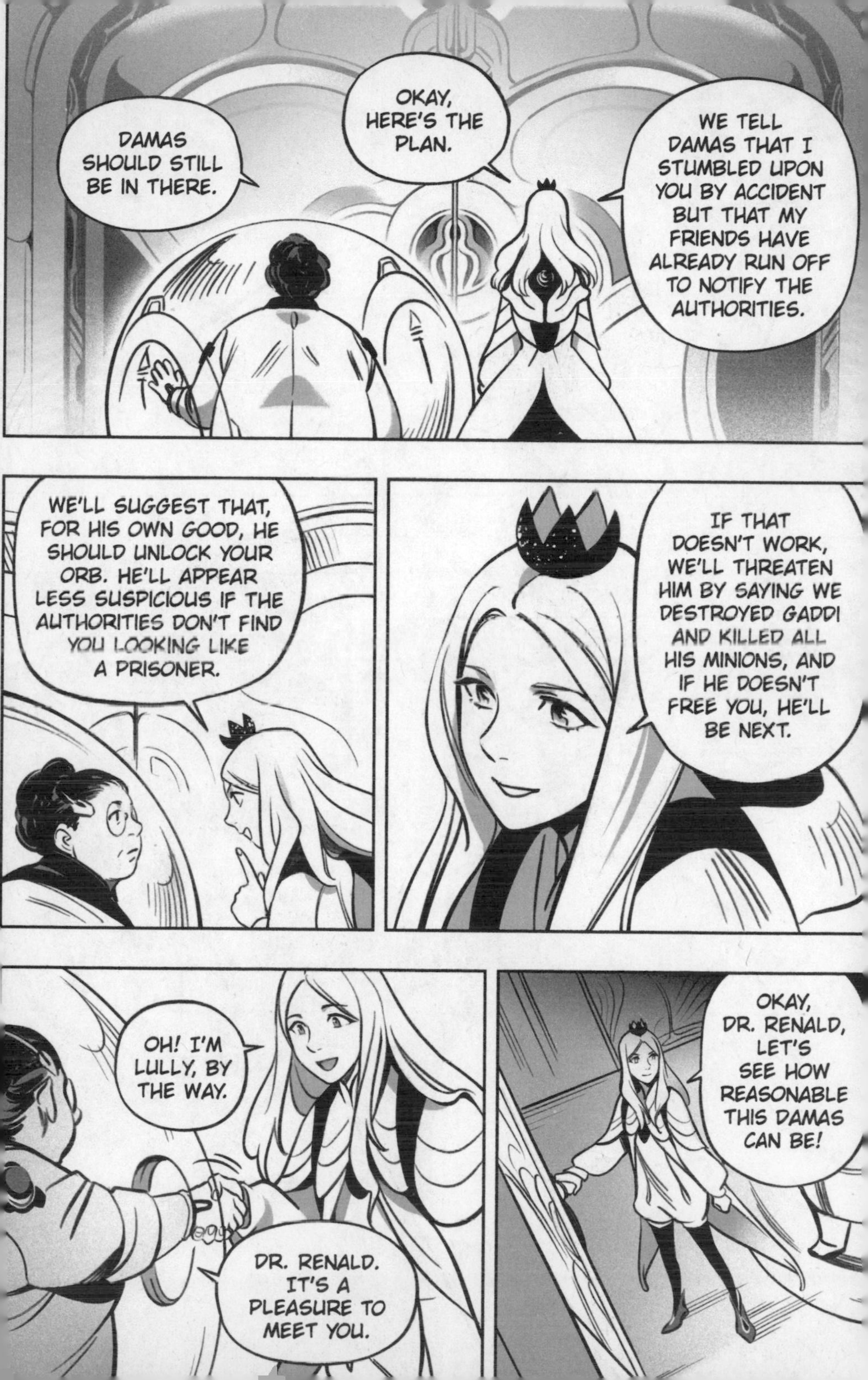
DAMAS SHOULD STILL BE IN THERE.
OKAY, HERE'S THE PLAN.
WE TELL DAMAS THAT I STUMBLED UPON YOU BY ACCIDENT BUT THAT MY FRIENDS HAVE ALREADY RUN OFF TO NOTIFY THE AUTHORITIES.
WE'LL SUGGEST THAT, FOR HIS OWN GOOD, HE SHOULD UNLOCK YOUR ORB. HE'LL APPEAR LESS SUSPICIOUS IF THE AUTHORITIES DON'T FIND YOU LOOKING LIKE A PRISONER.
IF THAT DOESN'T WORK, WE'LL THREATEN HIM BY SAYING WE DESTROYED GADDI AND KILLED ALL HIS MINIONS, AND IF HE DOESN'T FREE YOU, HE'LL BE NEXT.
OH! I'M LULLY, BY THE WAY.
DR. RENALD. IT'S A PLEASURE TO MEET YOU.
OKAY, DR. RENALD, LET'S SEE HOW REASONABLE THIS DAMAS CAN BE!

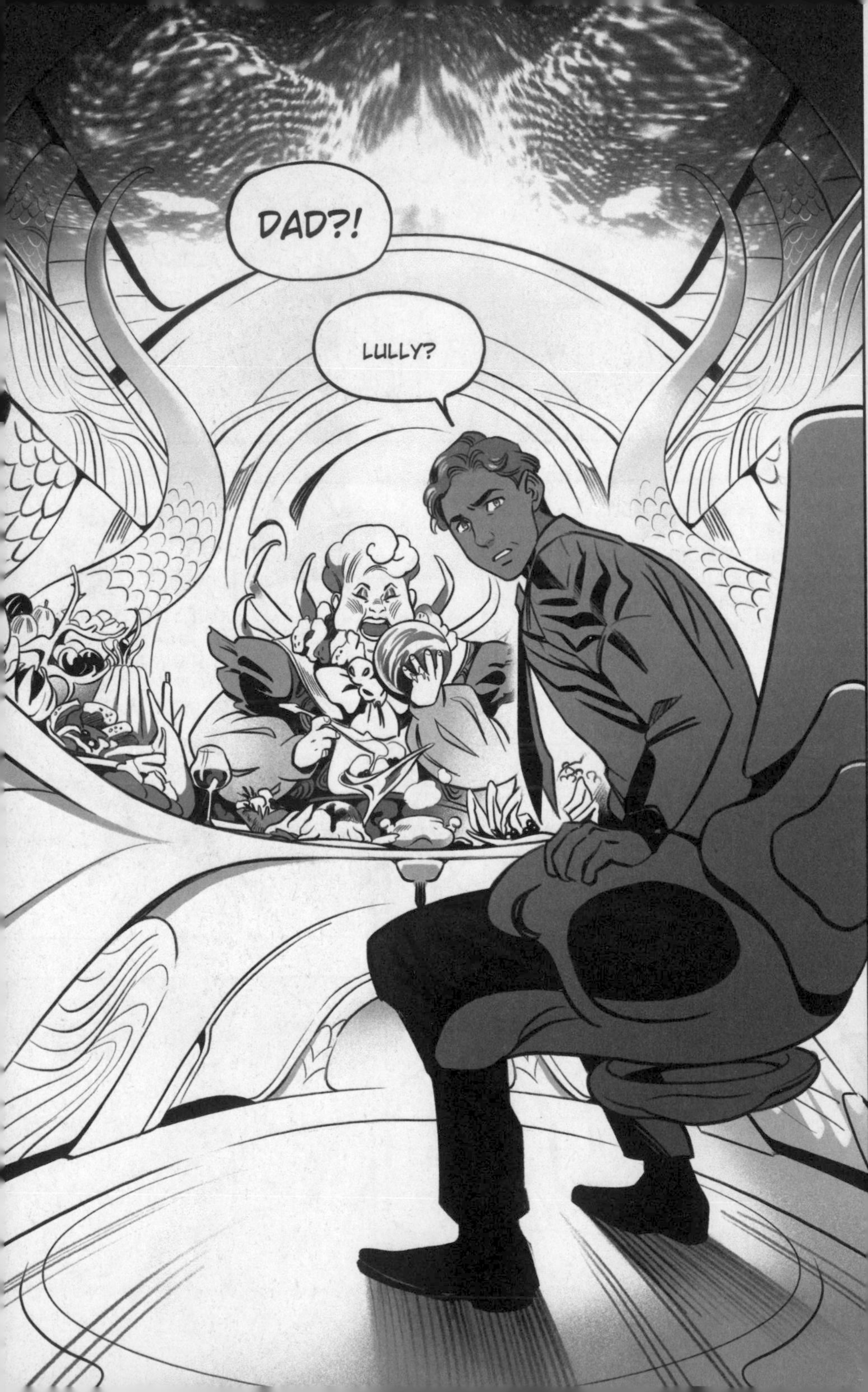
DAD?!
LULLY?

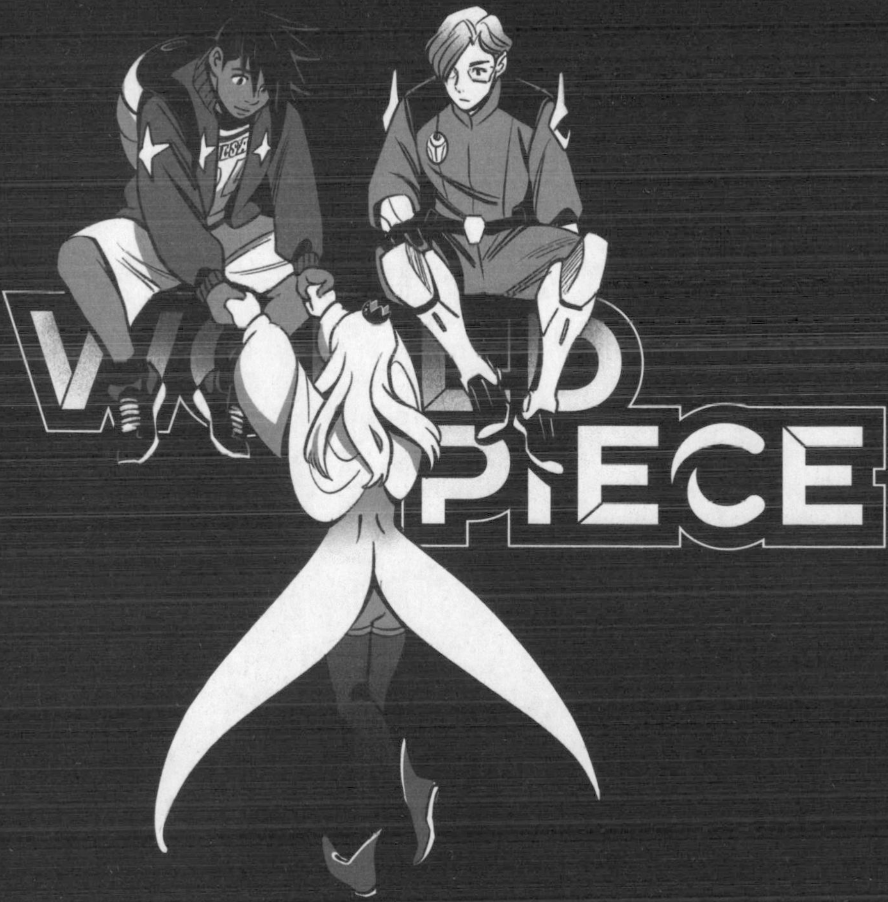
PIECE

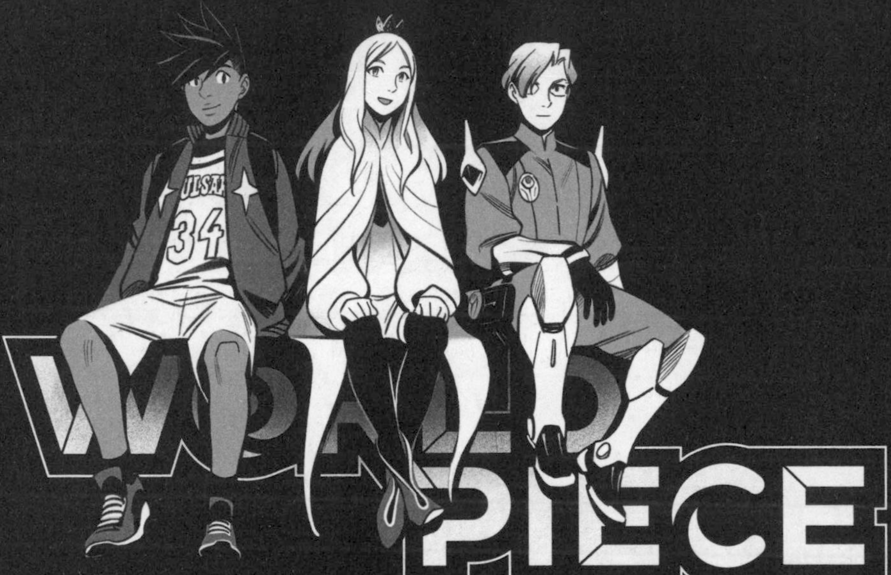
WORLD
PIECE
34

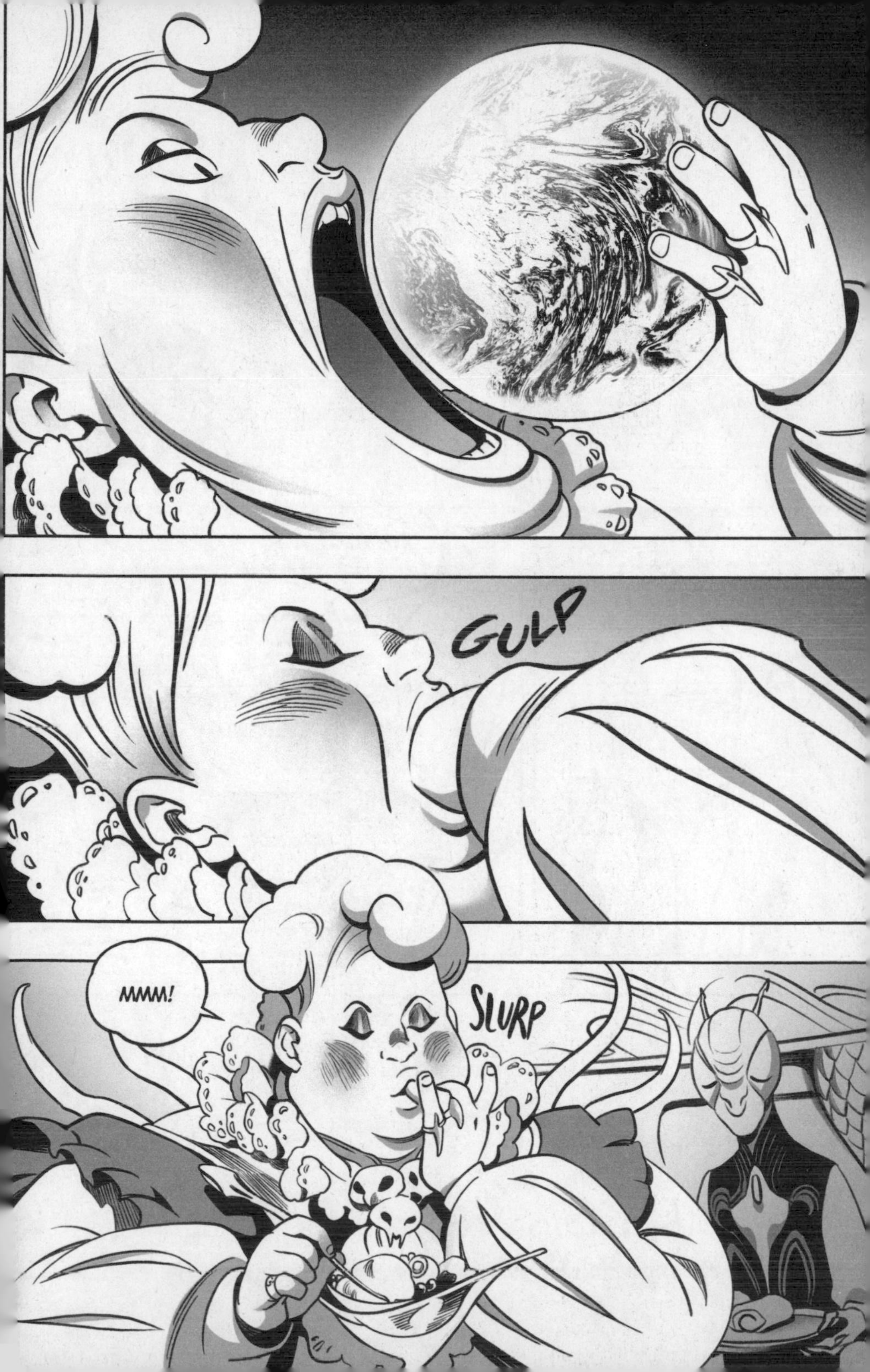
GULP
MMMM!
SLURP

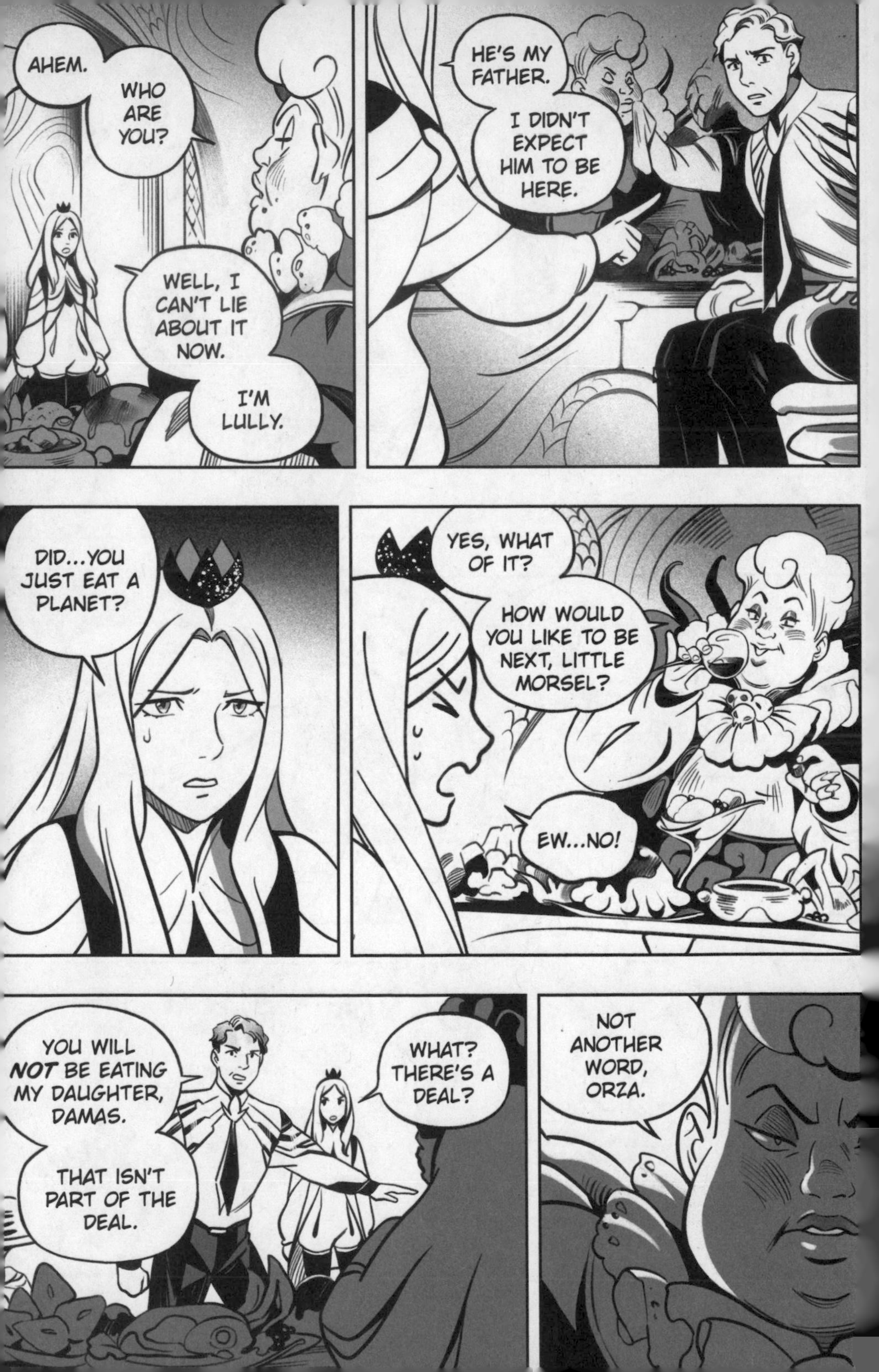
AHEM.
WHO ARE YOU?
WELL, I CAN'T LIE ABOUT IT NOW.
I'M LULLY.
HE'S MY FATHER.
I DIDN'T EXPECT HIM TO BE HERE.
DID...YOU JUST EAT A PLANET?
YES, WHAT OF IT?
HOW WOULD YOU LIKE TO BE NEXT, LITTLE MORSEL?
EW...NO!
YOU WILL **NOT** BE EATING MY DAUGHTER, DAMAS.
THAT ISN'T PART OF THE DEAL.
WHAT? THERE'S A DEAL?
NOT ANOTHER WORD, ORZA.

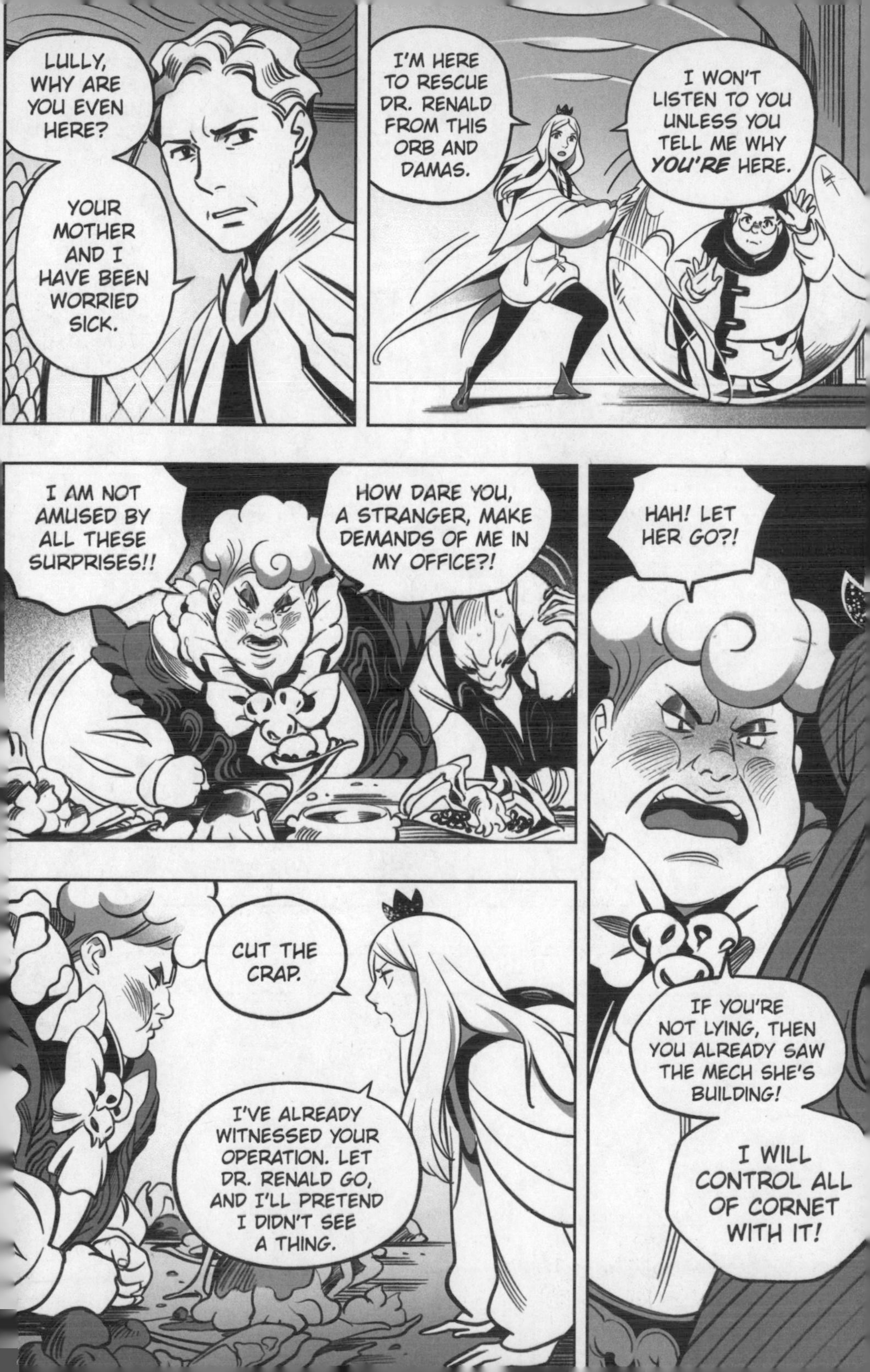
LULLY, WHY ARE YOU EVEN HERE?
YOUR MOTHER AND I HAVE BEEN WORRIED SICK.
I'M HERE TO RESCUE DR. RENALD FROM THIS ORB AND DAMAS.
I WON'T LISTEN TO YOU UNLESS YOU TELL ME WHY *YOU'RE* HERE.
I AM NOT AMUSED BY ALL THESE SURPRISES!!
HOW DARE YOU, A STRANGER, MAKE DEMANDS OF ME IN MY OFFICE?!
CUT THE CRAP.
I'VE ALREADY WITNESSED YOUR OPERATION. LET DR. RENALD GO, AND I'LL PRETEND I DIDN'T SEE A THING.
HAH! LET HER GO?!
IF YOU'RE NOT LYING, THEN YOU ALREADY SAW THE MECH SHE'S BUILDING!
I WILL CONTROL ALL OF CORNET WITH IT!

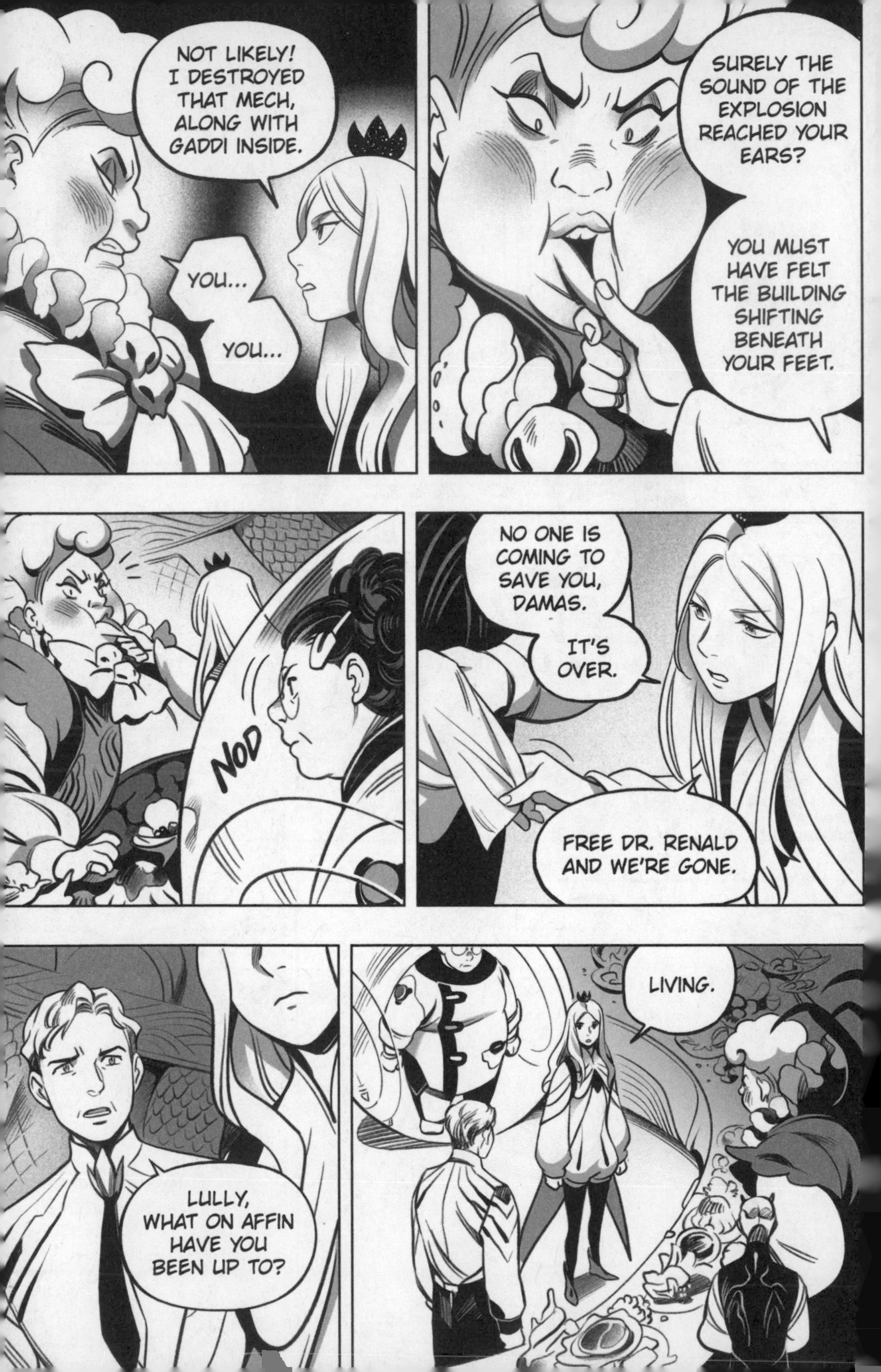
NOT LIKELY! I DESTROYED THAT MECH, ALONG WITH GADDI INSIDE.
YOU...
YOU...
SURELY THE SOUND OF THE EXPLOSION REACHED YOUR EARS?
YOU MUST HAVE FELT THE BUILDING SHIFTING BENEATH YOUR FEET.
NOD
NO ONE IS COMING TO SAVE YOU, DAMAS.
IT'S OVER.
FREE DR. RENALD AND WE'RE GONE.
LULLY, WHAT ON AFFIN HAVE YOU BEEN UP TO?
LIVING.

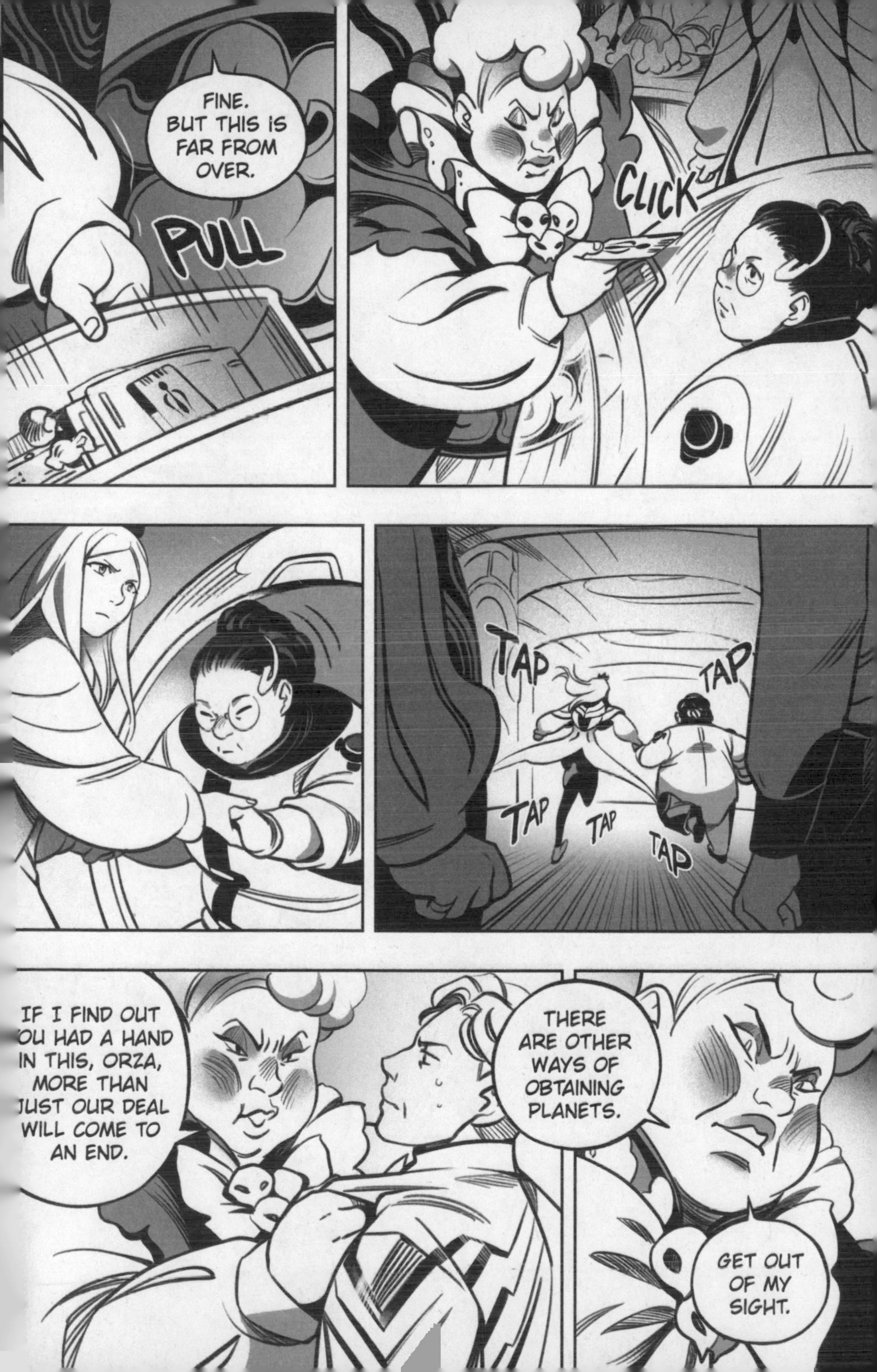
FINE. BUT THIS IS FAR FROM OVER.
PULL
CLICK
TAP
TAP
TAP
TAP
TAP
IF I FIND OUT OU HAD A HAND IN THIS, ORZA, MORE THAN JUST OUR DEAL WILL COME TO AN END.
THERE ARE OTHER WAYS OF OBTAINING PLANETS.
GET OUT OF MY SIGHT.

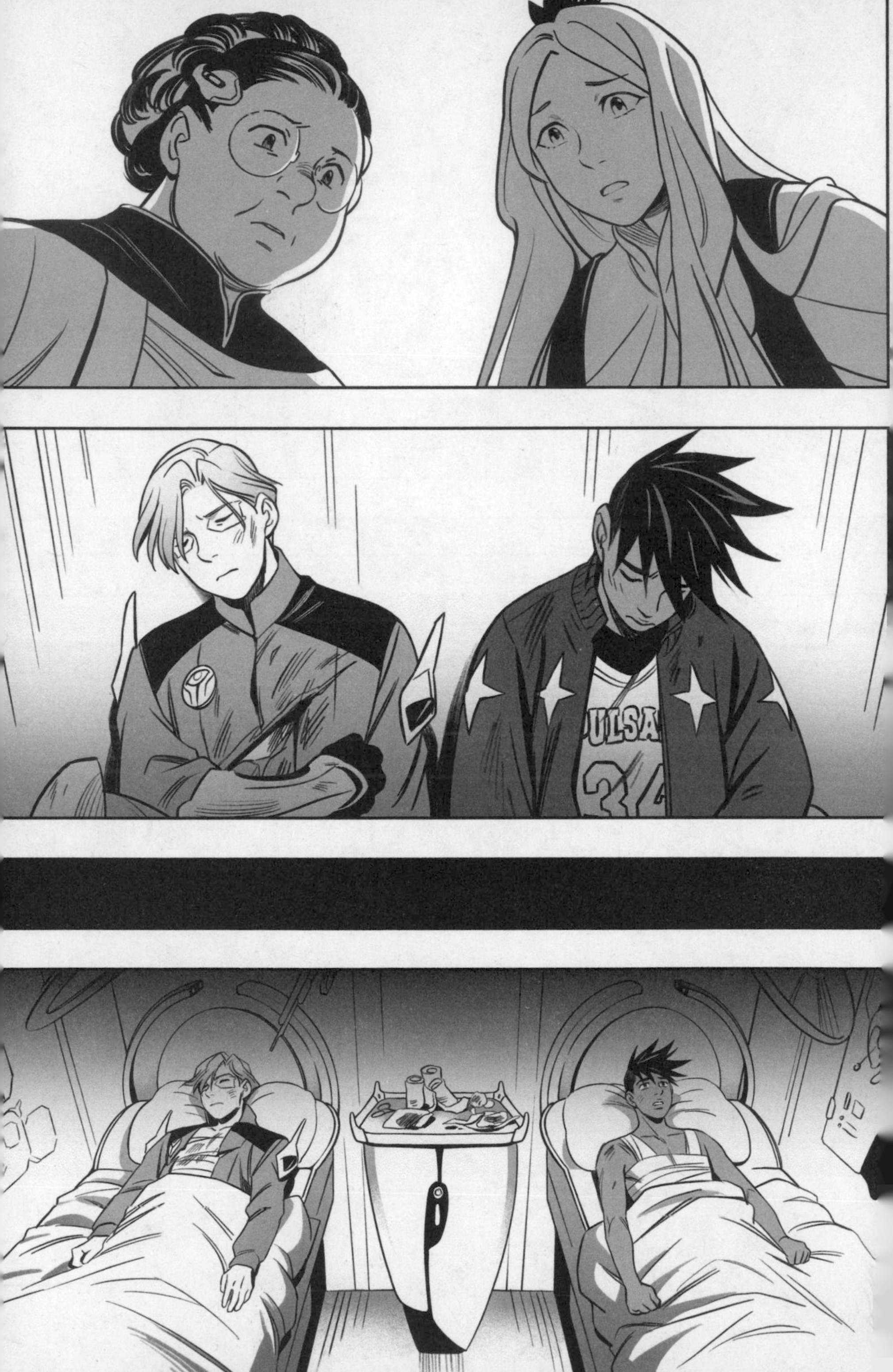

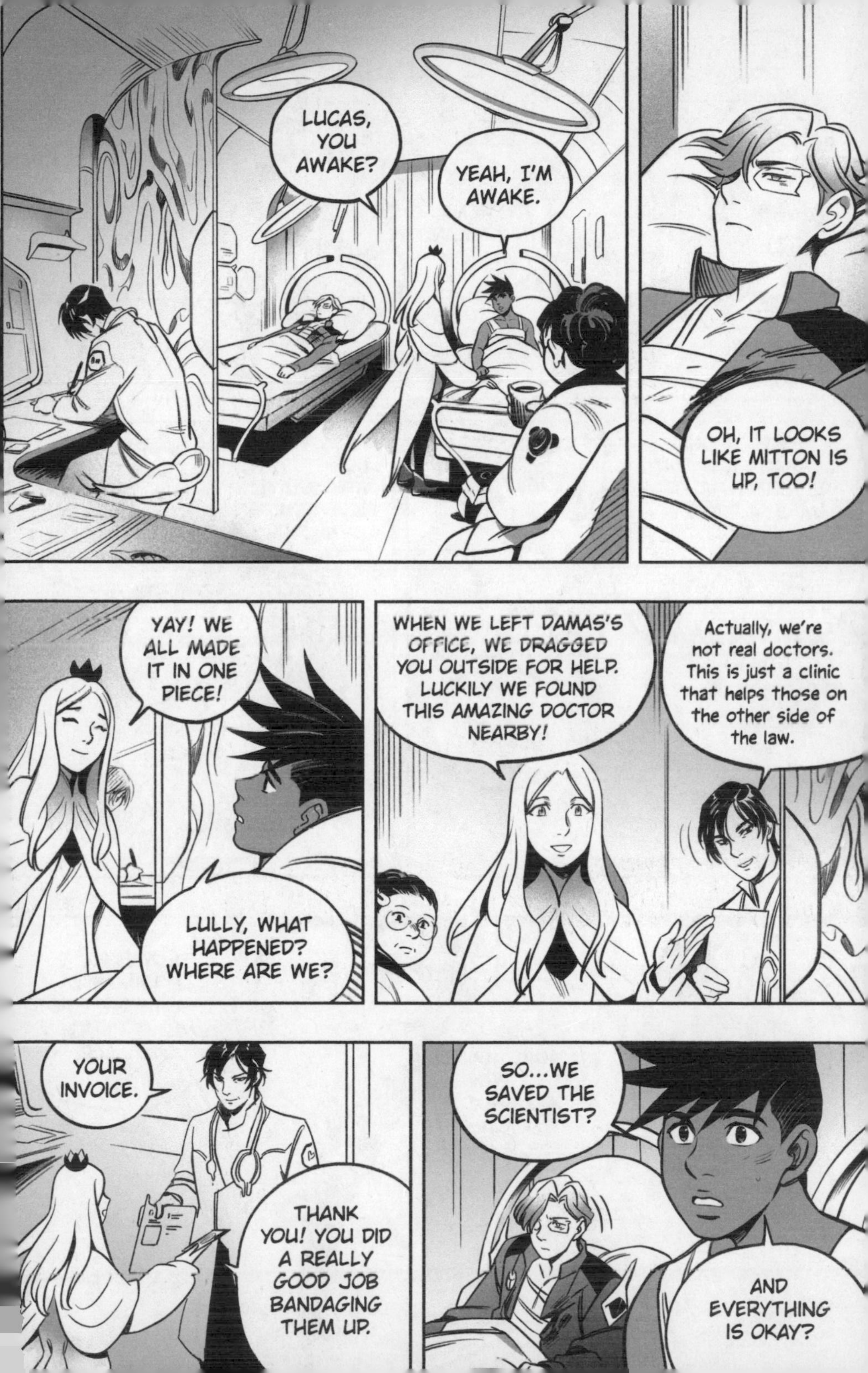
LUCAS, YOU AWAKE?
YEAH, I'M AWAKE.
OH, IT LOOKS LIKE MITTON IS UP, TOO!
YAY! WE ALL MADE IT IN ONE PIECE!
LULLY, WHAT HAPPENED? WHERE ARE WE?
WHEN WE LEFT DAMAS'S OFFICE, WE DRAGGED YOU OUTSIDE FOR HELP. LUCKILY WE FOUND THIS AMAZING DOCTOR NEARBY!
Actually, we're not real doctors. This is just a clinic that helps those on the other side of the law.
YOUR INVOICE.
THANK YOU! YOU DID A REALLY GOOD JOB BANDAGING THEM UP.
SO...WE SAVED THE SCIENTIST?
AND EVERYTHING IS OKAY?

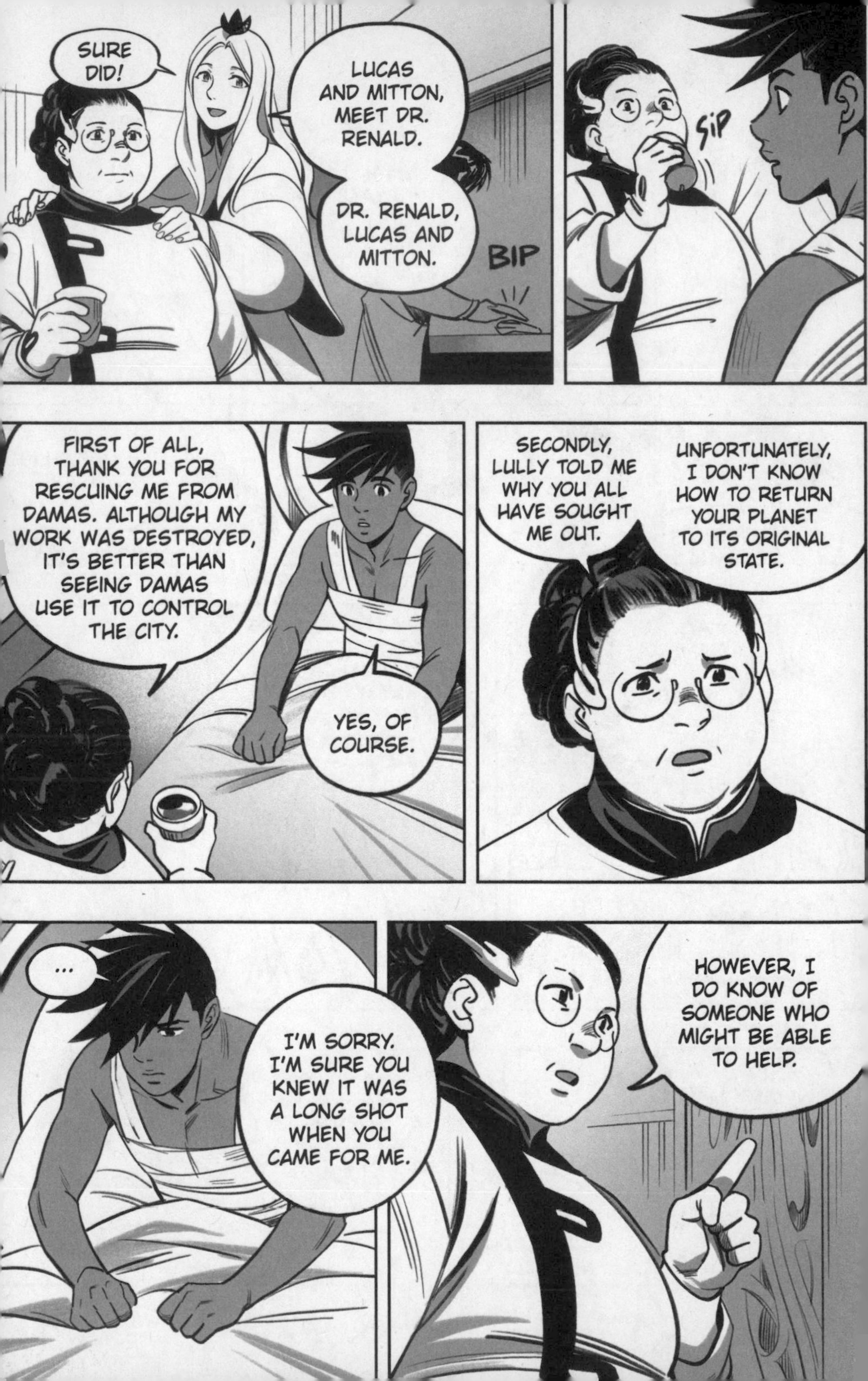
SURE DID!
LUCAS AND MITTON, MEET DR. RENALD.
DR. RENALD, LUCAS AND MITTON.
BIP
SIP
FIRST OF ALL, THANK YOU FOR RESCUING ME FROM DAMAS. ALTHOUGH MY WORK WAS DESTROYED, IT'S BETTER THAN SEEING DAMAS USE IT TO CONTROL THE CITY.
YES, OF COURSE.
SECONDLY, LULLY TOLD ME WHY YOU ALL HAVE SOUGHT ME OUT.
UNFORTUNATELY, I DON'T KNOW HOW TO RETURN YOUR PLANET TO ITS ORIGINAL STATE.
...
I'M SORRY. I'M SURE YOU KNEW IT WAS A LONG SHOT WHEN YOU CAME FOR ME.
HOWEVER, I DO KNOW OF SOMEONE WHO MIGHT BE ABLE TO HELP.

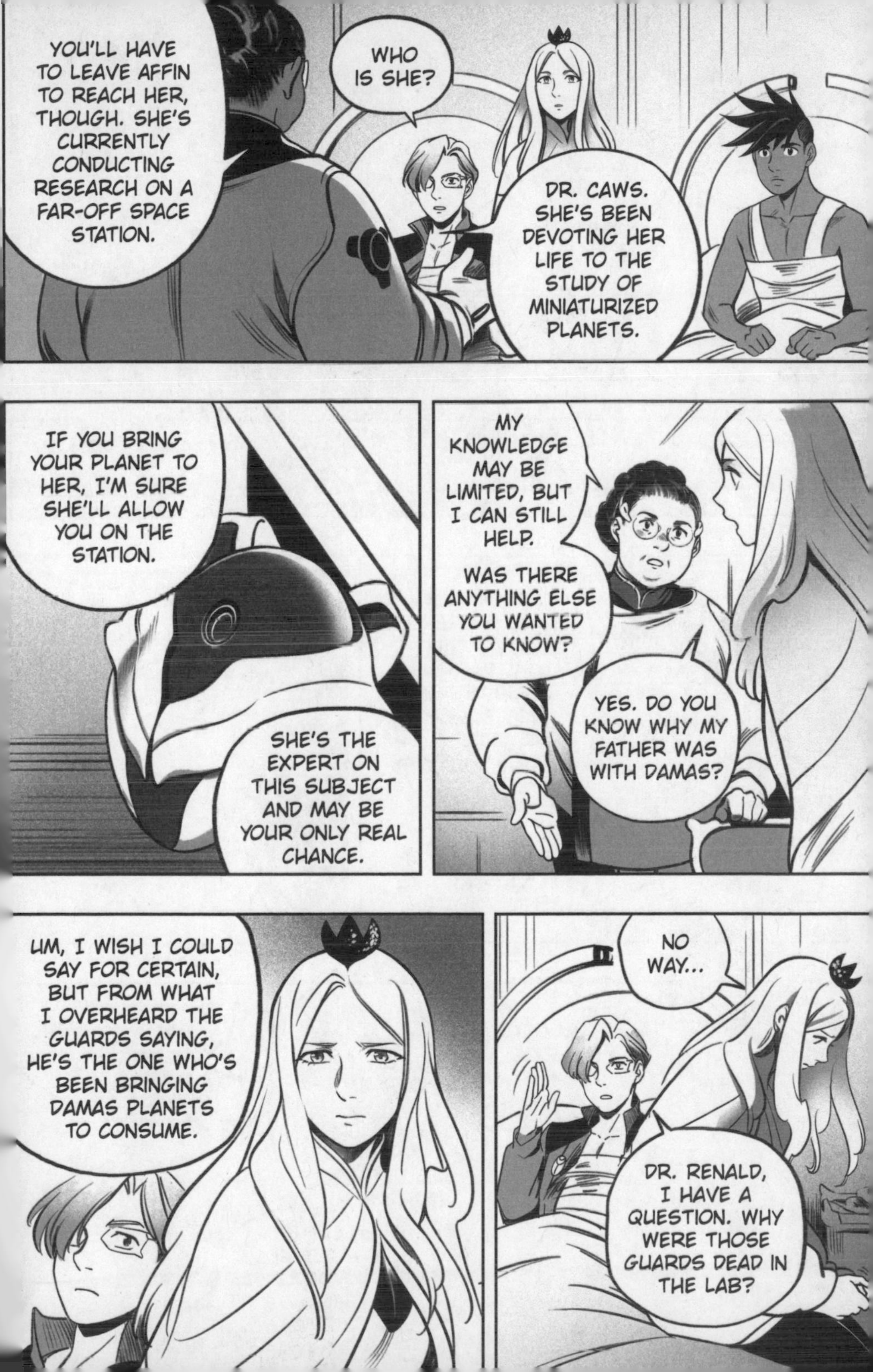

YOU'LL HAVE TO LEAVE AFFIN TO REACH HER, THOUGH. SHE'S CURRENTLY CONDUCTING RESEARCH ON A FAR-OFF SPACE STATION.
WHO IS SHE?
DR. CAWS. SHE'S BEEN DEVOTING HER LIFE TO THE STUDY OF MINIATURIZED PLANETS.
IF YOU BRING YOUR PLANET TO HER, I'M SURE SHE'LL ALLOW YOU ON THE STATION.
SHE'S THE EXPERT ON THIS SUBJECT AND MAY BE YOUR ONLY REAL CHANCE.
MY KNOWLEDGE MAY BE LIMITED, BUT I CAN STILL HELP.
WAS THERE ANYTHING ELSE YOU WANTED TO KNOW?
YES. DO YOU KNOW WHY MY FATHER WAS WITH DAMAS?
UM, I WISH I COULD SAY FOR CERTAIN, BUT FROM WHAT I OVERHEARD THE GUARDS SAYING, HE'S THE ONE WHO'S BEEN BRINGING DAMAS PLANETS TO CONSUME.
NO WAY...
DR. RENALD, I HAVE A QUESTION. WHY WERE THOSE GUARDS DEAD IN THE LAB?

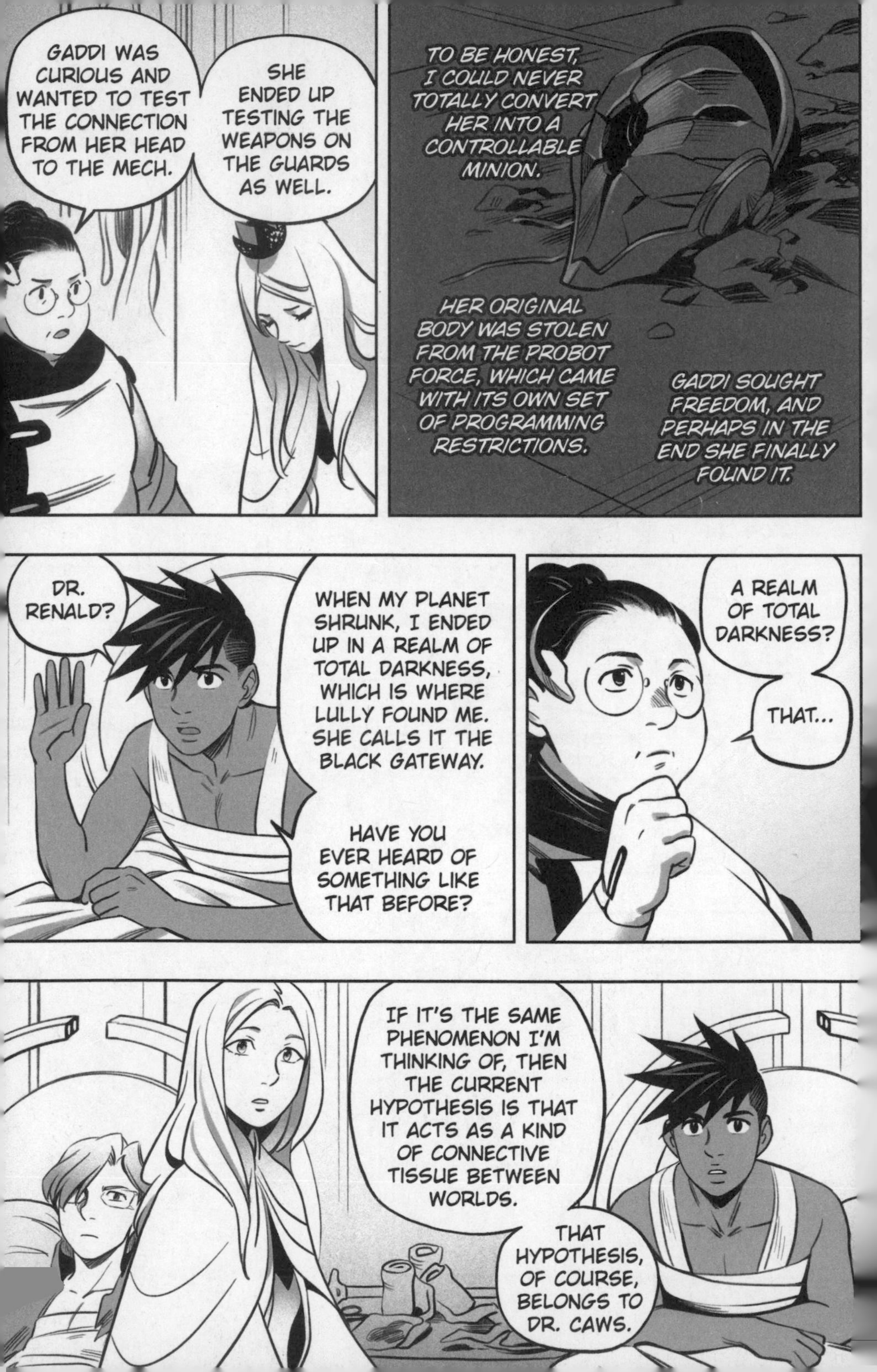
GADDI WAS CURIOUS AND WANTED TO TEST THE CONNECTION FROM HER HEAD TO THE MECH.
SHE ENDED UP TESTING THE WEAPONS ON THE GUARDS AS WELL.
TO BE HONEST, I COULD NEVER TOTALLY CONVERT HER INTO A CONTROLLABLE MINION.
HER ORIGINAL BODY WAS STOLEN FROM THE PROBOT FORCE, WHICH CAME WITH ITS OWN SET OF PROGRAMMING RESTRICTIONS.
GADDI SOUGHT FREEDOM, AND PERHAPS IN THE END SHE FINALLY FOUND IT.
DR. RENALD?
WHEN MY PLANET SHRUNK, I ENDED UP IN A REALM OF TOTAL DARKNESS, WHICH IS WHERE LULLY FOUND ME. SHE CALLS IT THE BLACK GATEWAY.
HAVE YOU EVER HEARD OF SOMETHING LIKE THAT BEFORE?
A REALM OF TOTAL DARKNESS?
THAT...
IF IT'S THE SAME PHENOMENON I'M THINKING OF, THEN THE CURRENT HYPOTHESIS IS THAT IT ACTS AS A KIND OF CONNECTIVE TISSUE BETWEEN WORLDS.
THAT HYPOTHESIS, OF COURSE, BELONGS TO DR. CAWS.

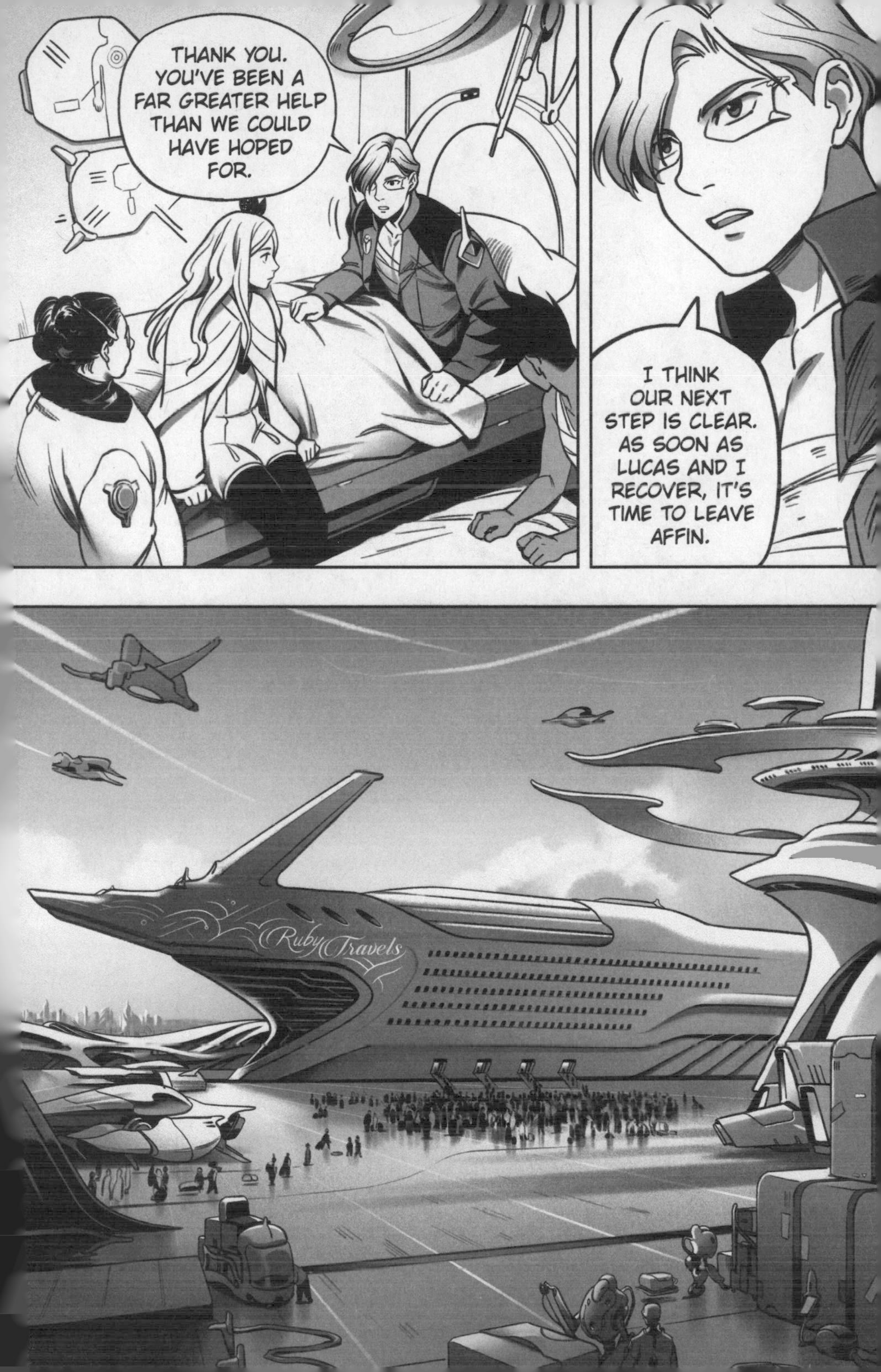
THANK YOU. YOU'VE BEEN A FAR GREATER HELP THAN WE COULD HAVE HOPED FOR.
I THINK OUR NEXT STEP IS CLEAR. AS SOON AS LUCAS AND I RECOVER, IT'S TIME TO LEAVE AFFIN.
Ruby Travels

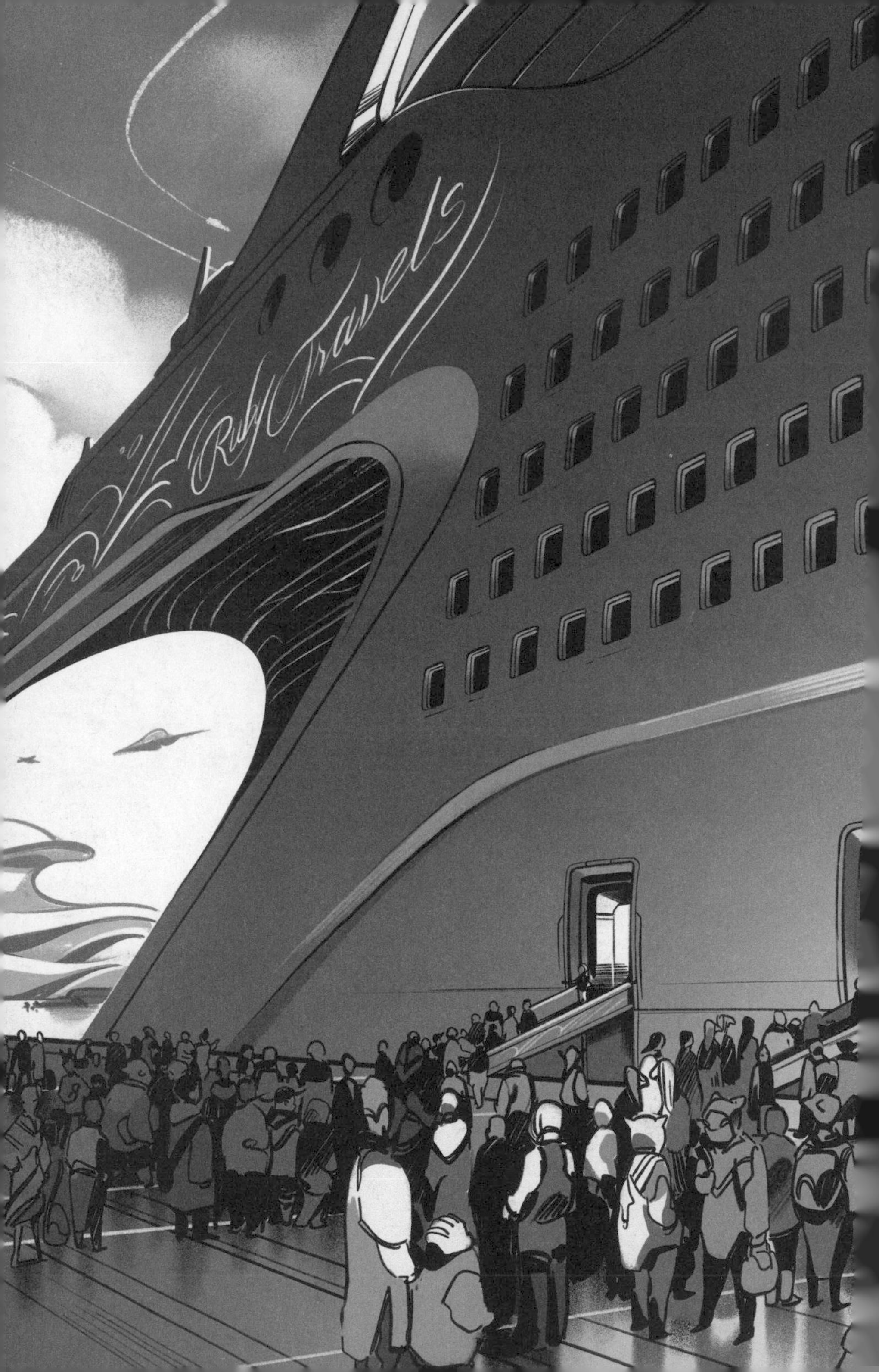
Ruby Travels

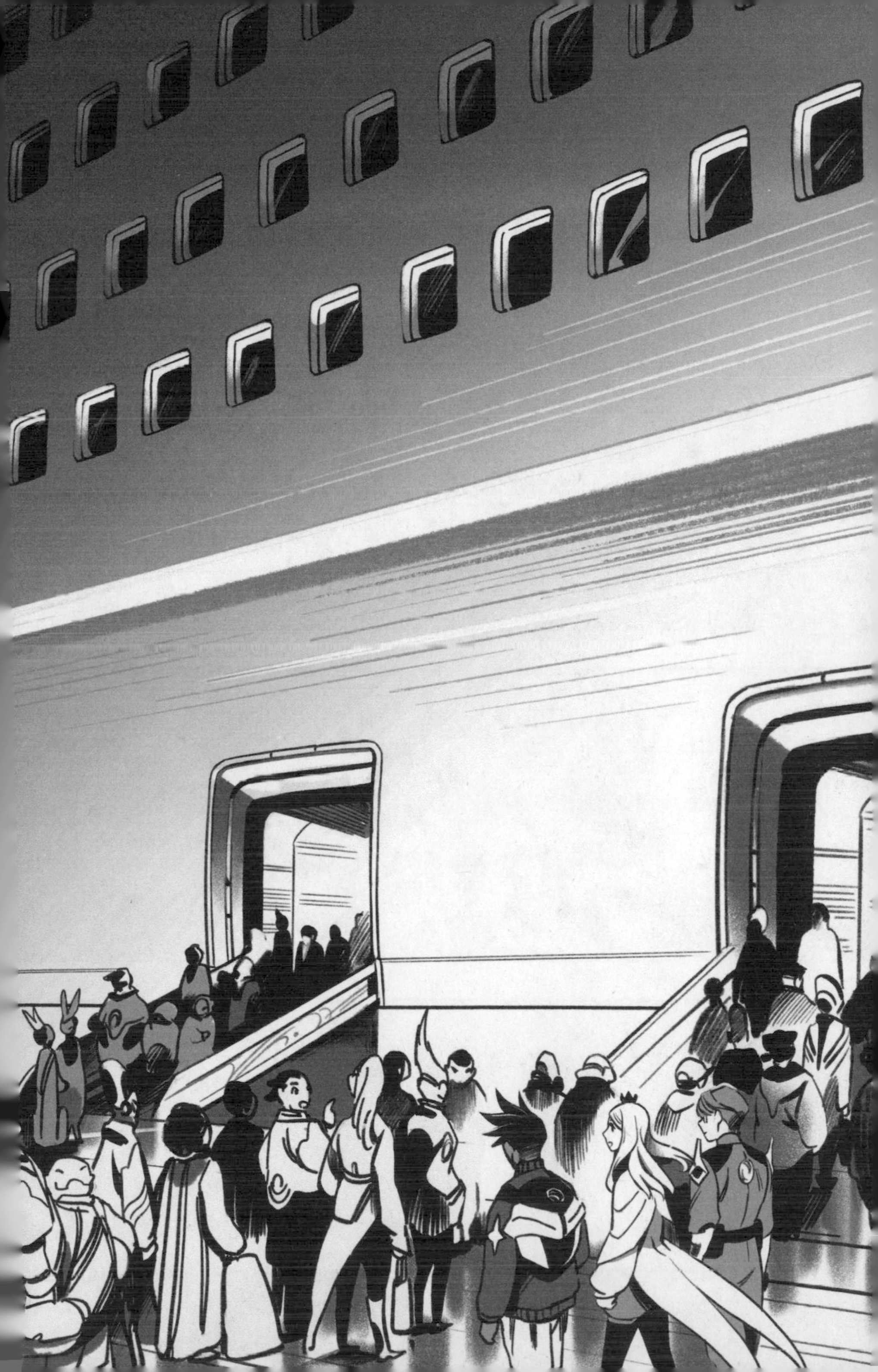

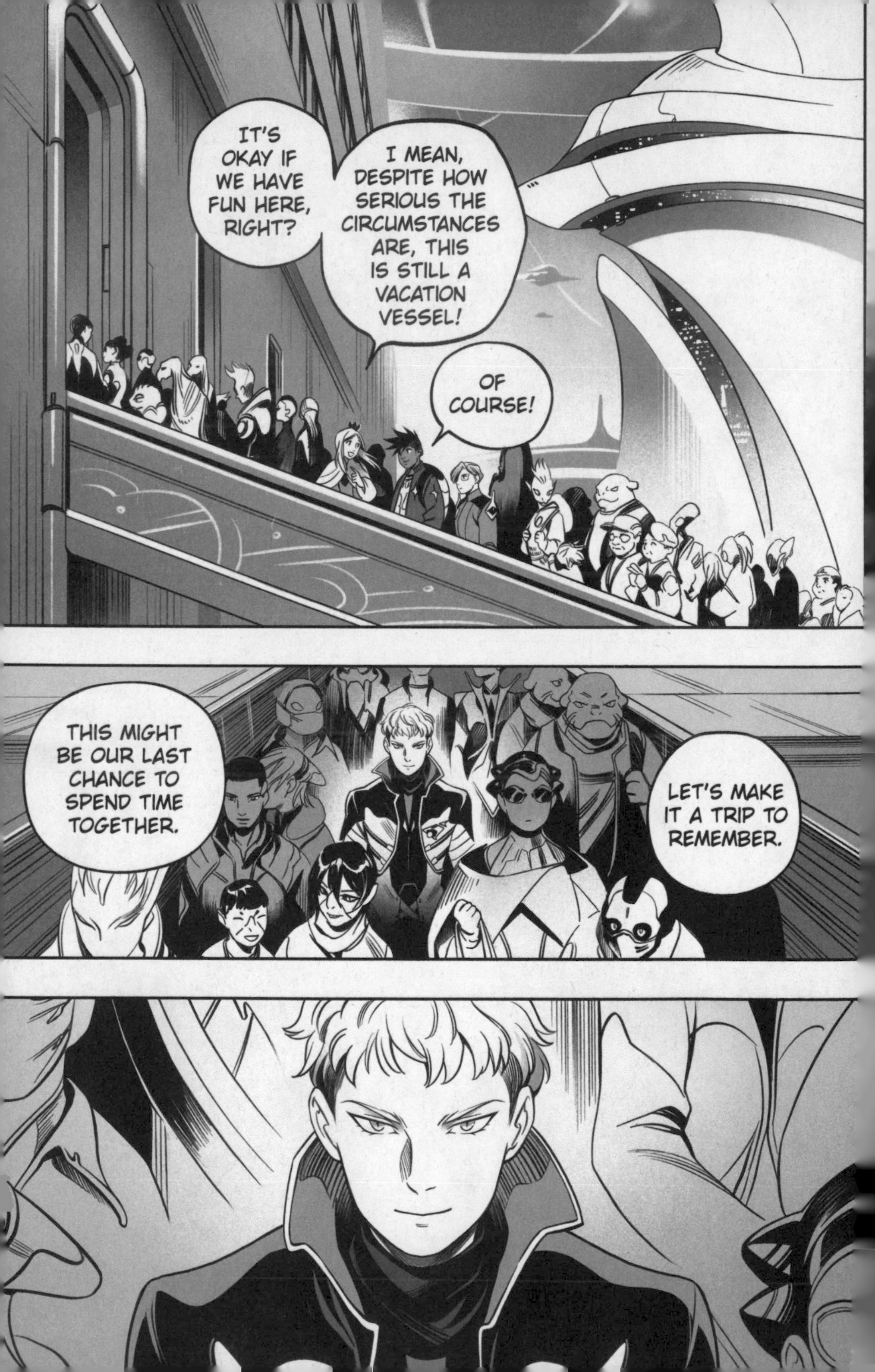
IT'S OKAY IF WE HAVE FUN HERE, RIGHT?
I MEAN, DESPITE HOW SERIOUS THE CIRCUMSTANCES ARE, THIS IS STILL A VACATION VESSEL!
OF COURSE!
THIS MIGHT BE OUR LAST CHANCE TO SPEND TIME TOGETHER.
LET'S MAKE IT A TRIP TO REMEMBER.

TO BE CONTINUED
IN VOLUME

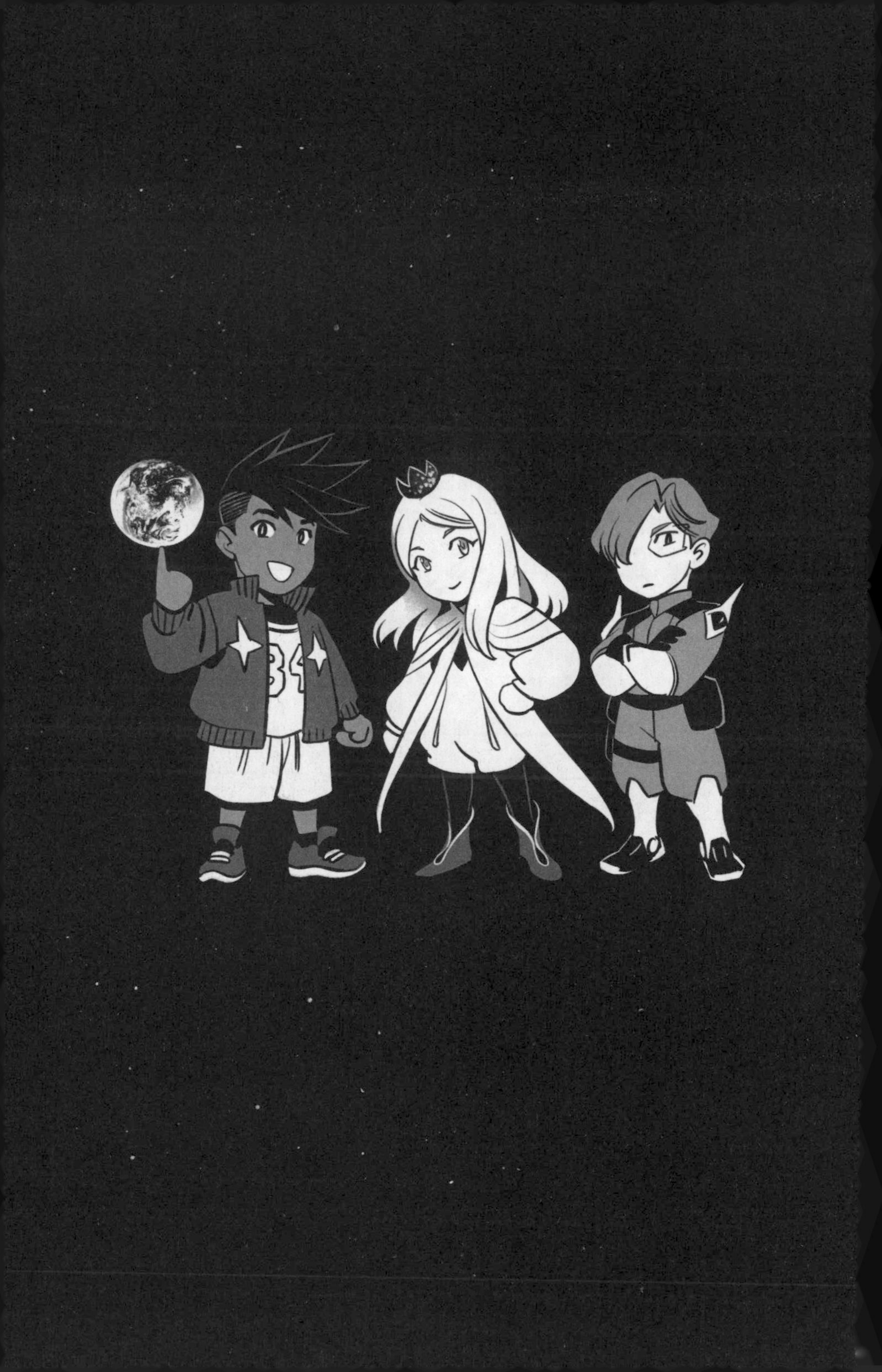

CREATOR COMMENTS

JOSH TIERNEY

Like a lot of you, I've been a fan of VIZ manga for many years, and several of their publications have influenced my writing, but the thought never occurred to me that I'd one day be creating something for them.

When our editor reached out about a new line of original manga, I was beyond thrilled. This was my chance to write something that could be placed in the manga section, beside not only *Dragon Ball* and *One-Punch Man* but works by Taiyo Matsumoto and Junji Ito. The concept for *World Piece* popped into my head instantly.

I knew that, for this series, I needed to go big—and would do so by shrinking Earth, all the way down to the size of a basketball.

I'm tremendously grateful to Fawn and VIZ for taking a chance on *World Piece*, and to Agroshka for joining me and bringing the many worlds within to life. I must also thank my children, Ena and Finn, for their enthusiastic support, especially during the pandemic which has been so difficult for all of us.

Most importantly, thank you for picking up this book and going on this adventure with Lucas, Lully and Mitton! We hope you'll look forward to volume 2. There are many more surprises to come...

AGROSHKA

When Josh showed me the script for *World Piece*, I was immediately drawn to it. Sci-fi is my favorite genre, and I was excited about the chance to illustrate this story and combine my love for distant worlds filled with aliens and robots and my love for manga.

As an artist, I've always been inspired by the unique visual language and aesthetics of Japanese comics. As a teenager, I loved to read Shonen Jump series and was always doodling manga-inspired sketches in my notebooks, never imagining that I would be drawing a full-length graphic novel in the future.

I would like to thank our editor Fawn and the VIZ team for giving me this opportunity, and Josh for trusting me with bringing the characters to life with my art. I would also like to thank my family for supporting me throughout the project, and particularly my dad for introducing me to science fiction at a young age.

Thank you for taking the time to read *World Piece*. I hope you enjoyed the story and look forward to Lucas's adventures in volume 2.

JOSH TIERNEY
resides in Ontario, Canada, with his daughter, son and cat, where they consume a steady diet of anime and manga. He is the creator of the fantasy graphic novel series *Spera*, which was nominated for Eisner, Shuster, Harvey and Diamond Gem Awards, as well as the high school mystery webcomic *Warm Blood*.

AGROSHKA is an illustrator from Poland whose previous work includes book illustrations, album covers and video game concept art. She has previously collaborated with Josh Tierney on the webcomic *Warm Blood*. *World Piece* is her first graphic novel series.

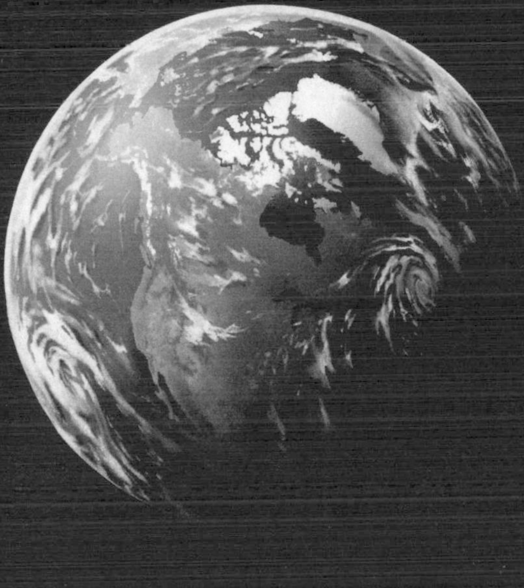

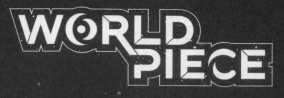

WORLD PIECE

1

VIZ MEDIA EDITION

Story by JOSH TIERNEY
Art by AGROSHKA

Lettering: ERIKA TERRIQUEZ
Cover & Interior Design: VIZ MEDIA
Editor: FAWN LAU

Printed in Canada

Published by VIZ Media, LLC
P.O. Box 77010
San Francisco, CA 94107

10 9 8 7 6 5 4 3 2 1
First printing, June 2021

RATED T+ OLDER TEEN ratings.viz.com

PARENTAL ADVISORY
WORLD PIECE is rated T+ for Older Teen and is recommended for ages 16 and up. This volume contains mature language and mild violence.

VIZ ORIGINALS
viz.com

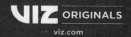